CONSTITUTING CRITIQUE

Post-Contemporary Interventions

Series Editors:

Stanley Fish and Fredric Jameson

CONSTITUTING CRITIQUE

Kant's Writing as Critical Praxis

By Willi Goetschel

Translated by Eric Schwab

DUKE UNIVERSITY PRESS   Durham and London 1994

© 1994 Duke University Press
All rights reserved
Printed in the United States of America on
acid-free paper ∞
Typeset in Aldus by Keystone Typesetting, Inc.
Library of Congress Cataloging-in-Publication Data appear
on the last printed page of this book.

CONTENTS

ACKNOWLEDGMENTS

I ALWAYS IMAGINED THE PRIMAL scene of hermeneutics to be somewhat like a scene in *A Fish Called Wanda*. There the avid Nietzsche-reading protagonist replies to the objection that monkeys—and therefore he too—cannot read: "Sure, they can read, they just do not understand." Realizing that the monkey is already in us might be an emancipatory step toward a liberated understanding that we, too, do not always understand.

If to some degree every translation is, as the Italian proverb has it, treason, Eric Schwab has taught me otherwise. Insisting that his task as translator be a challenge for the author, too, he prompted me to revise, reconsider, rephrase, add, and, most importantly, think through once more many of the issues. At moments of doubt when the worth of this whole enterprise of translation seemed doubtful, his sustained enthusiasm was welcome reassurance.

I have updated the discussion according to the research which has appeared since the publication of the German version. Occasionally, when necessary, I have changed the course of argumentation. The first part of the introduction is new. Comments on this section by Sam Kerstein, Gayatri Chakravorty Spivak, and an anonymous reader have proven helpful in clarifying the concept and agenda of critique. Material has been added in several chapters. Taking advantage of the privilege of knowing better how to write a book once one has written it, and having had the chance to put this knowledge to some use, I consider this the final version.

Dieter Henrich accompanied and inspired the project when it was just that. Karl S. Guthke generously accepted its progress, and James Engell, Jurij Striedter, and Maja Wicki-Vogt provided intellectual support as critical readers. Raymond Geuss took it upon himself to convince Ken Wissoker of the need for translation of this book, and Ken was a supportive editor. Maura High was the perfect copy editor. Pam Morrison provided unflagging editorial assistance. Alan Cameron gave kindly advice on English translations of Greek and Latin sources. I would also like to thank Claudia Brodsky Lacour for a generous and perceptive reading. Most of all I thank my English-speaking friends who, as they listened for countless years to my sneak previews of *Kant—The Movie,* forced me to rethink many of the scenarios.

This translation has been made possible by a grant of the Council on Research and Faculty Development in the Humanities and Social Sciences of Columbia University.

CONSTITUTING CRITIQUE

INTRODUCTION

Ⅰ T IS NO COINCIDENCE THAT CRI-
tique has become the rallying point for most current theoretical projects. It assumes the central function of legitimizing theoretical practice. Yet this is where consensus ends: there appears to be no agreement on what critique might mean. In fact, the question of what it means is treated in a surprisingly casual way, given the fundamental role it plays in the context of theoretical self-explanation and legitimation.

In the last two hundred years or so critique has become a critical term in itself. As a concept, it has enjoyed a long career, first as a philological technicality, and later to signify a certain form of aesthetic assessment. Kant added a new dimension to critique when he gave it an intrinsically philosophical meaning: it assumed an epistemological function and thereby achieved theoretical dignity. But Kant, redefining the theoretical as the genuinely practical, transformed critique into a concept with practical meaning. And this, for Kant, meant a concept of political relevance.

Critique is thus a concept with a history. And if this history is supposed to be more than simply critique's nemesis, the career of the concept needs careful historical investigation. For this seems the only way to ensure that history is not mistaken for *a priori* truths, contingency for necessity.

The concept of critique is intimately connected with history. The *Critique of Pure Reason* itself names its age the "Age of Critique." And it is evident from the revolutionary implications of the *Critique of Pure Reason* that this declaration points beyond theoretical claims to practical—that is, political—claims.

If *enlightenment* signifies both a period and a theoretical agenda, and if only a dual approach leads to an adequate understanding of enlightenment, then the approach to understanding critique should also be dual. Ever since Kant fused the two notions, enlightenment has carried critique deeply inscribed as its determination, and critique has become constitutively connected to enlightenment.

Connecting the concept of critique and the *Critique* with his age, Kant makes it clear that his project is not just an academic exercise. He takes the problem of determining the nature of critique to a new level, beyond the confines of scholarly debate, transforming critique into a new philosophical method, one grounded in a fundamental shift in epistemology. What seems crucial to this shift is not so much its technical implications but rather their philosophical-practical consequences. Kant himself never tired of emphasizing this connection. Academic division of labor, however, has resulted in the construction of an image of the critical enterprise that has theoretical analysis painted into one corner and practical philosophy into another. The intricate weave of Kant's critical argument, constituting the practical and theoretical spheres on the basis of their interdependence, has thus been neglected. And yet the importance of the *Critique* lies in its recognition of this nexus of the practical and theoretical aspects of reason.

Self-determination is the motive of Kant's *Critique*. Taking a cue from Rousseau, autonomy for Kant means self-legislation. Consequently, autonomy requires a reflection on the self itself. However, reflecting on the self gives rise to a question of methods; for, if the self prescribes the law to itself, how can we know such an autonomous self? Kant's eventual answer is that we can only recognize the aspects of the self that fall under the law of causality, but that we cannot know this self as far as its "intelligible character," that is, its freedom and self-determination, is concerned. Now, such an approach to dealing with the self—which after all, according to Kant, becomes the fixing point for critical philosophy—must have a direct impact on the question of presentation and representation for such a philosophy.

To respond to this exigency, which has its most radical expression in Montaigne and Hume, philosophical discourse had to be accommodated. Conventional styles of philosophy had proven to be insufficient for such a task. This is the situation when Kant enters his career in the late 1740s. Self-determination thus necessarily means, for him, self-determination as a writer. As a result, for Kant, critique assumes from the beginning a meaning connected to self-determination. Critique is only possible on the grounds of self-determination: this is one of Kant's implicit propositions. And, it follows, self-determination has specific discursive ramifications.

In its title the *Critique of Pure Reason* already hints at this fact. The duality of the genitive construction, in its objective and subjective aspects (the objective pointing to the critique *of Pure Reason*, the subjective to the

Critique of pure reason), opens up a circularity. Reflexive two-way thinking is thus already inscribed in the title of Kant's project. As an arrow bent back on itself, the double meaning creates a space beyond a mere two-way directionality: the double meaning expands into a surplus of sense. This interpretational space projects a procedure; the title and entitlement of critique, we can say, *is* its procedure. We might even detect in the title a suggestion that the task and definition of critique is one of its very own means and methods. The title thus enacts the project of critique as the process of self-referential theorizing about its own procedure. Quite apart from its title, the book itself announces the inauguration of a new philosophical genre with its publication; the title functions as the entitlement of this new philosophical genre by introducing it, the first work of its kind.

To grasp the full impact of the Kantian project, it is necessary to trace the so-called precritical stages of the development that lead Kant eventually to his new discursive strategy. A close look at his early writing career shows the degree to which Kant self-consciously perceives himself as a writer entering the *république des lettres*. His entry into the scene of writing is not of mere anecdotal interest but carries for Kant philosophical significance. Testing the ground serves first of all as a way to find a place to build a foundation for his writing. It is a literary process of philosophical self-constitution. Reaching the "critical" stage is thus not purely accidental but the result of systematically probing and working through a series of experiments in literary and philosophical writing, a search for an adequate mode of representation for critical philosophy.

It is significant that for Kant this process is not just an "aesthetic" enterprise but includes, rather, a fundamental rethinking of epistemology. For when Kant suggests eliminating aesthetics as an independent branch of knowledge and giving transcendental aesthetics a fundamental role instead in the process of knowledge formation, he changes the way in which the problem of representation is conceived. The arguments that have become a condensed summary by the time they are presented in the *Critique* developed slowly over three decades in the precritical writings. At the end of that period, it becomes clear that the essays have been moving toward an epistemological-critical, transcendental philosophy. The search for the formulation of critical philosophy is thus built into Kant's essays as their driving force. Over time, the development of the critical takes on a formal and, therefore, formal-literary dimension; this is what determines the philosophical essay as literary genre.

Kant's reformulation of the critical as the new philosophical method is thus not a sudden event. It is a long and complicated process establishing the critical as the central concept of philosophical method only on the

grounds of a philosophical framework that defines critical as an intervention with precise parameters.

Critique is, then, on the groundwork Kant established, a procedure that
defines itself—it is self-defining; it operates from the very beginning in
a self-conscious way within the framework of literary presentation. For
Kant, this means that critique itself follows procedural givens, rules stipu-
lated by its discursive form. Constructed thus, critique emerges as a discursive practice that is aware of the fact that it remains always tied to its
constitutive moments.

Thus, in Kant's writing, critical theory and critical thought imply the
necessity of considering the limits of writing as self-instituted conditions
of its possibility. To be critical—the only path that remains open, as Kant
maintains—denotes thus an altogether more differentiated program than
the usual accounts of the history of philosophy would have it. It can also
mean a reconsideration of the literary and linguistic medium, not only as
part of the answer but also as part of the question that critical philosophy
poses. As a result, the critical receives a different reading from what might
be expected. Critique, so to speak, has only become critical since Kant. But
to recognize Kant's critical—and that implies self-critical—potential, a
reading is called for that remains critical in and of itself.

What has come to be viewed as the solid rock of modern thought, the
secure fundament for all methodological thinking, looks more like an experiment. The experiment even functions for Kant as the paradigm for
paradigm change. The *revolution in thinking* is not established *against* experiment, but is introduced as a thought experiment itself.

Critique no longer means a simple, topical application of given standards.
Critique opens up, becoming a self-reflective process in which reason no
longer determines truth. Rather, reason engages in self-reflection, on its
own presuppositions. Kant's celebrated phrase speaks of the *conditions for
the possibility of knowledge* that critique must determine. Critique, in the
critical sense, has transformed the truth-finding process from the traditional ontological-metaphysical discourse to one where the discourse itself
is turned into the subject/object of examination. In shifting to the question
of what constitutes adequate procedure, the method emerges as the crucial
moment in philosophy. If the term *critique*, before Kant, denoted the philological task of restoring a text in order to establish its authenticity, Kant has
redefined it as a complex, self-reflective, epistemological procedure for constructing knowledge. As a result, authenticity is replaced by the transcendental method of critique. Knowledge has to legitimate itself from now on
as a self-constituting process. Reason assumes the place of the judge, critique represents the court, and the *Critique of Pure Reason* serves as the

record of the trial. It is no accident that legal metaphor plays such a prominent role in Kant's thought. One is reminded sometimes of Immanuel K.'s
poor brother, Joseph K., of Kafka's *The Trial.*

But Kant's point is not to advance legal procedure as a model for the
truth-finding process. On the contrary, his argument demonstrates that
examining the question "What is truth?" leads to a reformulation of the
concept of truth itself: it is recast as the product of the conditions of the
possibility of knowledge. "Truth" is no longer a fixed standard but a function of our epistemological practice. And so is representation. The court,
thus, comes to serve as a visualization of this process of knowledge production. It is the critical assessment of this operation, which points to the law
as a regulative idea of how knowledge is generated, and upon which in turn
its justification is based. As a descriptive device, therefore, the metaphor of
the court does not by itself serve any legitimating function. Rather, it
functions as a discursive device to re-represent the epistemological model.

With the emancipation of the epistemological subject, Kant subjects all
hitherto ruling forms of legitimation to the uncompromising investigation
of the court of reason. But Kant defines reason as nothing other than
universal reason, envisioned as the chorus of the voices of "everybody." His
epistemological model thus is intrinsically political. Law is the product of
practical reason and therefore only existant and valid to the degree it is
determined by practical reason. Consequently, reason is transformed from
the capacity to execute definition-based syllogisms into the practice of
expressing the *volonté générale.*

This is why the *Critique* is forced to generate a new model of representation. The performative and process-like character of the new concept of
critique implies a variety of styles, and to some extent also some sort
of heteroglossia. The self-aware, complex style so typical of the densely
packed construction of the Kantian periodic sentence assumes, in its mimetic moment, a transcendental quality. It is a style that at the same time
reflects and creates the conditions of the possibility for its epistemic framework. It produces the literary environment, that is, the discursive medium
and framework for voicing critique. The transcendental moment in Kant's
style is expressed by a distinctive literary gesture, reiterated in such a way
that it assumes the character of a syntactical habit or pattern, defined by its
urge for constant recreation of the complex ensemble of discursive conditions necessary to constitute a space for the practice of critique and of
critical discourse. The reiteration of this distinctive gesture is the literary
feature of what may be called "transcendental style." The "transcendental
style" not only sets a new stage for the discourse of philosophy but also
exerts a formative impact on the post-Kantian literature, from Kleist to

Kafka to Dürrenmatt and beyond. Governed by the stipulative imperative, the sheer redundancy of qualifying clauses inscribes the transcendental turn of modern literature as its critical moment.

Critique acquires thus a rather precise contour. In its very nature it is now recast as a constructive, radically self-reflective procedure. The transcendental, self-conscious discourse—and this is Kant's point—*is* critique.

Not a mere academic subtlety, this conceptual shift marks the revolutionary step Kant takes politically. His celebrated Enlightenment program, formulated in his essay "Answer to the Question: 'What is Enlightenment?' " is but the logical consequence of this shift. Public use of reason, as Kant comes to use it, precisely describes the parameters of the new polemical meaning of critique with which his critical project is charged. The "transcendental principle of publicity" illustrates the political role that the constitution of reason as critique has for Kant. For this principle assumes autonomous use of reason only to be possible as public use, that is, free from external authority. Publicizability thus comes to spell out the terms for the possibility of reason. Critique—and Kant's political testament, *Perpetual Peace: A Philosophical Sketch*, repeats this *expressis verbis*—deeply inscribes the notion of the political as the condition for the possibility of reason in general. More than just voicing another protest, critique carries the power of resistance and contradiction. It has the potential to reshape and recast what is, into what could be. Critique produces the critical difference of the status quo and what should replace it.

Kant's critique of reason denotes thus a project which, far from having come to an end, still awaits its realization. It represents the theoretical framework in which European philosophical discourse for the last two hundred years has been defined. And it has proven to be so powerful that bypassing it regularly has meant regressing to the precritical stage.

It remains a remarkable fact that the reception of the "father" of modern thought has experienced such a role reversal. Whatever Oedipal politics operate in the reception of Kant, the extreme ambivalence sometimes shown toward his character or some interpretations of his philosophy still serves too often to displace any discussion of his philosophy at all. Yet the transferential complicities of those who claim that, in order to be critical, the first step is to renounce Kant's project of critique *in toto*, compromise the possibility of critical practice. For as long as the fundament of critical thought lacks a serious assessment, contemporary critique not only must remain unaware of its own provenance and its implications but, even more decisively, will remain incapable of addressing its own blind spots critically.

It is for these reasons that this study attempts to steer clear of applying methodical recipes. (Perhaps Kant's motive for refusing his friend Hippel's suggestion that he critique the art of cooking—if he had taken it for more than a joke—was that he had an aversion to using any kind of recipe in his life and philosophy.) To the degree that prefaces promise what the books do not deliver themselves—as the head of the Marburg neo-Kantians, Hermann Cohen, so succinctly put it—a few words about this book's approach might be helpful. If this book proceeds in an interdisciplinary way, it is because the extradisciplinary quality of an interdisciplinary approach seemed the only rationale for discipline at all. A few readers of the German edition were somewhat confused about whether this study argues historically or systematically, as if a clear-cut divide between the two approaches were possible. For the fact remains that it is precisely their irreducible interdependence that produces constantly changing views of the systematic and the historical, and that nexus is short-circuited the moment they are taken as really existing entities. That Kant himself might have known better is a point that Kant reception has not yet been able to fully appreciate.

In such a situation, a chronological approach seemed most appropriate, even if it might be mistaken for the procedure of conventional histories of ideas. Chronology does not necessarily imply a teleological framework. Digressing from a so-called systematic approach (as if history would not have systematic options as well), a chronological presentation allows for a certain transparency of construction, which thus remains more susceptible to critique. Excluding contingency, a "systematic" approach seems to run the risk of obfuscating its constructed nature no less than a chronological one.

Other readers have realized that this investigation is not exactly an exegesis of style and rhetoric in Kant. Their observation has occasioned some disappointment on their side. Yet if style and the use of rhetoric is intimately connected to philosophical intentions, a study of individual sentence structures or stylistic idiosyncrasies misses the point as long as it does not account for their specific philosophical framework. In Kant's case, however, this framework requires in turn a careful interpretation of his writing practice. That such a study is only as good as its interpretation of Kant would not warrant mentioning if it were not for the fact that it has actually been argued otherwise.

It must be remembered that when Kant set out to write his essays, observations, and lecture programs, he was aiming at transcending the narrow borders of academic institutionalized speech. His project was enlightenment at large. However, read from a post-Kantian perspective, which conditions our perceptions to a much higher degree than we acknowledge, "philosophy" and "literature" might appear as well-established entities. This book will suggest that critical philosophy might teach otherwise.

It must be one of the many great ironies of the history of philosophy that one of the most-read and most-referred-to philosophers is also one whose work has scarcely been appreciated or explored in its totality. Kant never varied in his insistence that the *Critique of Pure Reason* be considered the primer and central text for all future philosophizing, but philosophy has taken on this task without ever having become fully conscious of its scope. Until now, philosophers have explained this astonishing fact in general terms, with recourse to doxographical questions of "content." The unceasing laments of his interpreters, deploring his writing as difficult, even incomprehensible, have always served as an excuse to treat the *Critique* as a sort of theory stockpile. Each interpretation legitimizes itself by using parts of the theory, *en gros* or *en détail*, and only as much as meets its current needs. This mentality, which treats Kant's text as a kind of quarry from which ideas can be removed, has left an unusual theoretical rubble behind. Only in exceptional cases has the "form" been recognized and taken into account in this seemingly unformed work, only here and there have the style of stylelessness and the structure of structurelessness, at the very heights of Kant's critical philosophizing, been understood as themselves meaningful constituents of its content. This is even more astonishing considering that Kant's very purpose here is to show the conditions of the possibility of knowledge. The attempt to reflect upon space and time as pure intuitions and upon the categories as constitutive of judgment raises precisely the problem of how to give written representation to such reflection, in the fullest depths of its philosophical significance. The mode of literary representation itself must be confronted as an object of knowledge. Only a specifically literary quality, moreover, can explain the extent and depth of the effect that the *Critique* has exercised, and continues to exercise. For—and this is one of the *Critique*'s points—the thought is always and eminently "form." And, as such, it must be ascribed a literary quality. If, therefore, the *Critique* can be fully and critically grasped only by recognizing this quality, then such an approach will likewise engender consequences that have been obscured until now. For even if calls for such an approach are as old as Kant's *Critique* itself—and only in this way can we understand all Kant's coquetry about the book's poor style and unintelligibility, which a talented writer might one day remedy—the approach must be made fertile, for an interpretation to succeed. Kant's coquetting has to be read as an artfully worn masquerade that demonstrates, *e contrario ad oculos,* what is hidden behind it: the question of what adequate philosophical expression is.

Too many have already been caught in his snare. For Kant, the irony at work here functions as a basic figure, the gesture of critical philosophy. Brutish seriousness can also be a form of stupidity, whereas reflection maintains an openness for itself. Still others pretend to find a clarity in Kant's thought which only they have been elected to understand. The consequence of this is that they, too, are compelled to ignore any form-induced quality or intention in the context of Kant's argument that would undermine their clarity-based approach to reading. At both of these extremes, philosophical translation is presented as an unproblematic necessity, but by the same token, these interpretations suffer a remarkable crisis when it comes to upholding any further claim of being an adequate match for Kant's *Critique.* They perceive only a doxographically propped-up Kant, while simultaneously ignoring the very medium in which his philosophy represents itself.

In contrast to these readings, this book attempts to bring Kant's specifically literary quality to light. To restrict its enquiry to the *Critique of Pure Reason* and the so-called critical phase, however, would be inadequate. Such a narrow focus would merely bring on all the vices of isolation that only such Cyclopean close reading exposes itself to. Rather, the deeper dimensions of Kant's historical-empirical context and the discursive-pragmatic implications of Kant's conception of himself as an author must be brought to bear in this interpretation. And here arises a different danger: on the basis of a reception aesthetics methodology, albeit one carrying all the distortions of its retrospective optics, the interpretation might merely reiterate the entire eighteenth century, in a litany of "historical influence" observations. For it seems only fair to postulate, in a discussion of Kantian philosophy, that the discussion must support the appropriate level of philosophical reflection. Otherwise it can claim a place within the literature theory industry only as a curiosity.

Thus the approach of the present investigation is to minimize its involvement in methodological problematics. Its chosen theme is Kant's development as a writer. This development involves an effort by Kant that is at times conscious, at other times less conscious, but at all times steadily directed toward the goal of creating a platform in his writing secured by a theory of knowledge, from which and through which a literary audience could also be produced. Kant's early writings will therefore be examined in regard to their specifically literary function, in order to highlight this eminently discursive-pragmatic side to the *Critique* in the context of its historical origins. The common denominator will be Kant's self-definition as a writer. The specific details of Kant's case can be fleshed out around this *leitmotiv*, while keeping in focus the theoretical implications of the *philosophe*'s public role as *écrivain* in the Enlightenment in general. Role models and contemporaries of Kant's will be pointed out whose significance is constitutive in this context, insofar as they cast a revealing light on his development. But the intention here is not to become entangled in the self-multiplying problems and *quisquilia* of identifying possible influences that bear little upon our question.

The approach of this book may be apt, in the first place, because Kant, as his friend and colleague Christian Jakob Kraus once said, read in an "unbound" way. As the tenant of a bookdealer and as an assistant librarian (and thus able to access new publications even before they were bound), Kant seemed to absorb knowledge from everything he came across. And as anyone who writes letters or diaries knows, it is often the most important things that get written about the least. The decisive role in the history of philosophy is often not played so much by the *philosophemes* and philosophical theories, as by the personalities of the philosophers who deploy them. Crucial here are not so much grand methodological premises as individual theoretical accordances. Here too, it seems that it is the practice of theory rather than the theory of practice that is essential. The role models Kant chose are decisive: Rousseau and Hume, but also Voltaire, Swift, Mendelssohn, and Aristotle. For him they were not figures that could not be questioned but examples of possible philosophizing, to which he felt his own was in some way related—although they, too, fall on the other side of the dividing line drawn so clearly by the *Critique of Pure Reason*.

Philosophical discourse operates within a context of deduction and proof, in which literary forms of expression must conform to the requirements of intersubjective verifiability. The literary-critical investigation of philosophical works differs from criticism of purely literary works because the former must concern itself with objective truth claims. Literary influences, in particular those involving literary form, play a different role, albeit one just as important. But they gain fundamental significance only in the course of the philosophical legitimation carried out by the work itself. Poetry and fiction can disregard such legitimation, however; for them, any paradigm of explanation or interpretation set out by an aesthetics of reception will have an entirely different sense. Thus it would appear expedient, in the absence of a comprehensive literary study of Kant, at least to consider his work itself more carefully as a literary endeavor. The task will be to show how the self-thematizing of the philosopher *as* a writer, progressing throughout all of his early works, clearly functions in a literary sense as a moment of crystallization, an attempt to define the condition of the possibility of the "I" [*Ich*] in general. This has to be understood from the very beginning as a critique of Descartes's tautological concept of the self. Kant attempts to break up Cartesian ontology, with all its conceptual poverty as regards the "I", without himself renouncing the self. In the end, this leads away from the fixity of an ultimately problematic concept of the "I" to Kant's concept of the transcendental subject of knowledge, which is able to function as an emancipatory vehicle of autonomy.

In this light, Kant's two first works, *Thoughts on the True Evaluation of Living Forces* and *Universal Natural History and Theory of the Heavens*, take on a precise meaning among his writings.

A further characteristic of Kant's early writings, from the first freely conceived book onward (that is, excluding both those written in Latin specifically to fulfill academic requirements and the *Thoughts*, as a work still completely ensconced within the boundaries of scholastic philosophy) is that they are all *attempts*, all essays [*Versuche*]. He entitles them "Attempt," "Essay," "Observation," "Dreams." The essay, as a genre favored in the Enlightenment for thought experiments that probe into the possible, is taken up by Kant in a creative fashion.

If Montaigne is considered to have given the essay its tone of privacy and individual subjectivity, and if Bacon introduced factual objectivity, then it is Kant who brought the essay a new, even deeper dimension. Given his search for a self-reflecting method by which to establish a foundation for the possibility of knowledge, it was only natural that he chose the essay as best fitted for his purpose. In the history of the essay, Kant thus marks a turning point. After him, the essay owes its position as a critical form to Kant's use of it to reflect upon the transcendental. This transcendental reflection, the implicit core around which his "attempts" constantly revolve, is what Kant inscribed upon the essay. Following Kant, the essay is no longer just the genre of skepticism (Montaigne), of individual reflection and self-reflection, any more than it is the genre merely of the artful aphorism (Bacon). Even its subsequent function, proceeding from Locke, Hume, and the Scottish Enlightenment, as the privileged genre of philosophical discourse struggling to free itself from the fetters of tradition, is eclipsed by Kant's efforts. It is no longer distinguished simply by a trend that is critical of metaphysics. Rather, following Kant, and indeed in a way that becomes irrevocable, transcendental reflection becomes an integral component of the philosophical essay. Any history of the essay that overlooks Kant's critical deepening of the form is thus constrained to follow the general tendency that defines the criteria of the essay as openness, incompleteness, and a view to the infinite. Such an approach will be unable to grasp the decisive criterion: transcendental reflectivity. What makes Kant's use of the essay so interesting, from the perspective of both philosophy and literary theory, is that it brought about a qualitative transformation in the philosophical essay as such, by employing the essay as a means of reflecting upon method itself.

Kant's essays can therefore be understood as a series of experiments, extending over decades, at the end of which stands a new literary genus, the *Critique*. It is a form derived from the essay. Yet to the extent that the *Critique* represents the essay in its fully developed transcendental reflectivity, it critically transcends this latter form, and establishes, in parting, a new form. Seen in this context, an abundance of literary peculiarities in the *Critique of Pure Reason* can be explained easily as genre-specific qualities. Features that until now have been considered mere weaknesses, insufficiencies, or simply awkward moments, once they are understood in terms of Kant's effort to develop a generic form adequate to critical philosophy, now appear to be determined by their genre, and only as such can their specific function be interpreted successfully. Thus, with the *Critique*, a new, philosophical species of literature was created. The scope of its influence in the history of literary forms can hardly be estimated (so great is the role it has played). But the first step to be taken here must be to lay out the interpretive potential of Kant's essays, insofar as they indicate, in the trajectory of Kant's development, the beginnings of what resulted in the *Critique*. This theme, to be fully articulated in chapters 1 through 7, will be summarized here only in its key points.

With his first publication, *Thoughts on the True Evaluation of Living Forces* (1755), Kant introduces himself as a writer into the *république des lettres* toward which this text is primarily directed. The preface serves as a sort of charter, set out by the author himself, that allows him to operate, generally, as an author: "I have already prescribed the track to which I will hold. I shall launch my career, and nothing shall hinder me from completing it" (preface, § vii).

The *Universal Natural History and Theory of the Heavens* (1755) adds greater depth to this "I", by extending it into the dimension of cosmology and cosmogony. This travelogue describing the *terra incognita* of space and time begins on a Promethean note, something Goethe later merely repeats lyrically: self-knowledge realizing itself in the universe in the form of its self-representation. Its genre is the essay, as a form whose possibilities Kant explores here for the first time. In a series of shorter essays, in journalistic articles and lecture announcements, Kant plays through various authorial roles. The year 1762 marks a turning point. The revolutionizing encounter with Rousseau's writings and the epistemological breakthrough open the way to a new concept of metaphysics. All this brings Kant to a new, fundamentally consolidated point of departure for his emergence into the public realm as an author. As such, he is instantly greeted by Germany's leading literary judge at that time, Moses Mendelssohn. Alongside this illustrious figure, Kant, although here anonymous, makes his appearance with the *Inquiry Concerning the Distinctness of the Principles of Natural Theology and Morality* (1764). In the *Attempt to Introduce Negative Magnitudes into Philosophy* (1763), presumably the last-conceived work of the group of texts dating from 1762, Kant provides a revealing literary self-portrait when he condenses the procedure of experimental thinking and writing into the image of the flash of light that explodes out of long-preserved, volatile material, once this is finally ignited in some way.

With the *Observations on the Feeling of the Beautiful and the Sublime* (1764), an essay whose composition demonstrates his virtuosity with the quill, Kant strives to delineate the border between aesthetics and ethics, in a critical counterstatement against prevailing positions that intermingled the two realms. Yet this is possible only to the extent that the literary hybrid form of the essay as observation is worked out from within, reflectively, so that the lines of demarcation are demonstrated once again within the genre itself. Kant's attempt to mediate Rousseau's *volonté générale* and the moral sense of the Scottish School by means of his own theory of "moral feeling" [*moralisches Gefühl*] can be formulated only within the framework of an essay within the essay.

As an "original experiment," his *Essay on the Sicknesses of the Head* (1764) shows how Kant, the "experimental moralist," develops the essay as a literary field of play, wherein he is able to cultivate a fruitful reciprocity between forms of thought and of writing, to produce a dialectic of open-ended tension, in a manner nearly reminiscent of Swift. The level of thought and expression Kant reaches here can be designated "prototranscendental."

Almost as a sort of cabinet piece, as it were, is his *Dreams of a Spirit-Seer, Elucidated by Dreams of Metaphysics* (1766). Here, in a fluctuating double satire, the skeptical method itself becomes the literary staging ground for critical reflection. Considered both in its content and in its place in the history of literary form, the *Dreams* delineates precisely the preliminary stage to the *Critique of Pure Reason* (1781). With this work, a new type of philosophical literature is inaugurated, one whose procedure not only embodies the literary representation of thought but that also generates this thought in the first place. This is decisive, and must remain so for every interpretation. The model of knowledge and the mode of representation converge in the *Critique;* its genre is its form of demonstration.

With the *Critique of Pure Reason,* the course of Kant's formal development, with respect to the formulation of his theoretical philosophy, comes to a close. In my closing chapter, I interpret Kant's enlightenment-oriented publications as a consistent continuation of what the *Critique* had established. Because these later works belong essentially to practical reason, their style is no longer a "zetetic-searching" one. As an explication of the concept "enlightenment" and oriented as they are toward a wider public, these texts are "practical," and hence ethical, meaning that they serve a moral-political function. Yet they, too, are distinguished by this same "transcendental" style, characterized by its extreme reflectiveness, its restraint and modesty in the midst of such certainty about what constitutes the subject of knowledge.

ONE

Project Career Trajectory

A SPECIFIC FUNCTION OF FIRST publications is to serve as a letter of recommendation for their authors, introducing them to the literary world. Indeed, Fichte, writing to Kant a half-century later, after Kant had established his authority, arrived at the same conclusion: an author writes himself his own recommendation letter.[1] Only thus does the writer really become an author, by becoming an enfranchised claimant to a voice in the "republic of letters"—an "authority."

In the realm of publicity, this simple, yet on the other hand puzzling, circular movement—the basic figure of authorial existence in general—remains both the central prerequisite for any reflection concerning a modern writer's existential experience and one of its defining moments. As the definition of the writer, this figure defines the author and authority as well. To be a writer means, from the very beginning, to demand authority as an author, or at least to claim it, but always already to *pretend* to such a status. For the philosopher to be an author, furthermore, means to *reflect* upon this status.

For Kant, this theme of authorial legitimation is present from the very beginning. It is such a loaded and challenging issue that the preface to his first published piece, *Thoughts on the True Evaluation of Living Forces [Gedanken von der wahren Schätzung der lebendigen Kräfte]*, is nothing but an argumentative self-justification for his very emergence as an author. Already, this first text acquires a latent meaning, to be found in Kant's subsequent titles also. In fact, the title itself contains a camouflaged self-reference.

To make his debut as an author, not just theoretically but, finally, for real, and in print, is of such significance to Kant that he discontinues his studies. In order to see his first piece published, he takes a position as a private tutor outside of Königsberg, in the provinces, far from the city and the university. To make his name as a writer becomes such high priority that his most urgent task becomes the procuring of funds for typesetting his first book.

Thus appears, in 1749, Kant's first publication, the *Thoughts on the True Evaluation of Living Forces*. The year 1746 stands on the title page, which is when the text was submitted to the censors by the faculty of the University of Königsberg and accepted. But it was actually completed in 1747 at the earliest. The dedication is dated on Kant's twenty-third birthday; paragraphs 107–113A and 151–156 contain extensive additions from the year 1747.[2]

It may well be that in terms of its contents the treatise was already outdated by the time it appeared.[3] Perhaps this cannot finally be decided, however, for such a decision would have to resort to historiographic premises that are scientifically problematic.[4] The most significant formulation of Kant's writerly failure here comes from Erich Adickes:

> Kant's expectations were deeply disappointed. His text proved to be a total washout. Granted, one cannot fault the twenty-two-year-old for not tempering the conflict in which greater personages were involved, for this is hardly a wonder. But one may very well fault his having proposed a solution that contained a violation of the law of inertia, and that thus sharply opposed the principles of healthy natural science. The path he chose leads to error.[5]

In a conciliatory gesture for this harsh verdit, Adickes adds, "But certainly even then, as a twenty-two-year-old, Kant was greater than his own works" (69)—an opinion often echoed about Kant by his contemporaries when he was much older, as well.[6] Arnoldt judges matters quite differently: "The seriousness of his investigations and the thoroughness of his demonstrations compel respect for this young man, page after page, from the reader."[7] Arnoldt subsequently distinguishes the scientific value of this text from its philosophical significance. As outdated as it may be in regard to its mechanics, it nonetheless has enduring value from a metaphysical perspective (Arnoldt, "Kants Jugend," 161). Of particular value is the recognition that metaphysics has yet to become a science. This distinction does indeed seem to provide for a fairer evaluation of Kant and has the added advantage of being an argument free of affect.[8]

Kant's title places his text within the tradition of Wolff.[9] This, in turn, makes his preface that much more remarkable. It is here that he right away sets his footing as an author. For his epigraph, he quotes Seneca's *De vita beata:* "Nihil magis praestandum est, quam ne pecorum ritu sequamur antecendentium gregem, pergentes, non qua eundum est, sed qua itur" [There is nothing more important than not to follow what has gone before us, like the beast in the herd does, going on the path where all have gone, rather than going where we ought to go.] Nietzsche's famous beginning to his second *Untimely Meditation*, "On the Uses and Disadvantages of History for Life," evokes a similar image: "Observe the herd, that grazes before you: they know not what yesterday, what today is, but merely prance about, and eat, and sleep."[10] Indeed the youthful freshness and sometimes ingeniousness that inspires Kant's preface resembles Nietzsche's. Adickes points out how, in respect to this text's actual accomplishments, there appears a tendency "to speak of oneself more often than necessary, as youth is wont to do." As to the somewhat peculiar quality of this preface, Adickes continues, "Kant's belief in himself and in his future is clearly no minor matter. Even so, his tone is not boastful, insulting, or taunting. What one hears in such words is, rather, a justified awareness of his innate value, coupled with a gallant audacity that is well-suited to youth, at least so long as it is matched by knowledge of sufficient resources to tip the scales in its favor."[11]

Certainly this is a far cry from the tone in Kant's dedication, where rather the "lowliness of the author" is mentioned (ww, 1:13).[12] So strongly felt is the need for justification of his authorship, that Kant launches into a quasi-legalistic defense, just to disarm any possible complaints in advance. The preface, in fact, pleads not only for acquittal, as would accord with tradition, but also asks that it not be considered a "crime" when the author takes the liberty of contradicting great men (1:15, §1). Kant continues this metaphor complex drawn from the legal world, in the second paragraph, where the readers are addressed as judges and precedents from legal history are cited. It is the case of Timoleon:

> Die Richter entrüsteten sich über die Vermessenheit seiner Ankläger. Allein Timoleon betrachtete diesen Zufall ganz anders. Ein solches Unternehmen konnte einem Manne nicht missfallen, der sein ganzes Vergnügen darin setzte, sein Vaterland in der vollkommensten Freiheit zu sehen. Er beschützte diejenige, die sich ihrer Freiheit so gar wider ihn selber bedieneten.

> The judges were indignant at the impudence of his accusers. And yet Timoleon viewed the case quite differently. Such an undertaking could not displease a man whose highest satisfaction was seeing his fatherland enjoy the utmost freedom. He protected even those who chose to use their freedom to attack him. (1:16)

Yet there still remains the prejudicial power of reputation: "If the author is unknown, with neither character nor accomplishments, then the book can hardly be worth spending time on" (1:16, §3). This predilection toward extolling only already famous authors is, in any case, a product of complacency and egotism. It serves as an excuse for closing an ear to new authors while at the same time remaining ignorant of the oft-praised established ones (1:17, §4). Here already, one of Kant's fundamental characteristics makes itself felt: instead of lamenting a situation, he finds a theory to explain it. Thus he applies the theory of prejudice to the public's reception of authors, and makes the result into an anticipatory gesture of self-legitimation.

The fifth paragraph goes on to counter the accusation of authorial self-presumptuousness, that whoever attributes errors to a great scholar must think him- or herself greater than that scholar. Kant's response is that whoever can isolate a specific topic of inquiry and generate new knowledge from it is hardly, for this reason alone, about to claim mastery (1:17ff.). Kant thus also clears the way for his own specific inquiry, as far as his competence as an author is concerned. No longer is the author compelled, for the sake of legitimacy, to offer a comprehensive solution, prior to taking on any single topic.

He follows this with the announcement that even though such "presumptuousness" is inexcusable, he is hardly willing to do entirely without it himself (1:18, §6). Coming from the same author who, a paragraph earlier, had called himself a "lowly and unknown writer," this claim is not without its own touch of imperiousness. Kant declares, "I have already prescribed the track [*Bahn*] to which I will hold. I shall launch my career [*Lauf*], and nothing shall hinder me from completing it" (1:19, §7).[13] The pictorial force of this metaphor—in the preface to a book titled, after all, *Thoughts on the True Evaluation of Living Forces*—is perhaps best explained by the fact that it is a figure drawn from the realm of physics itself. What is sublime here (in the sense of Kant's own later definition of the term) is that the pathos of freedom that he expresses is formulated in terms of a law of nature. As Gerland rightly maintains, "[h]is words here are so weighty that they can only be indications of his newly conceived lifetime project of the study of nature: the observation of the world, and then its explanation."[14] There is a play on words in the second sentence. The words, as they stand, are simply "prescribed the track," "launch my career." "Career trajectory" [*Laufbahn*] has to be synthesized by the reader. By association, this conjures the trajectory or flight path of an object. But objects do not prescribe themselves. They merely obey the strict laws of nature, and mathematical calculations prescribe their motion. The reflexive use of *prescribe* is an indication of the author's own reflective stance. In the second sentence, the expression "launch [a] career" connotes *agon* just as much as astronomy. Is the author a star or, more humbly perhaps, some small heavenly body, determining its own trajectory and then pursuing (and completing) it with the force of natural law? Or is he simply a determined competitor, defining his own career track? The ironies here are too complex to be reduced to a single sense. Yet in this one joke is mirrored all the reflectivity of Kant as he reflects upon his role as author.[15] At the same time, the expression "launch (a) career" connotes psychodynamic elements that can be fully accounted for only by a study such as Böhme and Böhme's analysis of the *Universal Natural History and Theory of the Heavens.*

Almost a half-century later, Kant writes to Fichte to encourage him in his work, itself very much connected to Kant's own. Kant reflects:

> Wie nahe oder wie fern auch mein Lebensziel ausgesteckt sein mag, so werde ich meine Laufbahn nicht unzufrieden endigen, wenn ich mir schmeicheln darf, dass, was meine geringen Bemühungen angefangen haben, von geschickten, zum Weltbesten eifrig hinarbeitenden Männern der Vollendung immer näher gebracht werden dürfte.

> As near or as far away as my life's end may be, I will not end the trajectory of my career unsatisfied, as long as I can flatter myself with the thought that what began with my trifling efforts will be carried ever nearer to completion by the hard work of skillful men, working towards the betterment of the world. (*Briefwechsel,* 639, May 12, 1793)

Fichte's answer points, *e contrario,* to the orbits of stars: "What can it be like, you great, good man, to be able to have sentiments such as these near the end of your *earthly* career [*irdischen Laufbahn*]. I confess, that the thought of you will always be my genius, which guides me" (*Briefwechsel,* 649, September 20, 1793). The trajectories [*Laufbahn*] of stars, however, are "revolutions."[16]

Just what Kant's use of the expression "career track/trajectory" was meant to suggest[17] is shown clearly in Arnoldt's portrayal of Kant's youth: it concludes with the observation that Kant's "track" [*Bahn*] developed quite willfully, though it was not the least bit simple or easy. On the contrary, his life progressed "in a most irregular fashion toward its aims."[18] And after Arnoldt illustrates this with biographical examples, he finishes his portrait of Kant: "Thus he reached the end of his track" (Arnoldt, "Kants Jugend," 210).

Irony functions as a defensive gesture, as a withdrawal to which Kant sees himself compelled. The presumptuousness of his declarations about his career stems from a claim he makes just prior to that passage, that "*the truth, which the greatest masters of human knowledge have struggled in vain to attain, has exhibited itself, for the first time, to my intellect*" (ww, 1:18, §6, Kant's emphasis). These words are not just presumptuous, as Kant himself concedes. They also play upon something that he returns to in *Dreams of a Spirit-Seer*, again ironically, when he admits to being in love with metaphysics, "even though I can boast of having won only the most infrequent evidences of her favor towards me" (ww, 2:982).[19] Yet now Kant boasts that the truth, sought after by all, has "exhibited herself" for the very first time, and to him.[20] With the claim that the truth has exhibited [*dargestellt*] herself to him, however, arises the problem complex of representation [*Darstellung*]. For this reason, Kant's audience is no longer denied access to the boudoir: "As a matter of course, a writer draws his reader, unnoticed, into that very same disposition in which he found himself as he wrote his text" (ww, 1:20, §8). But this does not happen until the necessary arrangements have been made. The writer's disposition, at the moment of writing, is that of being convinced of the truthfulness of his own thoughts. Kant justifies his tone of self-certainty with the assumption that the world will doubt him in any case, and in reading him will thus automatically correct for any overstatement, which he therefore programs into his writing in advance.

Kant's last point in the preface concerns literary presentation (1:22, §10). An inquiry that promises new truths is required to provide proof, and this in turn requires simplicity and clarity of presentation. The author "must therefore make his inquiry as simple and as easy as possible, so that he may, to the best of his judgment, assume there to be as much light and clarity in his own observations, as some other would expect to find, as far as he were able, in a much more intricate inquiry" (1:22f.). The way the preface announces its author as both self-confident and willing to leap those very bounds of convention that had just been given their due in the dedication, is remarkable. The writer's track, as the one Kant prescribed to himself, reveals a quality of philosophical reflectivity already manifest in both its language and its style. The ambiguity of the astronomical metaphor denotes the author's still-indeterminate self. This self has still to project itself into the universe, to seek out and get a feel for the conditions of its possibility. The process of self-definition as an author includes playing through various authorial roles, within which the writer probes for his own identity. These kinds of literary preludes represent texts necessary for self-understanding, and are thus far from trivial. Diffuse metaphors of the self, brought into play to function beyond the discourse as a means of authorial legitimation, become unnecessary only later, on the basis of his Rousseau experience. From that time on, in principle since the group of texts from 1762, the author's identity is consolidated.

Cassirer has pointed out that, although this first work appears inadequate as regards its content, its tone is nonetheless worth noting. Its "peculiar charm" lies not so much in what it contains as in what it "strives for and promises":[21] "We encounter here for the first time the subjective pathos of Kantian thought, in full force and definitiveness" (Cassirer, *Kants Leben,* 28). "From the moment that Kant comes onstage as a philosophical writer, it is as if all the narrowness and wretchedness of his external existence is extinguished, and there stands, alone, and with an almost abstract clarity, the defining law under which his being and intellect operate" (Cassirer, *Kants Leben,* 30). Although not yet reflective in a philosophically critical way,[22] this first text is still less of a natural philosophy treatise than it is "an essay on the methods of natural philosophy" (Cassirer, *Kants Leben,* 25). For Kant, it is a question of a *modum cognoscendi* (compare ww, 1:75, §50; also Cassirer, *Kants Leben,* 25). Thus already, in this first text, one discovers two moments that will acquire decisive significance for Kant's procedure: first, the use of the "skeptical" method as a means, as well as a mode of representation for, discovering the truth (ww, 1:85, §58); and second, the methodological reflectivity resulting from this. This latter moment involves ascertaining the condition of its possibility by posing the question back upon itself, "whether the conditions of the proof also contain in themselves the necessary definitions" (1:183, §128; cf. 1:114, §88f.). One perceives here, in its first stages, a genuine, self-sufficient voice seeking its own, autonomous tone. Its form is not yet clearly delineated, but it has already reached beyond the gestures of youth to find, in a critical tone, its balance.

This critical reflection on knowledge intrudes, at methodologically permeable points, on the theme of a treatise on physics, penetrating its cloak of scientific dignity. Simultaneously, by critically whittling away at the assumptions of objective science, such reflection begins to formulate a philosophical discourse aimed at the basic premises of objectivity. Having initiated its dissolution with methodological questions, Kant then turns the dogmatic discourse to his own purposes, gradually evolving it, step by step, first into a skeptical discourse, then a protocritical, and finally a transcendental-reflective one.

This process of critical reevaluation and step-by-step transformation of methodological premises is already recognizable in Kant's first text. That this is a serious systematic point for Kant is evident in, among other things, his sharp attack on Wolff's methodological approach, whose fixation on totality still counted as exemplary in Kant's time. Such "methodological panoply" may dazzle, but is unable to convince. As Kant further observes:

> Man kann sagen: dass die Hindurchführung seines Satzes durch eine grosse Reihe von vorhergehenden Sätzen, die vermittelst einer gestrengen Methode sehr genau zerteilet und vervielfältiget werden, der Kriegslist einer Armee zu vergleichen ist, welche, damit sie ihrem Feinde ein Blendwerk mache, und ihre Schwäche verberge, sich in viele Haufen sondert, und ihre Flügel weit ausdehnt.

> One can say: the way he draws his concluding sentence from a great series of preceding sentences, which have all been precisely divided and multiplied according to a strict method, is comparable to that military strategem in which an army creates a deception, and conceals its weakness from the enemy, by separating its number into many smaller groups and greatly extending its flanks. (1:139, §103)

It will be worth keeping in mind this critique of Wolff's deployment of concepts and his deception and bluff tactics when it comes time to consider the *Critique of Pure Reason*. There, Kantian syntax, in its fully developed form, will be considered in terms of the specific emphasis it lends to the critique of philosophy. His syntax arrives at this function only after a long process of development, involving much experimentation.

TWO

Cosmological Family Romance

ITH HIS FIRST MAJOR WORK, *Universal Natural History and Theory of the Heavens* [*Allgemeine Naturgeschichte und Theorie des Himmels*], Kant debuts, albeit anonymously, with astonishing self-assurance.[1] Indeed, to debut so self-assuredly and immediately to establish a first-person discourse calls for some initial anonymity: in order to avoid reproaches of arrogance and ridiculousness and instead foster the appearance of argument, this literary anonymity is theoretically necessary. Nonetheless, in practice it cannot be upheld beyond this initial stage, for otherwise this "youthful misadventure in the cosmos"[2] degenerates, literally, into an ego trip.

The history of *Universal Natural History*'s production reads like an excerpt from Jean Paul's *Schulmeisterlein Wutz:* stranded in the provinces, lonely, penniless, and thirsting for knowledge, the hero is able to afford only the annual book-fair catalogue, and so from reading just the titles, and with the help of his own fantasy, he rewrites the books for himself. "Jean Paul probably never suspected that a very similar undertaking had been attempted in real life by Immanuel Kant, about forty years previously."[3] Kant had read a report briefly summarizing Thomas Wright's *Original Theory or New Hypothesis of the Universe*, which had just appeared in 1751, in the *Freye Urtheile und Nachrichten zum Aufnehmen der Wissenschaften und der Historie überhaupt*, published in Hamburg.[4] But he was never able to inspect the book for himself during his seven years' absence from Königsberg.[5] We can assume that when Kant returned to Königsberg in 1754, he brought the manuscript of the *History*, already completed, with him. The *Universal Natural History* appeared, in any case, shortly after his return.

In 1754, Kant's article, "Investigation of the Question Whether the Earth Has Undergone an Alteration of Its Axial Rotation" ["Untersuchung der Frage, ob die Erde in ihrer Umdrehung einige Veränderung erlitten habe"], appears in the *Wöchentliche Königsbergische Frag- und Anzeigungsnachrichten.* At the end of this article, Kant himself announces an upcoming work with the title *Cosmogony, or an Attempt to Deduce the Origin of the Universe, the Formation of the Heavenly Bodies, and the Causes of Their Motion, from Newton's Theory of the Universal Laws Governing the Motion of Matter* [*Kosmogonie, oder Versuch, den Ursprung des Weltgebäudes, die Bildung und die Ursachen über Bewegung aus den allgemeinen Bewegungsgesetzen der Materie der Theorie des Newton gemäss herzuleiten*]. The book is "to be published shortly."[6] Although several articles on geography appeared before the *Universal Natural History*, it must be assumed that Kant first conceived of the book as a whole. Then, once the project was completed, and while he searched for a publisher, he reedited smaller portions into articles for newspaper publication. In this way, the *Universal Natural History* forms both the conceptual foundation and structural matrix that scientifically support the various articles conceived for popular consumption.[7]

The book appeared in March 1755, nine months after its announcement. In the May 1756 issue of the same journal that carried Kant's own announcement, in the section entitled "Things for Sale in Königsberg," comes the notice: "M. Kant's Universal Natural History and Theory of the Heavens is now available at the Book Printer Mr. Joh. Fried. Driest's" (AA, 1:545). But because the publisher was in bankruptcy, resulting in its storerooms being sealed off, the book was distributed late and under difficult conditions, and thus remained largely unknown. Only the energetic *Freye Urtheile und Nachrichten* (Hamburg, 1755, 429–32) printed a review. This was the same journal that had carried the original report on Wright's new theory, providing Kant with his starting point for this work. Adickes mentions six original editions of the *Universal Natural History* still existing in German libraries in 1925.[8] Although Kant repeatedly referred to this text, and to the priority its hypotheses merited, he decided against a new edition of the book.[9]

In his text, Kant offers the argumentative foundation for modern cosmogony. He formulates the hypothesis that later becomes significant as the Kant-Laplace theory.[10] The literary form he chooses is the *Versuch*,[11] the essay.

The *Versuch* is the German form of the essay. It is an open-ended investigation that strives to free itself from the rigidly ordered textbook form exemplified by Wolff and built around strictly numbered paragraphs, and from other fixed academic-literary forms as well, like the tractate. Having set out upon this course, Kant must simultaneously be on guard against drifting toward the opposite extreme and landing in the realm of poetry or fiction. From the very first, the essay has to establish its middle ground between scholastic philosophy and the literary novel, much in the same way the *Critique of Pure Reason* has to claim its little island of reason between rationalism and empiricism. This act of philosophically transcendental self-founding—so to speak—is what the essay tentatively strives for in its form. Such a mode of representation, which reflects upon its own presentation, guarantees philosophical candor through its nonclosure. This "tentative intention" makes the essay into the "critical form *par excellence.*"[12]

The *Versuch*, or essay, is one of the literary forms prevalent in the Enlightenment's "republic of letters." It is assigned to the "minor" or marginal genres such as letters, dialogues, observations, diversions [*Unterhaltungen*], and dictionaries. All of these have in common the basic idea of a form of communication in which thoughts can be easily exchanged.[13] Originally a marginal form, the essay developed, in the meditative, conversational style of Montaigne's essays and the pragmatic rationalism of Bacon's, to become the preferred literary genre of philosophical reflection in the French and English Enlightenment. Locke's investigations into the theory of knowledge, Leibniz's theodicy and his critique of Locke, Hume's essays and *Inquiries*, as well as Swift's literary escapades, for example his *Trictical Essay*, were all conceived of and written in the "form" of the essay.[14] In the Enlightenment, this form is associated not only with literary agility and elegance, but also with wit, *Witz, esprit*. The essay designates that free discursive space in which thoughts are allowed to develop without constraint. Not compelled to ascribe to any scholastic codex of regulations, the essay withdraws from rigid intellectual and formal structures, choosing instead to reside, as it were, in Diogenes' barrel.[15] This free form, predetermined in neither content nor scope,[16] provides a type of framework in which philosophy can proceed independently and yet systematically at the same time. As a marked departure from *mos geometricus*, the essay delineates the place where philosophical thought can experiment freely. This experimental quality, inherent to the essay, becomes a component of the argument—a part of critical reflection. Unencumbered by virtue of its newness, the genre literally becomes a locus of experimentation, in contrast to the summary generalities and textbook style of academic books and treatises. In this "laboratory of thought," individual problems can be extracted from the overarching and as yet unquestioned context, and investigated on their own.[17]

One indication of the role that the concept of the *Versuch* played for Kant is the fact that the term appears even in the early publication announcement of 1754 and was carried over to the later title, even though everything else was changed. Another indication is the presence of numerous epigraphs and quotations from poems by Pope, Addison, and "the most sublime among German poets," Haller (who was Swiss; ww, 1:335), all pointing to their predecessor, Montaigne, for whom classical citations were an element of any well-reasoned argument.[18] When Kant lectured, according to Reinhold Jachmann, "he practically undertook experiments [*Versuche*] in his listeners' presence, as if he were just then beginning to contemplate his object, and only gradually suggesting concepts to redefine it, modifying explanations already tried, step by step, finally arriving at a concept that was illuminated from all sides, exhausted in every aspect, and hence utterly conclusive. Thus he not only acquainted his strictly attentive audience with the object, he also guided them in thinking methodically."[19]

Cosmology comprises its own literary genre in the eighteenth century.[20] Didactic poems [*Lehrdichtungen*], like those of Pope, Haller, and Brockes, fall under this rubric. Even when older, Schelling was of the opinion that "there is no true didactic poetry, except that in which the universe [*das All*] itself, in mediated or unmediated form, as it is reflected in knowledge, is the object. Because the universe is *singular*, both in form and in essence, there can therefore be only *one single* didactic poem, ideally speaking, from which all others are mere fragments, namely, the poem on the Nature of Things."[21] *De rerum natura* is the subject of Kant's cosmogony, as well, placing it not only doxographically in the tradition of ancient Atomists, but also demarcating its genre-specific literary form. For indeed, Kant's cosmogony takes on Lucretius's classic didactic poem in all its epic scope, to a degree otherwise unheard-of in the eighteenth century.[22]

Well into the second half of the eighteenth century, natural science and literature were not separated within the language of cosmology. "The truth of Copernicus's discoveries, as Blumenberg pointed out, translated almost immediately into a shift in the history of consciousness itself, becoming, within a vast current of tradition, an integrated, at times even constitutive, moment of literary language" (Böhme and Böhme, *Das Andere*, 172). This is an essential aspect of the *Universal Natural History*, "that in the realm of cosmology, the differentiation between scientific, philosophical, and literary modes of discourse occurred only very late—namely after Kant's *Theory of the Heavens*" (173). Hence there can still be found, even in Kant's *Universal Natural History*, "natural-scientific exposition, philosophical reflection, and poetic enthusiasm, all so insolubly bound together, that one is forced, in this case, to speak of a peculiar species of cosmology whose structure can be grasped only under the rubric of 'new science'" (173).[23]

All of this is of foremost significance to an analysis of Kant, because any interpretation that ignores this peculiarity will run itself into the ground, or at best spin its wheels. Thus it would be, for example, "a senseless philological game—we have tested it out—to attempt to demonstrate just what sort of eclectic mumbo jumbo would result from reconstructing how this theory connects to every other physical and cosmological theory prior to and contemporary with it" (Böhme and Böhme, *Das Andere*, 193).[24] It is therefore necessary to concede that the only possible interpretation here is one fully conscious of the literary genres involved.

Remarkably enough, the fundamental character of Kant's cosmology has until now only been considered from a natural sciences perspective. For this reason, its place in the history of literary forms has been utterly ignored. Gerland has remarked pointedly that "the natural history of the heavens and the physical study of the earth form the natural, although entirely unconscious, preliminary stages for the *Critique of Pure Reason*, and the latter is thus connected to his geographical studies most narrowly." He calls these studies, "the outer garb of the first phase of his philosophical development."[25] And Munitz repeats this: "We cannot understand [his entire philosophical] career without giving due place and importance to the role that cosmological speculation had for him. . . . *The Critique of Pure Reason* cannot be fully understood apart from its continuity with the *Theory of the Heavens.*"[26]

It is a matter of logical consequence that Kant directs his attention to cosmology, and that he seeks to establish it as a modern science. The point where the act of knowing can take place must first be created. The knowing subject must first establish itself as such. It does this by speaking of the self. And Kant's narrative self, the "I", has surfaced already, with significant redundance, in the *Thoughts on the True Evaluation of Living Forces*, in whose preface every second paragraph begins with "I".[27] This is surprisingly emphatic for a philosophical discourse, and already, in 1746, it served as a means of asserting the writer's authorial self. What began there as a pragmatic-discursive, self-founding gesture, so to speak, is now extended into the cosmic realm. Once again, the redundancy of "I" references is astonishing in its sheer quantity. The work literally begins with "I". Of the first ten sentences in the preface, seven start with "I".[28] Of the twenty-four paragraphs that comprise the preface, eight begin with,[29] and seven more are constructed around, this "I".[30] The phrase "only I" [*Allein ich*] appears twice.[31] It designates Kant's self-constituting gesture with particular clarity, through its "Only I!" This speech pattern built around the "I" is, in fact, the figure establishing the Archimedean point of the text.[32] That it serves as Archimedean point is possible only "because nature can proceed in no other way, even in chaos, than with regularity and order" (ww, 1:235). For indeed, reason does not derive itself from nonreason, as the Atomists claimed, but rather from "certain necessary laws," to which matter, too, is bound (p. 234).

This narrative self, establishing itself through repetition of the "I", provides the groundwork for the central passage in the longest paragraph (§XVII), where the stage is also set, as it were, for the leap into speculation. It is in this context that Kant's comment, "Just give me matter, and I'll build you a world from it" ["Gebt mir nur Materie, ich will euch eine Welt daraus bauen."], wins such emphatic significance. Right away, he carries this over into metaphor: "Give me matter, and I will build a world from it! that is, give me matter, and I will show you, how a world is to be created from it" [Gebet mir Materie, ich will eine Welt daraus bauen! das ist, gebet mir Materie, ich will euch zeigen, wie eine Welt daraus entstehen soll] (237). The Archimedean point is transformed into a cognitive function, but it also preserves its primal function: to establish and to legitimate. But Archimedes' *dos moi pou* is also given a Promethean turn. Goethe's "Prometheus," which becomes the priming-powder for the Pantheism dispute, merely repeats this process once more, in a lyric mood. For Kant, it is radical self-knowledge, staking out its place in the universe; for Goethe, it is the self's deification, able to realize itself only in its self-representation.[33] Goethe himself later stressed the importance of the Copernican turn, whereby "those who embraced it felt justified and encouraged to assume a freedom of thought and a grandeur of disposition that was unknown and even unsuspected until that time."[34]

And there is just as much metaphysics at play for Kant as there is for Goethe. Kant's hymn to infinitude is where, in the text, subjectivity is constituted; hence it is form-defining for the *Versuch,* even for its linguistic basis. It is of utmost importance to observe "that scientific propositions of cosmogony must have had a primarily metaphysical meaning for the youthful Kant."[35] "Kant's critical position in regard to metaphysics grew out of a decades-long positive engagement with metaphysical questions. It is essential to note . . . that Kant was first of all, and most seriously, a metaphysician" (Schmalenbach, *Kants Religion,* 24).

Kant's passionate fling, his intoxicated enthusiasm for the infinite, cannot be reduced simply to poetic terms. On the contrary, poetry proves—bursting the framework of a decorative but still in-control rococo—to be the only possible form for initiating any philosophical reflection on the infinite. To this end, Kant's pantheism plays an undercurrent, but that much more important, role (for bringing to light this long-forgotten side of Kantian cosmology and theology, credit belongs to Herman Schmalenbach). This is relevant for the history of philosophy because it shows the effective breadth of the pantheistic tradition as a movement that also left its trace in Kant. It also allows one to understand, from a contrary position, Kant's later distancing of himself from Spinozism, confining it henceforth to the *mos geometricus,* as a disavowal of positions he had once held.

It has often been said of Kant's concept of God, that it suffers from an almost embarrassing blandness. But upon closer scrutiny—and this extends even to the *Critique*—one finds, "the same, essentially pantheistic concept of God that was founded, in both the *Proof* and even the *Cosmogony,* in the original pantheistic or pantheistic-metaphysical, but in any case sublime, experience of Kant's youth."[36] This "Nature Pantheism," "Kant's intimate linkage between God and world" (Schmalenbach, *Kants Religion,* 36), at last explains the literary form of the *Versuch:* a work as chaotic as it is orderly, because ultimately it just mirrors, monad-like, the divine cosmos.

The pathos of freedom and of being an author are both grounded in this Spinozistic moral consciousness: of themselves appearing "panentheistically," that is, in God, as God's expression, as *modi* of God's being. For this reason, the authorial "I" is also "a personal-sounding 'I' ";[37] its cosmological orchestrations manage not to alienate but instead to draw us closer to its personality.

Epicurus and Lucretius are the classical, and for that reason alone still admissable, code names in this discourse of Spinozism. Its essential nature is not really epistemological, but rather moral-political—indeed ethical. But these names can be cited only as borderlines, over and against which Kant seeks to define his position. What they have in common can be invoked only within a figure of self-distancing. This has to serve as a code of hidden references:

> Aber die Verteidigung deines Systems, wird man sagen, ist zugleich die Verteidigung der Meinungen des Epikurs, welche damit die grösseste Ähnlichkeit haben. Ich will nicht völlig alle Übereinstimmung mit demselben ablehnen. Viele sind durch den Schein solcher Gründe Atheisten geworden, welche bei genauerer Erwägung sie von der Gewissheit des höchsten Wesens am kräftigsten hätten überzeugen können. Die Folgen, die ein verkehrter Verstand aus untadelhaften Grundsätzen zieht, sind öfters sehr tadelhaft, und so waren es auch die Schlüsse des Epikurs, ohnerachtet sein Entwurf der Scharfsinnigkeit eines grossen Geistes gemäss war.

But it will be said, that to defend your system is at the same time to defend the opinions of Epicurus, for they bear the most similarity to your own. I will not disavow completely all agreement with him. Many have become atheists by the semblance of such reasons which, upon more precise deliberation, could have convinced them, on the contrary, and most powerfully, of the certainty of the supreme being's existence. The conclusions that a perverse intellect draws from flawless premises are more often than not quite flawed themselves, and this was also the case with Epicurus's conclusions, notwithstanding that his basic scheme reflected the acuity of a great mind. (ww, 1:233)[38]

One finds here a figure—subsequently cultivated by Lessing—of rescue. That same year, in 1755, Mendelssohn publishes his rescue of Spinoza, that states literally the "seed of truth in the midst of error" that Kant is after here. Both refer to the same intellectual-historical phenomenon. Spinoza and Epicurus are their common denominators. The only difference is that Epicurus had gained a sort of typological dignity in scholastic philosophy.[39]

"I am therefore not going to dispute that the theory of Lucretius or his predecessors, Epicurus, Leucippus, and Democritus, resembles mine in many ways" (233). After a brief report on each of these Atomists, Kant concludes:

So viel Verwandtschaft mit einer Lehrverfassung, die die wahre Theorie der Gottesleugnung im Altertum war, zieht indessen die meinige dennoch nicht in die Gemeinschaft ihrer Irrtümer. Auch in den aller unsinnigsten Meinungen, welche sich bei den Menschen haben Beifall erwerben können, wird man jederzeit etwas Wahres bemerken. Ein falscher Grundsatz, oder ein paar unüberlegte Verbindungssätze leiten den Menschen von dem Fussteige der Wahrheit durch unmerkliche Abwege bis in den Abgrund.

For my theory to have so much affinity with a school of thought that in ancient times truly denied the existence of God, does not, even so, draw it into their community of error. One can always notice at least some truth in even the most nonsensical opinions that have found approval among men. One false premise, or a few ill-considered connecting propositions, will lead a man from the path of truth, along unnoticed detours, into the abyss. (233–34)[40]

What is expressed here is the constitutive role, so far only analyzed in Goethe as an issue of poetic productivity, that pantheism plays. The authorial self is constituted by its inscription in the ontological matrix of Spinozan nature. Only in this way does the self become certain of itself as bound to existence. Kant's text, as a piece of didactic pantheism, performs precisely this function, securing its rootedness in its primeval substance. By achieving this grounding, it first makes possible, and serves as a prelude to, the self's philosophical enactment.

This is by no means just a case of "philosophical dreams" (242), Kant quickly reassures the reader: "Indeed, I have taken great care to banish from myself every bit of capricious invention [*willkürlichen Erdichtungen*]" (242). The emphasis is on *capricious*. For in fact later on, at the end of the appendix dealing with the topic "On the Inhabitants of the Stars," the reader encounters claims that are reasonable only to a certain degree—that are, in Kant's later terminology, the fictions of reasoning [*vernünftelnde Erdichtungen*]. We will return to this later.[41]

The experimental form of the *Universal Natural History* is characterized not only by the fact that Kant composed it as an essay. Along with this fact, a good deal of quite properly executed (or one could even say, artistically adept) theatrics play their part.[42] The central motif shaping the *Versuch* is the travelogue. One could also speak here of "science fiction" (Böhme and Böhme, *Das Andere*, 86). In the first paragraph of his preface, Kant himself maintains: "On the basis of a most modest conjecture, I have ventured on a dangerous journey, and already I glimpse the foothills of new lands. Anyone with courage enough in their hearts to press onward with the investigation, will set foot upon these lands, and will have the satisfaction of claiming them in their name" (ww, 1:227). Time and again it has been pointed out that Kant is a braggart on this subject, having almost never left Königsberg, and never having gone beyond Prussia. One might rather see this objection as an expression of the narrow tourist mentality among those who do travel. For in fact Kant had traveled, intellectually, throughout the universe, and this is his report on the journey.

Kant read travelogues voraciously,[43] and not merely because he had hardly traveled. Indeed, one of the numerous, utterly unfounded claims about Kant is that he was somehow unable to travel. Even students like Hamann and Herder, who lacked financial means, could travel if they wanted to. But Kant did not have the least intention of traveling (he actually declined all appointments to foreign universities, even the more lucrative ones). *Travelogues*, however, are not the same thing as traveling oneself. For Kant, travel and travelogue are related inversely, it seems, much in the way thinking [*Denken*] is related to thinking for oneself [*Selbstdenken*]. To not-travel is an act of renunciation, for the absolute journey would not be possible anyway—unless by way of the travelogue itself.[44]

In the grand tradition of the "connectedness of all things," Kant places an epigraph from Pope (in Brockes's German translation) at the beginning of part 1 of the *Universal Natural History:*

> Seht jene *Wunderkette*, die alle Teile dieser Welt
> Vereinet und *zusammenzieht* und die das grosse Ganz' erhält.
>
> Behold that great wonder-chain, that unifies and ties together
> All the world's parts, and upholds this great Whole. (255)[45]

Here already, Kant addresses the fundamental principle of the *plenitudo*, itself the basis of his cosmology.[46] A world of worlds follows from this principle, and with that the insight "that creation, in the whole infinite expanse of its greatness, is everywhere systematic and interconnected" (266).[47] In this system, the earth is hardly more noticeable than a grain of sand: "There is no end here, but rather an *abyss* of true immeasurability, into which sinks all human conceptual ability, even though this ability is also elevated by the help of numerical science" (267; emphasis added).

The epigraph to part 2 points the reader the way out of this confusion, away from this "abyss," and toward more familiar turf:

> Schau sich die *bildende Natur* zu ihrem grossen Zweck bewegen,
> Ein jedes *Sonnenstäubchen* sich zu einem anderen *Stäubchen* regen,
> Ein jedes, das *gezogen* wird, das andere wieder an sich zu ziehn,
> Das nächste wieder zu umfassen, es zu *formieren* sich bemühn.
> Beschaue die *Materie* auf tausend Art und Weise sich
> Zum *allgemeinen Centro drängen.*
>
> Behold, as form-giving nature proceeds in her great aim,
> As each sun-lit *fleck of dust* excites another *dusty grain,*
> As each one feels *pulled,* and *pulls* another one, in turn,
> Trying to encompass, indeed to *form* the other one.
> Contemplate how *matter,* in a thousand shapes and ways
> *Urges on* toward the *universal center.*[48]

The nucleus of the *Universal Natural History* is section 7 of part 2, "On the Creation in the Whole Expanse of Its Infinitude, in Respect to Space, as well as Time." It begins with the following words: "The world edifice [*Weltgebäude*] brings forth quiet astonishment [*stilles Erstaunen*] in us through its immeasurable scope and its infinite variety and beauty, emanating from it on all sides" (326). But this is not the "quiet simplicity" [*stille Einfalt*] that Winckelmann, that same year, had described as an aesthetic criterion; instead, what leads to such "quiet astonishment" is something extremely dynamic. It corresponds more to the "pregnant moment" described in Lessing's *Laokoon.* The concept of sublimity just beginning to get established in that work is closely connected with Kant's conception of nature. Even in

Kant's *Critique of Judgment,* art is still conceived of as merely a special case of beauty in nature [*das Naturschöne*]. Nature and knowledge are too intimately connected to allow art an autonomous space between them. And thus, from the very beginning, an epistemological character is ascribed to art, as a part of nature.

The writerly style of the *Universal Natural History* operates within the field of this aesthetic tension. It reaches its poetic high point in the "Addition to the Seventh Section," the "Universal Theory and History of the Sun in General." From a technical description of the sun, as the physical point of a system, the discourse soars into an imagined heliography that leaves every geographic fantasy behind. The fantastic voyage leads us right up to the sun's surface: "seas of fire," "furious storms," "scorched rocky crags, whose terrible peaks jut forth from flaming gullies"—in short, a grandiose drama of the "land of the sun" (350ff.). The demythologization of that heavenly body most laid claim to by theology is a task Kant can realize only by opposing the old metaphysics with a new intellectual poetics, in a sort of enchanting disenchantment. To do this he has to project.[49] Poetic fantasy is literally in danger here of getting too hot to handle.

Kant's first flight to the sun is a philosophical reformulation of the myth of Icarus. It is possible to avoid crashing only because the center has been displaced from the sun to a central mass, replacing the sun's theological significance. This preserves, free of confusion, the certainty of "approaching, albeit gradually, the destination of the highest perfection, namely the divine, but never being able to reach it anyway" (355).[50] But not until part 3, which declares that it will deal with "the inhabitants of the stars" (377), are the real heights of science fiction attained. "Poetic license" [*Freiheit zu erdichten*] (377) is expressly allowed, even justified here as a heuristic device, as long as it is kept within limits. Precisely because "poetic license" leads to philosophical knowledge in the first place, and to this extent is necessary, these limits are literally of fundamental significance. Kant's attitude toward everything novelistic, which bordered on aversion, stems from this close affinity of philosophical knowledge with it. It is Kant who first separates them; the separation represses the losses on both sides, in order not to awake suspicion.

Thus Kant's essay itself turns into sublime thought poetry. Pope's and Haller's verse seem to integrate into the essay completely. The language is mildly sublime throughout. Kant's extraordinary literary dexterity is indicated by the fact that his language never slips into pathetic or droll tones. "Who will show us the border where well-founded probability ends, and capricious inventions commence?" (393), he asks. He quotes Haller's lines as a response (394): "Perhaps it's radiant spirits, who live upon the stars, /

and as vice rules our world, so virtue rules theirs."[51] With a view to the implicit question here of the immortality of the soul and its migration through the universe, which is what is really at stake here, Kant declares: "We do not even rightly know what man, in his present state, is, even though our consciousness [!] and our senses [!] ought to have instructed us in this matter; how very much less, then, will we be able to guess at what he should someday become" (395).

In the appendix, "which contains an attempt [*Versuch*] to compare the inhabitants of different planets, based upon the analogies of nature," as the chapter heading announces (375), two passages bear closer consideration, because of their poetic density. A metaphor complex is developed in both of them that seems to have a dynamic all its own, but which also fully corresponds to Kant's tentative intention. The first passage gives us a surprisingly compromised portrayal of human existence: "If one observes the life most humans lead: this creature seems to have been created, like a plant, merely to draw juices into itself and to grow, to propagate its species, finally to become old, and to die" (382). The human being can be viewed as a creature. And for the majority of humans—whom the Greeks dismissively called the "many" [*hoi polloi*]—this may just be an accurate description. But this reduces the human to a plant. The classical image of man is given an ironical twist. For Pico della Mirandola, for instance, and even still for Pope and Haller, humans fall between the angels and beasts, in other words between reason and sensuality. But now—in contrast to the "great wonder-chain"—man is ironically reduced to a plant, something that simply vegetates, passive except to suck in its nourishment. This is also not a proud tree, which could stand as an emblem of nobility, but just a plant. An oral-infantile existence for the simple sake of reproduction. But this only *seems* to be the case. This creaturely root, keeping humans gravely, irreversibly earth-bound, is the starting point of any aspiration to an intelligible character. Hence the irony here is not biting, but humane. This is not deferred reassurance, but a spiritual view of the universe that is conciliatory:

> Er erreichet unter allen Geschöpfen am wenigsten den Zweck seines Daseins, weil er seine vorzügliche Fähigkeiten zu solchen Absichten verbrauchet, die die übrigen Kreaturen mit weit minderen, und doch weit sicherer und anständiger, erreichen. Er würde auch das verachtungswürdigste unter allen, zum wenigsten in den Augen der wahren Weisheit, sein, wenn die Hoffnung des Künftigen ihn nicht erhübe, und denen in ihm verschlossenen Kräften nicht die Periode einer völligen Auswickelung bevorstünde.

> Among all created beings, humans accomplish the purpose of
> their existence the least, for they exhaust their superior capabili-
> ties in such pursuits as the other creatures, with far fewer ca-
> pabilities, accomplish with far more certainty and propriety. Hu-
> mans would also be the most despicable of creatures, at least in
> the eyes of true wisdom, were they not elevated by their hope for
> the future, and by those strengths still slumbering within them,
> whose period of full development is still to come. (382ff.)

Human weakness is a necessary condition of human existence; cosmogony
is what first lets humanity come into its own in the shadow of galactic
systems.[52]

It seems surprising that such a passage could appear in the *Universal
Natural History and Theory of the Heavens*. It makes sense only when
understood within the discourse of a *Versuch:* an attempt within an attempt, an essay within an essay. Through this *"mise-en-abîme,"* Kant pur-
chases, as it were, his "poetic license."

The *Universal Natural History* reaches its most directly poetic emphasis
in the concluding sentences. These comprise the actual high point of the
Versuch, the destination Kant seems to be writing toward. We may recall
Kant's words of nearly a decade earlier, regarding the track whose course he
had prescribed, the career he had launched, and the discussion of those
metaphors: "Indeed, when one has filled one's mind with such observations, as well as the preceding ones: then the sight of a starry sky on a clear
[*heitern*] night can provide the sort of gratification only felt by noble souls
[*eine Art des Vergnügens, welches nur edle Seelen empfinden*]" (396). It is
still "a" sky. Kant's thoughts carry out the logical consequences of the idea
he had just proposed, of a plurality of worlds. For there may well be one
single all-encompassing sky, but this is made up of many, infinitely many,
individual starry skies. The clear night suggests more than meterological
conditions; it points to the Enlightenment, which itself draws its name
from meteorology.[53]

Kant continues, "In the universal silence of nature and the stillness of
the senses, the hidden cognitive capacity of the immortal spirit [*das ver-
borgene Erkenntnisvermögen des unsterblichen Geistes*] speaks an unnameable language, and gives undeciphered concepts that can no doubt be
sensed, but cannot be described" (396). It is the language of sentimentality
[*Empfindsamkeit*] that the author speaks here.[54] And yet it is nonetheless
strictly philosophical, and expresses poetically only what the *Critique of
Judgment* will later formulate within the system of transcendental philosophy. But Kant's language here is still undecided and ambiguous. Is the

"immortal spirit" that of the individual, or that at the basis of all things? The "unnameable language" is a poetic oxymoron, for language is precisely that which names. "Unnameable" can mean both that it does not name and that it cannot be named. Kant probably means both. That only "unde-ciphered concepts" are given must mean that these could be deciphered. But then they could also be described. And this is just what happens here— poetically. It is a speaking in silence (nature) and stillness (the senses).

THREE

Short Essays

URING THE YEARS 1754 THROUGH
1756, Kant published a series of articles on geographical questions in the
Wöchentliche Königsbergische Frag- und Anzeigungsnachrichten and its
publishing house.[1] These were produced mostly as sideline efforts in the
years Kant was chiefly occupied with preliminary work on the *Universal
Natural History*. Carefully crafted, self-contained prose pieces, they are
more than simply patched-together portions of his larger work-in-prog-
ress. Both their language and their content are nicely rounded, inducing a
meditative tranquility in the reader that was not yet to be found in the
cosmic travelogue's excited adventurousness. Vorländer describes their
function exactly when he remarks that these articles "strive more to be
thought-provoking viewpoint pieces, written for their popular appeal
among the readers of Königsberg's local papers and university programs."[2]

These pieces demonstrate a clarity and elegance that is grounded in an
enlightened, reflective sense of human engagement. Even while dealing
with geographical issues, one notices again and again that the fundamental
objects of Kant's contemplation are the conditions of human existence in
general. Whether it is the rotation of the earth, or the origin of winds and
monsoons, the Lisbon earthquakes that had been upsetting all of Europe, or
the volcanos on the moon, they all share in conditioning "that great lump
we inhabit" (Kant, *Geographische Schriften*, 44), and thus our lives as well.

Kant extracts these scientific questions about nature from the totality of
a worldview still dominated by theology. Approaching his questions by
way of investigating specific details does not result in a deficit of meaning,
because behind the analysis stands the process of a philosophy laying its

own groundwork. Although just beginning to develop, this philosophy is already able to transcend, critically, a pure description of the given.

Thus when answering "The Question Whether the Earth is Aging, Considered Physically" ["Die Frage, ob die Erde veralte, physikalisch erwogen"] (Kant, *Geographische Schriften*, 11ff.), Kant does not restrict himself to physical matters, but rather points to the universal nexus of becoming and passing away [*Werden und Vergehen*].[3] The question of the "coming to completion [*Vollendung*] and aging of the earth . . . (is) a well-founded and scientifically valuable topic of philosophical observation" (29). For this question, methodological considerations play a formative role:

> Ich habe demnach die aufgeworfene Frage von dem Veralten der Erde nicht entscheidend, wie es der unternehmende Geist eines kühnen Naturforschers erheischen würde, sondern prüfend wie es die Beschaffenheit des Vorwurfs selber mit sich bringet, abgehandelt. Ich habe den Begriff richtiger zu bestimmen gesucht, den man sich von dieser Veränderung zu machen hat.

> Accordingly, I have treated the question posed on the aging of the earth, not with an eye towards deciding it, as the enterprising spirit of a daring explorer of nature would demand, but rather as a means of examining what such a topic, by its very conception, entails. I have striven to define more correctly the concept to be derived here, the one that would describe this change. (32)

"Strive to define the concept more correctly" is Kant's program here. What this subsequently means is shown in light of the earthquake in Lisbon a year later, which made all of Europe extremely uneasy. Kant expressed his opinion right away in January 1756.[4] He not only writes off any theological connotations to the question of the Lisbon misfortune, but also places it, as a natural event, in the context of the earth's history, in order to grasp it as a purely scientific phenomenon. Even so, it retains philosophical relevance, to the extent that Kant assigns it a usefulness *post eventu:* denying the earthquake any divine purpose that we could possibly comprehend, Kant allows for the chandeliers in the churches to provide now their own good—secularized—sense, namely to show, as free-swinging pendulums, the direction of the tremors (69). Thus they demonstrate that nothing is condemned to lose its meaning, as long as we philosophize.

Kant inverts the usual theological lines of thought when he shows his willingness to extract such "utility" from an earthquake:

> Als die Menschen, die geboren waren, um zu sterben, können wir es nicht vertragen, dass einige im Erdbeben gestorben sind, und als

die hier Fremdlinge sind und kein Eigenthum besitzen, sind wir
untröstlich, dass Güter verloren worden, die in kurzem durch den
allgemeinen Weg der Natur von selbst wären verlassen worden.

As humans, who were born to die, we cannot endure that some
few died in the earthquake, and as strangers borne upon this
earth, who possess nothing, we are inconsolable that possessions
were lost, that all by themselves would have been lost soon
enough in the general course of nature. (73)

Inverting the point, and driving it home, he then asks, "Would it not be
better thus to reason: It was necessary that earthquakes occasionally dis-
rupt the earth's surface, but it was unnecessary that we build splendid
residences upon it?" (73)

In light of such an opinion of nature—and one ought to contrast this with
what Voltaire considered such an enlightened position in his *Candide*—all a
person is left with is thankfulness (Kant, *Geographische Schriften*, 76) and
the knowledge that "man [is] not born into this theatre of vanity to build
everlasting huts" (78f.). Thankfulness comes in as a form of acquiescence to
the contingent.[5] But in being directed toward nature, thankfulness is restricted to it as well. Natural history is, necessarily and at the same time,
the ground on which world history is written. Hence Kant's concluding
remark suddenly turns the observation of nature into a function of emancipation, giving final notice to the predominance of theology and at the
same time reminding secular rulers of their political duties:

Ein Fürst, der durch ein edles Herz getrieben, sich diese Drang-
sale des menschlichen Geschlechts bewegen lässt, das Elend des
Krieges von denen abzuwenden, welchen von allen Seiten über-
dem schwere Unglücksfälle drohen, ist ein wohlthätiges Werk-
zeug in der gütigen Hand Gottes und ein Geschenk, das er den
Völkern der Erde macht, dessen Werth sie niemals nach seiner
Grösse schätzen können.

A prince, who, compelled by a noble heart, allows himself to feel
moved by this calamity of the human race, and to divert the
misery of war from those whom it threatens from all sides with
the gravest incidences of misfortune, is a benevolent implement
in God's good hands, and is a gift He gives the people of the earth,
whose value they can never truly estimate in all its scope. (79)[6]

Kant repudiates the attribution of divine intention in natural disasters as
merely a hybrid, excessive self-presumption on the part of the human race.
Unable to overcome the blow to its narcissism in realizing it is not the

center of creation, humanity would rather feel it was chastised by some imagined willful force than admit to itself its own insignificance.

In the years following these articles directed to the newspaper-reading public, Kant published his lecture announcements, accompanied by short essays. One reason he had to do this was because the lecture announcements of adjunct lecturers were not included in the university's official course listings,[7] and so Kant, like others in his position, had to rely upon his listeners' ability to pay for them. This also explains the particular character of these program texts. Due to force of circumstance, they express themselves with clarity and promise. Although obligingly written, they have little literary value; even so, the author manages to give them an essay-like quality. The award in 1755 of a degree, closely followed by his academic inauguration, did force Kant to produce dissertations ("De igne," "Nova dilucidatio," "Monadologia physica"). Written in Latin, they are purely functional texts produced to fulfill academic requirements.[8] Kant's inaugural speech earned some notice, but only its title has survived: "On the Easier and Thorough Presentation of Philosophy" ["Vom leichteren und gründlichen Vortrag der Philosophie"].[9]

Whereas the "Theory of the Wind" ["Theorie des Windes"] (1756) and the "New System" ["Neuer Lehrbegriff"] (1758) are still clearly lecture announcements, the heading he gives his 1759 announcement, "An Attempt at Some Reflections on Optimism" ["Versuch einiger Betrachtungen über den Optimismus"][10] suggests something different.

In 1753, the Berlin Academy of Sciences had announced a prize competition for the year 1755, with the theme, "l'examen du système de *Pope*, contenu dans la proposition: *Tout est bien.*"[11] Kant sketched out a few thoughts, but never worked on them further. Unlike Lessing and Mendelssohn, who treated the competition question with amicable levity, Kant considered Pope to be of some significance, philosophically.[12] Lessing and Mendelssohn countered the academy's veiled attack on Leibniz pugnaciously, by summarily equating Leibniz with truth.[13] Running *hors de concours*, they reciprocated the academy's prank of exposing Pope, but having Leibniz in mind, by arguing that the philosopher's beard, which the famed academy now called for battle over, was a false one.[14] Their strict separation of philosophy from poetry in this instance is obviously polemically motivated, for the most part. Yet it is still worth noting that while Kant quite clearly settles on a comparison of Pope and Leibniz, Lessing and Mendelssohn seek to deter any such mixture of philosophy and poetry:

> The philosopher who climbs onto Parnassus and the poet wishing
> to descend into the valleys of serious and serene wisdom, meet

each other right at the halfway mark, where they exchange clothes, so to speak, and then go back the way they came. Each brings the other's external form back home with him; but nothing more than the external form. The poet has become a philosophical poet, and the philosopher has become a poetic philosopher. But for this reason alone, the philosophical poet is still not a philosopher, and the poetic philosopher is still not a poet. (Lessing, *Werke*, 3:27)[15]

Thus, the authors maintain, while Lucretius's poetry contains Epicurus's system, he is still "a versifier, but not a poet" (3:27). If one views Lucretius as a poet, however, as Kant undoubtedly did,[16] then Lucretius and Epicurus delineate precisely the field of potentiality in which Kant himself wrote: with epic scope, on the one hand (*Universal Natural History*), and philosophical speculations about nature, on the other (*Theory of the Heavens*).

Unlike Kant's previous sketches, his *Versuch* leaves Leibniz's theodicy problem, the question of the origin of evil in the world, on the margin. Instead, the focus turns to the methodological side of the question. In the sketches, reflections on the question of evil predominate, but in the *Versuch* these are reduced to a question of subjective values.[17] Now, Kant asks first and foremost about the best world in general—and this means about the best world for God. Even if the argument is hardly successful and somewhat confusing—Kant would later consider this essay in particular as a failure—there can be found here already a first application of the important distinction, introduced by Crusius, between real and epistemological grounds of rational argument [*Real- und Erkenntnisgrund*].[18] An inherent, indeed essentially constitutive part of the essays is the possible danger of failure or, as Kant puts it, "Subtle errors are a lure for one's vanity, which loves to feel its own strength" (ww, 2:587; DW, 71).

"Written in energetic language, almost poetic yet disdaining the phrase,"[19] Kant's consolation text, "Thoughts on the Occasion of the Precipitous Demise of . . . Johann Friedrich von Funk" ["Gedanken bei dem frühzeitigen Ableben des . . . Johann Friedrich von Funk"],[20] is conceived as an open letter and composed in the tone and style of Haller. Indeed, quoting Pope as well as Haller, it differs from the latter's work only in that it is not divided into lines of verse.[21] It is the only consolation text [*Trostschrift*] of this sort, and the question arises here, as for no other text of Kant's, as to its motivation. We must assume that the death of Funk, one of Kant's listeners, touched him extraordinarily deeply, so deeply that he felt called upon to direct an almost sermon-like epistle to the mother of the deceased.[22]

Funk died in his twenty-second year. This may suggest one reason, among others, why the teacher was so moved by the death of his esteemed student. It was at this same age that Kant completed his first literary work. The fact that a person could die so young that he never even had a chance to leave traces of himself behind in a work, may be part of what induced Kant to compose a consolation text in Haller's style to the mother of the young man. There is also a very personal side to this gesture. Kant lost his mother when he was thirteen. To console the mother of a student of his for the loss of her son functioned perhaps as a replacement, allowing Kant to mourn his own loss in the literary medium of a consolation text for another's—mother.[23]

FOUR

System Crisis

THE GROUP OF TEXTS THAT AP-
peared in 1762 mark the completion of one of the first phases of Kant's
thought. Four texts are produced in this period that all share the same
systematic foundation. As Dieter Henrich notes, it seems, "that Kant
proved himself to be a surprisingly prolific writer for just this reason, that
now he believed himself to be in possession of the basic elements of a new
concept of metaphysics, something that could be expostulated in various
applications."[1]

The texts are closely connected to one another, make reference to one
another, and together comprise the outline of a system.[2] In rapid succes-
sion, there appear (1) *Die falsche Spitzfindigkeit der vier syllogistischen Fi-
guren* [*The False Subtlety of the Four Syllogistic Figures*] at the beginning of
the winter semester, (2) *Der einzig mögliche Beweisgrund zu einer Demonstration des Daseins Gottes* [*The Only Possible Argument in Support of a
Demonstration of the Existence of God*] in the second half of December 1762.
And on the last day of December, the submission deadline for the Prussian
Academy's competition, comes (3) Kant's manuscript, *Untersuchung über
die Deutlichkeit der Grundsätze der natürlichen Theologie und Moral* [*In-
quiry Concerning the Distinctness of the Principles of Natural Theology and
Morality*], arriving in Berlin at the last possible moment for consideration.
In 1763 comes finally (4) the *Versuch, den Begriff der negativen Grössen in
die Weltweisheit einzuführen* [*Attempt to Introduce the Concept of Negative
Magnitudes into Philosophy*].[3]

With these four texts, Kant decisively shifts the concept of definition and
philosophical method. This revolutionary step is to reverse the prevailing

concept of definition, whereby the definition comes first and the singular specifics, logically deduced from it in a process of conceptual analysis, follow after. Reversing this order, Kant grasps definition as the goal—to be achieved, if at all, at the very conclusion of the process. The result of this reversal carries profound implications that not only affect the concept of philosophy but also pose an immediate challenge to the demands of literary presentation. Their effect can still be felt in the presentation of the *Critique of Pure Reason.*

The texts from 1762 attempt, first of all, and in the widest sense, to stake out the context in which this discovery is meaningful. But this group of texts does not constitute a closed system. Instead, with their overlapping, converging, and diverging contiguity, they reach beyond a system and induce a system crisis. This is indicated even in their literary form, where, in following several tracks at once, they epitomize the incomplete nature of ongoing experimentation. Their experimental character is the result of Kant's tentative progress in his theory of knowledge, which is still in flux at this point, a flux reflected in the concept-oriented presentation of these texts. They are formed by this movement and give expression to it, without yet being able to process it from a literary standpoint. But the conceptual work in epistemological theory carried out by the texts of 1762 marks the fundamental turn in the critique of knowledge. With this as his basis, Kant's literary development takes an experimental direction that is methodologically motivated.

The False Subtlety is an invitation to Kant's lectures (AA, 2:466), although he does not conclude it with a course listing, as he had done before becoming fully established as lecturer.[4] The text is written with a light and—particularly in the fifth section—witty touch.

By the end of July, Kant awaited daily the arrival of Rousseau's *Emile*, which he devoured immediately upon its appearance in Königsberg. This enthusiasm for Rousseau was to have a decisive effect on Kant. A philosophically systematic penetration of Rousseau came only later, gradually but all the more forcefully reaching its fullest extent after "the system concept crisis of 1762,"[5] as Henrich calls it. But the first marks of Rousseau already appear in the *False Subtlety.* Its title attacks scholastic philosophy just as sharply as Rousseau's own antitheses do, although Rousseau does so more completely and with more virtuosity.[6] Kant echoes Rousseau's acrid sarcasm, which is so often hostile to science. From his first discourse of 1750, Rousseau never tired of repeating the insight, which he practically made into a system in *Emile*, that the enlightenment had its own dialectic. Kant proves his reverence for this claim when he ironically notes:

Die wissenswürdige Dinge häufen sich zu unsern Zeiten. Bald wird unsere Fähigkeit zu schwach, und unsere Lebenszeit zu kurz sein, nur den nützlichsten Teil daraus zu fassen. Es bieten sich Reichtümer im Überflusse dar, welche einzunehmen wir manchen unnützen Plunder wieder wegwerfen müssen. Es wäre besser gewesen, sich niemals damit zu belästigen.

In our time, the things worth knowing keep piling up. Soon enough, our capability will be too weak, and our life will be too short, to grasp even the most useful part of them. An excess of riches offers itself to us, and to make place for this, we must once again discard other, useless bounty. It would have been better never to have burdened ourselves with it in the first place.[7]

Lecture announcement and cultural critique enter into a singular sort of synthesis here. In rejecting the academic way of procedure, however, Kant uses irony, to indicate that he now knows, along with Rousseau, what the issue really is:

Es gibt noch eine gewisse andere Brauchbarkeit der Syllogistik, nämlich vermittelst ihrer in einem gelehrten Wortwechsel dem Unbehutsamen den Rang abzulaufen. Da dieses aber zur Athletik der Gelehrten gehört, einer Kunst, die sonsten wohl sehr nützlich sein mag, nur dass sie nicht viel zum Vorteil der Wahrheit beiträgt, so übergehe ich sie hier mit Stillschweigen.

There is still another application for syllogistic reasoning, namely its use in an educated dispute, to outmatch whoever fails to be on guard. But since this belongs to academic gymnastics, an art that, although perhaps quite useful otherwise, nonetheless adds little to the advancement of truth, I will pass over it here in silence. (ww, 2:610ff.; DW, 101)

Herder's transcriptions of Kant's lectures on logic from 1762 are evidence of how open Kant's opposition was to the dominant scholastic philosophy of his time. There one encounters the statement, for example, about the relation of Wolff to Leibniz: "Wolf was Ali to Mahommed" ["Wolf war Ali gegen Mahomet"] (AA, 24:4).

In the *Only Possible Argument*, Kant picks up the thread of the *Universal Natural History*, which had been forgotten in the interim, and once more presents a summary of its hypothesis. His preface formulates a motif of Rousseau's that will subsequently grow to be a recurring theme in the *Critique of Pure Reason:*

Die Vorsehung hat nicht gewollt, dass unsre zur Glückseligkeit höchstnötige Einsichten auf der Spitzfindigkeit feiner Schlüsse beruhen sollten, sondern sie dem natürlichen gemeinen Verstande unmittelbar überliefert, der, wenn man ihn nicht durch falsche Kunst verwirrt, nicht ermangelt, uns gerade zum Wahren und Nützlichen zu führen, in so ferne wir desselben äusserst bedürftig sein.

Providence did not wish that our insights, of the utmost necessity for our happiness, should be based on the subtlety of delicate deductions, but rather that they be entrusted immediately to natural, common sense, which, so long as it is not confused by some false art, will not fail to lead us directly to true and useful conclusions, in so far as we are most in need of them. (ww, 2:621; DW, 111)[8]

The preface further introduces two metaphor complexes, variants of which Kant thenceforth uses repeatedly: the journey at sea, and a building metaphor.[9] The "bottomless abyss of metaphysics" is for him "a dark ocean without shores or lighthouses." Only those who seek a proof of God embark upon such a sea. "Like a sailor upon uncharted seas," one has to double-check, upon setting ashore, "whether some unnoticed ocean currents haven't confused one's course" (ww, 2:621f.; DW, 111). Meanwhile, a proof of God's existence "has still never been discovered" (ww, 2:622; DW, 111). Thus the "*Noonautica*"[10] is discontinued for the time being. Instead of setting out upon an expedition, a foundation shall be laid. Kant takes "argument in support" [*Beweisgrund*] literally: "What I am providing here is only the argument supporting a demonstration, a laboriously assembled framework [*Baugeräte*] . . . so that, from its usable pieces . . . the building can be completed" (ww, 2:622; DW, 111f.).

The difference between a demonstration and what Kant offers here has a ground-breaking significance for the mode of representation. He does claim a lack of time as the reason, why "the presentation [*Vortrag*] is the kind that shows signs of not being completely worked out"; but he holds firm to the claim that the observations set forth are "the outcome of extended contemplation" (ww, 2:622; DW, 112). So in conjunction with this long contemplation, the fact must be considered that Kant is willing, and indeed able, to give only a sketch, "the first outlines of an overall plan," from which subsequently "a building of no minor excellence . . . could be erected" (ww, 2:622f.; DW, 112). And indeed, as Kant hastens to add, not without a trace of irony, this would come "when more practiced hands give the drawing more correctness in its parts, and a completed symmetry to its whole" (ww, 2:623; DW, 112). The irony here is that Kant is actually questioning, from the ground upward, the very possibility of such a structure, whose basis he himself has pledged to construct. The *conditionalis* is unmasked as an *irrealis*, because such "practiced hands" can accomplish nothing here; only in this form, disguised with provisos, is it possible for Kant to justify his specific "kind of presentation."

The whole third paragraph of the preface (ww, 2:622f.; DW, 112f.) can thus be read as a single claim, concealed in various turns of phrase: that the author, although unsatisfied with the shape of his work, could not have rendered it otherwise without infringing on its intrinsic content, the very reason for its being written. The game he plays with his readers is not one of leading them about by their noses but rather a hide-and-seek where he constantly leaves them clues. The pursuit of these is left to all readers willing to think for themselves. In this way, they, too, take on an independent role in a text that stands open to them and forces them to think along with it continually, much like reading a musical score. In its complexity, this paragraph displaces Kant's undecidedness about the systematic place of the possibility of the *Only Possible Argument* onto a formal level. He designates, provisionally, the difficulty of being in philosophical flux as the formal ground for his own writing. The literary genre of the *Versuch*, the essay that is also an "attempt," thereby justifies precisely this type of writing as a legitimate way of reasoning. Equipped with the privilege of skepticism, this form of reasoning is able to describe itself respectably as a way of writing. It is a form—more proposal, sketch, or experimental attempt than something already executed—that posits a reflection on the conditions of the possibility of its own procedure at the very beginning:

> Ich habe bisweilen gemeine Verstandesurteile angeführt, ohne ihnen durch logische Kunst die Gestalt der Festigkeit zu geben, die ein Baustück in einem System haben muss, entweder weil ich es schwer fand, oder weil die Weitläufigkeit der nötigen Vorbereitung der Grösse, die das Werk haben sollte, nicht gemäss war, oder auch weil ich mich berechtigt zu sein glaubte, da ich keine Demonstration ankündige, der Foderung, die man mit Recht an systematische Verfasser tut, entschlagen zu sein.

> Occasionally, I have introduced common-sense judgments without reinforcing their form through the art of logic, as the building blocks of a system would require, either because I found it difficult, or because the preparations necessary for this would exceed the intended size of this work, or because I also believed myself to be justifiably spared what one rightfully demands of

systematic authors, since I never offered a demonstration. (ww, 2:623; DW, 112f.)

With this, Kant also justifies extracting and dealing with individual problems, hence freeing his writing of systematic constraints.

Just days after the *Only Possible Argument* appears,[11] in the middle of December, Kant concludes his *Inquiry*. These treatises are indeed quite closely connected. It is impossible to discern whether they were conceived and written sequentially or concurrently. There are some indications that certain essential insights, common to both, were formulated in the framework of preparations for the essay competition. Some of the formulations in the *Argument* sound more polished, leading to the assumption that Kant had recourse to a supply of knowledge already earned. The *Inquiry* seems still to be wrestling with these same formulations, and to settle for less pleasing locutions because of this. Thus, for example, the *Argument* summarily establishes, from the very beginning, what the *Inquiry* unfolds systematically: the separation of mathematics and philosophy and, related to this, the differentiation of the role of definition in both disciplines (ww, 2:630; DW, 116f.). It seems plausible to assume that Kant pressed forward with both treatises simultaneously, working sometimes on one, sometimes on the other.[12]

From a purely external perspective, the epigraphs that Kant gives these concurrent texts both come from Lucretius's *De rerum natura*, and this suggests an inner connection. By their very nature, their full meaning can be understood only by apprehending the resonance of their context. The lines at the opening of the *Basis* are taken from the beginning of Lucretius's didactic poem, and are basically his preface. Immediately preceding them comes a demand to the reader to heed the author's *vera ratio:*

Quod superest [nobis] vacuas auris [animumque sagacem]
Semotum a curis adhibe veram ad rationem,
ne mea dona tibi studio disposta fideli,
intellecta prius quam sint, contempta relinquas.

For the rest, ears unpreoccupied and keen intelligence detached from cares you should apply to true philosophy, that my gifts, set forth for you with faithful solicitude, may not be contemptuously discarded by you before they have been apprehended.[13]

And Lucretius continues, sketching out the extent of his work:

nam tibi de summa caeli ratione deumque
disserere incipiam et rerum primordia pandam.

For I shall begin to discourse to you upon the most high system
of heaven and of the gods, and I shall disclose the first beginnings
of things [the atoms].[14]

The final basis (of proof) of the heavens and the gods will thus be investigated.

The Berlin Academy's competition for 1763 was phrased, like its predecessor, as an attack on Wolff's school of thought. The theme for 1763 was
announced in 1761: "Are the metaphysical sciences capable of the same
evidence as the mathematical?"[15] Moses Mendelssohn's treatise, which is
essentially a defense of Wolff's position, captured first prize, by distinguishing comprehensibility [*Fasslichkeit*] from certainty [*Gewissheit*] and
fully conceding the latter to metaphysics.[16] But Kant was awarded the
accessit and the distinction of having his work published along with Mendelssohn's prize-winning treatise. Thus the *Inquiry* appeared in a form
unaltered from the way it was submitted to the Academy,[17] albeit without
naming its author, remarkably enough. It is introduced simply by the
epigraph: "Verum animo satis haec vestigia parva sagaci/ Sunt per quae
possis cognoscere caetera tute" [But for a keen-scented animal, these little
tracks are enough to enable you to recognize the others for yourself[18]—
except for the author, naturally!].[19] A year later, in his "Announcement
of the Program of His Lectures in the Winter Semester of 1765–1766"
["Nachricht von der Einrichtung seiner Vorlesungen in dem Winterhal-
benjahre von 1765–1766"], Kant makes his authorship known (ww, 2:910;
DW, 294). Kant also notes there, that this is simply "a short, hastily written
text." But it nonetheless holds up well in comparison with Mendelssohn's.
Although both texts agree on some points, Kant's *Inquiry* is incomparably
more original, for it independently forges the path to critical philosophy.[20]

For Mendelssohn, the difficulty of the proof of God's existence consists
solely in its presentation. He excludes as nonevident precisely those proofs
that Kant would admit—the physical-teleological ones—and is fully satisfied only with "logical" and ontological ones.[21] For Kant, these are merely
technical problems. Mendelssohn still sees the *ars combinatoria* as a self-
evident scientific ideal, with philosophy as a type of elevated mathematics.[22] Kant and Mendelssohn converge again on the question of moral certainty.[23] Both consider the chief maxim to be Wolff's definition of the
human being as perfection.[24] If Mendelssohn's emphasis on grounding
morality in freedom did not influence Kant, it must at least have recon-
firmed his views.[25]

In his treatise, Mendelssohn advocates quite eloquently the viewpoint that mathematics serves as the guide to all knowledge. This way of thinking, still well within the tradition of Wolff, is vehemently opposed by Kant:

> Die Methodensucht, die Nachahmung des Mathematikers, der auf einer wohlgebähnten Strasse sicher fortschreitet, auf dem schlüpfrigen Boden der Metaphysik hat eine Menge solcher Fehltritte veranlasst, die man beständig vor Augen sieht, und doch ist wenig Hoffnung, dass man dadurch gewarnet, und behutsamer zu sein lernen werde.

> The mania for method, the imitation of the mathematician striding securely forward along a well-trodden lane, has incurred a number of stumbles along the slippery surface of metaphysics, such as we see before us constantly, and yet there is little hope that anyone will take this as a warning, and learn to be more cautious. (ww, 2:630; DW, 117)

"The genuine method of metaphysics," in contrast, as the competition text formulates it, is "basically the same as the one *Newton* introduced into natural science" (ww, 2:756; DW, 259). This, to use Harnack's expression,[26] writes the death certificate for the Leibniz-Wolff metaphysics. And it is simultaneously legitimated with a tested trope that writers so often prefer: "Metaphysics is doubtless the most difficult of all human inquiries; for indeed, none has ever been written" (ww, 2:752; DW, 255). Experience steps in to replace logical deduction. With this, the extraction and independent handling of individual problems is justified:

> [S]uchet durch sichere innere Erfahrung, d.i. ein unmittelbares augenscheinliches Bewusstsein, diejenige Merkmale auf, die gewiss im Begriffe von irgend einer allgemeinen Beschaffenheit liegen, und ob ihr gleich das ganze Wesen der Sache nicht kennet, so könnt ihr euch doch derselben sicher bedienen, um vieles in dem Dinge daraus herzuleiten.

> Seek out, through reliable internal experience, i.e., an immediate, manifest consciousness, those distinguishing characteristics that are certain to be included in the concept of some general property, and even though you do not yet know the whole essence of the matter, you can still very well make use of those characteristics in order to derive many things about it. (ww, 2:756; DW, 259)

This advance in the theory of knowledge[27] rests on Kant's consistent separation of mathematics from philosophy, and the new understanding of definition itself that results from it. Countering the predominant epistemological ideal of the *mos geometricus*, Kant emancipates metaphysics from mathematics, where it was still regarded as *more geometrico demonstrata*, and sets it free as an autonomous discipline. The beginning of this movement is given consistent expression in the group of texts from 1762. It transcends conventional forms of systematic philosophical discourse, skeptically calling them into question, and reaches for a new form, yet to be created. The process of reasoning shapes itself searchingly. Thus the form of the discourse is forced at first to sketch out only the outlines of itself:

> Lange vorher, ehe man eine Erklärung vom seinem Gegenstande wagt, und selbst dann, wenn man sich gar nicht getraut, sie zu geben, kann man viel von derselben Sache mit grössester Gewissheit sagen. . . . Oft kann aus diesem, was man vor aller Definition von der Sache gewiss weiss, das, was zur Absicht unserer Untersuchung gehört, ganz sicher hergeleitet werden.

> Long before anyone would dare to offer an explanation of their object, and even in the case when one dares not attempt it at all, there is still much that can be said about it with the greatest certainty. . . . Often, from what we know for certain prior to any definition, we can deduce quite assuredly some part of what our inquiry intended. (ww, 2:629f.; DW, 117)

In mathematics, the concept of the object originally stems from the object's explanation; in philosophy, however, the concept of what has to be explained is always already *given* (ww, 2:762). Definition in mathematics is the inverse of that in philosophy. In mathematics, it is what basically comes first, because it is what first produces the object to be known (i.e., a genetic definition),[28] whereas in philosophy it is "most every time the very last thing" (ww, 2:753; DW, 256. Cf. ww, 2:759; DW, 261).[29] "Had we as many correct definitions as appear in books under this name, just imagine with what security one could deduce and draw conclusions from them. But experience teaches just the opposite" (ww, 2:753; DW, 256f.). Once experience is given, concepts must then be extricated from it analytically (ww, 2:759; DW, 261). This decisive "overturning" [*Umkippung*][30] frees up the way, as Kant repeatedly explains, "to be able to say much about an object with certainty . . . without having explained it" (ww, 2:759; DW, 261f. Cf. ww, 2:754; DW, 257f.). He speaks ironically of "the overly refined wisdom of those who put secure and useful concepts into their logical crucibles and exaggerate, distill, and refine them until they finally evaporate into volatile salts and steam" (ww, 2:634; DW, 120). Yet these concepts must be dissolved "down to these atoms" if "demonstrative certainty" is ever to be reached. Such analysis is what first leads to the consistent differentiation between real and cognitive reasons [*Real- und Erkenntnisgrund*], and to the resultant distinction between "real repugnancy" [*Realrepugnanz*] and logical contradiction (ww, 2:647; DW, 130). From this comes finally the recognition that the "ontological" proof of God runs a logical circle.[31] Throughout this, Kant is aware of the dialectic he is moving in when he undermines the tenets of definition (going "before all definition") and journeys *in terra incognita* to lay new grounds:

> Indessen legt die so sehr abgezogene Natur des Gegenstandes selbst aller Bemühung der grösseren Aufklärung Hindernisse, so wie die mikroskopischen Kunstgriffe des Sehens zwar das Bild des Gegenstandes bis zur Unterscheidung sehr kleiner Teile erweitern, aber auch in demselben Masse die Helligkeit und Lebhaftigkeit des Eindrucks vermindern.

> Meanwhile, the utterly abstract nature of the object itself creates impediments to all efforts towards greater clarification, much the way the artifices of microscopic vision can indeed enhance the image of the object to where very small parts can be distinguished, but only in the same degree that they diminish the luminosity and vitality of the impression. (ww, 2:640; DW, 125)

Regarding the impossibility of rationally deducing the existence of God, it may indeed be, as the concluding sentence of the *Only Possible Argument* expresses it, "utterly necessary that one convince oneself of God's existence; but it is not quite so necessary that one demonstrate it" (ww, 2:738; DW, 201). But if this is the case, then the cosmological proof of God is to be preferred to the ontological one, the former being "as old as human reason, it seems to me" (ww, 2:734):

> Und da es ohne Zweifel von mehr Erheblichkeit ist, den Menschen mit hohen Empfindungen, die fruchtbar an edler Tätigkeit sein, zu beleben, indem man zugleich den gesunden Verstand überzeugt, als mit sorgfältig abgewogenen Vernunftschlüssen zu unterweisen, dadurch, dass der feinern Spekulation ein Gnüge getan wird, so ist, wenn man aufrichtig verfahren will, dem bekannten kosmologischen Beweise der Vorzug der allgemeinen Nutzbarkeit nicht abzusprechen.

> And since it is doubtless more important to enliven one's fellow men with lofty sentiments, which bear the fruit of noble deeds, in that one persuades the healthy intellect directly, rather than instructing it with meticulously weighed-out rational deductions

that aim to satisfy rarified speculation, so then, if one is to proceed openly, the well-known cosmological proof cannot be denied preference as regards its general usefulness. (ww, 2:736; DW, 200)

And with sublime and often sentimental speech, the *Only Possible Argument* seeks to do justice to this demand. This hypothesis, repeated from the *Universal Natural History*, necessarily brings sentimental language into play, as is evident from the preceding analysis of that work. In addition to this we find new passages of remarkable sublimity. Thus, for example, Kant thinks of God as speaking to Himself in human language and calls this thought, "the sublimest of all" (ww, 2:724; DW, 191).[32] In another passage, he evokes the grandeur of the chain of being by gazing from a snowflake out into the universe, and recognizing the same harmony everywhere (ww, 2:709; DW, 179).

So it is no wonder that Kant runs across the same problem he had already confronted in the *Universal Natural History*. While seeking to buttress himself against poetic invention, he simultaneously avails himself of it as a heuristic method. The meaning of the concept *poetic invention (Erdichtung)* fluctuates meanwhile between negative and positive connotations.[33] A half-year later, in June 1763, the faculty files record the last title of this group of texts, the *Attempt to Introduce the Concept of Negative Magnitudes into Philosophy*. This essay further elaborates the idea of differentiating "real repugnance" and logical contradiction. With a view to Böhme and Böhme's analysis of the *Universal Natural History* and the two highly influential principles of attraction and repulsion that are its basis, the *Attempt* can be seen as gathering up metaphysical principles into the methodological discourse now taking shape. It continues, as it were, the *Universal Natural History*'s discussion by other, newly acquired means:

> Denn es sind die negative Grössen nicht Negationen von Grössen, wie die Ähnlichkeit des Ausdrucks ihn hat vermuten lassen, sondern etwas an sich selbst wahrhaftig Positives, nur was dem andern entgegengesetzt ist. Und so ist die negative Anziehung nicht die Ruhe, wie er davor hält, sondern die wahre Zurückstossung.

> For negative magnitudes are not the negations of magnitudes, as might be assumed from the similarity of the expressions, but rather something in themselves truly positive, that are opposed to other magnitudes. And so negative attraction is not a state of rest, as *Crusius* claims, but in fact true repulsion. (ww, 2:781; DW, 209)[34]

One objection to the imitation of mathematics in philosophy is that ultimately, "that troublesome *non liquet* does not yield a bit to all this pomp [*Gepränge*]" (ww, 2:779; DW, 207). The direct application of mathematics is only meaningful in the case of "insights connected to natural science" and the calculation of probabilities. Thus to introduce negative magnitudes into philosophy implies that these will be given a new definition that will be justified on a strictly philosophical basis.

For this reason, a delicate irony runs throughout this *Versuch*. While not devolving into open ridicule until the conclusion, it is present as an undercurrent from the very beginning. Parodying Cartesian and Spinozist psychology, it measures passions and feelings against one another, strictly apportioning each. There is a paradoxical, distinctly literary intention in what Kant leaves unsaid,[35] in what he merely hints at and yet manages to convey nonetheless. Indeed, this application of negative magnitudes demonstrates practically *ad oculos* how mathematical concepts transform into philosophical ones, as soon as one leaves mathematics and moves onto a philosophical footing. Unlike mathematics, which works with purely quantitative magnitudes, philosophy is concerned strictly with qualitative magnitudes. To measure these against each other is impossible. Kant's examples play with just this idea, producing a dialectic which pursues such measures *ad absurdum*. What applies in physics (ww, 2:785; DW, 212f., a ship's journey) and in mathematics (ww, 2:793; DW, 220, bookkeeping), is absurd in morality. Kant's parody of the classroom exercise involving a patriotic Spartan mother illustrates this, for to argue that her love of a country is $4a$, and the loss of her son is a, leaving a final sum of $3a$, sounds at least amusing, if not downright absurd (ww, 2:792f.; DW, 291f.).[36]

Kant's examples render unmistakably what the competition text had investigated systematically: that philosophy and mathematics must be scrupulously differentiated from one another as distinct realms of expertise. The *Versuch* explores their borderline, probing for transgressions. Kant's exposition shows just how much explanatory power the concept of negative magnitudes actually has when understood philosophically, particularly in those passages that reflect Kant's own position. Thus, for example, he describes abstraction as a positive process, rather than as a lack of the concrete. This enables him to fix more sharply on the complex of problems stemming from speculative vagueness. Abstraction involves "a *negative attentiveness* [*negative Aufmerksamkeit*], i.e., a bona fide action and an interaction opposed to that action, whereby a mental representation becomes clear; by combining these, the zero, or the lack of a clear mental representation [*Vorstellung*], emerges" (ww, 2:803; DW, 228—Kant's emphasis).

But another application of the concept of *negative magnitudes* offers the most revealing insight. This comes in a literary self-portrait that not only carries implications about the conditions underlying writing but also casts a surprising light on Kant's own conception of himself as a writer:

> Es ist eben nicht nötig, dass, wann wir glauben in einer gänzlichen Untätigkeit des Geistes zu sein, die Summe der Realgründe des Denkens und Begehrens kleiner sei als in dem Zustande, da sich einige Grade dieser Würksamkeit dem Bewusstsein offenbaren. Saget dem gelehrtesten Manne in den Augenblicken, da er müssig und ruhig ist, dass er etwas erzählen und von seiner Einsicht soll hören lassen. Er weiss nichts, und ihr findet ihn in diesem Zustande leer, ohne bestimmte Erwägungen oder Beurteilungen. Gebt ihm nur Anlass durch eine Frage, oder durch eure eigene Urteile. Seine Wissenschaft offenbart sich in einer Reihe von Tätigkeiten, die eine solche Richtung haben, dass sie ihm und euch das Bewusstsein dieser seiner Einsicht möglich machen.

> It is not necessarily the case, in moments when we believe ourselves to be utterly inactive mentally, that the sum of real impulses in our thinking and desiring is any smaller than in situations where we are conscious of some degree of such activity. Go and say to the most educated of men, in a moment when he is idle and relaxed, that he ought to tell you about something, and share some of his insights. He knows nothing, and in this situation you will find him empty, without any definite suggestions or judgments. So induce him with a question, or with a judgment of your own. His knowledge reveals itself in a series of activities, directed in such a way as to make it possible for yourself and him to become conscious of his insight. (ww, 2:813; DW, 236)

And following this comes an analogy of the philosopher, introduced with an explanatory "likewise" [*so*], that literally plunges every other metaphor of enlightenment into darkness:

> Ohne Zweifel waren die Realgründe dazu lange in ihm anzutreffen, aber da die Folge in Ansehung des Bewusstseins Zero war, so mussten sie einander in so ferne entgegengesetzt sein. So liegt derjenige Donner, den die Kunst zum Verderben erfand, in dem Zeughause eines Fürsten aufbehalten zu einem künftigen Kriege, in drohender Stille, bis, wenn ein verräterischer Zunder ihn berührt, er im Blitze auffährt und um sich her alles verwüstet.

No doubt, the real impulses within him had long been available, but in so far as their result in respect to consciousness was zero, they must have offset one another. Likewise, that thunder invented by human skill to its own ruination rests in a prince's arsenal, set aside for a future war, in ominous silence, until, when touched by some treacherous spark it explodes in a flash of lightning and devastates all that surrounds it. (ww, 2:813f.; DW, 236f.)[37]

This type of experimental thought and writing represents most succinctly how Kant works as a writer. That he understood himself in this way casts a new light on the specific literary conditions under which the *Critique of Pure Reason* was produced: a decade of unbroken silence, followed by three months of intense writing. This conforms precisely to the analogy of explosives. And the *Critique* had just such an effect. Redundancy creates the conditions of possibility, the foundation upon which the experimenter makes himself understood, both to himself and to the public. Kant excuses himself ironically to "readers of enlightened insight" for his long-winded explanations, remarking that they should bear in mind "that there is yet another, unteachable breed of critics [*Beurteilern*] who, by spending their lives with just one single book, comprehend nothing but what it contains, in regard to whom even the most extreme long-windedness is not superfluous" (ww, 2:797; DW, 223). On the other hand, "the thorough [*gründlichen*] philosophers, as they call themselves," are, "proliferating daily" (ww, 2:816; DW, 239). And "when it comes to metaphysical intellects whose insight is complete, one would have to be quite inexperienced to imagine that something more could be added to their wisdom, or that something could be subtracted from their foolishness (ww, 2:782; DW, 210). From behind the mask of modesty, he lets the "gallant magister" emerge, and jokes about the "educated populace" [*des gelehrten Pöbels*], letting drop the following *aperçu:* "It knows nothing, it comprehends nothing, but it talks about everything, and what it talks about, on that it insists" (ww, 2:815; DW, 238). And, one page later, Kant again puts on the mask of irony: "I, who make no secret of the weakness of my insight, being that I am generally least able to grasp what everybody else thinks is easiest to understand" (ww, 2:816; DW, 239).

Because Kant opposes the "language of the educated populace" so vehemently, the form of the essay becomes highly important to him. It has the ability to insure against any sort of "deception"[38] by means of the highest possible transparency. As Kant explains:

[S]ehe ich es einer so schlüpfrigen Erkenntnis, wie die meta-
physische ist, vor viel gemässer an, seine Gedanken zuvörderst
der öffentlichen Prüfung darzulegen in der Gestalt unsicherer
Versuche, als sie sogleich mit allem Ausputz von angemasster
Gründlichkeit und vollständiger Überzeugung anzukündigen,
weil alsdenn gemeiniglich alle Besserung von der Hand gewiesen
und ein jedes Übel, das darin anzutreffen ist, unheilbar wird.

When I see such a slippery sort of knowledge, as metaphysical
knowledge is, it seems much more suitable for such thoughts to
be presented to public inspection, first of all, in the form of uncertain experiments rather than announcing them straight-away in
their full regalia of pretended thoroughness and utter conviction,
for in that case all improvements are most commonly rejected,
and every misfortunate turn one finds in them is beyond remedy.
(ww, 2:802; DW, 227)

Enlightenment, critical philosophy, and specific literary form comprise an
intimate, constitutive unity for the philosophical writer. Immediately after
Kant has introduced his two "postulates of energy preservation,"[39] he once
more indicates this connection:

Ich habe diese zwei Sätze in der Absicht vorgetragen, um den
Leser zum Nachdenken über diesen Gegenstand einzuladen. Ich
gestehe auch, dass sie vor mich selbst nicht licht genug, noch mit
genugsamer Augenscheinlichkeit aus ihren Gründen einzusehen
sind. Indessen bin ich gar sehr überführt, dass unvollendete Versuche, im abstrakten Erkenntnisse problematisch vorgetragen,
dem Wachstum der höhern Weltweisheit sehr zuträglich sein
können.

I have presented these two sentences with the intention of inviting the reader's reflection upon this object. I also admit that they
are not illuminating enough, even for me, nor are their reasons
sufficiently evident. Nonetheless I am very much convinced that
unfinished experiments, presented so as to problematize abstract
knowledge, can contribute greatly to the flourishing of higher
philosophy. (ww, 2:811f.; DW, 235)

With these texts, Kant achieved his long-desired breakthrough as a writer.
Mendelssohn wrote reviews on three of them, which appeared in *Briefe, die
neueste Litteratur betreffend*.[40]

FIVE

Observation as Indirect
Literary Strategy

OBSERVATIONS AND ESSAYS SHARE
an experimental character—but *observation* can imply many things. Empirical findings can be distinguished according to whether they are the product of systematic experiments or are simply contingent, singular statements of fact. *Observation* can thereby stand for an unsystematic attempt [*Versuch*], as opposed to an arranged series of attempts, that is, an experiment. But equally it can mean the condition of data not yet put in order, prior to their being arranged—experimentally—into a system.[1]

As instances of the process of experimentation, observation and essay [*Versuch*] relate to each other as subject and object. Observation contains a subjective moment. It is already inscribed with infinite regress, whose epistemological consequence finds its literary expression in the travelogue and which subsequently crystallizes into the notion of the transcendental. The travelogue can thus be seen as representing, in literary form, epistemological theory's search for a standpoint. Both the *Universal Natural History* and the geographical writings made use of the travelogue in this respect, almost as if their object made it a practical necessity. And indeed the choice of the object is no accident. From a literary standpoint, the shift from cosmology to anthropology can take place only in the setting of a poetological *tertium comparationis*. The travelogue, as a literary genre, offers the requisite inspecificity, on the basis of which this shift is first able to unfold.

By October 8, 1763, the text bearing the title *Observations on the Feeling of the Beautiful and Sublime* [*Beobachtungen über das Gefühl des Schönen und Erhabenen*] had been submitted to the dean of the University of Königsberg. It appeared in December, presumably, but was in any case available in January (AA, 2:482).[2]

The title of this text signals its specific function. Although it must be considered as one of the essays, the subjective spin of the term *Observations* [*Beobachtungen*] denotes an especially free, open form of essay. Functionally, its literary quality serves a complicated strategy: not to treat aesthetic issues, as one might expect, but to delineate the *feeling* [*Gefühl*] of the beautiful and the sublime and their limits. For this to be done consistently, the demands of feeling must be articulated within their legitimate sphere of jurisdiction. Only from there does it become possible to formulate these limits and then to establish the realm of ethics and epistemology autonomously. Hence the *Observations,* as a literary undertaking, are assigned an epistemological-critical intention from the very beginning. But the text can realize this intention only as a genuine literary *Versuch*. Thus when Kant casts his gaze upon the object, "more with the eye of an observer than of a philosopher" (ww, 2:825; G, 45),[3] he is not saying that a philosopher is not needed here, but rather the contrary: that the philosopher must *also* be, first of all, an observer. Observation requires philosophy, which is necessary but not yet sufficient. For indeed, "the field of observation . . . of human nature" stretches wide and has a rich source of discoveries at its disposal, "that are just as charming as they are instructive" (ww, 2:825; G, 45). And this can only mean that besides the realm of the beautiful ("charming"), something philosophical in the narrower sense, hence "instructive," must be meant as well.

"It would be quite a pleasing text if the words *beautiful* and *sublime* were not in the title at all, and were seen more seldomly in the little book itself. It is full of the most delightful remarks about humankind, and one sees his fundamental principles already beginning to sprout."[4] Goethe's remark points ironically to the weak spot: Kant's dichotomizing of all appearance into either beautiful or sublime. Yet at the same time he recognizes that the text's actual meaning derives less from its aesthetic accomplishments than from its particular epistemological intentions. Schiller's letter replies: "What you wrote about Kant's little text is also what I remember feeling when I read it. The exposition is merely anthropological, and one learns nothing from it about the ultimate principles of the beautiful. But as a physics and natural history of the sublime and the beautiful, it contains some fruitful material. For such serious subject matter, the style seemed to me a bit too playful and flowery; a peculiar error, coming from Kant, but then again quite understandable."[5]

These *Observations* do indeed present a "natural history." And just as in Kant's first major work, the literary form plays a crucial role as the chosen medium in which the idea develops. To that extent, Goethe's and Schiller's admonitions about its relevance for aesthetics contain an anachronism, one moreover first made possible thanks to Kant's work itself. Elements still mixed together in a pre-Kantian context get differentiated for the first time: the sphere of feelings of the beautiful and the sublime in its specific difference from the sphere of morals. The differentiation here is not yet final, but it marks the start of a path leading through the *Observations* and, by this route, to the *Critiques*. Only when Kant becomes critical—and this constitutes one of the chief concerns of the *Critique*—do anthropology, ethics, and epistemology get severed irrevocably from each other. As long as this has not happened, however, it is not only a legitimate way but also the only possible way to address this theme by means of miscellaneous remarks.

The point of departure and impetus for the *Observations* come largely from British authors, particularly Edmund Burke and his *Enquiry*,[6] but from Hutcheson and others as well. Nonetheless it is Rousseau who gives the decisive direction—"Rousseau set me aright" ["Rousseau hat mich zurecht gebracht"][7] is the notorious phrase describing this circumstance. Although the word *observation* does not appear in the title of Burke's work, Mendelssohn considered the concept of observation to be closely connected with Burke's *Enquiry*. Burke himself uses *observation* occasionally to designate his investigation (esp. Burke, *Philosophical Enquiry*, 54; cf. 175). In one passage from the *Rhapsodie über die Empfindungen*, Mendelssohn writes of Burke: "The author . . . is a great observer of nature. He heaps observations upon observations, all of them just as well-founded as they are incisive; but indeed, as often as it comes time to explain these observations by reference to the nature of our soul, his weakness shows itself."[8] But precisely Burke's methodological orientation on Newton must have been compelling for Kant. Indeed after criticizing Newton for having been untrue to his own method, Burke draws the following conclusion in a way that is reminiscent of Kant: "That great chain of causes, which linking one to another even to the throne of God himself, can never be unravelled by any industry of ours. When we go but one step beyond the immediately sensible qualities of things, we go out of our depth. All we do after, is but a faint struggle, that shews we are in an element which does not belong to us" (Burke, *Philosophical Enquiry*, 129f.). Among the British during this time, aesthetics and ethics represented still-undifferentiated realms of philosophical discourse. Shaftesbury's enthusiasm-pantheism differed in degree, but not in principle, from Hume's and others' recourse to sentiment, even when this advances into some sort of "moral" quality for Hutcheson. Aesthetic reflections could quickly turn into moral ones, or moral ones into aesthetic. This very differentiation was the object of Hutcheson's efforts, but in principle it was Rousseau who first managed the breakthrough to the fundamentals.[9] Hutcheson's significance consists primarily in having thematized the problem with the concept of *moral sense,* which raises the question of the connection between reason and feeling and hence defines the realm of the ethical. His insistence on this problem as the fundamental question for all moral philosophizing, and the aporia his approach exposes, must have been attractive to Kant, who was as dissatisfied with the existing solutions as Hutcheson was.[10] For Kant, only Rousseau's vision could show the way to go beyond this.

Rousseau's achievement, which in Kant's eyes pioneered a new course for philosophy, came in the specific form of literary style. It should come as no surprise that this also won it a formative influence on Kant's work. What Cassirer formulates in general terms must therefore be kept in mind when considering the literary form of the *Observations.* Here, Kant thematizes the *principium* of morality, that is, feeling [*Gefühl*] or conscience [*Gewissen*] implicitly, in a particular literary manner, in that he elicits by way of "observation" the specificity of what the *Observations* calls *feeling.* The differentiation that follows from this is exactly the reason why this text must also have literary quality. As Cassirer comments ("Kant and Rousseau"): "We hear their [Rousseau's sentences'] echo and reverberations in the most essential and crucial theses of the Kantian ethics. . . . And we may surmise that Rousseau not only influenced the content and systematic development of Kant's foundation of ethics, but that he also formed its language and style."[11]

Just how much the actual Rousseau discussion is carried on *between* the lines here is made clear by the *Bemerkungen zu den Beobachtungen* [*Remarks on the Observations*], which are notes Kant entered in his copy of the *Observations.* There, he thematizes this influence himself, when he writes: "I have to read Rousseau long enough that the beauty of the expressions no longer disturbs me and only then can I begin to study him at all rationally" (AA, 20:30). Kant read Rousseau unlike any other author: as a philosopher, resisting his rhetorical force. Intensive rereading must have made the philosophical content clearer. But this immersion must also have enabled Rousseau's literary power, against which Kant sought to defend himself, to express its full force subliminally, against Kant's will. These *Bemerkungen*—written in the year the text appeared and the following one[12]—are an elaboration and commentary on the Rousseau discussion implicitly carried on in the *Observations.*[13] Yet let us turn, before taking a closer look at the *Bemerkungen,* back to the *Observations* themselves, to view them first without the *Bemerkungen,* which we will deal with afterward.

The fact that Kant's view is directed more to the aesthetic theories of the Scottish philosophers than to Rousseau, who first gets named as a subtext in the *Bemerkungen,* has nothing to do with Kant's reception of Rousseau, the particular dates of which are difficult to fix in any case.[14] Instead, it involves the very intention of the work. This is not directed as much toward the aesthetic per se as toward the resolution of its borders. Hence Rousseau cannot be the central focus, for Kant actually shares his perspective. Likewise, he cannot justify his views with recourse to Rousseau, and this compels him instead to seek argumentative justification. For both, it is a question of disentangling feeling from ethics. Moreover, Kant's strategy here is not dogmatic, but rather zetetic, or searching.[15] Instead of simply decreeing borders in advance, he does the reverse: the borders of the aesthetic are not defined from the viewpoint of ethics—extraterritorially and heteronomously, so to speak—but rather autonomously, from within the realm of feeling itself.

When Rousseau is quoted in the concluding sentence, without quotation marks and without being named, it shows that his view serves as the sort of reference point toward which the path of knowledge has to lead. And certainly this path will require laborious conceptual work in order to traverse the entire dialectic of ethics and aesthetics, particularly since it denies itself the elevating wings of Rousseau's eloquence. For this very reason, Herder was able to greet (and to misunderstand) Kant as "a German Shaftesburi [*sic*]."[16] Kant's concluding words in the *Observations* not only recall Rousseau's theory, much discussed at that time, but quote the beginning of *Emile* as well:[17]

> dass das noch unentdeckte Geheimnis der Erziehung dem alten Wahne entrissen werde, um das sittliche Gefühl frühzeitig in dem Busen eines jeden jungen Weltbürgers zu einer tätigen Empfindung zu erhöhen, damit nicht alle Feinigkeit bloss auf das flüchtige und müssige Vergnügen hinauslaufe, dasjenige, was ausser uns vorgeht, mit mehr oder weniger Geschmacke zu beurteilen.

> but especially that the secret of education, as yet undiscovered, be rescued from the old illusions, in order to elevate early-on the moral feeling in the breast of every young world-citizen to a lively sensitivity, so that all delicacy of feeling may not amount to merely the fleeting and idle enjoyment of judging, with more or less taste, what goes on around us. (AA, 2:884; G, 115–6)

This allusion was clear enough for Kant's contemporaries. Thus Hamann could conclude his review of the *Observations* with a paraphrase of Kant's concluding sentence, along with the parenthetical comment that this secret of education was one "already betrayed, presumably, by Jean Jacques."[18] It is to be assumed that Hamann, who at this time was a close associate of Kant's, is on the mark here about Kant's intention, if he was not actually guided to it by Kant himself.[19]

This indirect strategy is what first renders the specific character of these *Observations* understandable. It explains not only their literary form, but also the epistemological interest that strives to exceed this form, and which finds its justification only in the inner aesthetic delineation of borders between the realms of the moral and the aesthetic.[20]

The second paragraph ironically reflects the author's situation, when Kant writes of "stout persons, whose most gifted authors are their cooks and whose works of fine taste are in their cellars" (ww, 2:825; G, 45), against whom, Kant seems to suggest with a wink, other gifted authors of fine taste will have difficulty competing.[21] But another use for authors is imaginable, the author goes on to admit, namely, providing readings that serve as a comfortable soporific. Such bitterly humorous irony—all the more significant for beginning on the very first page of the work and thus setting the tone—provides an index for how important this problem is for the author. It touches him so deeply that he believes himself compelled to seek recourse in irony in order just to be able to communicate. Such a harsh degree of pitiless self-reflection is not called upon again until Heine.

If we grant that the perspective from which Kant considers the entire moral character of human nature is an aesthetic one here, that is, it sees human nature in terms of what is beautiful and sublime about man, then the overall picture, according to Schmucker, expresses itself as *splendor* [*Prächtigkeit*]. And splendor, according to Kant, is the conjunction of the beautiful and the sublime, such that beauty is spread across a sublime design in a way that leaves the sublime expression visible even through all the beauty.[22] Certainly Kant lets the sublime show through beauty again and again; by doing this he can point to what it evokes, the moral dimension. But there is a continuing tone of irony in the way Kant presents all this. It indicates that the main orientation here is in fact not the "splendid," but rather the separation and emancipation of beautiful and sublime feelings from ethics, which is done in order to emancipate morality from feeling. So this text reveals itself to be less a capricious detour into open fields, whither easy booty tempts the author, than a necessary excursion along a path that he follows in search of the right method.

Kant is more inclined to distance himself from the "splendid." He expresses this inclination by allowing for splendor generally as the "gloss of sublimity" [*der Schimmer der Erhabenheit*], but adding disparagingly that it is "a strong conspicuous color that conceals the inner content of a thing or person, which perhaps is only base and common, and deludes and moves us by its appearance" (ww, 2:843; G, 68).[23] The conclusion of the second section precisely delineates the relative value of splendor. Following an amusing summary of the good-hearted but naive character and the egotistical, ambitious one (to which we will return later), Kant announces: "Thus the different groups unite into a picture of splendid expression, where amidst great multiplicity unity shines forth, and the whole of moral nature exhibits beauty and dignity" (ww, 2:849; G, 75). Given the context, this can only be understood as serious *and* ironic, as is so often the case with Kant. The irony of the context reveals the "splendid perspective" as questionable.

"Understanding is sublime, wit is beautiful" ["Verstand ist erhaben, Witz ist schön"] (ww, 2:829; G, 51). Thus begins the second section, "Of the Properties of the Sublime and Beautiful in Man in General." With pointed aphorisms like this one, arranged antithetically in a way that at times assumes the lapidary brevity of telegraphic style, Kant seeks to winnow out the contraries of the sublime and the beautiful and its attributes. Viewed stylistically, this passage could hardly be outdone in its language and is thus itself an example of the beautiful and the sublime, in their specific tension.[24] Merely witty would be beautiful; just understandable, sublime. For a philosophical observer, however, both must converge:

> Die Werke des Verstandes und Scharfsinnigkeit, in so fern ihre Gegenstände auch etwas vor das Gefühl enthalten, nehmen gleichfalls einigen Anteil an den gedachten Verschiedenheiten. Die mathematische Vorstellung von der unermesslichen Grösse des Weltbaues, die Betrachtungen der Metaphysik von der Ewigkeit, der Vorsehung, der Unsterblichkeit der Seele enthalten eine gewisse Erhabenheit und Würde.

> Works of understanding and ingenuity, in so far as their objects also contain something for feeling, likewise take some part in the differences now being considered. The mathematical idea of the immeasurable magnitude of the universe, the meditations of metaphysics upon eternity, Providence, and the immortality of the soul contain a certain sublimity and dignity. (ww, 2:834; G, 57)

Thus it becomes conceivable why Haller had to be Kant's prototype, whereas Homer and Milton appeared too adventurous, Ovid's *Metamorphoses* "grotesque," and the anachreontic poems "generally very close to trifling," and only Vergil and Klopstock are esteemed noble (ww, 2:834; G, 57). The fictitious [*romanhaft*] charade of the novel is defined only generally, "in so far as sublimity and beauty exceed the known average" (ww, 2:832; G, 55, note).

If Hamann and Herder occasionally criticize Kant's predilection for quibbling in the *Observations*,[25] in another instance Herder quotes an entire page from the *Observations*, accompanied by the following remark: "I find the observations of my philosopher to be so precise and discriminating, that I wish to have them as a worthy prototype to imitate and to reach for in the course of attaining my goal."[26]

The "beauties of written style" ["*Schönheiten der Schreibart*"] (ww, 2:846; G, 71)[27] naturally play an important role in this *Versuch*, but not the lead role. The sublime is tempered here by beauty, and both are cast together as aesthetic viewpoints to be considered relative to their significance for ethics. The paragraph that concludes the second section makes this clear. It problematizes a theme that was already introduced, but now becomes the essential issue: the topic of principles [*Grundsätze*]. The irony Kant brings into play here is crucial, and it is remarkable how often this irony is simply overlooked.[28] Kant introduces these principles as "not speculative rules, but the consciousness of a feeling that lives in every human breast" (ww, 2:836; G, 60). In what follows he explains more closely what this means, namely, the "feeling of the beauty and the dignity of human nature" (ww, 2:837; G, 60). By this, in turn, he means universal respect [*allgemeine Achtung*], which still later serves as the basis for ethics in the *Foundations of the Metaphysics of Morals*. Whether Kant still equates this with Hutcheson's *moral sense*, [29] or whether he already has in mind Rousseau's idea of conscience, is difficult to decide. The one indication Kant gives us can be gleaned from a careful reading of the second section's conclusion. For I believe that precisely the irony found there, in that it signifies a degree of reflectivity, points away from Hutcheson and toward Rousseau. This holds true even though Rousseau himself seems to point to an answer yet to be discovered, rather than being already able to offer one, as such.

> Dererjenigen unter den Menschen, die nach *Grundsätzen* verfahren, sind nur sehr *wenige*, welches auch überaus gut ist, da es so leicht geschehen kann, dass man in diesen Grundsätzen irre und alsdenn der Nachteil, der daraus erwächst, sich um desto weiter erstreckt, je allgemeiner der Grundsatz und je standhafter die Person ist, die ihn sich vorgesetzt hat.

> Among men, there are *few* who behave according to *principles*—which is extremely good, as it can so easily happen that one errs in these principles, and then the resulting disadvantage extends all the further, the more universal the principle and the more resolute the person who has set it before himself. (ww, 2:848f.; G, 74)

How exactly Kant wants his readers to understand these sentences has been carefully prepared in the second section. We are meant to conclude that the principles do not have to be surrendered, and instead are of key significance precisely because of this danger. But these consequences can be expressed so vividly only by just such an ironic twist.[30] The sentences are a sort of negative of what Kant is aiming at, thus making the aporia of the problem of principles evident. For if Kant considers the *adopted* virtues beautiful and charming, then genuine virtue—it appears, in opposition to the others, only in the singular—is sublime and venerable. It indicates a noble heart and righteousness, in short it "rests on principles," whereas the other virtues, although requiring a good heart, are blinded by their very goodheartedness (ww, 2:837; G, 61).

Now Kant defines the relationship of principles themselves to the virtues resting on them through the not very simple metaphor of "grafting" [*Aufpfropfen*] (ww, 2:836; G, 60). This metaphor represents the interpretive crux of Kant's concept of ethics, as he understood it in this phase of his thought. He has in mind a certain causality, but the metaphor of grafting definitely safeguards it from any simple logical implications. If "grafting" means a necessary condition, namely here that of principles, then eventually the metaphor also includes the question of whether these alone are adequate. In visual terms, it introduces questions of growth and the ensemble of external conditions that affect it.[31] Although Kant is serious in claiming that for principles, "the more general they are, the more sublime and noble [virtue] becomes" (ww, 2:836; G, 60), just the opposite is the case when they grow into weeds (ww, 2:848f.; G, 74). The metaphor of "grafting" must include this option, as well.

The third section deals with the "Distinction of the Sublime and Beautiful in the Interrelations of the Two Sexes" (ww, 2:850; G, 76). For Kant, these qualities represent the basic distinguishing characteristics of man and woman. The sexist aspect shows through in the lack of reflectivity at the moment when the transition from pure observation to normative judgment occurs.[32] In the process, however, he does provide a miniphenomenology of the relations of the sexes, one that right away takes on a personal tone. He points this out himself *en passant*, that in such cases, "the author always appears to depict his own inclination" (ww, 2:860f.; G, 88). Kant's personal perplexity with this theme conjures up virtually poetic passages of contemplation. And it is not only an understatement, but a misleading displacement of emphasis when Kant biographies regularly furnish these moments with commentaries to the effect that Kant felt "human impulses" or the like. It is more than that.[33] Evidence of this is that the *Observations* speak of the meaning of life at this point. Precisely where Kant is writing of perhaps the most difficult subject, love, we see just how masterfully he guides his quill.

First of all, a closer look needs to be taken at the partitioning of understanding, from an aesthetic perspective, into the beautiful and the sublime. "The fair sex has as much understanding as the male, but it is a *beautiful understanding*, whereas ours should be a *deep understanding*, an expression that signifies identity with the sublime" (ww, 2:851; G, 78). Kant stresses repeatedly that he is not proceeding on a moral footing here, but rather is only observing the phenomena in their effect on the senses. Yet the demarcation of reason is affected as well. The *moral sense* remains ultimately just that—a sense:

> Der Inhalt der grossen Wissenschaft des Frauenzimmers ist vielmehr der Mensch und unter den Menschen der Mann. . . . Man wird ihr gesamtes moralisches Gefühl und nicht ihr Gedächtnis zu erweitern suchen, und zwar nicht durch allgemeine Regeln, sondern durch eigenes Urteil über das Betragen, welches sie um sich sehen.

> The content of woman's great science, rather, is humankind, and within humanity, man. . . . One will seek to broaden her total moral sense and not her memory, and do so indeed not by universal rules, but by some judgment upon the conduct they see around themselves. (ww, 2:853; G, 79–80)

The emancipation of practical from theoretical reason by means of *moral sense* is not possible as long as this sense is based on a sexist distinction that distinguishes it from "universal rules." "Deep meditation and a long-sustained reflection are noble but difficult," and are as little suited to women as "laborious learning or painful pondering" (ww, 2:852; G, 78): "The beautiful understanding selects for its objects everything closely related to the finer feeling, and relinquishes to the diligent, fundamental, and deep understanding abstract speculations or branches of knowledge that are useful but dry" (ww, 2:852; G, 78f.).

Kant also knows what women ought to be reading: no geometry, and only as much metaphysics as is appropriate for salon conversations (ww, 2:852; G, 78f.). And the refrain of his sister-in-law, who never tires of thanking him repeatedly for sending her a handbook for the household entitled *Die Hausmutter in allen ihren Geschäften* [*The Housewife in All Her Occupations*], illustrates what his recommendation means.[34] The "lack of book learning" is for women a virtue. As a matter of consequence, Kant imagines only men as (his) readers. Not that women are excluded from reading. On the contrary. In the history of philosophy up until then, certainly, it was always men who were authors and readers, and the question was never raised. But Kant cannot overlook that in his century, a large segment of the reading public is made up of women. So while they are not completely excluded from reading, for them reading functions rather to compensate for any lack of attractiveness: "Gradually, as claims upon the charms diminish, the reading of books and the broadening of insight could fill unnoticed the vacancy left by the Graces, with the Muses" (ww, 2:864; G, 92). So women are not only incapable of principles (ww, 2:855; G, 81), but Kant practically denies women their humanity, with the words: "Nothing of duty, nothing of compulsion, nothing of obligation" (ww, 2:854; G, 81). Yet these very ideas underlie what later, according to the "critical" Kant, makes human beings human.

Kant considers these matters self-evident, and this attitude defines the *Observations.* Just how true this is becomes clear when the beauty and sublimity of humans themselves becomes the subject of his investigation. Judging from its heading, one may have expected this to have been the subject of the preceding section ("Of the Properties of the Sublime and Beautiful in Man in General"), where in fact a purely psychological interest predominated. But here, "as it is our purpose to judge the sensations, it cannot be unpleasant to bring under concepts, if possible, the difference of the impression that the form and features of the fair sex make on the masculine" (ww, 2:859; G, 86). With this, Kant reaches beyond purely aesthetic concerns and addresses the realm of sensation, whose task is to represent the actual center point of sentimentality: love. The word itself does not occur even once in all of this. Rather, it constitutes the unspoken motif. The way Kant manages this thus casts a light on the literary intentions of the *Observations.*

The "beauties of written style" and the "delicate enchantments of love" (ww, 2:846; G, 71) are intimately connected.[35] The author seems to unite them. First, Kant recognizes both beauty and moral sensation as being distinct from charm, which is an erotic feeling connected externally to physical qualities. Likewise, there is a beauty of written style, to which the same distinction applies that Kant draws between a beautiful woman, on the one hand, and a merely pretty one on the other:

> Man findet, dass diejenige Bildungen, die beim ersten Anblicke nicht sonderliche Wirkung tun, weil sie nicht auf eine entschiedene Art hübsch sein, gemeiniglich, so bald sie bei näherer Bekanntschaft zu gefallen anfangen, auch weit mehr einnehmen und sich beständig zu verschönern scheinen; dagegen das hübsche Ansehen, was sich auf einmal ankündigt, in der Folge mit grös-

serem Kaltsinn wahrgenommen wird, welches vermutlich daher kommt, dass moralische Reize wo sie sichtbar werden, mehr fesseln, imgleichen weil sie sich nur bei Gelegenheit sittlicher Empfindungen in Wirksamkeit setzen und sich gleichsam entdecken lassen, jede Entdeckung eines neuen Reizes aber immer noch mehr derselben vermuten lässt; anstatt dass alle Annehmlichkeiten, die sich gar nicht verhehlen, nachdem sie gleich anfangs ihre ganze Wirkung ausgeübt haben, in der Folge nichts weiter tun können, als den verliebten Vorwitz abzukühlen und ihn allmählich zur Gleichgültigkeit zu bringen.

One finds that those features that at first glance do not have any particular effect, because they are not pretty in any decided way, generally appear to captivate far more and to grow constantly more beautiful as soon as they begin to please upon closer acquaintance; on the other hand, the pretty appearance that proclaims itself at once is later received with greater indifference, which is probably because moral charms, when they are evident, are all the more arresting because they are set in operation only on the occasion of moral sensations, and let themselves be discovered in this way, each disclosure of a new charm causing one to suspect still more of these; whereas all the agreeable features that do not at all conceal themselves, once they have exercised their entire effect at the beginning, can subsequently do nothing more than cool off the enamored curiosity and bring it gradually to indifference. (ww, 2:862f.; G, 90)

With the words, "Along with these observations, the following comment quite naturally presents itself" (ww, 2:863; G, 90), Kant attaches the following paragraph to these remarks, in which he crosses over into circumspectly handled but allusion-filled self-thematization. The discussion revolves around what Freud will later term *sublimation,* which gives rise to the problem of *Civilization and Its Discontents,* namely the fact that persons "of such delicate sentiment" are so seldom happy (ww, 2:863; G, 91). As for unhappiness in matters of love—apparently still one more "quite naturally following remark" in the *Observations*—Kant laconically concludes, "It is never to be lost sight of that in whatever way it might be, one must not make very high claims upon life's happiness and human perfection" (ww, 2:864; G, 92).

In the fourth, concluding section, Kant treats "national characteristics" with regard to the beautiful and sublime. He comes to speak here of national determinations of style and type of speech. For if France is the home of "naturally flowing writing," then in England "thoughts of profound content" predominate, including "tragedy, the epic poem, and in general the solid gold of wit, which under French hammers can be stretched into thin leaves with great surface" (ww, 2:870; G, 99). Indeed, Kant makes similar comments in the *Bemerkungen* in regard to Rousseau (AA 20:30), and he may have had him in sight here as well, even if he meant to avoid publicly criticizing one to whom he owed so much. In a footnote, he calls Rousseau "the shrewd Swiss" (*den scharfsichtigen Schweizer*) (ww, 2:873; G, 102), undoubtedly a more correct designation for the *citoyen de Genève* than simply to list him as French. As a Swiss, he consequently may even have moved into proximity with Haller, that other Swiss so venerated by Kant for his poetry. So in Kant's eyes, Rousseau does in fact remain his role model as a writer, an exception to the critique of the French.

> In der Metaphysik, der Moral und den Lehren der Religion kann man bei den Schriften dieser Nation nicht behutsam genug sein. Es herrschet darin gemeiniglich viel schönes Blendwerk, welches in einer kalten Untersuchung die Probe nicht hält. Der Franzose liebt das Kühne in seinen Aussprüchen; allein um zur Wahrheit zu gelangen muss man nicht kühn sondern behutsam sein.

> In metaphysics, ethics, and theology, one cannot be cautious enough of the publications of this nation [the French]. Commonly there prevails in them much beautiful delusion, which in a cold inquiry does not hold up under the test. The Frenchman loves bold declarations; but in order to attain the truth, one must be not bold but careful. (ww, 2:872; G, 101, note)

For Kant, the Germans essentially stand between the French and the English, as regards their "national character." Kant's position on German literature can be interpolated from this. Although he does not devote much exposition to his views, he does point out the "richness of our German language" (ww, 2:875; G, 105). He also grants that the language is "stiff and awkward," and its predilection for titles loads it with "bombast" that hinders "the beautiful simplicity other people can give to their style" (ww, 2:876; G, 106).

Burke's observation that rhetorical and poetic language is incapable of the exact description of which painting is capable marks the turn away from a Cartesian ideal of knowledge. Whereas painting produces an imitation, a counterfeit, poetry functions with an incomparably greater intensity, for it is charged with expressing the forces of the soul.[36] For language, to cite Leibniz's coinage, is the "mirror of the mind."[37] To delineate the border between painting and poetry in this way is to emancipate style from its traditional obligation to provide something like an "objective," "pure" representation. "In reality poetry and rhetoric do not succeed in exact description so well as painting does; their business is to affect rather by sympathy than imitation; to display rather the effect of things on the mind of the speaker, or of others, than to present a clear idea of the things themselves" (Burke, *Philosophical Enquiry,* 172).[38] Language as an instrument of the mind, when reflected upon for its own sake, thus becomes an essential part of method. Consequently, style becomes the medium for representing the transcendental moment of knowledge.

When Kant began—probably soon after the *Observations* appeared— recording his remarks in his personal copy of the text, he may have conceived them with a new edition in mind, but he may also have written them out simply to clarify things for himself. Notebook-style memoranda alternate with fully formulated continuations of arguments. Sometimes his personal copy may have served merely as a convenient place to write down thoughts that would otherwise have ended up on loose scraps of paper.[39] This double function as book and notebook makes the *Bemerkungen* a quite informative commentary on the *Observations,* claiming for them an interesting literary middle position.

The new edition of the *Bemerkungen,* which has been carefully retranscribed, edited, and commented on by Marie Rischmüller, demonstrates the workshop character of Kant's extensive marginalia.[40] A reading of the *Bemerkungen,* Rischmüller points out, promises new insights into "Kant's thinking, which is rich in images and yet at the same time associative and concentrated" (*Bemerkungen,* xxii). Thanks to Rischmüller's commentary, Kant's intricate dialogue with literary fiction can be grasped in its full implications. In the remarks he jotted down, Kant establishes an empirical archive for moral psychology, where he files all his findings gathered in his adventures into the literary world of novels and travelogues. It is noteworthy that Kant's observing gaze is not so much "a distanced one, directed towards human nature in general," as Rischmüller claims (xiii), but instead assumes a constitutive function. Oscillating between external projection and introspection, the authorial "I" becomes entangled in the search for the self. The clue-like allusions, intimations, *aperçus,* and thought sketches illustrate to what degree literature and fiction serve to compensate for the lack of empiricism and experience. At the same time, they assume as a medium for communicating the author's own experience.

The *Bemerkungen* thus do not present so much mere rhapsodic observations, nor aphorisms,[41] but rather building blocks for an ongoing project of self-reflection. The fact that this search for self takes its point of origin in literature is as little a coincidence as the choice of its object for reflection.

The organization of such a psychological repository of knowledge along the lines of the dichotomy between the beautiful and the sublime has its deeper reasons. The continuous thematization of gender differences, the almost compulsive repetition of addressing gender and sex differences as constructions of the beautiful and the sublime, point to Kant's underlying efforts to address the implications of philosophy and sexuality, precisely at the point where they would appear to constitute each other mutually. In this way, these "Reflections" function as self-reflections. Proceeding through repeated recourse to the alterity of sexual difference, they represent iterative attempts at self-definition. The virulence of this precarious self-communication, mirroring one's self-reflections onto repeatedly new attempts at inscribing gender and sex difference, displays some of the economy of self-reflection at work even as Kant labors to stake out his philosophy. The function of the *Bemerkungen* for Kant's precritical experimental philosophy consists in this complex moment of self-reflection and conceptual legitimation. By looking at Kant's associative note jottings, we can see what the philosophical rationale is behind his combination of a theory concerning the beautiful and the sublime with an effort to transfix gender and sexual difference. Kant expresses here what he otherwise cannot bring into focus: the observation of his self.

As has been pointed out above, the continuing Rousseau commentary one finds in these remarks reveals a new dimension to the *Observations,* allowing for a more precise understanding of them. In his encounter with Rousseau, Kant formulates his concept of himself as a writer. The famous "Rousseau set me aright" (AA, 20:44) merely expresses this with formulaic brevity. But Rousseau is actually just as trailblazing as he is irritating for Kant. Rousseau has to be read against the grain. Hence Kant exempts the "shrewd Swiss" (WW, 2:873; G, 102) from his claim that French writers are simply rhetoricians:

> Der Erste Eindruck den ein verstandiger Leser der nicht blos aus Eitelkeit oder Zeitkürzung lieset der Schriften des Hn. J. J. Rousseau bekömt ist dass er eine ungemeine Scharfsinnigkeit des Geistes einen edlen Schwung des Genies und eine gefühlvolle Seele in so Hohem Grade antrift als vielleicht niemals ein Schriftsteller von welchem Zeitalter oder von welchem Volke er auch sey vereinbart mag besessen haben. Der Eindruck der hernachst folgt ist die Befremdung über seltsame u. wiedersinnische Meinungen die demjenigen was allgemein gangbar ist so sehr entgegenstehen dass man leichtlich auf die Vermuthung geräth der Verfasser habe vermoge seiner ausserordentlichen Talente

nur die Zauberkraft der Beredsamkeit beweisen und den Sonderling machen wollen.

The first impression that an intelligent reader who reads not just for vanity or pastime gets from the writings of J. J. Rousseau is that he is encountering an uncommon shrewdness of the mind, a noble sweep of genius, and a soul full of feeling in such a high degree as perhaps no other writer may have possessed united within him, whatever his era or his nationality. The impression that follows is one of astonishment toward strange and nonsensical opinions that are so opposed to those that are generally met with that one easily arrives at the supposition that the author on account of his extraordinary talent wanted only to prove the charming power of eloquence and to display his originality. (AA, 20:43f.)

Mendelssohn also found fit to declare similar reservations about Rousseau. Having translated, on Lessing's advice, the two *Discours* of 1751 and 1755, he sent them to Lessing along with an open letter (*Sendschreiben*, 1756) containing a critique of Rousseau.[42] He suspected Rousseau's "language from the heart" of actually being the "mighty enchantress of honest minds,"[43] who has the "thunder of eloquence" at her disposal.[44] And five years later, in his review of *Nouvelle Héloise*,[45] he reports that the novel is a book, "that people are ripping out of each other's hands in Germany, and is spoken of all over, in all social circles."[46] Even before *Emile* appears, Mendelssohn speaks of the "disturbing eloquence we have grown accustomed to from the citizen of Geneva, which nothing, not even the most obdurate despair, can resist."[47]

Not only does Kant grant Rousseau a prominent place as a philosopher, but he actually speaks of a "Rousseauian method" (AA, 20:17): "Rousseau. Proceeds synthetically & begins with natural man. I proceed analytically & begin with moral man" (16). Kant subsequently contrasts Rousseau with Newton. He counts Rousseau as the discoverer of the "deeply hidden nature of man from among the variety of forms [*Gestalten*] he assumes" (58).[48] What Rousseau and Newton have in common is that both discovered the underlying laws governing phenomena: for Newton, the mathematical laws underlying the physical; for Rousseau, laws of the human world. Kant expresses their significance with the emphatic words: "After Newton & Rousseau God is justified & now Pope's theorem is true" ["Nach Newton u. Rousseau ist Gott gerechtfertigt u. nunmehr ist Popens Lehrsatz wahr"] (59).

To Kant, Rousseau was, even more than Newton, a philosophical revolutionary. Thus he viewed Rousseau as his real predecessor, one who in

Kant's eyes served as the model for an exemplary writer.[49] Cassirer has described perhaps most precisely just what Rousseau's decisive influence on Kant in this epoch was:

> We know that Kant not only prized Rousseau's style, but that this was exactly what led him to turn again and again to Rousseau's writings. It could hardly be otherwise. For in just that period of his life in which he felt Rousseau's influence, Kant had not yet become the pure analyst concerned merely with the 'dry dissection of concepts.' He was equally a stylist and a psychological essayist, and in this respect he established a new standard for the German philosophical literature of the eighteenth century. His *Observations on the Feeling of the Beautiful and the Sublime* display a precision of observation and a lucidity and facility of presentation Kant never again attained in any later work. At this time he must have possessed a sensitive ear for Rousseau's distinctive literary style.[50]

Rousseau's style may have also led Kant to the insight that authors who "put a ban on wit" might "appear thorough," but only in the way "crude people seem to be honest" (AA, 20:159). The appearance of beauty can be just as misleading as the appearance of erudition. Philosophy, Kant maintains, is "not a matter of necessity but rather one of amenity" (131; see 175), and hence also subject to aesthetic demands. One may no more prescribe a form to philosophy than a truth to it, from the outside. And "the truth has no value in and of itself . . . Only the way one attains the truth has a definite value because what leads to error can also do this in practical things" (175). What is true of humans in general also counts for those who are searching after the truth: "All life's satisfactions have the greatest allure while you pursue them. Possession is cold" (186).

Truth, understood in this way, achieves its form in the shape of doubt. The zetetic approach or, as Kant translates it, the searching approach, becomes the element by means of which the discourse develops, the medium in which philosophical thinking occurs. Freely experimenting, philosophical doubt generates an adequate literary form for itself: "The method of doubt is useful in that it predisposes the mind to proceed not by speculation but rather by healthy understanding & sentiment. I seek the honor of Fabius Cunctator" (175). Searching, deferment, and hesitation—these comprise the force that shapes Kant's philosophical thinking. Their form of expression is the *observation, essay* [*Versuch*]. Sloppily formulated: "Truth looks good only in a nightgown, in a habit *de parade*—appearance" ["Wahrheit schickt sich nur im Schlafrocke im Habit *de parade* der Schein"]

(179).[51] But whereas for instance Montaigne positions his own self at the focal point of his *Essays* and Descartes becomes a narrator, at least protreptically, in seeking recourse in the ego, Kant seeks to avoid retreating into the private sphere. He honors the maxim that one "should never speak of oneself," and indeed even adds in parentheses, "not even in books." His postscript, "unless one wanted to say something of oneself that can be laughed at," shuts the self out of philosophical discourse completely, and assigns it to the sphere of the nonserious (143).[52] With the "honor of Fabius Cunctator," Kant directs his attention to the *res publica*, which until this point had always seemed to be exempted from doubt and whose discourse—laws, decrees, commands, tracts, summations—directly embodies the doctrinary as such. Kant's zetetic method turns against this privatizing of doubt; it requires breaking out of the individualization of doubt handed down from antiquity and ratified by Montaigne and even Descartes, and exposing it as *res publica*, as a public affair. Accordingly Kant, induced by Rousseau, subjects the concept of virtue to an intensification that extends it beyond the private sphere:

> Man redet immer soviel von Tugend. Man muss aber die Ungerechtigkeit aufheben ehe man tugendhaft seyn kann. Man muss die Gemächlichkeiten die Üppigkeit u. alles was andere unterdrükt indem es mich erhebt abstellen damit ich nicht einer von allen sey die ihr Geschlecht unterdrüken. Alle Tugend ist unmöglich ohne diese Entschliessung.

> There is always so much talk about virtue. But injustice has to be abolished before we can be virtuous. We have to make an end to the conveniences, the luxury, and everything that oppresses others, in that it elevates me so that I am not one of all those who oppress their own kind. All virtue is impossible without this resolution. (151)

The love of truth is the "foundation of all social virtue" (153), and this in turn provides a constitutive meaning of doubt. Kant speaks of "stupid" and "wise ignorance" (142). Employed as a method, "wise ignorance" finds its most fitting form in the sparingly composed essay.[53] Whoever wishes to teach others to be "wise without their needing to know a lot" must certainly know a lot, but teach with a view to communicating just a little of that knowledge: "It is much to be wished that this skill were more developed" (142). Literary communication, "to be wise with little knowledge," thus is a skill that requires art [*Kunst*]. It cannot be learned but can be merely "developed." To instruct someone is not simply an intellectual process. In addition to a "good & correct understanding," "a certain goodness of the heart" must be presupposed (32f.). Therefore Kant declines the use of piquant satire, for "satire never improves character" ["Satyre bessert niemals"] (106). But jokes are a different case (159).[54] Alongside the difficulties with which a writer has to struggle emerges a new problem in the age of Enlightenment: the steady increase in the production of books. Following the laws of universal developmental tendencies, this production translates into a book market:

> Unter den Schaden welche die Sündfluth von Büchern anrichtet womit unser Welttheil jährlich überschwemmt wird ist einer nicht der gringsten dass die wirklich nützlichen die hin und wieder auf dem weiten ocean der Büchergelehrsamkeit schwimmen übersehen werden und das Schicksal der Hinfalligkeit mit dem übrigen Spreu theilen müssen. Die Neigung viel zu lesen um zu sagen dass man gelesen habe.

> Among the damages incurred by the deluge of books that annually floods our part of the world a not insignificant one is that the really useful volumes that now and again float by on the wide ocean of book-learning are overlooked and must share the fate of perishing with the other chaff. The tendency to read much in order to say one has read. (42)

Like Lessing, Mendelssohn, and others, Kant feels less constrained by this as a writer than challenged to participate even more, staking his faith in open competition:

> Man muss jetzo gar keine Bücher verbieten das ist das eintzige Mittel dass sie sich selbst vernichten. Wir sind jetzo auf den Punkt der Wiederkehr gekommen. Die Flüsse wenn man sie ihre Überschwemmungen machen lässt bilden sich selbst Ufer. Der Damm den wir ihnen entgegensetzen dient nur ihre Zerstöhrungen unaufhörlich zu machen. Denn die Verfasser unnützer sachen haben zu ihrer Entschuldigung die Ungerechtigkeit anderer vor sich.

> From now on, no books at all are to be forbidden: that is the single means by which they will eliminate themselves. We have now reached the turning point. Rivers form their banks on their own if we allow them to flood. The dikes we set against them only serve to make their devastations unceasing. The authors of useless products have as their excuse the injustice of others before them. (105)

This self-contained dynamic of reception being altered by an expanding book market[55] has consequences not only for a writer's self-esteem, but exercises a constitutive significance for the way that writer's work is presented. And ultimately, for all concerned, it is a question of the "destiny of man."[56]

The *Observations* were conceived as an aesthetic discussion (including ethical phenomena as well, but from an aesthetic perspective). But having once delineated the borders here, Kant henceforth moves ever more decisively in the direction of ethics. His "remarks" show clear traces of the gradual transition to the primacy of practical reason, first formulated in the *Dreams*. It is *moral* freedom that stands as the highest principle of all virtue (31), and it is *moral* knowledge of God that alone is certain (57). Finally, morality has to be placed above religion and thereby recognized as autonomous (153). In doing this, morality is compared with the "medicinal art" ["*Arzneykunst*"], so that for the most part it is defined negatively: "The best doctor is the one who teaches me how I can be spared of sicknesses & medicines. The art of this is easy & simple. But that which lets everything decay & alleviates it afterward is artificial & confused" (122).

The last remarks already point directly to the *Dreams*, which was to appear shortly after this. They thus link the *Observations* to what becomes the continuing consideration: "One could say that metaphysics is a science of the limits [*Schranken*] of human reason" (181).[57]

In a postscript to a review of Isaak Iselin's *Wissenschaft der Gesetze* in March 1762, Mendelssohn calls Iselin, a Swiss, to task for his emphasis on the importance of observations as instructive aids for determining moral precepts. He points out that observations serve as the source for both normative as well as historical moral theories. Yet since observation can never come to a conclusion, moral precepts, too, seem doomed to remain imperfect:

> I think that until now philosophical moral theory has been neglected in France and historical moral theory in Germany. Hence the profound system of one such as Wolff lacks pragmatic application to history, and the subtle observations of one such as Montesquieu lack general systematic principles. A work that would combine the profound depth of Wolff with the shrewdly observant mind of Montesquieu would, in my opinion, be the most perfect masterpiece of human reason; maybe this is an ideal that transcends human capacities, but the greatest minds of our time should try to approximate it, as much as possible.[58]

Kant seems to adhere precisely to this program when he employs aesthetics to frame the question, at the center of his *Observations,* of the conditions necessary for the foundation of moral principles. His attempt at mediating the "French" and "German" extremes may merely be a fulfillment of Mendelssohn's appeal.

SIX

Wit as a Formal Principle

H̲AVING PASSED BEYOND THE
ego's cosmological trial phase, followed by the gender-specific and nation-
ality-oriented anthropology of the *Observations*, Kant arrives at the next
phase of his career path. This is a new level in the process of sounding out
the philosophical conditions of the possibility of the "I" and, with this, his
definition as a writer, understood in the widest sense. After exploring the
limitless universality of cosmological generality and then proceeding
through universal-anthropological observations, Kant's gaze now focuses
itself, like a zoom lens, on individual anthropology. From there he will
venture further, in the *Dreams*, to position himself at the very borderline of
epistemological theory within human limits.

As can now be recognized, this path consists of a series of literary experiments [*Versuche*], developing according to an internal law that is both
logical and practically necessary. Methodologically self-conscious of his
every step, Kant's goal is to inscribe the path *of* method as the path *to*
method. Once again, content and form define each other reciprocally. The
journey out of outer space, and ever deeper into the mind and soul, to the
center point of the subject, and then to the epistemological subject, gradually transforms itself along the way from essay [*Versuch*] into protocritical
discourse.

One miniature expedition—Kant's first and only one—does come at the
beginning of this new phase. And sensibly enough, it is a journey that aims
not to travel great distances, but rather, reversing this, to venture into the
unexplored strangeness of the human psyche's interior. Kant first begins to
"travel" in the moment that travel, as the gathering of data about foreign

cultures, is no longer the issue; instead, the expedition takes the form of a journey inward.

As subjectivity increases objectively, namely the subjective nature of Kant's object, the literary framework defining the discourse is displaced. Thus, by way of this formal impact, the thematic context undergoes adaptation as well. In Swiftean style, the law of associative connection becomes the formal principle, in a Lockean sense. This can be seen as the philosophical basis that motivates the specifically playful yet experimental literary quality of the "Essay on the Sicknesses of the Head" ["Versuch über die Krankheiten des Kopfes"].

In mid-January 1764, just as the *Observations* appeared, there came a "goat prophet" from Galicia to the Königsberg region. Wandering with his son and a herd of sheep and goats, he was marveled at by his contemporaries as a sort of natural man, and soon he drew public attention. Kant's publisher and bookdealer, Kanter, even organized an excursion to visit this attraction, as much to satisfy the curiosity of his customers as their enlightened, scientific interest. Kant participated in it along with others (Vorländer, *Kant*, 1:162). Hamann, the editor of the *Königsbergische Gelehrte und Politische Zeitung*, printed Kant's thoughts about his experience, together with a description of this "appearance of the new *Diogenes*," this "spectacle of human nature,"[1] as a short "*Raisonnement*" in the third issue that year. It is generally not included in editions of Kant's works, and even in the *Akademieausgabe* it is relegated to a footnote. As a small masterpiece of Kantian prose—and in light of the complex sentence structure, editorial intervention by some stranger's hand can be ruled out, particularly because Hamann as chief editor (one of the most peculiar stylists and idiosyncratic writers of the eighteenth century) must have been philologically far too conscientious to correct another author—it does merit some interest.

Its significance is due, among other things, to its being the shortest complete journalistic text Kant composed, thus representing the only example of his mastery of short form. The short form often enables writerly qualities to be recognized whose absence might otherwise be disguised easily. Surprisingly, one finds in Kant an ability to condense and abbreviate, aphorism-like. This allows him to make fruitful use of essayistic disjunction, by stylistically avoiding having his argument play itself out in flat either-or constructions, and instead turning it into an open-ended dialectic. To this extent, the "*Raisonnement*", as a short form, operates as a *Versuch in nuce*:

> Bei dem Anschauen und Anhören des begeisterten Faunus und seines Buben ist für solche Augen, welche die rohe Natur gerne ausspähen, die unter der Zucht der Menschen gemeiniglich sehr

unkenntlich wird, das Merkwürdigste—der *kleine Wilde*, der in
den Wäldern aufgewachsen, allen Beschwerlichkeiten der Wit-
terung mit fröhlicher Munterkeit Trotz zu bieten gelernt hat, in
seinem Gesichte keine gemeine Freimüthigkeit zeiget und von
der blöden Verlegenheit nichts an sich hat, die eine Wirkung der
Knechtschaft oder der erzwungenen Achtsamkeiten in der
feinern Erziehung und, kurz zu sagen (wenn man dasjenige weg-
nimmt, was einige Menschen schon an ihm verderbt haben, die
ihn lehren Geld fordern und naschen), ein *vollkommenes Kind* in
demjenigen Verstande zu sein scheint, wie es ein Experimen-
talmoralist wünschen kann, der so billig wäre, nicht eher die
Sätze des Herrn *Rousseau* den schönen Hirngespinsten beizuzäh-
len, als bis er sie geprüft hätte. Zum wenigsten dürfte diese Be-
wunderung, zu welcher nicht alle Zuschauer fähig sind, weniger
zu belachen sein, als diejenige, darin jenes berufene schlesische
Kind mit dem goldnen Zahn viele deutsche Gelehrte versetzt hat,
ehe sie durch einen Goldschmidt der Mühe überhoben wurden,
mit der Erklärung dieses Wunders sich länger zu ermüden.

Watching and listening to the inspired Faunus and his boy is for
the eyes of those[2] who enjoy scouting out raw nature, which so
often becomes scarcely noticable among cultivated men, and the
most remarkable thing is—the *little wild child,* who grew up in the
woods and learned to defy all the discomforts of exposure to the
elements with a joyful cheer, whose face shows an uncommon
frankness, without any trace of the timid confusion that results
from serfdom or the forced attentiveness of a fine upbringing,
and in short (if we take away what a few men have already
spoiled in him, in teaching him to elicit money and sweets), he
seems to be a *perfect child,* understood in the sense that an experimental moralist might wish, were he fair enough not to attribute
the hypotheses of *Rousseau* to the list of beautiful intellectual
chimeras until he had taken the time to test them himself. In the
very least, this sense of amazement, which not all onlookers are
capable of, should merit less derision than the amazement of so
many German scholars that was elicited by that acclaimed Sile-
sian child with the golden tooth, at least prior to their being
relieved, by a goldsmith, of the laborious task of having to explain this miracle. (AA, 2:489)[3]

The dominant position given to Rousseau is indicative of the time at
which Kant wrote these words. The irony of playful levity is simulta-

neously an expression of the seriousness of his engagement with Rousseau, a way of announcing the critique of him he is just then formulating. Kant's designation of himself as an "experimental moralist" is particularly revealing, because he sets himself in a differentiated relationship to Rousseau here, even syntactically. This move carries a number of implications, right down to the formulaic brevity with which Kant expresses his own self-perception. As an oxymoron that encapsulates the contradiction between empiricism and rationalism by locking it into a single concept, this phrase bears, to a certain degree, the mark of Rousseau's own method. It does not signify a synthesis, but rather problematizes method itself. Kant's playfulness is an indication of how indefinite and searching his own self-definition continues to be, as a writer and as a philosopher, and both of these aspects are contained in the title "experimental moralist." In fact, the form of this expression is itself a sort of experiment. "Moralists" is what essayists were called who carried on the tradition of social criticism from Montaigne and Bacon.[4] In this context, Kant's ironic self-designation as "experimental moralist" clearly shows his understanding of himself as a writer who literally *experiments,* both within and through his essays, his *Versuche.* He thus indicates the necessity of finding a methodical solution to the problem addressed in the *Observations:* how to synthesize the two separate strains of philosophy—the deductive, general, and the inductive, experimental; the normative and the descriptive. That Kant arrives at this self-description in what could be called the shortest form of the *Versuch* shows just how experimental this understanding still is at this point in time. Furthermore, it casts light on the role of experimental philosophy, which, as formulated by Bacon and others, represents the modern understanding of the world:[5] the search for a method that has become a method unto itself.

Kant's piece was followed by an announcement: "We hereby announce at once the first original essay [*Originalversuch*] in our upcoming issues, and for the satisfaction of our readership we have engaged additional contributions from the kindness of this incisive and scholarly patron" (AA, 2:489). The two sentences of the *"Raisonnement"* thus represent a kind of preview to the upcoming *Originalversuch.* Although this designation may have come from Hamann, it is clearly based nonetheless either on an impression of Kant's own intentions or from a reading of the beginning of the *Versuch* itself, which was ready to run in the next issue—if the announcement was not from Kant himself.

The "Essay on the Sicknesses of the Head" appeared in the following issue of the *Königsbergische Gelehrte und Politische Zeitung* anonymously, as was the custom for newspapers in that period. But for Königsberg's readers, the identity of the author was no secret. Rousseau's influence on the "experimental moralist" is appreciable throughout the entire *Versuch*. Right at the beginning, Rousseau's philosophy of culture is cited, when Kant states, "The simplicity and sufficiency of nature requires and forms only crude concepts and a plump sincerity in man, while the contrived compulsion and luxuriant growth of the civil constitution churns out jokers and pedants, and occasionally fools and cheaters too" (ww, 2:887).[6] This emulates rhetorically the powerful opening words of the *Emile*.[7] Hence a course is set for the *Versuch:* in the free form of the essay, it follows Rousseau's thoughts on the self-sufficiency of the natural man who becomes perverted through artifice and culture. This, in turn, although historically irreversible, also brings forth new possibilities. In its fundamentals, the historical skepticism of Rousseau is still repeated in the *Critique of Pure Reason*, where it is justified in epistemological terms (B, 859/A, 831; S, 651f.). Such sharp irony can be preserved only in the framework of Kant's (and Rousseau's) enduring humanity, which does not serve to temper the irony but rather is what first gives it its full weight.

Although the *Versuch* claims to be "a little onomasticon of mental maladies," this is not meant completely seriously in view of its object. Fools and lunatics in even the most extreme stages (who thus form a parody of the chain of being, as well) are discussed in clean, precise pathological terms. But a consequence of this discussion is the implication that this pathology is really all-encompassing, that no one can escape it. As a cultural critique, the point here—and it is only possible thanks to Rousseau—is that the natural man does not exist (anymore), and whoever claims to be one provides his or her own diagnosis. "Degenerate [*ausgeartete*] man has strayed from his natural place, and is attracted by everything and bound by everything" (ww, 2:890). But "degenerate" is less an individual ailment than a historical category, to be distinguished from natural man, that is, from man in the state of nature. For the individual, there is only the particular way chosen, in each case, to overcome this loss of naturalness by compensating with a greater or lesser degree of secondary gain.

One sees just how complicated Kant's own situation appears to him when he continues: "To the fool [*Tor*], we oppose the *sensible* man; but whoever is without foolishness, is a *wise man*. This *wise man* can be sought, for example, on the moon; there, perhaps, people are free of passion and have infinite amounts of reason" (890). The universality of foolishness is thus insured, at least as relates to earth-dwellers.[8] The classification of diverse deficiencies of reason actually underscores more readily what they have in common, rather than bringing to light the accidental differences in each particular case. This gesture of offering classifications is not without its own intended critique of method, a gesture we see repeated later on in

Kant's critical works. This "hair-splitting" [*Wortklaubereien*] must be understood in its critical function. Indeed, it is not to be mistaken for some repeatedly disguised inability or system-oriented traditionalism, for it is precisely these things that it criticizes behind the mask of irony.[9]

In further, seemingly endless subdivisions, Kant distributes the ailments into despicable and pitiable ones. Those that merit our pity are separated into those of impotence (imbecility) and those of perversion (distemper). Under the rubric of derangement [*Verrückung*] he includes the "perversion of concepts of experience" [*die Verkehrtheit der Erfahrungsbegriffe*] while he names insanity [*Wahnsinn*] the disordered power of judgment, and madness [*Wahnwitz*] is named "reason that has become perverse in regard to more universally held judgments" [*die in Ansehung allgemeinerer Urteile verkehrt gewordene Vernunft*] (892f.).[10] Kant conceives of derangement more precisely as a natural capacity that becomes taken for granted. "Creative poetic ability" [*schöpferische Dichtungsfähigkeit*] is thus a necessary capacity for a healthy condition, as well. Its activity is one and the same whether we are asleep or awake. What sensations [*Empfindungen*] are when awake, become chimeras during sleep: "Thus this phantasm [*Hirngespinst*] itself has to be considered a real experience, even when we are awake and our reason is well and soundly functioning" (893). The question of exactly how sensations are to be distinguished from chimeras has to be determined, first of all. What Kant makes into the theme here will soon grow into an entire epistemological problem complex in the *Dreams of a Spirit-Seer*. The answer he gives, "at least whoever has been enchanted by these chimeras can never be led to doubt the reality of his supposed sensations by means of reasoning," (894) points to the noticeable lack of a theory. Where one is lacking, its place is taken by—a story. Thus Kant shifts over into a self-portrayal, using the narration of his personal history of hypochondria as a substitute for theory. Only on the basis of this narrative does it become possible, in the *Dreams* that follow this essay, or more precisely in this *Originalversuch*, to develop a theory of the critique of the sensations. The biographical necessity inherent in such philosophical-historical development is decisive here.[11]

The sketch of the "melancholy person" given in the *Observations* finds its sequel here under the appellation of "Fantast." The "delusory sensation [*Blendwerk von einer Empfindung*] of his own condition" (895) makes the "hypochondriac" melancholy. The fact that Kant is describing himself forces its way to the surface, as the narrator's standpoint is gradually displaced into the mental space of this "inner fantasy." Because the description is objective at first, and the self-description transparent for any of

Kant's friends in Königsberg, one is led to conclude that the remainder of the text represents observations in experimental psychology.

"He is most fond of speaking of his own indisposition, enjoys reading medical books and finding his own occurrences throughout, and while socializing his good mood often comes to him unnoticed, and then he laughs much, dines well, and generally has the appearance of a healthy person" (895). This self-portrait is not difficult to confirm from the biographies; it is that of the "gallant scholar." Kant himself confirms having studied medical books a few pages later (900). But the way he continues this self-description is surprising:

> Die innere Phantasterei desselben anlangend, so bekommen die Bilder in seinem Gehirne öfters eine Stärke und Dauer, die ihm beschwerlich ist. Wenn ihm eine lächerliche Figur im Kopfe ist (ob er sie gleich selber nur vor ein Bild der Phantasie erkennet), wenn diese Grille ihm ein ungeziemendes Lachen in anderer Gegenwart ablockt, ohne dass er die Ursache davon anzeigt, oder wenn allerhand finstere Vorstellungen in ihm einen gewaltsamen Trieb rege machen, irgend etwas Böses zu stiften, vor dessen Ausbruch er selbst ängstlich besorgt ist, und der gleichwohl niemals zur Tat kommt: alsdann hat sein Zustand viel Ähnliches mit dem eines Verrückten.

> As pertains to the inner fantasy of this person, the images in his brain frequently take on an intensity and duration that he finds troublesome. When he gets some ridiculous figure in his head (even if he himself recognizes it instantly as just a fantasy image), and when this whim elicits an unseemly laughter from him in the presence of others, without his explaining the cause of it, or when all sorts of gloomy thoughts excite a forcible drive within him to bring about some evil deed, an outburst whose very possibility causes him fearful concern, and which all the same is a deed he never commits; at that moment his condition has much in common with that of a deranged person's. (895)

Melancholy has been considered traditionally to be the attribute of the wise man, a suffering caused by hyperreflectivity. Socrates, Plato, Aristotle, and Montaigne,[12] all Kant's models of exemplary philosophers, were melancholy.[13] The mood in which reflection is carried out is one of melancholy. It is the source of genius. The time of day when the owl of Minerva begins its flight, it is said, is at the crack of dawn, when everything appears gray on gray.[14] Thus the critical philosopher is always already confronted with melancholy as the cultural convention for the way he (or she) perceives him- (or her-) self. For Kant, however, it is not only the attribute of the wise man, but in fact the condition of the possibility of knowledge in general. The thematization of melancholy has a systematic context. The connection between melancholy and the sublime undertaken in the *Observations* only now becomes recognizable in its fullest extent. There, Kant interprets melancholy as an expression of the sublime, and hence—in opposition to the prevailing opinion[15]—as an expression of moral vigor. Thus he attributes the melancholy disposition to one of true virtue.[16] Now this appreciation of its motivating principle finds its application. The moral rehabilitation of melancholy is the prerequisite for the self-portrayal in the *Versuch*, is what makes it even possible. Without this shift in emphasis, it would lack the theoretical dignity it needs as an explanatory device. As a principle that generates knowledge, the investigation of the self has a systematic place assigned to it, in order, as it were, to reserve a free space for that knowledge which has yet to be attained.

When Kant again takes up the discussion of the melancholy and hypochondriac dispositions over thirty years later, it has once more been disassociated from its original context of epistemological motivations and has reverted to being a biographical subtheme. The description is disburdened of any of the knowledge-producing functions once they have found comprehensive presentation in the *Critique of Pure Reason*. Therefore, once the original task of melancholy has been accomplished, it is freed from the compulsion connected with the production of theory. The title of the essay deals as it were symptomatically with the success of this emancipation: "On the Power of the Mind to Become Master of One's Morbid Feelings through Mere Determination" ["Von der Macht des Gemüts durch den blossen Vorsatz seiner krankhaften Gefühle Meister zu werden"] Melancholy has become a theme for anthropology.[17] The melancholy person may well be "a fantast in regard to life's evils" (896). But life often has need of fantasts, and least in the eyes of those whose "dull and often ignoble feeling(s)" lead them to view those who "are excited by a moral sensation the way they would be by a principle" as fantasts (896). Thus Aristides and Epictetus were just as much fantasts in the eyes of their contemporaries as Rousseau was to the doctors of the Sorbonne (896). Kant continues: "This ambiguous appearance of fantastry in moral sensations that are good in and of themselves is *enthusiasm*, and nothing great in the world has ever been accomplished without it" ["Dieser zweideutige Anschein von Phantasterei, in an sich guten moralischen Empfindungen, ist der *Enthusiasmus*, und es ist niemals ohne denselben in der Welt etwas Grosses ausgerichtet worden"] (896).

The proximity of the fantast to the fanatic makes Kant's fascination with Swedenborg understandable. He feels challenged by him, but he also needs to distinguish himself sharply from him. Kant sounds more imploring than convincing when he immediately adds: "The situation is quite different with the *fanatic* (*visionary, religious enthusiast* [*Schwärmer*])" (896). And directing his words at attempts to arrogate religious authority, which he will repeat against Swedenborg in the *Dreams*, Kant declares: "This [fanatic] is actually a deranged person who claims to have unmediated inspiration [*Eingebung*] and great intimacy with the powers of heaven. Human nature knows no delusion more dangerous" (896). All the same, his "power of understanding is actually not affected" (897), for which reason pathology is subsequently unable to substitute the criterion of knowledge here.

Kant closes his Rousseauean circle in the *Versuch* with a paraphrase of Rousseau's description of the state of nature and its degeneration into the "civil constitution" [*bürgerliche Verfassung*] (898f.). But a witticism closes the larger circle, one which had come into play already through the denial that wise men are found on earth (890, see above). Wit (*Witz*) thus proves itself to be a fundamental formal principle. This wit consists not only of agility in grasping and remembering something, but also the capability of presenting it [*Darstellung*], "in other words, ease in expressing it properly" (888). For Kant, knowledge and the capacity to represent it [*Darstellungsvermögen*] are thus thoroughly correlated: "Difficulty in being able to express oneself proves nothing at all about the capacity of understanding, but instead only that one's wits are supplying insufficient assistance in clothing one's thought in various symbols, a few of which will suit it most aptly" (888).

As a principle of knowledge, wit attains a formative significance. The *Versuch* expresses this in both its form and its content, in that it not only treats of wit but also itself represents a joke, a witticism. The concluding paragraph serves to reiterate this with utter clarity. That the sicknesses of the head are ailments of the intellect (900) plays upon ideas which have thus far remained implicit. Kant's conclusion will put these allusions into their proper context, which has also merely been hinted at: that of an attempt in critically reorienting epistemological theory.

Kant refers his readers to an explanation of the origin of such sicknesses, namely, in the digestive organs. This explanation had also been brought to bear on the "goat prophets,"[18] and Kant uses it here to give his essay one last twist. Just after pointing out this possible cause, he concludes:

Denn da nach den Beobachtungen des *Swifts* ein schlecht Gedicht
bloss eine Reinigung des Gehirns ist, durch welches viele schäd-

liche Feuchtigkeiten, zur Erleichterung des kranken Poeten abge-
zogen werden, warum sollte eine elende grüblerische Schrift
nicht auch dergleichen sein? In diesem Falle aber wäre es ratsam,
der Natur einen andern Weg der Reiniging anzuweisen, damit
das Übel gründlich und in aller Stille abgeführet werde, ohne das
gemeine Wesen dadurch zu beunruhigen.

For if according to the observations of *Swift*, a bad poem is merely
a purification of the brain, through which many harmful humors
are evacuated to relieve the ailing poet, then why should a miser-
able, brooding text not do the same thing? In this case, however, it
would be advisable to direct nature to a different path of purification, so that the foulness gets evacuated thoroughly and in utter
silence, without thus upsetting the common good. (901)[19]

With this, the last consequence is drawn and the essay is inscribed with the
strongest possible self-reflectivity. It is transcendental to the extent that it
reflects upon the conditions of the possibility of knowledge in general and
finds a way to represent this process. On the path to the *Dreams,* and from
there to the *Critique,* this *Versuch* denotes a crucial point of transition. The
epistemological standpoint Kant reaches here could perhaps thus be called
"prototranscendental."

SEVEN

Double Satire and Double Irony

O<small>N</small> F<small>EBRUARY</small> 7, 1766, K<small>ANT SENT</small>
seven copies of the *Dreams of a Spirit-Seer, Elucidated by Dreams of Meta-physics* [*Träume eines Geistersehers, erläutert durch Träume der Metaphysik*]
to Moses Mendelssohn, to be distributed in Berlin. In the letter that accom-panied them, he speaks of "a few overwrought dreams" as being "a text that
practically had to be forced out."[1] Two months later, he responds to "the
astonishment you [Mendelssohn] expressed about the tone of the little
text," with an extensive explanation. He tells of his "reluctance," and the
absurd disposition he felt himself to be in while writing this work. In this
letter, Kant not only develops the text's background, but emphasizes its
systematic position within the context of the search for a method. On the
question of literary representation, the metaphor of clothing is particularly
telling:[2] "Indeed, it was difficult for me to devise a method of clothing my
thoughts in such a way that I would not be exposing myself to public
ridicule" (*Briefwechsel,* 51). In one concise sentence, Kant names the liter-ary pattern for the *Dreams:*

> das dogmatische Kleid abzuziehen und die vorgegebenen Ein-sichten skeptisch zu behandeln, wovon der Nutzen freilich nur
> negativ ist (stultitia caruisse), aber zum positiven vorbereitet:
> denn die Einfalt eines gesunden, aber ununterwiesenen Ver-standes bedarf, um zur Einsicht zu gelangen, nur ein Organon;
> die Scheineinsicht aber eines verderbten Kopfs zuerst ein Kathar-tikon.

> to remove the cloak of dogma and to deal with the preexisting
> insights skeptically, which admittedly is useful only in a negative

way (*stultitia caruisse*) but prepares the way for positive uses: for the simplicity of a healthy but uninstructed intellect requires merely an *organon* in order to attain insight, but the pseudo-insights of a ruined mind first need a *kathartikon*. (*Briefwechsel*, 52f.)

The *Königsbergische Gelehrte und Politische Zeitungen* printed an extensive review on March 3, 1766. Herder was its author. He points out the literary affinity with Sterne's *Tristram Shandy*, and sets forth Kant's critique of Swedenborg as a paradigm of how such writers are to be dealt with.[3] But for this student of Kant's who is otherwise so positively inclined toward him, the *Dreams* left behind a mixed impression: "The text, as a whole, would seem to lack unity, and each part does not seem connected enough to the others. The author presents the truths from both sides, and like a certain Roman, he says, 'One of you, say no! the other, yes!' You Romans, whom do you believe? Meanwhile, it hones one's attentiveness that much more, and one sees at every turn that the author has the genius of philosophy for his friend, just as Socrates conferred with his daemon in holy dreams."[4] So is the critique of dreams itself a dream? One year later, in a brief announcement of the *Dreams* in the *Allgemeine deutsche Bibliothek*, Mendelssohn also maintains, "The droll profundity in which this short work is written often leaves the reader in doubt as to whether Mr. *Kant* wants to render metaphysics laughable, or make the seeing of spirits seem credible."[5]

Kant's text is one that presents itself like a literary Hussar on a take-no-prisoners mission. What starts off in a tone of fairy-tale cheer and seems to abscond into the colorful land of fables unmasks itself at the end as a literary exercise, a practice session in logically consistent, critical philosophy. Its literary-philosophical point is that this excursion into the realm of fantasy becomes a necessary point of passage for the constitution of Kant's critical method. The virtuosity of Kant's quill emerges here with dazzling artistry, so that it manages elegantly to gloss over the need for such a passage, diverting the reader with amusing, artistic skill. In this way, Kant has seduced readers into overlooking the specific philosophical function of the text's aesthetic quality. Yet this high point for the writer signifies a crisis for the thinker, a decisive turning point, and a complex problem emerges in determining just how to approach his text. Kant gives literary shape to philosophical substance, which also means expressing what is philosophically inexpressible. This makes a rigorous philosophical interpretation just as uncertain as it makes a literary interpretation inviting. But the fusion of the two elements is exactly what condemns any one-sided approach to mere reductionism. The systematic place in Kant's thought highlighted by this crisis determines the coordinates along which a reading must orient itself. Failure to take these into account would make one disoriented as the headlong-charging narrator is, himself.

The mode of presentation is literary for several reasons. The perspective it takes seems necessary to its theme, but this theme is itself in turn tailored to literary conditions. The reciprocity of content and form constitutes its literary quality. This hinging point of content and form is where the code of the *Dreams* is to be deciphered, as it were. The specific narrative character of its philosophical-historical discourse seems to have smoothed over the join to create a seamless transition that only a keen eye might discern. On the transition from the precritical to the critical Kant, Ueberweg states, for instance, "For Kant, however, extracting himself from scholastic metaphysics and turning toward popular writing did not mean the end, but rather the beginning of a more serious engagement with metaphysical problems."[6] The observation that the genesis of critical philosophy could be causally connected to the idea of writing is not carried any further by Ueberweg. To begin with, it would need to be reflected upon. Instead, Ueberweg simply carries on with his report.

Kuno Fischer points out the "cheerful and joking sort of approach" and Kant's proximity to the style of the English humorists, as well as the stylization of the chapter headings.[7] Cassirer calls the *Dreams* "a text that in its literary form and its stylistic trappings already overthrows the whole tradition of academic philosophical literature."[8] Schilpp writes: "This essay is probably the most fantastic that Kant ever wrote,"[9] and Ward adds that the *Dreams* are "the strangest and most tortured of Kant's writings."[10] Elaborating this, Ebbinghaus explains that the essay is

> written in a style that makes it a pearl of the comic-satirical species that is so rare in Germany. If our literary historians knew what was good for them and . . . would cast their glance on the miracles of literary form that have emerged in our fatherland, then they would have been able to discover long ago, in the *Dreams of a Spirit-Seer,* that concealed in the Magister Kant was a literary talent which in all likelihood could be placed alongside that of Wieland, or Lichtenberg, and that would even rise above these others through the weight of its insights, which he holds right under the noses of his readers, and he holds them there all the more closely, the more the reader believes himself to be fooled-with.[11]

Vleeschauwer notes a "change in tonality" and attributes this to Rousseau's influence.[12] The epigraph from Horace's *Ars poetica,* "velut aegri somnia, vanae finguntur species,"[13] sets dreams, sickness, and fiction on an equal footing—in enjambment.[14]

In his preface, the anonymous author lays out a series of reasons that might account for the text having been written. These have been readily taken up in Kant research in order to satisfy the text's obvious need of legitimation as to its motives. The situation is a good deal more serious, however. The "Preface, Which Promises Very Little for the Execution of the Project," accordingly expects to be taken seriously in its capacity as satire. It consists of a framework of repeated *mises-en-abîme,* which like a hall of mirrors reflects the author twice, and therefore, by double-projecting, makes the author fade away. In three times three sequences, Kant names basic patterns of how to behave in response to sightings of spirits. For the philosopher, the following questions are raised:

> Soll er die Richtigkeit aller solcher Geistererscheinungen gänz-lich ableugnen? Was kann er vor Gründe anführen, sie zu wi-derlegen?
>
> Soll er auch nur eine einzige dieser Erzählungen als wahr-scheinlich einräumen? wie wichtig wäre ein solches Geständnis, und in welche erstaunliche Folgen sieht man hinaus, wenn auch nur *eine* solche Begebenheit als bewiesen vorausgesetzet werden könnte? Es ist wohl noch ein dritter Fall übrig, nämlich sich mit dergleichen vorwitzigen oder *müssigen* Fragen gar nicht zu bemengen und sich an das *Nützliche* zu halten.

> Should he completely deny the truth of all such apparitions? What reasons can he adduce to refute them?
>
> Should he admit the probability of even one of these stories? How important such an admission would be! And what astonish-ing implications would open up before one, if even *one* such occurrence could be supposed to be proven? There is, I suppose, a third possibility left, namely, not to meddle with such prying or *idle* questions, and to concern oneself only with what is *useful.* (ww, 2:923f.; DW, 305f.)[15]

With regard to his motives for writing a book, Kant lists three: (1) to have found out nothing ("already a sufficient reason"), (2) "the vehement urging of known and unknown friends," and (3) having purchased and, "what was worse," having read, Swedenborg's *Arcana coelestia.* "Such are the origins of the present treatise, which, the author flatters himself to hope, will fully satisfy the reader as to the nature of its subject matter, in that he will not understand its most refined parts, will not believe other parts, and will laugh at the rest" (ww, 2:924; DW, 306).

Clearly, this highly stylized typology is meant to mirror a series of "reasons" for writing the text. Their actual value as justifications has to be taken into account cautiously, however, for the typology marks a literary strategy that locates every such motive *a priori* in the context of a literary composition, where it is presented under the guise of a *façon de parler*. The preface represents a perfect hall of mirrors, in which the reader's face is reflected back, regardless of which mirror he or she looks into. For each of the reasons Kant mentions, if they were taken seriously, encloses the reader within an interpretive circle, whose result is a hermeneutic short circuit. And even if Kant's readers were to stumble upon the real reason, they would only find themselves laughing back at themselves from the mirror. For by means of this device, an insurmountable difference between reality and fiction is created.[16]

Thus already, in the opening words, a contrasting image is evoked, even though its positive counterpart, Candide's garden, is not cited until the closing words. Only then does the full meaning of Kant's opening become clear: "The realm of shadows [*das Schattenreich*] is the paradise of fantasts. Here, they find a land without borders, which they can cultivate however they please" (ww, 2:923; DW, 305). In contrast to this realm of night and dreams, however, Kant invokes the paradise of "realists." This is an expanse that, admittedly, is limited, and even shrinks down to an island in the *Critique of Pure Reason*, nor can it be cultivated "however they please," but rather only according to the precepts of reason.

Kant's argument with Swedenborg and his distancing of himself from him are crucial, because the latter's way of playing with idealism is bound to propel Kant's own conception into a questionable light. Transcendental idealism, as Kant intends to develop it, represents the only possible way to overcome the dilemma posed by empiricism and rationalism. The satire is as sharp as it is because Swedenborg's abstruse theory is blocking the way to an idealistic solution. Hence a refutation of him is required, first of all, to clear a path that is philosophically acceptable. This is a precarious operation, which is why it requires a satirical tone. The affinity is too compromising to tolerate; it has to be overpowered and drowned out by a tone that will nonetheless preserve the dignity of philosophy from the ridiculousness of superstitious belief in ghosts.

Kant forestalls any mockery by mocking himself, first of all. Moreover, on the matter of superstitious beliefs in spirits and ghosts, it was considered a mark of enlightened achievement during the Enlightenment—and the epidemic extent of the countermovement to such enlightenment was already observed by the enlightened themselves[17]—to see through these beliefs. Kant does not proceed with his literary crusade in the least bit arbitrarily, and he adheres closely to philosophical conventions. This can be illustrated by comparing his approach with a statement by Spinoza, made one hundred years previously, on the question of the existence of ghosts. In their essential points, Kant's and Spinoza's approaches correspond exactly: beginning with an initial posture of tactful, agnostic restraint, but leading finally to the last possible recourse, laughter, in the face of such phantasms and overwrought dreams: "I still do not know what they [ghosts] are, either, and nobody has been able to enlighten me on this subject. If the philosophers want to call everything that is unknown to us ghosts, then certainly I will not contradict them; for there is infinitely much of which I have no knowledge."[18] The outcome of this is that spirits, just like harpies, griffins, and hydras, are nothing more than "dreams . . . , that are as different from God as nonbeing is from being."[19] Thus the dreams themselves have nothing to do with the truth of the stories that get passed around, but rather pertain to the conclusions that are drawn from them. If these are false, then there remains for the philosopher just one option: "In short, I refer to Julius Caesar, who laughed upon hearing the testimony of Sueton and yet was happy. . . . And in the same way, when contemplating the effects of limitless imaginings and passions, we all can only laugh about these things, despite the dreams and fancies that Lavater and others present as evidence in support of their object."[20]

Alongside his argument with spirit seeing, Kant is also contending with rationalistic scholastic philosophy, thus with the "Dreams of Metaphysics." This involves the critique of conceptual "realism," which believes in the possibility that concepts alone can create knowledge, in a metaphysics that posits substances as the grounds of reality, and in the Cartesian epistemological model. The "building materials" of metaphysics seem no less flighty than those of spirit seeing. Hence the text's very title brings together two apparently widely divergent things: ghosts and metaphysics. The humor lies in the parallelism thus revealed between the two discourses. From this arises what Kuno Fischer calls a "double satire": "For Kant, Swedenborg and the metaphysicians were, to borrow a phrase, like two flies he could strike with *one* swat."[21] But the tactic is dialectical. It is rather that of the brave little tailor of the Grimm fairy tale, who, with a few well-tossed stones, manages to pit the two giants against one another, so that they vanquish each other. From this dialectic, a tactic evolves that doubles the irony, directing it not only toward the reader, but toward the narrator as well, and this in turn becomes the driving force behind the text. As opposed to traditional irony, which reverses the direction of its thrust only once, and to the later so-called romantic irony, which can only be formulated on the basis of transcendental philosophy, Kant's double irony takes a positive stance—in a critically reflective way—toward what it negates.

In Kant's writing, irony has an essentially methodological character. The fact that it is simultaneously an eminently literary category is something Kant exploits to the very end. His wordplays and witticisms show him to be surprisingly adept at guiding his pen. Subordinating this entire amusing interplay to an overarching purpose, while keeping it fully integrated, is what constitutes the art of literature. This is the criterion of an art work, as Kant himself later formulates it in the *Critique of Judgment*. Here already, he not only masters this art, but even makes it into an object of reflection.

Much like "romantic" irony, Kant's double irony plays with his readers, addressing and also continually keeping an eye on them. In this way, his readers are brought into an ongoing dialogue with the author.[22] But whereas "romantic" irony takes on a sublime but consistently authoritative posture by essentially making a fool of the reader, Kant's narrative strategy differs to the extent that it poses the question, "Who is the fool?" ["Wer ist der Narr?"] free of any predisposition. The fact is that Kant knows no more than his readers do, and he fully acknowledges, in a theoretically consistent fashion, their equal capacity to judge for themselves.

Utilizing the literary medium of poetic, free-playing narrative, Kant strives to formulate his position. His playfulness is not a game, however, but an indication of actual indecision. Indeed, the repeatedly acclaimed charm of this text, as well as its literary quality, stems precisely from this freely admitted *docta ignorantia*. The outcome is a literary masquerade: in the costume of a journey, fragment, story, anticabbala, report, and anecdote, as the chapter headings declare. In this respect, the question arises as to the work's literary genre. It is an essay, a *Versuch* in the most extreme sense: a literary masquerade that grants itself free rein in its parody. And just as the text is in search of its genre, and the "I" in search of its identity, Kant the writer is also in search of himself here. These are all closely intertwined in a way that overdetermines the text, and on the basis of this the *Dreams* get overstated, appearing almost too literary. Such literariness bordering on excess becomes the travesty of satire itself, the "double satire" satirizing itself. It reflects the conditions of its possibility in a way that is not yet systematic, but that instead drags these conditions out onto the narrative stage one by one. Behind this disguise, the first outlines of Kant's undertaking in the *Critique* already become visible.

The parallel pursuit of two strains of discourse (Swedenborg and metaphysics) makes it worth tracing these strains individually, at first.

"A Tangled Metaphysical Knot, Which Can Be either Untied or Cut as

One Pleases" is the heading of the first part. In it, the author plunges *in medias res* and attempts to answer, analytically, the question as to what spirits are. At the beginning, he maintains, "I do not know, therefore, whether spirits exist, and what is more, I do not even know what the word '*spirit*' means" (ww, 2:926; DW, 307). Yet just two pages later, he gives a precise definition (ww, 2:927f.; DW, 309). Likewise, Kant does allow for the possibility of the existence of spirits, for, since they transcend the basis of common concepts of experience, they can be just as well assumed as denied. Kant finds the traditional theological idea that spirits are incorporeal[23] to be beneficial for the body-soul problem, and thus for the question of the identity of the self. The spirit hypothesis serves for Kant as a critique of the Cartesian model. The question, "Where is the place of this human soul in the corporeal world?" proves unanswerable. Thus begins the search for the self, the "I": "I would therefore rely on ordinary experience and say, for the time being: where I feel, there I *am* [wo ich empfinde, da *bin* ich]. I am just as immediately in my fingertips as I am in my head. It is I myself whose heel hurts and whose heart beats with emotion" (ww, 2:931; DW, 312).

Whether spirits exist or not cannot be answered. They can be just as well assumed as denied. As for the self—and this is the thrust of Kant's involvement with this metaphysical knot—the problem of spirits, as it is conceived here, proves to be inadequate for the specific complexity of this question. Kant's irony here signals that his polemic is directed not so much toward answering the question as it is against the question's fixation on a pre-given conception of the problem: "The methodological babble of the universities is often just an arrangement in which questions that are difficult to solve are evaded through variations in the meanings of words, simply because the comfortable and for the most part reasonable "*I do not know*" is frowned upon in the academies" (ww, 2:925; DW, 307). In contrast to this, Kant formulates his own "I do not know." He allows for the existence of spirits—now, however, considered simply as immaterial beings—but with the stipulation that the spirit-like being to be dealt with will be precisely that one we designate as "I": "I confess that I am very much inclined to assert the existence of immaterial natures in the world, and to count my own soul among this class of beings" (ww, 2:934; DW, 314f.). With this, admittedly, Kant has neither cut through nor untied the knot, but rather, conversely, he has tied still another one. And in so doing, he has revealed not only Swedenborg's hidden philosophical core, but the speculative nature of a metaphysics of substances, as well.

Set forth immediately and abruptly as a "Fragment," the second section ironically mimics just that pretence of logical decisiveness that constitutes the essence of esoteric philosophy. Thus the "Fragment of Occult Philosophy, That Will Reveal Our Community with the Spirit-World," begins with the solemn words:

> Der Initiat hat schon den groben und an den äusserlichen Sinnen klebenden Verstand zu höhern und abgezogenen Begriffen ge-wöhnt, und nun kann er geistige und von körperlichen Zeuge enthüllte Gestalten in derjenigen Dämmerung sehen, womit das schwache Licht der Metaphysik das Reich der Schatten sichtbar macht.

> The initiate has already accustomed his crude intellect, which clings to the external senses, to higher, rarified concepts, and now he can see spirit-forms, stripped of their bodily trappings, in that particular twilight in which the weak light of metaphysics makes visible the realm of shadows. (ww, 2:936; DW, 316)

And after not even thirty octavo pages (fourteen in modern print), he continues: "Let us now, therefore, following the arduous preparation we have endured, venture forth on this perilous pathway" (ww, 2:936; DW, 316). Vergil's words (*Aeneid*, bk. 6, ll. 268f.) are then introduced, both as reaffirmation and as an obscure sort of oath: "Ibant obscuri sola sub nocte per umbras,/ Perque domos Ditis vacuas et inania regna" [Like shadowy forms they wander through the lonely night among the ghosts, traversing the desolate abodes and the empty realms of Pluto] (DW, 450).

Following this initiation, Kant returns to the discussion that began with the question of the identity of the "I." Now, he comes to speak of the presumed existence, "if not with the clarity of a demonstration, so then at least with the presentiment of a not-untrained intellect," of an "immaterial world (mundus intelligibilis)" (ww, 2:937; DW, 316f.). The justification for this assumption follows an argument Leibniz uses against Descartes, namely, that in addition to the mechanical explanation of "dead matter," the organic dimension of the world also requires explaining. But once an immaterial world is presupposed, then it must further be presumed that the beings of this spirit world will interact with each other, according to an analogy with mechanics, "pneumatically" [*pneumatisch*].

This brief, partial fragment (ww, 2:936–42; DW, 316–21) is again broken up, ironically. This is done first with a footnote of a distinctly humorous bent (ww, 2:940f.; DW, 319f.), and then again unmistakably with the frank declaration:

> Es wird mir nach gerade beschwerlich immer die behutsame Sprache der Vernunft zu führen. Warum sollte es mir nicht auch erlaubt sein, im akademischen Ton zu reden, der entscheidender

ist, und so wohl den Verfasser als den Leser des Nachdenkens überhebt, welches über lang oder kurz beide nur zu einer verdriesslichen Unentschlossenheit führen muss.

It is by [now] becoming tiresome for me to proceed at all times using the cautious language of reason. Why should I not also be allowed to speak in an academic tone, which is more decisive, and which spares the author as well as the reader of any need to think things over, which sooner or later would only lead both of them into an annoying state of indecision? (ww, 2:941; DW, 320)

Following this, Kant launches into an eloquent cadenza: "Accordingly, it is as good as proven, or it could easily be proved, if one wanted to go into the details, or even better, it will someday, I know not where or when, yet be proved . . ." (ww, 2:941; DW, 320). With this, the thread of the argument of this passage—which connects chain of being, irritability, sensory subject, dual citizenship of the soul—is once more unraveled, very much in the manner of Penelope, just when Kant pretends to be tightening the knot. He continues:

Es würde schön sein, wenn eine dergleichen systematische Verfassung der Geisterwelt, als wir sie vorstellen, nicht lediglich aus dem Begriffe von der geistigen Natur überhaupt, der gar zu sehr hypothetisch ist, sondern aus Beobachtung könnte geschlossen, oder auch nur wahrscheinlich vermutet werden.

It would be a beautiful thing if such a systematic constitution of the spirit-world, as we imagine it to be, could be deduced, not just from the concept of spiritual nature in general, which is simply too hypothetical, but instead from some sort of actual, universally admissible observation, or if it could at least be assumed from this with some probability. (ww, 2:942; DW, 321)

Following this, "with the reader's indulgence," comes a *Versuch*, which is distinctly and graphically offset with three stars at its beginning and end. As if in a sort of *mise-en-abîme*, "which does lead me off my path somewhat, and also seems quite far from evident" (ww, 2:942; DW, 321), this essay deals with the current status of Kant's attempts to resolve the issue of moral philosophy set in motion by *moral sense* philosophy and the encounter with Rousseau. His approach here is suddenly free of irony. Yet to this extent, it is also a "fragment of occult philosophy":[24] the metaphysics of morals in an embryonic state.

The mediation of the *moral sense* theory with Rousseau's concept of the *volonté générale* is not realized accidentally, as an experiment within a literary free space. Rather, this literary space is what first makes its formulation possible. It is a *Versuch* within a *Versuch* that provides Kant with a medium for presenting his philosophical concerns. Hence, the tendency toward formalization[25] is indebted to Kant's literary inclinations. Only in a disguised codification, a *mise-en-abîme* framed with irony, can Kant express the still undeveloped, immature state of his thoughts on the evaluation of the "forces that move the human heart" (ww, 2:942; DW, 321). This *mise-en-abîme* enables Kant to utilize the unconstrained freedom to experiment, so that a discourse can unfold that presents itself in an utterly unprotected way. Such a freely developing discourse allows Kant to lay open the underlying associations elicited by the complex problems surrounding the question of moral philosophy. Only in this way can the most delicate innervations of Kant's intellectual tendencies be given adequate expression. But precisely because these tendencies are not secured by any discursive apparatus, and instead are formulated in the experimental space of a crucible, it is possible for Kant's thought to emerge here in a form that expresses its original intentions. Thus this short fragment is able to show, *in nuce*, the movement of Kant's thought in its entire, multilayered breadth: the complex intermingling of motives, from the most personal stirrings of the heart, to conditions that encompass society as a whole, in short, "the forces that move the human heart." This *Versuch* draws together the complete, voluminous span of philosophical and natural-scientific reflections, causing the diverse threads of knowledge to ball up into one great, complex tangle of associations, from which the energy of Kantian thought draws its sustenance.

If indeed the "moral impulses" spring from "the will of others outside ourselves," then this external force can be understood as the "rule of the general will." And from this, "a moral unity and systematic constitution, according to purely spiritual laws, arises" (ww, 2:943; DW, 322). "Moral sense" (or "sentiment"), however, can be understood only as a symptom or manifestation of "what really goes on inside of us, without the causes thereby being determined" (ww, 2:944; DW, 322). This moral constitution can be conceived of as analogous to Newton's law of gravity, a description that is equally unable to determine underlying causes. If one allows for a certain analogy between gravitation and moral sentiment, as Kant suggests here (albeit only experimentally and with the utmost rhetorical restraint), the result is an analogy that points to the reality of an ideal state: "All morality of actions, following the order of nature, can never be completely effective in the corporeal life of humans; but in all probability, this can happen in the spirit world [*Geisterwelt*], in accordance with pneumatic laws" (ww, 2:944; DW, 323). Thus the decisive connecting point is established. What Newton recognized in the world of physics and nature, Rousseau recognized in the world of morals and freedom. But Rousseau was not yet able to provide an analysis, in the way Newton did. In bringing these two trains of thought into parallel, Kant tries to lead Rousseau's insight onto a level where it will eventually be possible to formalize it. With all the provisionality and uncertainty of a dialectic of literary form, Kant takes what has to be said, but which borders on the unsayable, and renders it sayable—but only by once again playfully suspending its propositional value.

Following this excursus, Kant steers back onto his previous course of attempting to give a scientific explanation for spirit seeing. In a long, detailed footnote, he even concedes, in opposition to philosophical tradition, that his thoughts while asleep "may be clearer and more extensive than even the clearest ones we have when awake" (ww, 2:947; DW, 325). Because we are no longer able to remember these once we awaken, this obviously does not help very much. And when Kant goes on to note dryly that sleepwalkers "occasionally show more intelligence in such a state than they show otherwise," one recognizes the prick of satirical mischief hidden behind the rambling scholarly prose and which could so easily be overlooked. Such irony makes it difficult to get a firm grasp on what Kant intends with this footnote. In spinning out its parody on the theme of the soul's dual citizenship, now applied to being asleep and being awake, it reads like a subtext that ironically mirrors the main text. By means of this strategy of creating a dynamic between the text and what is relegated to a footnote, the definition of dreaming provided in the footnote gains its own relative importance. Whereas Kant dedicates several pages of discussion to the definition of spirits in the very beginning of the main text, the central concept of dreams—on whose basis the *Dreams* as a text is even possible—seems to be summarily demoted, its definition delegated away from the discursive continuum of the main text. The specific definition of dreams thus owes its very place to its marginality, formally delineated by its position in the text:

> Die Träume dagegen, das ist, die Vorstellungen des Schlafenden, deren er sich beim Erwachen erinnert, gehören nicht hierher. Denn alsdenn schläft der Mensch nicht völlig; er empfindet in einem gewissen Grade klar und webt seine Geisteshandlungen in die Eindrücke der äusseren Sinne. Daher er sich ihrer zum Teil nachhero erinnert, aber auch an ihnen lauter wilde und abgeschmackte Chimären antrifft, wie sie es denn notwendig sein müssen, da in ihnen Ideen der Phantasie und die der äusseren Empfindung untereinander geworfen wird.

Those dreams, however, that is, those thoughts a sleeping person remembers upon awakening, are not included here. For in these cases, the person is not fully asleep; his senses are clear, to a certain degree, and the actions of his spirit are woven in with impressions from his external senses. Hence he remembers some part of them afterward, but he also encounters in them nothing but wild and absurd phantasms, as is necessarily the case, since they contain ideas of fantasy and those of the external senses all jumbled together. (ww, 2:947; DW, 325)

Dreams—this is the point—come from an interspace between the physical and the intellectual world. They are hybrids, appropriating sensuality (perception) as well as the faculty of intellect (fantasy), and this is what makes them phantasms, chimeras. They confound the faculties. And this is also what metaphysics and spirit seeing have in common, and what Kant labors to separate: dreams as a "syndrome."[26]

Having reached this definition, the change in tone and shift in focus explored during the excursion are again brought back on track with the main argument. What was addressed prior to the excursus in the context of irritability, a scientific concept first introduced by Haller (ww, 2:939; DW, 318), now has the nomenclature of pathology applied to it:

> Diese Art der Erscheinungen kann gleichwohl nicht etwas Ge-meines und Gewöhnliches sein, sondern sich nur bei Personen eräugnen, deren Organen eine ungewöhnlich grosse Reizbarkeit haben, die Bilder der Phantasie dem innern Zustande der Seele gemäss durch harmonische Bewegung mehr zu verstärken, als gewöhnlicher Weise bei gesunden Menschen geschieht und auch geschehen soll.

> These type[s] of symptoms cannot be something common or normal, however; but rather they occur only in persons whose organs have an abnormally great irritability so that the images of their fantasy are amplified in a harmonic movement proportional to the internal condition of their soul, to a greater degree than normally takes place, or even should take place, in healthy persons. (ww, 2:949; DW, 327)

Such "delusion(s) of the imagination" ultimately indicate "an actual illness." From this, "wild chimeras and wonderous grotesques are hatched" (ww, 2:950; DW, 328), as Kant now figures it, playing upon the epigraph from Horace. Thus he concludes: "Henceforth, one can no longer be at a loss to offer some apparently rational explanation for those ghost stories that so often cross the path of the philosopher, and likewise for all the sorts of spirit influences that now and again are mentioned" (ww, 2:950; DW, 328). But once again, Kant does not stay put, for only now does he close the circle of his argument. The explanations are "apparently rational." And so, having only just pronounced a diagnosis for the spirit seer, he slips one in for the metaphysician as well. Thus he mocks:

> Ich würde der Scharfsichtigkeit des Lesers zu nahe treten, wenn ich mich bei der Anwendung dieser Erklärungsart noch aufhalten wollte. Denn metaphysische Hypothesen haben eine so ungemeine Biegsamkeit an sich, dass man sehr ungeschickt sein müsste, wenn man die gegenwärtige nicht einer jeden Erzählung bequemen könnte, so gar ehe man ihre Wahrhaftigkeit untersucht hat, welches in vielen Fällen unmöglich und in noch mehreren sehr unhöflich ist.

> I would be offending the reader's shrewdness, were I to dwell any longer upon the application of this type of explanation. For metaphysical hypotheses have something about them so uncommonly pliable, that one would have to be quite unadept if one were unable to accommodate the present hypothesis to each and every story, even before investigating whether that story was plausible or not, which in many cases is impossible, and in even more cases is quite impolite. (ww, 2:950f; DW, 328)

Rather, the gift of spirit seeing resembles a gift of the Danae, in any event, the one "with which *Juno* honored *Tiresias*, when she first made him blind, so that she could grant him the gift of prophecy" (ww, 2:951; DW, 328). Spinning out this simile, Kant elaborates that for the "intuitive knowledge of the *other* world," some aspect of the understanding must be forfeited that is necessary for this world. This "harsh condition" also applies to "certain philosophers" (ww, 2:951; DW, 328f.). Thus Kant concludes, significantly enough, not with a mockery of spirit seers, but with an anecdote from Tycho Brahe. This proves likely to be Kant's own version of the anecdote, which tells of Thales's fall into the well. One evening, Tycho Brahe ventured to claim that he could find the shortest route for his coach by following the stars. Upon hearing this, his coachman replied, "Good Sir, you may indeed understand the heavens quite well, but here on earth you are a fool" (ww, 2:951; DW, 329).[27]

The third section, an "Anticabbala," parodies the title of the second section, whose "profound speculations" are now "wholly superfluous" (ww, 2:958; DW, 335), by summarily negating it: "A Fragment of Common Philosophy, That Will Cancel Community with the Spirit World."

It is not entirely clear whether the opening sentence, "Aristotle says somewhere," is simply an error on Kant's part, or whether it is to be taken as a parody of the scholastic style that begins every inquiry by invoking Aristotle.[28] Be that as it may, by citing Aristotle (and this means by taking up a philosophical tone), Kant also inscribes his chapter sequence with a tripartite structure. Whereas the first chapter introduces the concept "spirit" straightforwardly, thus in a certain sense "empirically," the second chapter brings spirit seeing itself into play. So now, as a countermove, metaphysics speaks. The concluding chapter of the first part, then, finally strikes a first balance.

The words Kant attributes to Aristotle actually stem from Heraclitus (AA, 2:501): "Heraclitus says that people awake enjoy one world in common, but of those who have fallen asleep, each roams about in a world of his own."[29] In Kant's version, the passage reads: "When we are awake, we share a common world, but if we are dreaming, then each of us has his own" (WW, 2:952; DW, 329). By transforming this into an implication, Kant is able to pull a simple reversal, so that now he can formulate it: "If, among different people, each one has his own world, then it must be assumed that they are dreaming." With this, Kant strikes a counterblow at metaphysics, among whose "builders of castles in the sky" he counts Wolff and Crusius, for the dreamers of reason reveal "a certain affinity" with the dreamers of the senses (WW, 2:952; DW, 329).

"Dreamers of the senses" are those whose internal disturbances cause them to see things projected as external appearances that they have actually only imagined. "The displacement of the nerve tissue can cause the *focum imaginarium* to be shifted that way [toward the outside]" (WW, 2:958; DW, 334). In speaking of the *focus imaginarius* (WW, 2:955–8; DW, 332–4), Kant arrives at a psychological theory of sensory deception. Seen from this perspective, "the prevalent concept of spiritual beings [*geistige Wesen*], such as we spin together from conventional figures of speech, above, (is) also very much in conformity with this type of deception [*Täuschung*]." Since they involve sensory deception, these delusions and "figments of the imagination" [*Hirngespenster*] prove to be resistant to reason, "because the sensory perception itself, true or apparent, precedes any judgment of the understanding" (WW, 2:958; DW, 335).

Once the secret [*geheime*] philosophy has been cancelled by the common [*gemeine*] one, the dual citizenship of the soul is again revoked: "Accordingly, I will not fault the reader in any way if he chooses not to view spirit seers as semicitizens [*Halbbürger*] of the other world, but instead dispenses with them without further ado as candidates for the hospital, and thus spares himself the need of any further investigation" (WW, 2:959; DW, 335).

And like the "Essay on the Sicknesses of the Head," the next step in the explanation of spirit seeing and of metaphysics leads to a gastrointestinal diagnosis. In order to make idealism once again acceptable on a critical level, the infernal path of critique must pass through its low point: "When a hypochondriac wind churns through one's innards, what matters is what direction it takes, for if it travels downwards, then it becomes a f——, but if it travels upwards, then it is an apparition, or a holy inspiration" (ww, 2:960; DW, 336).[30]

This is followed by the fourth section, which concludes the first part of the *Dreams*, under the heading "Theoretical Conclusion from All the Reflections in the First Part." Here, Kant introduces the metaphor of the scales of understanding as an allegory for the relationship of theoretical and practical reason. He calls the primacy of practical reason the "bias of the scales of understanding," one of whose arms, bearing the inscription "Hope for the Future," has a mechanical advantage (ww, 2:960; DW, 336f.). What seems to consist of nothing but air when placed on the "speculation" side of the scale can take on decisive weight the moment it is placed on the side of hope. Once again, we stand before, or rather we *hang* in the balance. In addition, the scale has a "deceptiveness," its only inaccuracy, but nevertheless one that, as Kant formulates, "I probably cannot remove, and indeed wish never to be removed" (ww, 2:961; DW, 337).

Thus Kant reaches a "critical" stage of ignorance, a state of indefinite suspension that can easily be tipped off balance. Now, surprisingly—given all that has been said—Kant again inverts the point, and declares:

> Eben dieselbe Unwissenheit macht auch, dass ich mich nicht unterstehe, so gänzlich alle Wahrheit an den mancherlei Geistererzählungen abzuleugnen, doch mit dem gewöhnlichen obgleich wunderlichen Vorbehalt, eine jede einzelne derselben in Zweifel zu ziehen, allen zusammen genommen aber einigen Glauben beizumessen.

> This very same ignorance also keeps me from venturing to deny outright any and all truth to the various stories about spirits, albeit while reserving the right, as conventional and yet wonderous as it may seem, to call into doubt each and every single one of them, even while attributing some measure of truth to them, taken collectively. (ww, 2:961; DW, 337)

With a hint of malice, Kant continues, "The reader is free to judge for himself."

And here the narrator, too, is to be judged. For just after the third section has canceled the second, we learn: "But as far as I am concerned, there is enough advantage on the side of the arguments of the second section for me to remain serious and undecided when listening to the various strange tales of this type" (ww, 2:963; dw, 338). Yet the conclusion of the "theory of spirits," moving in the opposite direction, states "that this reflection, if properly used by the reader (!), will mark the completion of all philosophical insight regarding such beings, and that perhaps in the future one will be able still to have all sorts of *opinions* about them, but will never be able to *know* anything more" (ww, 2:963; dw, 338). This is supposed to be the case because spiritual nature cannot be thought positively, since we do not find the requisite data anywhere in our sensations. Thus we have to make do with negations, "in order to conceive of something so very different from anything sensory, that even the very possibility of such a negation rests neither upon experience, nor upon inferences, but rather upon a fiction in which reason, stripped of all other remedies, seeks its refuge" (ww, 2:963f.; dw, 339). The word "fiction" [*Erdichtung*] has been mentioned, and for the first time in a—seemingly—positive sense. So then, in conclusion, and just before the Swedenborg anecdotes that follow, Kant declares, "Henceforth, I will lay aside this whole subject of spirits, an extensive portion of metaphysics, as settled and complete" (ww, 2:964; dw, 339).

What follows this is "fiction." The heading of the second part reads: "A Story, the Truth of Which is Recommended to the Reader, to Investigate as He Pleases." In fact, the "story" is three anecdotes that have been told by Swedenborg, whose name only now receives mention, in the last third of the text.[31] In recounting these anecdotes, Kant takes Swedenborg severely to task. Indeed, he does not shy away from maligning "Schwedenberg" against his own better knowledge.[32] Alongside the "fairy tales of a *fool's paradise* [*Schlaraffenlande*] of metaphysics," Swedenborg's fairy tales fit quite well (ww, 2:968; dw, 343). But once again, the matter is not actually decided, for again Kant leaves it up to the reader, "to resolve . . . in this strange story . . . the various elements of that dubious mixture of reason and gullibility" (ww, 2:969; dw, 343). Whoever considers those "ghost stories" to be a matter of importance, however, ought to make "a journey to investigate firsthand," Kant recommends (ww, 2:970; dw, 344). With this suggestion, Kant makes the transition to the next chapter, which promises an "Ecstatic Journey of a Fanatic [*Schwärmer*] through the Spirit World."

Before he delivers on this promise, however, Kant lets us first see the cards he is holding. His remarks on the "procedure" he observed while writing this text provide indications, on a methodical level, of the function of literature for the production of theory. It now becomes clear that even his placing the dogmatic part of the treatise before the historical part has an ironic twist. He is mimicking the "device so frequently and successfully employed by philosophers" (ww, 2:971; DW, 344). This consists of setting out the arguments of reason at the beginning, before turning to actual experience, and then afterward trailing them into the account of the experience, unnoticed, so that they emerge at the conclusion, surprisingly enough, as the result. That this can be accomplished at all, and so convincingly, is due to the fact "that all knowledge has two ends where it can be got hold of, the one a priori the other a posteriori" (ww, 2:971; DW, 344). However, this has led to the situation where some "students of nature" have tried to begin with experience, in order, as it were, "to catch the eel of science by the tail":

> Allein ob dieses zwar nicht unklug gehandelt sein möchte: so ist es doch bei weitem nicht gelehrt und philosophisch gnug, denn man ist auf diese Art bald bei einem *Warum*, worauf keine Antwort gegeben werden kann, welches einem Philosophen gerade so viel Ehre macht als einem Kaufmann, der bei einer Wechselzahlung freundlich bittet, ein andermal wieder anzusprechen.

> Regardless of whether this might not be such an unwise procedure, it is still far from being scholarly or philosophical enough, for in this way one soon arrives at a *Why*, to which no answer can be given, which does about as much honor to a philosopher, as would be merited by the merchant, who, when asked to settle a bill of exchange, kindly requests that his creditor call again some other time. (ww, 2:971; DW, 344f.)

But it is equally problematic to "begin from the extreme opposite limit, namely from the highest point of metaphysics" (ww, 2:971; DW, 345).

It is significant that Kant speaks of a "limit" here. This shows that he no longer has in mind an epistemological theory of fixed demarcations, but instead has already begun to reflect on the conditions of knowledge, produced by and through knowledge itself. These conditions are no longer endpoints, to be fixed objectively, but rather now must be grasped as limits. Thus, for both procedures, the *a priori* as well as the *a posteriori*, the aporia holds true, "that one begins, I know not *where*, and arrives, I know not *whither*" (ww, 2:971; DW, 345).

The aporetical uncertainty concerning the starting point of philosophical explanation is methodological in nature. Any reflection upon this question has to come in the form of a critique of method. Kant's transition in reverse, moving from the dogmatic to the historical discussion, is marked by the quotation from Vergil, placed there as an epigraph: "Sit mihi fas audita loqui" [May I be permitted to say what I have heard] (ww, 2:965; DW, 340).[33] Philosophy necessarily recurs to the "historical," "to the real experience or story" (ww, 2:971; DW, 345). The experience or story, as a narrative, provides a parallel to the arguments of reason, which "would probably stretch out beside each other into the unthinkable," were it not that

> [E]in jeder nach seiner Art den Anfangspunkt zu nehmen und darauf, nicht in der geraden Linie der Schlussfolge, sondern mit einem unmerklichen *Clinamen* der Beweisgründe . . . die Vernunft so zu lenken, dass sie gerade dahin treffen musste, wo der treuherzige Schüler sie nicht vermutet hatte, nämlich dasjenige zu beweisen, wovon man schon vorher wusste, dass es sollte bewiesen werden.

> Each chooses a starting-point his own way, and from there he guides reason so as not to follow a straight line to the conclusion, but rather, with an imperceptible *clinamen* of his arguments . . . he guides it so that it arrives inevitably at just that point where the true-hearted student never suspected it, namely in proving precisely what everyone knew beforehand was meant to be proved. (ww, 2:971f.; DW, 345)

In the image of the *clinamen*—an inclination, or more specifically *declination*, that a theory of atoms requires, but which is logically inexplicable, and without which the atoms could never converge—Kant offers perhaps the purest designation for philosophy's contingent character. This is what constitutes its "literary" quality, or the extent to which it requires narrative for its medium. Admittedly, it can come to have an actually fictional quality, and Kant's extreme caution, indeed his nearly panic repetition of phrases condemning everything in any way "fictionalized," can only be explained by taking into account his view of the mutually constitutive character of theory and narrative.

In his image of the novelist, Kant is able to get an ironic fix on this inescapable dilemma. Irony here only serves to make the universal validity of what he describes that much clearer:

> Nach dieser sinnreichen Lehrart haben verschiedene verdienstvolle Männer auf dem blossen Wege der Vernunft so gar Geheimnisse der Religion ertappt, so wie Romanschreiber die Heldin der Geschichte in entfernte Länder fliehen lassen, damit sie ihrem Anbeter durch ein glückliches Abenteuer von ungefähr aufstosse: et fugit ad salices et se cupit ante videri. Virg.

> Following this ingenious method of theory, various accomplished men have actually stumbled upon secrets of religion along the plain pathways of reason, much the way novelists have the hero-

ine in their stories flee to faraway lands, just so that in some felicitous adventure she can accidentally bump into her lover: et fugit ad salices et se cupit ante videri. Verg. (ww, 2:972; dw, 345f.)[34]

Kant is quick to trot out the reassurance that he himself has not made use of this device, one reason for this being that since he has already spilled the secret, it would no longer work. But this cannot be too convincing, since his analysis is based upon this being a problem underlying *all* philosophizing. Philosophy is thus compelled, *eo ipso*, to work with such "devices." Hence he basically undermines his own attempt to convince, offering a hypocritical question that comes around like a boomerang and makes the irony fully evident: "What help would it be to me now, anyway, since I can no longer fool anybody, having already spilled the secret?" (ww, 2:972; dw, 346). And so, by lamenting his "misfortune," that "what resembles my own mental offspring so uncommonly well, also looks so desperately misconceived and foolish," Kant drives the accursed parallelism to the fore, via paralipsis. Indeed, he overdoes the satire, by stating further, "that as far as such personal comparisons [between Kant and Swedenborg] are concerned, I have no sense of humor." For in fact, the *Dreams* are constructed on precisely such a principle of satirical wit, if they are constructed on any principle at all. This results in a paradox, a case of Kant being at cross-purposes with himself, dialectically. He brings poets into play—seemingly in a purely negative sense—but then detects, and pursues, systematic conclusions in his discussion of them that reach beyond mere ridicule.

Kant does not attempt to conceal the concordance between Swedenborg and "my system," of "how poets, in their ravings, occasionally prognosticate, as many people believe, or at least as the poets themselves say, when and if they happen to meet with success" (ww, 2:972; dw, 346). In its pretensions of pure contingency, however, Kant's "system" reflects, in even the most extreme fits of insanity, nothing but the "imperceptible *clinamen* of the arguments." The irritating factor in all this, and what makes satire into a necessary literary expedient, is therefore not contingency itself but the systematic necessity of contingency for the process of philosophizing.

When Kant imitates a poetic tone, in addressing Swedenborg as "my hero," he switches the theme along with it. Whereas, just previously, he had had his eye on the aporia of philosophical beginnings and accordingly had spoken with a subtle, self-reflective irony, Kant now shifts over to the attack, his satire sallying forth with slick invective. What follows is a critically illuminating analysis of the theoretically scant framework displayed by this "monstrous and gigantic fantasy, perhaps the outgrowth of an old, childish idea" (ww, 2:980; DW, 352). In both language and content, it is a brilliant, concise portrayal of Swedenborg: a "faithful excerpt made available for the convenience and economy of the reader (who does not lightly choose to sacrifice £7 sterling to a minor curiosity)" (ww, 2:981; DW, 353). With the result "that all this work comes to nothing in the end," this section concludes; "[a]nd thus we retreat with a degree of shame from a foolish experiment, with the reasonable but tardy reminder: that smart thinking [*das Klugdenken*] is an easy thing, for the most part, but unfortunately only after one has allowed oneself to be deceived for a while" (ww, 2:981f.; DW, 353).

With this note, Kant has found his way back to subtle irony. For however "ashamed" he claims to be, his *Versuch* proves, in all its foolishness, to be irrevocable.[35] The fact that he arrives at knowledge only as a result of the experiment, *post festum*, is precisely what necessitates philosophy's unfolding in the medium of literature. One has to be "deceived for a while," and that means surrendering to fantasy, to imagination. At this point, Kant breaks off the literary discourse and proceeds in the language of the philosopher. With this change in tone, he marks the point of entry for philosophy, the transition from narrative to theory. The seeming lack of intention (one could call it a purposeless purposiveness) is a ploy, underpinning what is really a judiciously formulated, eminently philosophical critical turning point. On this basis, metaphysics is given a new meaning. The task of metaphysics, as Kant now formulates, has been to track down, "the more hidden qualities of things by means of reason" (ww, 2:982; DW, 354). But alongside this task, a second assignment is added, that of seeking insight into the conditions of the possibility of knowledge, namely, "to discern whether the task is also defined according to what one can possibly know" (ww, 2:982; DW, 354).

Metaphysics is hence defined as "a science of the limits of reason" (ww, 2:982; DW, 354), or a "critique of reason," as formulated in the concurrently produced *Announcement of the Program of His Lectures for the Winter Semester, 1765–1766* [*Nachricht von der Einrichtung seiner Vorlesungen in dem Winterhalbjahre von 1765–1766*] (ww, 2:914). Via logic, the concept of critique is thus introduced into metaphysics.[36] The transformation of this concept from an originally philological to a philosophical one is essentially a redrawing of the limits. And this takes place on a literary footing.

The metaphor complex that expresses this process gets repeated once again almost word-for-word in the *Critique of Pure Reason* (ww, 2:983; DW, 354; cf. B, 295/A, 236; Smith trans., 257). It is worth noting in this case that the rigorous restriction of empiricism happens here precisely on the basis of "extended experience." Henceforth, Kant will engage empiricism, as well as rationalism, only from a critical perspective. Experience is to be presented here as mediated by its narrative function, as the attempt [*Versuch*] to represent reality free of metaphysical premises.

> [U]nd da ein kleines Land jederzeit viel Grenze hat, überhaupt auch mehr daran liegt, seine Besitzungen wohl zu kennen und zu behaupten, als blindlings auf Eroberungen auszugehen, so ist dieser Nutze der erwähnten Wissenschaft der unbekannteste und zugleich der wichtigste, wie er denn auch nur ziemlich spät und nach langer Erfahrung erreichet wird.

> [A]nd since a small country always has many borders, and in general puts more stock in knowing and asserting what it possesses than in blindly setting out after further conquests, so likewise, this use of the aforementioned branch of knowledge is the least-known and simultaneously the most important, for it is only arrived at somewhat late, and after extended experience. (ww, 2:983; DW, 354)

Kant describes the principle of literature with the paradox, "I have thus wasted my time, in order to save it. I have deceived my readers, in order to serve them" (ww, 2:983; DW, 354). By this principle, reading also involves wasting or killing time, so that in the creative process of the act of reading, time is won, in the sense that experience is generated.[37] Thus the "ecstatic journey of a fanatic," in which we have traveled in fantasy via the spirits through the beyond and conversed with spiritual forms, now comes to a sober end with a sentence that will later become almost a byword: "Courage, gentlemen, I see land."[38] Kant attributes this saying to "*Diogenes*, who, it is said, thus reassured his yawning listeners as he came to the last page of a boring book" (ww, 2:983; DW, 354).

Following this roller coaster of irony in Kant's satire of spirit seeing and metaphysics, the seriousness of his tone in the "practical conclusion" lends that much more emphasis to the founding role to be played henceforth by the "practical" in Kant's thought. Erudition is to be countered by wisdom. Not without some mirth, Kant equates learnedness with a craze for knowledge, bounded only by its own incapacity. In contrast, he emphasizes the fundamental significance of philosophy. For Kant, philosophy's transcendental nature proves to be of comprehensive significance for self-reflection: "Among the innumerable tasks that present themselves, to select that one alone that is of consequence to man, is the achievement of *wisdom*" (ww, 2:984; DW, 355). In this way, philosophy recoups its losses on the side of theoretical speculation by what it gains in practical perspective.

Such legitimation, based upon "extended experience," has to come in the experimental form of a *Versuch*. This is only now revealed as the perfectly logical consequence of an argument that must inquire into its method by itself, experimentally, beyond the problematic epistemological forms of *a priori* and *a posteriori*. This is precisely what is indicated by the reference to Socrates that follows (ww, 2:984; DW, 355). As the paradigm of the philosopher in the age of Enlightenment—and this counts for Kant's contemporaries as well as for Kant himself—Socrates represents the literary guiding light toward which all philosophical writing orients itself.[39]

A summary of the status of Kant's positions regarding the epistemological limitations of the postulate of identity and contradiction (ww, 2:985; DW, 356), as well as the problems surrounding causality (ww, 2:986f.; DW, 357), leads us directly to the finale.

The language becomes elevated, yet remains transparent in its complexity, even simple. Elements of Rousseau's social criticism, the *commonsense* theory of Shaftesbury and Hutcheson, as well as traces of pietism are all melted together in a vision of ethics that leaves sentimentality far behind, when Kant declares, "For indeed, true wisdom is the companion of simplicity, and since in her case it is the heart that instructs the intellect, she generally makes the voluminous equipment of scholarship superfluous, and to her purposes she does not require such means, as can never rest within the power of all men" (ww, 2:988; DW, 358). The language of the heart should be somewhat astonishing, at this point. But once the theatrical spell of passing through the spirit realm in the *Dreams* has dissipated, the path of simplicity, of words and of style, appears to be the one path that alone remains open. To fully orchestrate the innate sense of this newly achieved tone, Kant makes use of the slowly fading din and smoke of the preceding narrative scenarios as a background against which his new approach is contrasted and defined. The way Kant stages all this enables him to represent the full scope of his intentions for the first time, so that now he can write, quite plainly, emphatically, and yet with reserve: "Does not the heart of man contain within itself immediate moral instructions [*unmittelbare sittliche Vorschriften*], and is it necessary that we relocate the machinery completely to another world, in order to move in accordance with our destiny, in this one?" (ww, 2:988; DW, 358f.). Thus calmness becomes the stylistic element of self-reflective philosophizing: "Let us henceforth relinquish all the clamorous theories [*lärmende Lehrverfassungen*] about such remote topics to the speculation and worry of idle minds" (ww, 2:989; DW, 359).

If it is true that the beginning and the end of a book, read together, can offer revealing insights about a book's contents, then this is especially true for *Dreams*. As was pointed out above, the conclusion is contained already, negatively, in the book's opening words. Viewed thus, the *Dreams* could be defined as the path from negative to positive. The book closes with the words: "But since our destiny in the future world may very much depend, presumably, upon how we have administered our posts in the present one, therefore I close with what Voltaire gave to his honest *Candide* to say, after so many futile scholastic disputes, at the conclusion: *Let us attend to our happiness, go into the garden, and work*" (ww, 2:989; DW, 359).

The tableau-style final note of *Candide* must be grasped in its full significance. It brings the novel, with the impressive force of its philosophical composition, into remarkable proximity with Lessing's *Nathan the Wise*. Both works seek to realize the transition from theory to practice, and find themselves compelled, nevertheless, to express the gesture in words. This results in elevated imagery and pervasive allegory. The delicate irony at the end is refined for a practical purpose: the expression of critical and reflective affirmation of life, on the basis of autonomous self-determination. The emphasis is expressed by Candide's honesty. It alone—and this means the primacy of practical reason—is what turns philosophy into wisdom. Kant dissociates the bitterness of Voltaire's ridicule from its nonbinding denunciatory stance, and reformulates it to produce a philosophically systematic breakthrough in his own thought. Kant's "practical conclusion" can be read as a sort of commentary to *Candide*,[40] so that these same words from Voltaire's *Candide*, paraphrased by the author of the *Dreams*, can signal the very reverse of resignation: the beginning of critical philosophy. Kant's philosophizing lends depth to a limitation Voltaire felt was forced upon him, by giving it argumentative underpinning: in withdrawal, entry, and concentration upon the small, island-like terrain of reason: "*Let us attend to our happiness, go into the garden, and work*" (ww, 2:989; DW, 359).

There can admittedly be suspicions that a skeptical attitude is at work in Kant's conclusion.[41] Although style and composition betray something approximating skepticism to some degree,[42] our analysis has shown that in place of simply appropriating skeptical positions, Kant takes up skeptical elements in a way that leads rather to its own, self-sufficient literary shape of the *Dreams*. The radical orientation toward morality, from which philosophy fundamentally re-forms itself here, decisively transcends any form of skepticism. The skeptical method[43] becomes the *Double Government Methodology*, as Butts calls it,[44] which begins to organize antagonistic statements as statements about appearances or apparitions, on the one hand, and as statements about intelligible entities, on the other. This strategy of disentanglement does operate in a skeptical way, but it does so now with principally moral intentions. The difference, however—brought to full systematic explication only in the *Critique of Pure Reason*—is expressed in and by literary form. The fact that the path from the skeptical to the critical method sets its course through the medium of literary expression therefore has a constitutive meaning for philosophy. This path has taken the reader from the spectacular opening of the *Dreams,* with its view of the "realm of shadows" as a "land without borders," on a long and winding road that eventually ends up at the garden of self-cultivation and self-determination. This signals the transition from a skeptical, resigned method to the new critical path Kant is about to open up. That Kant resists allowing literary considerations to play such an important role and, moreover, that he can only do so in the disguise of a literary discourse may ultimately explain at least some of the motivation for the surprising brutality of his attack on Swedenborg:[45] "Kant's philosophical investigation and his retelling of Swedenborg's stories are necessary and provisional proxies for the educational novel that has to follow."[46]

Kant's own lack of clarity about the interconnecting motivations for the *Dreams* is documented in the way he feels compelled to explain his intentions in his letters. Perhaps with a view to the writing of the *Dreams,* which he was just completing, Kant explains to Lambert:

> Sie klagen, mein Herr, mit Recht über das ewige Getändel der Witzlinge und die ermüdende Schwatzhaftigkeit der itzigen Skribenten vom herrschenden Tone, die weiter keinen Geschmack haben, als den, vom Geschmack zu reden. Allein mich dünkt, dass dieses die Euthanasie der falschen Philosophie sei, da sie in läppischen Spielwerken erstirbt, und es weit schlimmer ist, wenn sie in tiefsinnigen und falschen Grübeleien mit dem Pomp von strenger Methode zu Grabe getragen wird. Ehe wahre Weltweisheit aufleben soll, ist es nötig, dass die alte sich selbst zerstöre, und wie die Fäulnis die vollkommenste Auflösung ist, die jederzeit vorausgeht, wenn eine neue Erzeugung anfangen soll, so macht mir die Krisis der Gelehrsamkeit zu einer solchen Zeit, da es an guten Köpfen gleichwohl nicht fehlt, die beste Hoffnung, dass die so längst gewünschte grosse Revolution der Wissenschaften nicht mehr weit entfernet sei.

> You complain, good Sir, rightfully about the eternal sniping of dilettanti and the tiresome urge to gossip that predominates in the tone of today's authors, who have a taste for nothing further than to write about taste itself. Indeed, it seems to me that this is the death by euthanasia of false philosophy, amidst frivolous singsong; it is worse by far when it is carried off to the grave accompanied by morose and phony broodings and all the pomp of

rigorous method. Before true philosophy can come to life, it is necessary that the old one destroy itself, and since putrefaction is the most perfect dissolution, which always comes before a new creation is to begin, so too, the crisis of scholastic learnedness, coming at a time when there is no lack of good minds, gives me cause to hopes that the long wished-for, momentous revolution of the sciences is no longer far away.[47]

This sounds programatically clear, and for Lambert, this letter from Kant could only be understood in such a way at this point in time. But in relation to Kant's own status at this point, these lines attain the character of a justification for his literary adventure, *post eventu,* even before it reaches the public. And this in a way that would have to appear to Lambert as justified *a priori.*

The literary strategy of double satire proves itself to be irresolvable. The necessity of its literary form consists in precisely this irresolvability. Only thus, with this sort of flexibility, could the *Dreams* represent an adequate medium of experimentation, of *Versuch,* that could give a new definition to philosophy as "world wisdom," in a critically self-reflective way.

EIGHT
Toward the Form of Critique

W E HAVE NOW ARRIVED AT THE *Critique of Pure Reason*. Proceeding further will mean deciding whether and to what extent the interconnections between philosophy and literature explored in the preceding texts have found their way into Kant's systematic major work. If connections can be shown effectively, then the present investigation will be justified in its systematic intentions, which reach beyond mere historical interest. Kant's texts from his early years will no longer appear (only) in the light of his critiques. Instead, they will, for their own part, allow the *Critique of Pure Reason* to be comprehended as the logically consistent continuation of a philosophical endeavor that finds its adequate mode of representation in a new literary genre for philosophy.

An analysis of the *Critique of Pure Reason* is by no means an unproblematic undertaking. Whereas Sleeping Beauty lapsed into a sleep that lasted only one hundred years, time spans in philosophy seem to be measured in incomparably more generous portions, so that the two hundred years that have elapsed since the appearance of the *Critique* seem to mark just the beginning of Kant interpretation. The *Critique*'s inexhaustable potential for interpretation places it in proximity with those works of art distinguished by something irreducibly enigmatic, that demand ever-new attempts to find ways to approach and to explain them.

On the basis of the foregoing effort, the attempt will be made to cast the *Critique* as a literary work, with reference to its structure, composition, stylistic characteristics, and its use of metaphor. As a heuristic guiding point, we may take Kant's selective use of a great variety of different styles, as instances of what Mikhail Bakhtin calls *heteroglossia*.[1] Stylistic variation takes on an epistemological function, allowing Kant to apply, at a given moment, whatever mode of discourse suits the discussion of the given object. The difficulty and incomprehensibility of the *Critique*,[2] so often deplored, has to be understood in this light as an intricate process of self-clarification. It is a process in which the author seeks to articulate and to develop his preconceptions into a cogent and effective approach to the problem. This project requires exposing the faculty of reason to self-criticism, generating a highly complex self-reflectivity that results, *eo ipso,* in implications that cannot yet be fully grasped conceptually. Such in-comprehensibility may derive simply from the fact that reason [*Vernunft*] comprises more than just understanding [*Verstand*]. However, these im-plications contribute to the inherent philosophical difficulty of such an undertaking, and this difficulty inevitably mirrors itself in the literary aspects of its presentation. This has been pointed out by Dieter Henrich:

> I believe that the weight of an *innovative* text is always accom-
> panied by a certain *obscurity* regarding the conjunction of the
> various intentions, a task that necessarily follows from actually
> writing out this text. Because of this, these texts are essentially
> obscure texts, and what matters is to elucidate this obscurity by
> way of an enlightenment that allows the conjunctions to be indi-
> cated, as well as the relative weight—differing according to the
> various levels of theoretical development—of these jumbled-
> together intentions.[3]

Making matters more difficult, another question arises, namely, how the two editions of the *Critique* relate to one another. It is one of the perils of such decisive—as so many are—philosophical questions that, regardless of how they are decided, their solutions are based upon predispositions that are themselves problematic.

In the introduction to the *Prolegomena,* in connection with his account of the actual writing of the *Critique,* Kant comes to speak of the problem of literary representation. The ongoing theme here is "Mallets and chisels may suffice to work on a piece of lumber, but for an engraving one needs an etching-needle" (ww, 5:118; lwb, 7).[4] Kant describes the path to the *Critique* as a *Versuch*.[5] In the exposition that follows, he addresses the com-plaints being voiced by a majority of readers, practically in unison, about the *Critique*'s incomprehensibility. His response to these complaints is re-vealing, expressing the tension that is inherent to any critical undertaking. On the one hand, Kant's inquiry requires the precision of scholastic philo-sophical discourse, but as a result it sounds pedantic. At the same time, on the other hand, Kant is striving to address his public directly, as an author to his readers, by laying claim to a critical procedure based upon recognition and knowledge of a concept of the world that transcends scholastic philosophy. Thus he states:

> Aber die Weitläufigkeit des Werks, so fern sie in der Wissenschaft selbst, und nicht dem Vortrage gegründet ist, die dabei unvermeidliche Trockenheit und scholastische Pünktlichkeit, sind Eigenschaften, die zwar der Sache selbst überaus vorteilhaft sein mögen, dem Buche selbst aber allerdings nachteilig werden müssen.

> Es ist zwar nicht jedermann gegeben, so subtil und doch zugleich so anlockend zu schreiben, als *David Hume,* oder so gründlich, und dabei elegant, als *Moses Mendelssohn;* allein Popularität hätte ich meinem Vortrage (wie ich mir schmeichele) wohl geben können, wenn es mir nur darum zu tun gewesen wäre, einen Plan zu entwerfen, und dessen Vollziehung andern anzupreisen, und mir nicht das Wohl der Wissenschaft, die mich so lange beschäftgt hielt, am Herzen gelegen hätte.

> But the long-windedness of this work, insofar as it stems from science itself, and not from its presentation, and the unavoidable dryness and scholastic precision that accompany it, are all characteristics that may be advantageous to the subject matter itself, but in any case must become detrimental to the book.

> Indeed, it is not for everyone to write as subtly and yet at the same time as enticingly as *David Hume,* or as thoroughly and yet elegantly as *Moses Mendelssohn;* but granted, I probably could have given my exposition (as I flatter myself to think) popular appeal, if my intention had been only to propose a plan and to commend its completion to others, and if I had not been so concerned for the well-being of that science which has kept me occupied for so long. (ww, 5:121; lwb, 10)[6]

Such concern for his readers on the part of the philosopher is rather rare—for Hegel, for instance, who seems to address the absolute Spirit as his reader, it would be unthinkable. This concern reveals Kant's serious aspirations as a writer. Behind the otherwise scholastic guise of the composer of the *Critique,* we catch a momentary glimpse of the vulnerable author: "for it required, by the way, much perseverance and no small amount of self-denial, as well, to postpone the enticement towards an earlier, favorable reception in favor of the prospect of a somewhat late, but enduring applause" (ww, 5:122; lwb, 10). It also sounds a little like sour grapes, when, in concluding the introduction, Kant retreats ironically to the philosophical prerogative for obscurity, and writes,

dass endlich die so beschriebene Dunkelheit (eine gewohnte Be-
mäntelung seiner eigenen Gemächlichkeit oder Blödsichtigkeit)
auch ihren Nutzen habe: da alle, die in Ansehung aller andern
Wissenschaften ein behutsames Stillschweigen beobachten, in
Fragen der Metaphysik meisterhaft sprechen, und dreust ent-
scheiden, weil ihre Unwissenheit hier freilich nicht gegen an-
derer Wissenschaften deutlich absticht, wohl aber gegen echte
kritische Grundsätze, von denen man also rühmen kann: *ignavum, fucos, pecus a praesepibus arcent.* Virg.

that ultimately, obscurity (a customary cover-up for his own
complacency or weak-sightedness), so often deplored, does have
its uses. For all those who observe a cautious silence in respect to
other sciences, speak masterfully about metaphysical questions,
and make their decisions boldly, since their ignorance here obviously does not stand out as clearly in contrast to other sciences,
although not, I suppose, in contrast to genuine critical principles,
of which one can thus proclaim: *ignavum, fucos, pecus a praesepibus arcent.* Virg. (WW, 5:123; LWB, 12)[7]

A late observation of Kant's from the 1790s makes it clear once again why
the theoretical discussion is allowed to be difficult, as long as the aspects
relevant for praxis remain clear enough. With a surprising richness of
meaning, the *Critique*'s confusion is expressed here in terms of its intentions. Its dialectical moment is inscribed in its complexity:

[U]nd was die Verwirrung betrifft, so ist eine solche Critik nicht
abgefasst, um den Einfaltigen, sondern den subtilsten Vernünft-
lern vorgetragen zu werden, welche sich keine Sache zu hoch
(dacht) zu seyn meyneten. Da dann diese Critik eben beweisen
soll, dass sie ihnen (wirkl) und jedermann (für die S) zur spekulativen Einsicht viel zu hoch sind, und sie in dem Wahn der letzteren zu verwirren (da es ihre eigene Schuld ist darinn zu behar-
ren), (ist die Vorbereitung) um sich zu derselben niedrigen Stufe,
der alle Menschen fähig sind, herabzulassen, für welche jene
Glaubenssachen eben so zugänglich seyn müssen als dem subtilsten Nachforscher.

[A]nd as pertains to confusion, such a critique is not composed
for presentation to the most simple-minded, but rather to the
most subtle-minded practitioners of reason, who would claim
that no matter is too lofty (to think). For in that case, the idea that
this critique should prove itself to be too lofty for them (really)

and for everyone (for S) to attain speculative insight, and leave them confused by the error of the latter (since it is their own fault for persisting in it), (is the preparation) for condescending to that same lowly level, of which all men are capable, for whom these matters of faith have to be just as accessible as for the most subtle inquirer. (*Reflexion* §6317, in AA, 18:628f.)[8]

Kant valued the professional precision of scholastic philosophy, and adopted it as the "standard measure" for his own method. But by the same token, he clearly recognized its dangers, and therefore sharply protested against an identification with philosophical scholasticism, considered in a pejorative sense. In *Reflexion* §5089, he notes:

Die gewohnliche Scholastische und doctrinale methode der Metaphysik macht dumm, indem sie eine mechanische Gründlichkeit wirkt. Sie verenget den Verstand und macht ihn unfähig, Belehrung anzunehmen; sie ist nicht philosophie. Dagegen Critic erweitert die Begriffe und macht die Vernunft frey. Die Schulphilosophen machen es wie Freybeuter, welche, so wie sie auf einer unbesetzten Küste anlanden, sich so gleich verschanzen.

The usual scholastic and doctrinal method of metaphysics stupefies, by effecting a mechanical thoroughness. It constricts the understanding and renders it incapable of accepting instruction; it is not philosophy. Critique, in contrast, expands the concepts and frees up reason. Scholastic philosophers go at it like freebooters, who, the moment they set foot on an unoccupied shore, entrench themselves immediately. (AA, 18:84)

This central metaphor of seafaring will have to be given even closer consideration in the context of what follows. It signals certain expectations, directed at the reader, and Kant does not shy away from calling them by name: "This is hard work, and demands a resolute reader, who (seeks) to think his way gradually into a system that presupposes nothing as given, except for reason itself" (ww, 5:135; LWB, 21f.). And he declares confidently, "Should my reader complain about the inconvenience and difficulty I will cause him in solving this task, he has the right to attempt to solve it on his own in an easier fashion" (ww, 5:138; LWB, 25). This challenge is repeated four years later, in 1787, in the preface to the second edition of the *Critique* (B, xliif.), and again in 1788, in the preface to the *Critique of Practical Reason* (ww, 7:115f; A, 20f.).

Let us now turn to the prefaces of the two editions of the *Critique of Pure Reason*, and consider each individually. In the first preface, one allegory is maintained throughout: the battlefield of metaphysics, reminiscent of knightly combat. It declares that metaphysics will be the queen of all the sciences, as it was at one point in time (A, viii; S, 7. See endnote 2). But now she (i.e., metaphysics) resembles Hecuba, a lamenting matron (A, viiif; S, 7f.).[9] Cast out of her queenly role into the chaos of anarchy, where even the skeptic's indifference proves to be merely an affectation, there is only one recourse: to institute a tribunal. If we consider more closely how this language of a tribunal is introduced into the discourse, we notice how artfully it is actually done. The chain of associations can be followed back almost to the first words of the preface, which reveals itself to be much more densely woven than its freely imaginative language suggests on first reading. Across the battlefield of metaphysics, past the queen and Hecuba, finally reaching skepticism, the thread of Kant's argument weaves its way consistently toward indifference,[10] which he apostrophizes, not as a weakness, but instead as the "mature judgment of the age." Kant prepares the terrain with a footnote, attached to *judgment,* about the age of critique:[11] "Our age is the true age of the critique, to which everything must submit" (A, xi; S, 9, note). The next sentence makes it clear just how comprehensive Kant intends his claim regarding the *Critique*'s proof of its legitimacy to be: "*Religion,* through its *sanctity,* and *law giving,* through its *majesty,* generally seek to exempt themselves from it." Worldly and spiritual authorities find themselves called into question directly and subjugated to reason, whose approval now becomes the prerequisite for granting them their privilege. The footnote continues in legalistic, practically courtroom language: "But in doing so, they [religion and law giving] only excite a justifiable suspicion against them, and cannot lay claim to unmitigated respect, such as reason grants to that alone which has been able to withstand reason's free and public trial." Thus, once directed back to the main text, the reader is presented with a strict philosophical discourse that has been enriched by a political and jurisprudential sense. This is the age that no longer allows itself to be enthralled by specious knowledge [*Scheinwissen*], and that fact demands that reason plunge ahead to self-knowledge. In these few words, Kant sketches and sculpts his vision of the age of philosophical reflection and of the critical inventory and examination of all that crosses reason's path.

This eminently political concept of reason, espoused by the first preface and unfolded progressively in the *Critique,* explains why reason, understood so emphatically, can become a political agenda for Kant. It involves, "calling upon reason to take up anew the most difficult of all its occupations, namely, that of self-knowledge, and to institute a tribunal . . . and this is none other than the *Critique of Pure Reason* itself" (A, xif; S,9). With this,. the image of the tribunal is indelibly inscribed in the text of the *Critique*. It is a metaphor identifying reason's legal empowerment as a form that has overcome despotism and religious fanaticism, and hence political and religious hegemony. This metaphor's development out of the (legal) case of Hecuba designates the *Critique*'s situation, within the history of philosophy, as the extreme form of self-reflectivity: a legal proceeding.[12]

Before we turn to the systematic unfolding of the metaphor of the tribunal as an emblem of critical philosophy, the discussion of the two prefaces needs to be completed.

It is not merely preening, on Kant's part, when he acknowledges the reader's demand for certainty and clearness as justified. Instead, it shows that he considers the problem of literary representation to be significant. Granted, judgment regarding certainty is left up to the reader, "because it befits the author to present the arguments, but not to judge what effect they should have upon those who judge him" (A, xv; s, 11). But Kant subsequently distinguishes between "discursive (logical) clearness," which concerns concepts, and "intuitive (aesthetic) clearness," which pertains to intuitions, hence examples or other illustrations *in concreto*.[13] This definition, already employing an abbreviated form of the fundamental distinction between concept and intuition, is not a frivolous excuse. Instead, it must be taken seriously in its systematic significance. As long as it accords with the demands of logic, the "dry, merely scholastic exposition" is justified, even if it disappoints aesthetically. According to the preface, the *Critique* represents a closed work, whose contents depend solely upon logical, not aesthetic, form.

Six years later, the preface introducing the second edition introduces the expression, famous ever since, of the "revolution in thinking" brought about by the Copernican turn initiated by the *Critique*. It is worth noting, in this instance, how Kant repeatedly cites the interconnection of experience, experiment, and *Versuch*. It seems that this connection of the formative elements of the *Critique* first becomes really clear to him from a distance. What began as an attempt [*Versuch*] is now apodictically proven:

> Man versuche es daher einmal, ob wir nicht in den Aufgaben der Metaphysik damit besser fortkommen, dass wir annehmen, die Gegenstände müssen sich nach unserem Erkenntnis richten, welches so schon mit der verlangten Möglichkeit einer Erkenntnis derselben a priori zusammenstimmt, die über Gegenstände, ehe sie uns gegeben werden, etwas festsetzen soll.

> Let us then attempt, for once, to see whether we do not make better progress in the tasks of metaphysics if we assume that

objects have to orient themselves to our knowledge, which thus would accord already with the possibility we required, of some knowledge of them *a priori*, by establishing something about the objects prior to their being given. (B, xvi; s, 22)

The problematic issue of clearness and certainty addressed in the first preface is now—after the initial reactions have come in[14]—displaced onto the distinction between popular and scholastic philosophy. Kant's differentiation of these is worth exploring, because it contains the first indications of Kant's conception of where, exactly, the *Critique* will situate itself within contemporary philosophical discourse. When we take a closer look at the images Kant offers to illustrate the *Critique*'s mode of representation, there emerges an imagery whose systematic application implicitly suggests what would, if carried out explicitly, necessarily lead to accusations of immodesty on the author's part, as well as giving rise to the suspicion of theoretical overhastiness. Philosophy is distinguished by its "mere groping" [*blosses Herumtappen*]. But the procedures of mathematics and physics, as well, were also a "mere groping" at the beginning, just as metaphysics is now. Both mathematics and physics required a "revolution"—"a felicitous whim" [*einen glücklichen Einfall*] to find their way onto the path of secure science. This did occur, and it gave their "attempts" [*Versuchen*] the decisive turn that constituted them as science. The "revolution in the way of thinking" is their shared basis. To realize this, the author announces, is the *raison d'être* of the *Critique*.

It is interesting to note that Kant assigns the *Critique* a place in the "history of experimental method" (B, xiii; s, 20, note). By doing so, he gives expression to the necessarily experimental character of all previous philosophical endeavours (including his own attempts until then, as well). At the same time, however, this raises an unmistakeable claim to the same theoretical dignity assumed by the other sciences. It may be that the repeated references to the methodically experimental character of all previous philosophy is meant to set the *Critique* apart from the other sciences that much more distinctly. But this talk of experimentation also betrays to what extent the *Critique* still bears traces of an experimental, essayistic character, at least more than Kant may have been comfortable with. This is necessarily the case, if we are to consider the metaphor of the "revolution in the way of thinking" to be valid here the way it is for mathematics and physics. For it is not the case that such a "revolution" presents an unproblematic shift in paradigms. In both the examples that Kant introduces, it is much more a matter of endeavors that have lasted generations, in the one instance, and decades, in the other. The pathway had to be laboriously prepared, first, before it could be traveled on. Regardless of whether the "experiment of pure reason" (B, xxii; S, 24, note) succeeds, its experimental character remains essential to it. This is not at all altered when Kant asserts:

> Ich stelle in dieser Vorrede die in der Kritik vorgetragene . . . Umänderung der Denkart auch nur als Hypothese auf, ob sie gleich in der Abhandlung selbst aus der Beschaffenheit unserer Vorstellungen von Raum und Zeit und den Elementarbegriffen des Verstandes, nicht hypothetisch, sondern apodiktisch bewiesen wird, um nur die ersten Versuche einer solchen Umänderung, welche allemal hypothetisch sind, bemerklich zu machen.

> In this preface, I am presenting the change in how we think . . . expounded in the Critique . . . merely as a hypothesis, for I want to direct notice here to the first attempts at such a change, which are always hypothetical, even though in the treatise itself, this is to be demonstrated apodictically, not hypothetically, from the very constitution of our ideas of space and time and the elementary concepts of the understanding. (B, xxii; S, 25, note)

Thus, in Kant's eyes, all previous endeavors in philosophy become mere attempts, at whose end the *Critique* now stands as the first transcendental philosophy, having overcome the status of an attempt [*Versuch*].[15]

Since the *Critique* is a "treatise on the method," and as yet "not a system of the science itself" (B, xxii; S, 25), the question arises as to the type of text required for such an undertaking. As generic designations, "critical inquiry" (A, 237/B, 296; S, 258), "inquiry" (A, 302/B, 358; S, 302), and occasionally "investigation" (A, 738/B, 766; S, 592), all point to juristic procedure. Hence ideas of experiment and attempt merge into a legal metaphor:

> Die Vernunft muss mit ihren Prinzipien, nach denen allein übereinkommende Erscheinungen für Gesetze gelten können, in einer Hand, und mit dem Experiment, das sie nach jenen ausdachte, in der anderen, an die Natur gehen, zwar um von ihr belehrt zu werden, aber nicht in der Qualität eines Schülers, der sich alles vorsagen lässt, was der Lehrer will, sondern eines bestallten Richters, der die Zeugen nötigt, auf die Fragen zu antworten, die er ihnen vorlegt.

> Reason, holding in one hand its principles, according to which alone concordant appearances can be admitted as equivalent to laws, and in the other hand the experiment which it has devised

in conformity with these principles, must indeed approach nature in order to be taught by it, but reason must not do so in the capacity of a pupil, who listens to everything the teacher wishes to say, but rather in the capacity of an appointed judge, who compels the witnesses to answer the questions that he submits to them. (B, xii; S, 20)

The second part of the preface spells out the idea that the *Critique* is essentially negative, but that this has a "positive use" (B, xxv; S, 26). The example used to illustrate this is the police, whose positive use is essentially a negative one, namely, "to stand in the way of the violence that citizens fear coming from other citizens, so that each can pursue his business in peace and security" (B, xxv; S, 27). Whatever negative and positive pretensions emerge from the *Critique* can be expressed easily in the assortment of images surrounding the tribunal, even though the tribunal itself is not actually mentioned here again, in contrast to the first preface. Thus the "thorough investigation of the rights of speculative reason" is bound to "obviate, once and for all, the scandal that sooner or later will erupt among the people, resulting from the petty disputes in which metaphysicians (and this includes finally the clergy, too), lacking a critique, invariably entangle themselves, and who even falsify their theories afterwards" (B, xxxiv; S, 31f.). Kant repeatedly makes it clear that a *quaestio juris* is at stake here (B, xxxvf; S, 31f.).

Kant's position on the question of popular versus scholastic philosophy illustrates just how central for him the realm of metaphors emanating from the tribunal is, conditioning even his conception of the *Critique*'s form.[16] Against the "dogmatists," who give themselves over to the illusion of the Enlightenment's effectiveness, Kant maintains that the public effectiveness of the Enlightenment is ultimately restricted to the small circle of schools of thought, for whom it is only a matter of power struggles, in any case. In arguing this, Kant redraws the lines of the conflict. The philosopher of the *Critique* steps forward as the guardian of human rights against various incursions (B, xxxiv; S, 31f.). His delineation of prerogatives reshapes the landscape of philosophy to such a degree, that he now becomes the notary of justified claims:

> Die Veränderung betrifft also bloss die arroganten Ansprüche der Schulen, die sich gerne hierin (wie sonst mit Recht in vielen anderen Stücken) für die alleinigen Kenner und Aufbewahrer solcher Wahrheiten möchten halten lassen. . . .
>
> Gleichwohl ist doch auch für einen billigeren Anspruch der

spekulativen Philosophen gesorgt: Er bleibt immer ausschliess-
lich Depositär einer dem Publikum ohne dessen Wissen nützlichen Wissenschaft, nämlich der Kritik der Vernunft.

The change thus affects merely the arrogant claims of the
Schools, who would gladly declare themselves in this matter (as
they rightfully could otherwise in many other things) to be the
sole arbiters and guardians of such truths. . . .

Nevertheless, a more moderate claim for the speculative philosopher has also been provided for: he will always remain the
exclusive depository of a science that benefits the public without
their knowing it, namely the critique of reason. (B, xxxiiif; S, 31)

In both prefaces, legal metaphors are dominant. Artistically woven together, they run through the entire *Critique* in a web of associations, sometimes with a juridical conceptuality, other times with a language merely
reminiscent of the legal realm. The full extent of pertinent vocabulary is
traversed, from that of the parliamentary advocate (A, 789/B, 817; S, 625),
to that of the witness (B, xiii; S, 20; A, 708/B, 731; S, 570), as well as
documents (A, 209/B, 255; S, 232), the "never-superannuated claims" (A,
777/B, 805; S, 618), the "probing and scrutinizing examination, irrespective
of a person's reputation" (A, 738/B, 766; S, 593), self-defense, the jury, the
judge, the court, jurisdiction, standard measures, the law, the trial, the *non
liquet*, and finally, to the verdict—all elements relevant to the legal procedure are named.[17] The process leading to proof is accordingly conceived
using the model of a legal proceeding, following strict rules and having to
justify itself from the outset. This makes it into a self-justifying (reflective)
process, constituting itself, and hence its right, on its own.[18] At the conclusion of the "Transcendental Doctrine of Elements," Kant fixes the results in
an image of government offices and legal archives: "[T]hus it was advisable
to draw up the transcripts of this trial in full detail, as it were, and to deposit
them in the archive of human reason, to protect against similar sorts of
errors in the future" (A, 704/B, 732; S, 570).

These legal metaphors are opposed to those of combat, the rule of the
strong. This is a never-ending state of war, for brawling can never prove a
cause just.[19] Throughout, the combatants are depicted as hopelessly anti-
quated knights in armor, pounding each other with swords. For all their
knighthood, they are rather reminiscent of Don Quixote:

Denn der einzige Kampfplatz für sie würde auf dem Felde der
reinen Theologie und Philosophie zu suchen sein; dieser Boden
aber trägt keinen Kämpfer in seiner ganzen Rüstung, und mit

Waffen, die zu fürchten wären. Er kann nur mit Spott oder Grossprecherei auftreten, welches als ein Kinderspiel belacht werden kann.

For the only possible battleground for it [reason] would have to be sought in the field of pure theology and psychology; but this ground cannot bear the weight of a combatant in full armor, and with weapons worth fearing. He is able to step forward armed only with ridicule or boastfulness, and these can be laughed-off like child's play. (A, 743 / B, 771; S, 596)

"Thus, rather than plunging in with a sword," Kant advises, we should withdraw to the "secure perch of critique," and watch the battle peacefully from there (A, 747/B, 775; S, 598). For only the critical judge is capable of recognizing that this matter involves "shadow boxers" (A, 756/B, 784; S, 604) caught up in "never-ending feuds" (A, 776/B, 804; S, 617).

The tournament is at once both a representation and a critique of the skeptical method.[20] Kant begins to reflect critically upon what had been his own practice in the *Dreams*. The argumentative chaos of the *Dreams* is here brought back into alignment by a clear narrative technique, as the antinomy of reason is now subdivided into theses and antitheses set opposing each other on juxtaposing pages. The problem that the *Dreams* deferred rather than solved in its double satire now finds its adequate presentation here.[21] In an indicative turn toward the self, battle henceforth becomes admissable only as defense: "Hypotheses are thus allowed only as weapons of battle on the field of pure reason, not to establish rights upon it, but only to defend them. We must seek the opponent at all times, however, within ourselves" (A, 777/B, 805; S, 617f.). The point of Kant's use of these metaphors of battle consists precisely in exposing their historically feudal character as an anachronism. A genuine "military metaphor"[22] with a positive meaning does not occur in Kant, significantly enough. Rather, if anything, it is subjected to critique here. Kant does not choose contemporary styles of waging war for his metaphors, although he was quite well informed about them, having had close, friendly contacts within the military. So the fact that he chose instead to retrieve historical metaphors from the attic illustrates—quite literally—the strain of pacifism in the *Critique*, which Kant indeed never tires of indicating. These metaphors of battle are deployed as a self-destroying parody. Kant's concept of reason revolves precisely around overcoming every form of war, and constituting a legal procedure to insure peace.[23]

The strangeness and peculiarity of what crosses each reader's path in the

"Transcendental Aesthetic" is expressed in the particular use of the concept "aesthetic," with which Kant pursues his program. In a long footnote at the beginning of the "Transcendental Aesthetic," Kant proposes letting the designation *aesthetic*—in the sense of the science of the beautiful, as introduced by Baumgarten—"wither away once again, and to reserve it for that doctrine which is true science" (A, 21/B, 35; S, 66). The "Transcendental Aesthetic" is not the nominal rival of aesthetics, in a contingent sense, but on the contrary lays claim to this name for good, systematic reasons. For if we accept Kant's proposal—which already introduces, at the beginning of the "Transcendental Aesthetic," the distinction between *phaenomena* and *noumena*, dividing knowledge in the ancient sense into *aistheta kai noeta*—then the concept of aesthetics that results from it is employed differently from the concept grounded in the metaphysics up until that time. This is not merely a matter of preventing equivocations. Rather, the systematic reorientation that Kant is undertaking necessitates a new definition of the concept of aesthetics:

> Die Deutschen sind die einzigen, welche sich jetzt des Worts *Ästhetik* bedienen, um dadurch das zu bezeichnen, was andere Kritik des Geschmacks heissen. Es liegt hier eine verfehlte Hoffnung zum Grunde, die der vortreffliche Analyst Baumgarten fasste, die kritische Beurteilung des Schönen unter Vernunftprinzipien zu bringen, und die Regeln derselben zur Wissenschaft zu erheben. Allein diese Bemühung ist vergeblich. Denn gedachte Regeln, oder Kriterien, sind ihren *vornehmsten* Quellen nach bloss empirisch, und können also niemals zu *bestimmten* Gesetzen a priori dienen, wornach unser Geschmacksurteil richten müsste, vielmehr macht das letztere den eigentlichen Probierstein der Richtigkeit der ersteren aus.

> The Germans are the only ones who currently make use of the word 'aesthetic' to designate what others call the critique of taste. At the root of this is a disappointed hope, conceived by Baumgarten, that superb analytical thinker, to bring the critical evaluation of the beautiful under principles of reason, and to elevate the rules of this practice to a science. But this is a futile effort. For the imagined rules or criteria are merely empirical, even in respect to their most *refined* sources, and thus can never serve as *definite* laws *a priori*, by which our judgment of taste would have to orient itself, for in this case, rather, it is the latter that functions as the actual touchstone of the correctness of the former. (A, 21/B, 35; S, 66)

A short time later, Kant must have realized that this program obviously could not be fully upheld in its terminological requirements. In the second edition, therefore, he added an "or" to the demand to let the designation *aesthetics* expire: "or else to share this name with speculative philosophy and to consider aesthetics partly in its transcendental sense, and partly in its psychological meaning" (B, 36; S, 67). The movement toward transcendental questions in aesthetics displaces the nexus of meanings away from "clear/unclear," for now its meaning gets placed in a transcendental-reflective context. The gradual transition from unclear to clear, asserted by the Leibniz-Wolff philosophy, rests upon presuppositions that are only valid as long as the "monadology," or some other corresponding theory of substance, is still in effect. But if the difference between sensory perception and intellect is understood, along with Kant, not as a question of gradations, but rather as a transcendental question, then the conceptual grasp of clearness extends only within the realm of intellect. Because of this, however, the criterion of clearness becomes a formal one. This means that the mode of representation [*Darstellung*] and the content [*Inhalt*], which for Leibniz still comprise an essential unity (*ars combinatoria*), are now distinguished from each other: "The difference between an unclear and a clear mental representation [*Vorstellung*][24] is merely logical, and does not pertain to its content"[25] (A, 43/B, 60f; S, 83). On a different level, namely that of transcendental logic, the synthetic unity of content and the mode of (external) representation [*Darstellung*] is given, for this very reason, even more deeply: as the condition of knowledge. For "as soon as we take away our subjective constitution, the imagined object, with the characteristics that sensory intuition bestows upon it, (cannot) be encountered . . . anywhere, ever" (A, 44/B, 62; S, 84). Accordingly, the mode of representation is no longer a criterion of knowledge, but is rather itself a principle of knowledge, an epistemological principle. A different function is attributed to it; this is not to give shape to the fixed set of truths in this or that way, sometimes more sensually, at other times more abstractly, but instead to generate experience itself, on its own, in the first place.

Once space and time are demonstrated as pure forms of sensory intuition, the next step is to investigate the pure capacity to think. Thinking is investigated in terms of the functions by which it constitutes knowledge, that is, in terms of concepts. "By *function*, I mean the unity of the activity by which various mental representations are arranged under one common one. Concepts thus base themselves on the spontaneity of thought" (A, 68/B, 93; S, 105). Since the faculty of understanding judges by means of concepts, all the functions of the understanding can be found, "if we can represent, in their entirety, the functions of unity in judgments" (A, 69/B,

94; S, 106). From the table of judgments, Kant is able to derive the table of categories in a way that is valid without forcing the issue: "This division has been conceived systematically from a common principle, namely the capacity to make judgments, (which is basically equivalent to the capacity to think,) and not rhapsodically" (A, 80f./B, 106; S, 114).

It is worth noting that at precisely the point where Kant's discourse seems best equipped, even presenting the reader with tables, the discourse gets caught up in the urge to legitimate itself. Kant very nearly overdoes it in satisfying this urge. In doing so, his discourse only calls that much more attention, and indeed suspicion, to its purported nonrhapsodical quality. In specifying what it is not, Kant makes it conversely clear that it is the system's very structural arrangement—upon which rests the "interconnection of all things" [*Zusammenhang aller Dinge*]—toward which imagination, as the fundamental transcendental capacity, is wont to stray. Kant's reassurance that the table of categories is not "born of a haphazardly undertaken search for pure concepts" (A, 81/B, 106; S, 114), along with his contrasting of his procedure with Aristotle's, who, lacking a principle, had to gather up whatever fundamental concepts came his way (A, 81/B, 107; S, 114), gives us an inkling, *ex negatione*, of just how experimental Kant's own procedure was originally. The fact that he distances himself here so critically does not mean that he is selling out on the experimental, *Versuch*-quality of the *Critique*. Rather, this gesture announces an essentially different sort of motivation, namely his claim to transcendental-philosophical validity for his endeavor.

The transcendental deduction is intended to substantiate a legal claim: "namely, how *subjective conditions of thought* are to have *objective validity*" (A, 849/B, 122; S, 124). This problem is a key to the entire *Critique*. Moreover, as a reformulation of the traditional but problematic approach, it enters new territory. Indeed, Kant warns that the ineluctable difficulty of this problem must be clearly realized in advance, so that the reader will not complain about obscurity, since it is actually the issue itself that is so deeply veiled (A, 88/B, 121; S, 123).

The difficulty of the deduction does not lie in the groping quality that adheres to it. Its lines of thought are themselves so compressed together that the result is a confusing density.[26] Instead of one simply continuous thread, the deduction can be described as the very spinning of this thread, in which manifold single fibers are intended to combine into a whole. Even the question to what extent the first edition differs from the second yields so few conclusive answers that a comparison between the two is inextricably bound to an excess of conjecture. Rather, one learns from such a comparison what a dense weaving the intricate strains of the deduction presented to Kant, even after the completion of the first version. The deduction forms a labyrinth of the concept of the "I" [*das Ich*], out of which only the self-spun thread of the synthetic unity of apperception is able to guide us. The synthesis that is its prerequisite, however, is a product of the imagination [*Einbildungskraft*] and, in particular, "of a blind, albeit indispensible, function of the soul, without which we would have no knowledge whatsoever" (A, 78/B, 103; S, 112). Thus it is pure imagination that rests, "at the basis of all *a priori* knowledge . . . as a fundamental faculty of the human soul" (A, 124; S, 146). On this point, the second version of the deduction basically alters nothing. It only situates imagination deeper, systematically, and removes its dominant character, by simultaneously anchoring it that much more definitely in the concept of synthesis (B, 151f.; S, 165).[27]

If we consider the deduction in respect to the question of how the "I" is introduced, then out of the complexity of the problem a specifically narrative function emerges. For if neither the Cartesian tautology of the *cogito, ergo sum* nor an empirical derivation is acceptable, then only an "I" reflecting this aporia can be brought into play here, in accordance with Kant's critical initiative. It is rendered conceptually as the original-synthetic unity of apperception, but in such a way that imagination is implicitly shown to be what simultaneously escapes its conceptualization. Self-knowledge and knowledge of objects are linked together inseparably and condition each other reciprocally (B, 155f.; S, 167f.), and this reciprocity is reflected in the obscurity of the deduction.

By mediating between intuition and concept, the schematism incorporates imagination irrevocably into the cognitive process. As the rule guiding imagination's synthesis, the schema is a sort of monogram of pure imagination *a priori*, by and through which images first become possible (A, 140ff./B, 180f.; S, 182f.). In this way, however, schematism brings thinking and fiction into systematic relationship with each other (A, 469/B, 497; S, 426).[28] As activities of pure reason, thinking and fiction are allotted a function in constituting knowledge. Subsequently, critique consists of distinguishing between truth and fiction. Because the latter continually interferes with the former—as a sort of necessary evil—their disjunction takes on a crucial relevance. The idea that perhaps a point of difference does not even exist is the secret suspicion of the *Critique*.

The possibility of a point of *indifference* between thinking and fiction leads to an ambivalence in the repeated use of the word *Dichtung*, that is, poetry or fiction. The *Critique*'s repeated attempts at distinguishing itself from fiction are conspicuous.[29] Yet these, too, are ambivalent. For at the same time, Kant always reminds the reader indirectly that there is a special type of fiction at stake here.[30] The ambivalence is of a systematic nature—

but for this very reason, it cannot be resolved any further. It can be critically reflected upon, and then we find ourselves in an infinite regression, represented by the multiple mirrors of self-knowledge.[31] But it cannot be clarified any further. It is the accomplishment and intention of the *Critique* to have led to this problem, in all its complexity. The result here is that it is impossible to go back any further; every step further, as ineluctable as it may be, leads into the dialectic.

Language itself is understood as the "semantic *a priori*," which therefore always already precedes thinking and fiction, in a transcendental correlation of reason and language.[32] In this regard, Kant's defensive posture shows that he has already anticipated and guarded against Herder's language-based metacritique of the *Critique:* in the painstaking separation of knowledge and fiction. Thinking and fiction are not disengaged from reality but are founded upon perception: "Without perception, even fiction and dreams (are) not possible" (A, 377; S, 350). For Kant, dream and fiction are synonyms. The dream is "the subjective interplay of things I imagine," which is thought of as something objective (A, 202/B, 247; S, 227). As they did in the *Dreams,* so too in the *Critique,* dreams play an important, latent role, as what is to be excluded by the *Critique* itself.[33]

This can be expressed otherwise: "Were [the object of thought] not real within [the space], i.e., immediately given through empirical intuition, it could never be fabricated [*erdichtet*], either" (A, 375; S, 349). Thus the entry point for fiction is designated: "From perceptions, therefore, either through a mere play of the imagination, or also by means of experience, knowledge of objects can be generated" (A, 376; S, 350). Ideas—and this is the point of Kant's Plato discussion—are, to a certain degree, fictions—fictions of reason.[34] If ideas and ideals relate to each other like original and copy, then both partake in such fictionalization. Thus it is surprising that ideals, designated as copies, are not "figments of the brain," but rather "an indispensable standard gauge for reason" (A, 569/B, 597; S, 486). One difficulty of the *Critique* is this stubbornly maintained conjunction of the exclusion of fiction and its simultaneous requisition, buried in a flurry of stipulations:

> Das Ideal aber in einem Beispiele, d.i. in der Erscheinung, realisieren wollen, wie etwa den Weisen in einem Roman, ist untunlich, und hat überdem etwas Widersinnisches und wenig Erbauliches an sich, indem die natürliche Schranken, welche der Vollständigkeit in der Idee kontinuierlich Abbruch tun, alle Illusion in solchem Versuche unmöglich und dadurch das Gute, das in der Idee liegt, selbst verdächtig und einer blossen Erdichtung ähnlich machen.

> To wish to realize the ideal in an example, i.e., in appearance, for
> instance as in the wise man in a novel, is impracticable, and
> moreover has something paradoxical and hardly edifying about
> it, since the natural limitations, continually detracting from the
> completeness of the idea, render the whole illusion of the attempt
> impossible, and in doing so render suspicious what is inherently
> good in the idea, as well, making it resemble a mere fiction. (A,
> 570/B, 598; S, 486f.)

This stipulation is directed, to take one example, against Wieland's
Geschichte des Agathon, whose epigraph announces the novel's intention in
its very title: "quid Virtus & quid Sapientia possit / Utile proposuit nobis
exemplum."[35] Precisely in his irony, Wieland clearly shows that, even
when reflected upon, the novel form cannot ultimately satisfy genuine
philosophical criteria.[36] To elude the closure of novelistic fiction in the very
medium of the novel itself is an idea worthy of Münchhausen, one that—
this is Kant's serious critique—finally negates the ideal itself, by representing as an appearance what by nature is strictly and exclusively intelligible.
Although Wieland successfully broke the novel's stigma as trivial literature, renewing the German novel with his *Bildungsroman,* this very effort
must have been counted a failure in Kant's eyes, nevertheless. The pretension of philosophy, as formulated by Kant, fundamentally differs from the
precritical philosophy that Wieland's *Agathon* so playfully masters. The
conditions of the possibility of knowledge having changed, *Agathon*'s philosophy, and with this his form of representation, become obsolete.[37]

Alongside the complex of legal metaphors encompassing the interrela-
tion of tribunal and battle, there is a second, less dominant realm of imagery. Yet through its strategic position at the "hingepoints" of the *Critique,* it
takes on a decisive function.[38] First, however, a nominal question arises.
The designation "legal metaphors" only inadequately characterizes the set
of associations encompassing politics and civil law, among other things,
that the *Critique* has in sight. In much the same way, in deciding whether to
designate this second metaphor complex as geographic, colonialist, or ar-
chitectural, it is a question of where we choose to begin. Once again, it is
the breadth of his vision that leads Kant, in elucidating the *Critique*'s intentions, to deploy metaphors whose imaginative power reaches beyond what
is merely conceptual.[39]

It is an essential function of metaphor to allow relationships and contexts
to show through that could not be formulated otherwise. In this way,
metaphor produces a synthesis that anticipates, on the level of imagery, the
synthesis of reflection. The journey at sea, land surveying, and architecture

are to be understood, therefore, not as single images lending literary flair to particular moments, but rather as part of an ongoing metaphor complex. Their importance derives from their function as a unity. Kant, who at one point calls Hume "the geographer of human reason" (A, 760/B, 788; S, 606), would in this case have to be considered the cartographer of it.[40] The definition of man lies ultimately in the delineation of borders, on land and at sea. Faust demonstrates this at the end too, in his own way. It is neither the storm-tossed sea nor the land that Kant speaks of here, but rather the border between them. Its emblem is the island, the border that is reduced to a point by the vast sea surrounding it. At the conclusion of the "Analytic," during the transition to the "Dialectic," at the decisive crossing point, the section "The Ground of the Distinction of all Objects in General into Phenomena and Noumena" begins with a passage which, on account of its geographical imagery, reads like an excerpt from a travelogue:

> Wir haben jetzt das Land des reinen Verstandes nicht allein durchreiset, und jeden Teil davon sorgfältig in Augenschein genommen, sondern es auch durchmessen, und jedem Dinge auf demselben seine Stelle bestimmt. Dieses Land aber ist eine Insel, und durch die Natur selbst in unveränderliche Grenzen eingeschlossen. Es ist das Land der Wahrheit (ein reizender Name), umgeben von einem weiten und stürmischen Ozeane, dem eigentlichen Sitze des Scheins, wo manche Nebelbank, und manches bald wegschmelzende Eis neue Länder lügt, und indem es den auf Entdeckungen herumschwärmenden Seefahrer unaufhörlich mit leeren Hoffnungen täuscht, ihn in Abenteuer verflechtet [A: verflicht], von denen er niemals ablassen, und sie doch auch niemals zu Ende bringen kann. Ehe wir uns aber auf dieses Meer wagen, um es nach allen Breiten zu durchsuchen, und gewiss zu werden, ob etwas in ihnen zu hoffen sei, so wird es nützlich sein, zuvor noch einen Blick auf die Karte des Landes zu werfen, das wir eben verlassen wollen, und erstlich zu fragen, ob wir mit dem, was es in sich enthält, nicht allenfalls zufrieden sein könnten, oder auch aus Not zufrieden sein müssen, wenn es sonst überall keinen Boden gibt, auf dem wir uns anbauen könnten; zweitens, unter welchem Titel wir denn selbst dieses Land besitzen, und uns wider alle feindselige Ansprüche gesichert halten können.

Now we have not only travelled through the Land of Pure Reason and carefully inspected every part of it, but we have also measured it throughout, and have defined the place of each thing upon it. This land, however, is an island, enclosed by nature itself with immutable borders. It is the Land of Truth (an enticing name), surrounded by a vast and stormy sea, which is the true home of Appearance, where many a bank of fog and floe of ice, quickly melting away, tell lies of new lands, ceaselessly deceiving the wayward-straying seafarer with empty hopes of discoveries, entangling him in adventures from which he cannot relent, and yet also can never bring to an end. But before we venture out upon this sea, to explore its every latitude, and to learn for sure whether anything is to be hoped for in it, it will behoove us first to cast our glance upon the map of this land we wish to leave behind us, and to ask first of all whether we could not be satisfied, in any case, with what it contains, or, too, whether we must be satisfied out of necessity, if there is otherwise no firm ground anywhere else upon which we could settle ourselves; secondly, under which title we ourselves possess even this land, and by which we can consider ourselves secured against all hostile claims. (A, 235f./B, 294f.; S, 257)

This excerpt alludes, as Kathleen Wright has shown,[41] to a passage in Hume's *Treatise of Human Nature.* But its intertextuality allows us to discern how Kant's idea of *critique* differs specifically from Hume's skepticism. Certainly it means, in Kant's case, that we cannot recur directly to Hume's *Treatise,* for although Kant knew Hume's work very well, he read him only in translation.[42] It is particularly interesting that the only excerpt from the *Treatise* translated into German before 1790 is precisely the one that became so influential for Kant's "awakening."[43] The passage includes Hume's seafaring metaphor, as well. It comes at the end of the first book of the *Treatise,* and for Hume, like Kant, it marks a transition. In Hume's original text, the passage ridicules the pretensions of philosophers with skeptical irony, in order to present Hume's own program that much more effectively. In Hamann's translation, however, this same passage is given a different twist by being set off as a "meditation" and given the heading, "Night Thoughts of One in Doubt" ["Nachtgedanken eines Zweiflers"]. Because of their different contexts they differ in tone as well, but the original has a nihilistic bent that Hamann must have welcomed. Hamann leaves out Hume's first sentence, which announces the passage as a continuation of the *Treatise,* in order to maintain the illusion of a self-sufficient text. Thus even the openings of the original and the translation are different. Hume's original reads: "But before I launch out into those immense depths of philosophy, which lie before me, I find myself inclin'd to stop a moment in my present station, and to ponder that voyage, which I have undertaken, and which undoubtedly requires the utmost art and industry to be brought to a happy conclusion."[44] Little resembling a happy ending remains in Hamann's version, however, since he has the "Night Thoughts" begin with the sentence that follows the one just quoted: "I seem to myself to be like a person who has stumbled across bottomless depths, and who, in crossing a small gulf, has escaped a shipwreck in utter peril, and yet who still, nonetheless, has the audacity to set out to sea upon his now leaky and weather-beaten vessel."[45]

Thus the same excerpt that led Kant to the problem of the antinomies also procured for him his ocean metaphor. The self-assurance expressed in Kant's rendition, as opposed to Hume's, gives implicit formulation to the difference between skepticism and the path followed by the *Critique*. Because this hope is ultimately grounded in practical reason, its adequate expression has to come in the literary medium of indirectness, in imagery. What is remarkable is the density of the imagery. It is as though after a long journey, with a resignation that comes from mental exhaustion, the voyager returns home to indulge in recounting his adventures. Motifs from the *Odyssey*, from the expeditions of explorers, and from the founding of states all come together in this passage. It strikes one almost as a paraphrase of *Candide*, when the entire, adventurous journey comes down to the search for firm ground "upon which we could settle ourselves."

Yet the structure of the exploration and discovery narrative in Kant differs a great deal from the circular or, for that matter, spiral progress of the story of Odysseus's homecoming. During his journey, Odysseus undergoes the rites of passage that prepare him for his return. In the modern world of newly discovered continents, however, the explorer/discoverer's narrative works in a different way. Whereas Odysseus's journey is a tale of visitation where the hero finds himself subject to the fixed rules and mores of the various places he visits, the story of the emerging capitalist universe involves expansion and annexation. This story shapes its discoveries in the image of the discoverer. It is the fiction of the uncolonized land awaiting cultivation, the *tabula rasa* of plain matter, immaculate nature, virgin land ready for conquest, occupation, and civilization. However, a closer look at Kant's colonial story tends to undermine the discourse it seems to advance. The sheer length and complicated imagery of this passage, as well as its imaginary power, display an overdetermined narrative. As such, it serves as an astounding exception in the discursive flow of the *Critique*, one that presents a coming together of the crucial motives of Kant's critical project.

The excursion narrative starts with ourselves already standing on the Island of Truth. The remarkable news of this passage—and a logical consequence of the transcendental-critical vantage point—is that colonization is what we are always already doing when we set out to determine the grounds and limits of reason. Colonization, Kant's narrative illustrates, takes place the moment our epistemological subject acts, that is, produces knowledge. Knowledge is a result of a kind of colonization. Knowledge presupposes colonization as its model. The enterprise of the critique of reason by itself tacitly implicates what only at this juncture of the *Critique* is spelled out: that the scientific and philosophical production of knowledge can only operate within the limits of an epistemic model that, in turn, takes as its model the colonization of the world (of experience). As a metaphor, Kant's Island of Truth serves to mediate, and indeed to contain, both of these models.

Near the end of the paralogisms chapter, the second, highly revealing "geographical" metaphor occurs:

> Nichts, als die Nüchternheit einer strengen, aber gerechten Kritik, kann von diesem dogmatischen Blendwerke . . . befreien, und alle unsere spekulative Ansprüche bloss auf das Feld möglicher Erfahrung einschränken, nicht etwa durch schalen Spott über so oft fehlgeschlagene Versuche, oder fromme Seufzer über die Schranken unserer Vernunft, sondern vermittelst einer nach sicheren Grundsätzen vollzogenen Grenzbestimmung derselben, welche ihr nihil ulterius mit grössester Zuverlässigkeit an die herkulische Säulen heftet, die die Natur selbst aufgestellet hat, um die Fahrt unserer Vernunft nur so weit, als die stetig fort laufenden Küsten der Erfahrung reichen, fortzusetzen, die wir nicht verlassen können, ohne uns auf einen uferlosen Ozean zu wagen, der uns, unter immer trüglichen Aussichten, am Ende nötigt, alle beschwerliche und langwierige Bemühung, als hoffnungslos aufzugeben.

> Nothing other than the sobriety of a strict yet fair critique can free us from this dogmatic delusion . . . , and restrict all our speculative claims merely to the field of possible experience, not, for instance, through the stale ridicule about experiments that have so often miscarried, or through pious sighs about the limits of our reason, but instead by means of a definition of reason's boundaries, carried out according to secure principles, which post their *nihil ulterius* with utter certitude on the Herculean pillars[46] that nature herself has erected, so that we will continue in our journey of reason only as far as we can reach upon the steady, continuous coasts of experience, which we cannot leave without

> venturing upon a shoreless ocean, one whose ever-deceptive prospects compel us in the end to surrender all our arduous and tedious efforts as hopeless. (A, 395f.; S, 361)

Just as the first geographic metaphor represented "an image in the text (as) an image for the text,"[47] this excerpt also represents a gesture of Kant's belonging to the stylistic uniqueness of the *Critique*. Although the arctic fantasy landscape with fog-banks and melting icebergs does not lose its charm, its entrance is barred with the stop signal, *"Nihil ulterius!"* Reason is restricted to a coastal journey. Admittedly, this journey takes place on an island that has been reduced to a point: reason turning in circles. In the distance, the ocean of dialectic beckons. Precisely this is mirrored in the problematic of paralogism. On top of this, the image of the Herculean pillars merits particular interest, because it embodies a radical gesture of Kant's that becomes a stylistic element: the redundancy of the figure "nothing other than/nothing but" [*nichts (anderes) als*]. This figure is highly significant in the *Critique*.[48] It is the expression of radicality itself: a *dictio negativa* that expresses, on a linguistic level, the movement of critique as *correctio;* as Galay remarks: "The NO (the lexological name of the negation) permits content to be, at one and the same time, present in and banned from philosophical discourse."[49]

Land and water metaphors are brought into connection with one another in the section "The Discipline of Pure Reason in its Dogmatic Employment." Here, the transition from water to land is given systematic significance and the imagery takes on a new, deeper dimension. "Bracketed" by the phrase *"instabilis tellus, innabilis unda,"* land and sea now designate what lies beyond the boundaries of experience. "To reach the charming regions of the intellectual realm" is impossible, and "thus it is necessary to wrest away the last anchor from our fanciful hopes, as it were" (A, 726/B, 754; S, 585). The verdict pronounced by epistemology is to remain at anchor. This fixed anchorage brings the disjunctive metaphors of land and sea into relation, *ex negatione*. Although the epistemological-critical Odysseus is denied the right to return home, the prospect is nonetheless expressed, at least as a "fanciful hope."[50] However, the sober fact remains that wherever coastal seafaring is practiced, and the Herculean stop sign is heeded, there one finds reality.

Barred from the open sea, the "actual dignity of philosophy" consists in "making the ground even and solid enough to build those majestic moral edifices, ground in which all sorts of mole tunnels are to be found, dug by reason while searching in good faith, but in vain, for treasures, and making our edifice unsteady" (A, 319/B, 375; S, 313f.). With this task defined, the colonization of the island has begun. More than mere cultivation of the ground, the *Critique* is understood also as the collection of "building materials" (A, 834/B, 862; S, 655), even if these "are to be taken from the ruins of collapsed older buildings" (A, 835/B, 863; S, 655). Thus the "previous undertakings" of the history of philosophy are imagined as "buildings, though only in ruins" (A, 852/B, 880; S, 666). The "Architectonic of Pure Reason" is given the task of conceiving a plan from the building materials gathered under the auspices of the *Critique*, and constructing a system. Kant defines *architectonic* as "the art of (building) systems" (A, 832/B, 860; S, 653). He stresses that he conceives of the whole "in sections (*articulatio*)" and "without altering the proportion" (A, 833/B, 861; S, 653f.). In the process, Kant distinguishes technical from architectonic unity. Only from the latter "is it possible for what we call science to emerge, whose schema contains the contour (*monogramma*), as well as the distribution of the whole into sections, in conformity with the idea, i.e., *a priori*" (A, 833f./B, 861f.; S, 654).

In a move typical for Kant, the geographical, almost cosmological curve of metaphors is drawn to a close. From the unlimited natural force of the high seas to the island constituting and constituted by experience, and from its buildable ground to the possible architecture built upon it, and finally to the fully planned "interior decoration" of this edifice, Kant's metaphor complex sets forth the literally *fundamental* function of imagination, in a continuous, associative chain of images. It is expected that plaster will be used only sparingly; all those who form themselves according to the reason of somebody else may very well have appropriated historical knowledge, but they have not produced knowledge themselves. As Kant says of the philosopher who merely adopts another's (such as Wolff's) system, "He has properly grasped and retained, i.e., learned, and is the plaster cast of a living human" (A, 836/B, 684; S, 656). By connecting the concept of a system with the architectonic, and by equipping this connection with a metaphor that provides it with a richly associative geographical and cosmological background, Kant explodes the traditional concept of system. In its place, he presents an expanded concept that describes the very dynamics of systematization in general.[51]

Following these remarks, directed against the whole plaster cast cultural aesthetic, comes the crucial passage where Kant not only distinguishes the learning of philosophy from learning to philosophize (A, 838/B, 866; S, 657), but also begins building a bridge to morality. The philosopher is not a mathematician or a natural scientist; nor does he resemble them, therefore, as a skilled practitioner of reason [*Vernunftkünstler*]. Instead, he is the lawgiver of human reason (A, 839/B, 867; S, 658): "[B]ut as he nowhere exists, while the idea of his legislation is found everywhere in every person's faculty of reason, we shall therefore restrict ourselves entirely to the latter." Understood in this way, philosophy involves "the whole vocation of man, and the philosophy about this is called morals"; and therefore the philosopher functions once again as the moralist, as he did in former times (A, 840/B, 868; S, 658), the only difference being that his pretensions throughout the *Critique* are fortified against all possible or even conceivable attacks, and his competence is firmly and entirely based upon practical reason itself.[52] In a legal-political respect, reason is defined by Kant as precisely what Rousseau calls the *volonté générale*. Its "verdict [is] at all times nothing other than the agreement of free citizens" (A, 738/B, 766; S, 593). It recognizes no other judge, "than, again, universal human reason itself, in which everyone has his say" (A, 752/B, 780; S, 602). This chorus of reason, however, if it indeed comprises the essence of reason, must be "represented" in the *Critique*.

These different metaphors, in all their variety, nonetheless point to some common sphere enclosing them all, which can best be described as the political sphere. What all these metaphors share is that they all express functions of the political. Deeply influenced by Rousseau, and with epistemological-critical revolutionary sensibilities sharpened by him, a philosophical practice forces its way to the surface here whose essence consists precisely in the intimate reciprocity of epistemology and political theory. This practice takes the shape of the critique of knowledge. Kant's concept of the political—still closely linked to a conception of legality that it nonetheless transcends critically, at the same time—emancipates itself from its antique and medieval forms and contents. For Kant, the idea of the political finds its form instead in an ensemble of metaphors that thematize all the ways in which human life orders itself. The legal, governmental, economic, architectonic, and other metaphors all point to something encompassing them all, whose central, fundamental context finally begins to reveal itself precisely through them—metaphorically—in the midst of Kant's epistemological—political project: the realm of the political.

The only clear-sighted discussion of this issue is Hans Saner's *Kant's Political Thought: Its Origins and Development*,[53] which Hannah Arendt rightly acclaimed as the best treatment of Kant's political philosophy, but which seems otherwise to have hardly been taken into account. Saner not only emphasizes the "pervasive political imagery" of the *Critique of Pure Reason* (*Kant's Political Thought*, 218) but also observes how the parallel discourses of metaphysics and politics reciprocally affect one another in the course of Kant's historical development, generating an interdependence in Kantian thought. Saner demonstrates, "the thoroughgoing proximity to the political way of thinking" (303) as a constitutive element in all of Kant's works. In respect to Kant's metaphors, this means that "not only the *Critique of Pure Reason* but his work as a whole is replete with imagery from the political realm" (303). To this extent, Kant's entire philosophy can be understood as political philosophy. As Onora O'Neill points out, "It is no accident that the guiding metaphors of the *Critique of Pure Reason* are political metaphors."[54] Kant's metaphysics becomes a propaedeutic to political thinking, and Kant's politics becomes a concrete case study of his metaphysics (313).[55] Understood in such a way, the form of legal procedure is given a new twist: it is not only a model of knowledge, but moreover a mode of representation. The title already expresses this, for with it, *critique* is first constituted as a literary genre. As such, however, it consequently sets the rules that define its mode of presentation. This happens in part implicitly (it being the first work of its genre) but in part explicitly enough, when it defines the critical method. Its method is sketched out as follows:

> Der kritische Einwurf, weil er den Satz in seinem Werte oder Unwerte unangetastet lässt, und nur den Beweis anficht, bedarf gar nicht den Gegenstand besser zu kennen, oder sich einer besseren Kenntnis desselben anzumassen; er zeigt nur, dass die Behauptung grundlos, nicht, dass sie unrichtig sei. . . . Der kritische (Einwurf) ist allein von der Art, dass, indem er bloss zeigt, man nehme zum Behuf seiner Behauptung etwas an, was nichtig und bloss eingebildet ist, die Theorie stürzt, dadurch, dass sie ihr die angemasste Grundlage entzieht, ohne sonst noch etwas über die Beschaffenheit des Gegenstandes ausmachen zu wollen.

> The critical objection, by leaving the sentence untouched in regard to its value or lack thereof, and assailing only the proof, does not need to know the object any better, or to have any pretensions to some better knowledge of it; the objection shows only that the proposition is unfounded, not that it is incorrect. . . . The critical (objection) is, to put it bluntly, of the type that overturns a theory by simply showing that one is assuming something for the sake of his proposition that is void and simply imaginary, and in this way it deprives the theory of its presumed foundation without otherwise claiming anything about the constitution of the object. (A, 388f.; S, 357)[56]

This procedure is one that not only has literary consequences but must even be understood as eminently literary, for its own sake. Its medium is always already the literary genre in which it expresses itself.

Substantial stylistic fluctuations are not to be censured as weaknesses on the part of the author, but must rather be read as experiments [*Versuche*]: attempts to approximate, in linguistic gestures, those objects that ultimately are synthesized by the capacity of knowledge itself.[57]

Along with short, dialogue-like passages (A, 594ff./B, 622ff.; S, 502ff., A, 843/B, 871; S, 660f.), the discussion of imperatives (A, 802/B, 830; S, 632f., A, 809/B, 837; S, 638), even a divine monologue (A, 613/B, 641; S, 513),[58] and moral maxims (A, 668/B, 696; S, 548),[59] the representation of the antinomy has to be cited as a figure that interjects itself into the very layout of the text. Kant's stylistic peculiarities engender a sort of emphasis, even radicalization of what is being said, and this is underscored even further by redundant, occasionally repetitive formulations. Schlegel, with a literary critic's acute sensibility, once observed "Kant's musical repetitions of the same theme—the best wit for combinations is Kant's."[60] "Nothing but," "in general," and "as if" are the sort of words that appear with significant frequency.[61] Kant's Latin use of periods and clauses, his stringing together of secondary clauses, oftentimes in highly complex sequences,[62] testifies to the compulsion to define things to the point of overdetermination. Yet this complexity also supports a precision in diction and clarity in even the most minimal epistemological step. It mirrors Kant's procedure down to the very construction of his sentences; delineation and mutual opposition spin themselves into the yarn that forms the epistemological net. This is not a tangle; rather, it is a knitting pattern upon which reality can be "given," that is, upon which experience can be produced. In the imitations of Kant's philosophical descendants, the result of this repetitive spinning of the argument is most often a whipped-up froth, but for Kant, it is an essential stylistic medium. The potential to generate and constitute knowledge can only be formulated as passage through this *stretto*.

Kant's use of language moves in the balance between professional precision and philosophical discretion.[63] Wolff's thoroughness remains exemplary in Kant's eyes, but his pompous tone betrays a dogmatic overassurance that Kant prefers to avoid. He would rather dispense with "some of the elegance of language . . . than . . . burden the scholastic usage with the slightest incomprehensibility" (A, 345/B, 403; S, 331, note). He repeatedly emphasizes that the genuine use of our concept of reason seems "to have allowed for the modest and reasonable language of the philosophers of all ages" (A, 701/B, 729; S, 568), and that it can "in no way be harmful to the good cause . . . to tone down the dogmatic language of the scornful sophist to one of moderation and humility" (A, 624f./B, 652f.; S, 520f.). This is not simply a question of taste but of the aspiration of the *Critique* itself. The concordance of its content and its form, of its language and its diction, comprise a *conditio sine qua non*, because, for Kant's *Critique*, legitimation can be found only in its procedure.[64]

In its contemplative quality, the occasionally labyrinthine complexity of Kant's syntax reflects the one path that remains open to critique.[65] This contemplative complexity can perhaps best explain Kant's puritan-sounding, but actually emancipation-oriented directive, "that it is unbecoming for philosophy . . . to flaunt itself with a dogmatic strut and adorn itself with the ribbons and titles of mathematics" (A, 735/B, 763; S, 591).[66] Humility has become a category of epistemological critique. The abstinence that such a critique requires also defines its form. With the *Critique of Pure Reason*, Kant has realized the next step beyond the essay, which literally *essayed*, or gave the appearance of doing so, in any case, and into a new form of inquiry. This form transcends in a critical way the model of a standard inquiry by recognizing and granting every individual realm of investigation its own mode of procedure according to its own laws, and allowing for a mode of representation in conformity with these. The fundamental self-reflectivity required by philosophy is thus not only acknowledged here, but also perceived as a formal problem, in all its consequences. Because composition, structure, and argument reveal themselves to be a function of its architecture, the *Critique* is able to exceed a mere static meaning and to take on a dynamic significance. This expresses itself in the *Critique*'s form; the form of philosophy is, indeed, transformed, so that it is no longer merely an aesthetic *point d'honneur*, but a transcendental-aesthetic problem in its own right.

In this way, *critique* becomes a self-sufficient literary genre whose results are still being felt. The genre designation "critique" proves henceforth to be as much evidence of this as does the inflationary use of the concept "critique" itself. Due to Kant's transformation of it, *critique* has become an emblem of intellectual prestige. Ever since the appearance of the *Critique*, this genre designation has provoked and inspired. It has led to anticritiques and metacritiques, but it has also taken on an independent meaning and role in forming schools of thought. From Marx up to today's postmodern plurality of "critical theories," there is an increasing tendency to use the expression "Critique of . . . " as an *oeuvre* title or trope. In the transcendental-philosophical rationalizations that stem from this, *critique* has become code for the philosophically self-evident conception of what philosophical discourse is supposed to be about, and toward which it ought to strive. *Critique*, having become the *conditio sine qua non* of philosophy, has thus quickly managed to attain a universal meaning. Following Kant, every form of critique finds itself always already having to refer back to its ground- and sourcebook, the *Critique of Pure Reason*. A purely conceptual theory is not capable of accounting for an influence of this scope, as long as the genuine literary quality of the *Critique* remains uncomprehended. And it is precisely this that constitutes a decisive portion of the argument, namely, the "demonstration," understood in the most literal sense of the word.

NINE

Publicizing Enlightenment: Kant's Concept of Enlightenment

W ITH THE ''IDEA FOR A UNIVER-sal History with a Cosmopolitan Purpose''[1] ["Idee zu einer allgemeinen Geschichte in weltbürgerlicher Absicht"], which comes three years after the first publication of the *Critique* and a year after the appearance of the *Prolegomena*, Kant begins the phase of his career centered on publicizing enlightenment. Even in a purely linguistic respect, Kant's specific usage of the term *enlightenment* signals a deepening of its meaning, in a historical-philosophical sense. The term appears here for the first time with remarkable frequency in Kant's work.[2] In the process of publicizing enlightenment, as such, Kant develops it into an operative concept. The fact that the definition of the term remains open is tied to Kant's understanding of definition itself; it does not imply that Kant lacks a precise conception of it.[3] The case is rather that enlightenment only becomes possible as an operative concept by being rooted in the transcendental-philosophical groundwork of the *Critique* and through the conceptual access that this affords. By virtue of this underpinning, and the critical and epistemological sophistication it provides, Kant's concept is more subtle than those definitions of enlightenment that are argued on the basis of precritical presuppositions.

The title of this 1784 essay carries a well-aimed barb, hidden playfully behind the ambiguity of the word *idea*. Introduced to the journal-reading public as a "favorite idea" [*Lieblingsidee*],[4] the "Idea for a Universal History" unmasks itself as a philosophical-historical program derived directly from the *Critique*. As such, it throws a new light back on the *Critique* itself. *Idea*, as defined by the *Critique*, is the opposite of "favorite idea," which in this context suggests something like home-made metaphysics for household use. This is precisely what the *Critique* labors against, in its every intention; it is the struggle to restore the idea once more to its full philosophical dignity and to its rightful place established by practical reason. Read as an explication of the *Critique*, the "Idea for a Universal History" illuminates the *Critique*'s moral-political core. This reading allows for a precise delineation of Kant's own position *vis-à-vis* his conception of philosophy and the presuppositions that necessarily follow from it. The *Critique* reveals itself to be conscious of enlightenment in the innermost sense. Moreover, precisely because this consciousness is reflective, it manages to steer clear of the reefs and shoals of extremist tendencies in uncritical Enlightenment discourse.

What Kant demands for world history here is an "attempt [*Versuch*] at a philosophical history" (ww, 11:50; HR, 53), something he has already accomplished, in a specific way, for the history of reason. This also explains his playful-contemplative tone. The parallels between world history and the history of reason that arise throughout the essay point less toward a transition, on Kant's part, from a philosophical to a political mode of argumentation and more toward their underlying interconnection.[5] Their conjunction lies at the historical-philosophical core of Kant's thought. Such a core is present only implicitly in the *Critique*, but it is no less fundamental on account of this, and here it is given its due explication.[6]

The repeated talk of attempt, exercise, and even overturning contains direct allusions to the *Critique*'s own undertaking.[7] The whole nexus of thoughts associated with a "perfectly just civil constitution as nature's highest task for mankind" (ww, 11:39; HR, 45f.), which sets the sort of conceptual framework for the "Idea for a Universal History," equally comprises the framework for the *Critique*. The dialectic of reason finds its analogy in the dialectic of "unsocial sociability" [*ungesellige Geselligkeit*]:

> Der Mensch will Eintracht; aber die Natur weiss besser, was für seine Gattung gut ist: sie will Zwietracht. Er will gemächlich und vergnügt leben; die Natur will aber, er soll aus der Lässigkeit und untätigen Genügsamkeit hinaus, sich in Arbeit und Mühseligkeiten stürzen, um dagegen auch Mittel auszufinden, sich klüglich wiederum aus den letztern heraus zu ziehen.

> Man wishes concord; but nature knows better what is good for his species: nature wishes discord. He wishes to live in comfort and satisfaction, but nature wishes that he should leave behind his indolence and idle complacency, and plunge himself into labor and hardships, in order that he should instead devise some means of cleverly extricating himself once more from them. (ww, 11:38f.; HR, 45)

Yet what is most remarkable is the passage that forms the world-historical parallel to the "conclusion" of the *Critique of Practical Reason*. This comes in the "Eighth Proposition" of the "Idea for a Universal History," when Kant declares,

> Es kömmt nur darauf an, ob die Erfahrung etwas von einem solchen Gange der Naturabsicht entdecke. Ich sage: *etwas weniges;* denn dieser Kreislauf scheint so lange Zeit zu erfordern bis er sich schliesst, dass man aus dem kleinen Teil, den die Menschheit in dieser Absicht zurückgelegt hat, nur eben so unsicher die Gestalt ihrer Bahn und das Verhältnis der Teile zum Ganzen bestimmen kann, als aus allen bisherigen Himmelsbeobachtungen den Lauf, den unsere Sonne samt dem ganzen Heere ihrer Trabanten im grossen Fixsternensystem nimmt.

> The question comes down to whether experience reveals to us some such progress in nature's purpose. I say *some small part,* for this cycle seems to require such a long time until its completion, that, from the small portion of this purpose that humanity has passed through, we are able to define the contours of its path and the relation of the parts to the whole with only as little certainty as we have managed, using all the observations of the heavens to date, to define the course taken by our sun, along with its whole army of satellites, within the vast system of fixed stars. (ww, 11:45; HR, 50)

With this, Kant ties the undertaking of the *Critique* to the progress of world history, taken in a philosophical sense. The "law within me" and the "law above me" from the practical, second *Critique* represent the individual analogy for what Kant is pursuing here, the idea of cosmological harmony. The unity of the two *Critiques,* and thus of theoretical and practical reason, is hinted at in the metaphor of the starry heavens.[8]

In the *Critique,* Kant had striven to disarm any suspicion that being an "idealist," even if this involved transcendental idealism, made him a mere poet or fiction writer. But Plato, from whom he feels so compelled to distance himself, is really a part of Kant himself.[9] Thus here, again, he sees himself forced to protect his "Idea for a Universal History" against the reproach that, in writing it, he is setting forth "merely a novel" (ww, 11:48; HR, 51f.).[10] This concern acts as the subtext when Kant pleads for an "evenly measured pace in the improvement of constitutional government," for this requires a quasi-historical narrative presupposition, "that some germ of enlightenment was always left over, which, developing more with each revolution, prepared a subsequent, even higher level of improvement" (ww, 11:49; HR, 52). Here already, enlightenment is no longer just the declared title of an era, as it still is in the *Prolegomena* (ww, 5:263; LWB, 130). Rather, it has become a category of history, receiving a constitutive significance for history, to the extent that history is understood to have a universal and civic purpose.

Kant's argument here is directed against a one-dimensional understanding of enlightenment. His concept of enlightenment is launched from a deeper level, for it undergoes, first of all, a process of historical-philosophical reflection.[11] In contrast to some who affiliated themselves with the Enlightenment and who generally had a technological and political orientation, Kant grounds his conception of enlightenment in his theory of practical reason and gives it an essentially moral impetus. To cite one instance, Mendelssohn, two months previously and in the same place, namely the *Berlinische Monatsschrift*, described enlightenment, culture, and education as being essentially identical concepts.[12] Kant, in contrast, maintains their separation: "We are *cultivated* to a high degree by art and science. We are *civilized* to a point of excess with all sorts of social courtesies and properties. However, to consider ourselves to be already *moralized*—in this, we are still very much lacking" (ww, 11:44; HR, 49). There is a "certain commitment of the heart" connected to enlightenment (ww, 11:45; HR, 50). Each human must "invent" herself or himself. Each is his or her own product (ww, 11:36; HR, 43).

One month later, in the December issue of the *Berlinische Monatsschrift*, the short essay appears, "An Answer to the Question: What Is Enlightenment?" ["Beantwortung der Frage: was ist Aufklärung"] (ww, 11:53–61).[13] As was the case with the "Idea for a Universal History," this essay contains a reference to its direct instigation. This time it is a remark made by Pastor Zöllner in his contribution to the *Berlinische Monatsschrift*: "What is enlightenment? This question, which is nearly as important as 'What is truth?' really ought to be answered, I should think, before we begin enlightening! And I still have not found it answered anywhere!"[14] Hence, Kant does not merely quote a question that has been raised but also summons up the context of an ongoing discussion. His program of enlightenment can be understood adequately only when considered as a contribution to a debate, already in progress, concerning the definition of enlightenment.[15] Such consideration must not be obscured by the general position, lately regarded as nearly thetical, and hence "official,"[16] that holds this essay up as a timeless document.[17]

Reasserting the timeliness of Kant's essay is especially necessary as regards its casuistry, whose fixedness of purpose can be evaluated only in the context of the contemporaneous discussion. Thus, for instance, the criticism that freedom of discussion appears in Kant's essay only in conjunction with unconditional obedience to the law misses precisely the radicality of what Kant intends. The conjunction could only be defined so restrictively, if it were claiming that it merited serious consideration. Nothing would be further from the mark, here, than to accuse Kant of accepting some base compromise, as is clear from the cautious but so much the better-aimed irony that he brings into play whenever he speaks of sovereign authority. In fact, the juridical definition of enlightenment suggests with this "overturn" a crucial point: the concept of legal majority [*Mündigkeit*], the age at which one is competent to use one's understanding without another's guidance, actually serves as a way to redefine enlightenment in terms of self-determination. Instead of treating majority as a legal notion,[18] Kant turns it into an expression of the ability to utilize one's understanding autonomously. And the autonomy of understanding is grounded, of course, in reason, now critically understood. This redefinition is decisive, because Kant's standard metaphor of constitutional government as a legitimating procedure is hence not grounded in itself, but rather—and this was the *Critique*'s concern—in his concept of reason. Within this difference lies the radical potential of the Kantian concept of enlightenment. This is why the concept of majority—used far more in polemical negation as tutelage—is such a heavily loaded term.[19] Because right is constituted by reason, it is not derived or established juridically. Rather, it is legality that functions as an expression (albeit a preferred one) of an underlying, dynamic concept of reason. The particularity with which Kant distinguishes the public from the private use of reason, which even puzzled his contemporaries,[20] only becomes comprehensible when viewed thus as a juridical way of harnessing a complex, problematic issue. One can almost speak of a linguistic-political regulation on Kant's part: "What Kant was now calling 'private,' was until then always called 'public'; the public use of reason, on the contrary, [he called] 'private,' with respect to the political position of [the person] who used it."[21] This "provocative twist" sharpens the contradiction, and brings the two meanings of "public" in the eighteenth century—on the one hand, what is openly accessible and comprehensible for all, and on the other, what pertains to society and government—into conceptual opposition.[22] For Kant, the *private* use of reason is privative, that is, deprived or partial.[23]

Kant is concerned with "legalizing," so to speak, the scholar as a writer, and thus as a critic. To understand this motion as a legalizing of repressive governmental structures would miss Kant's point. Kant is moving here within the framework of a provisionally defined conception of cultural norms (legality) that he seeks to render productive for the project of enlightenment. To wish to see a legitimation of these norms in this would short-circuit an interpretation.[24] On the contrary, Kant's formulation carefully directs a small ironic barb at Frederick the Great, who, for instance, in practically the same year, 1784, expressly forbade, in a rescript, any public criticism of himself: "A private person has no right to pass *public* and perhaps even disapproving judgment on the actions, procedures, laws, regulations, and ordinances of sovereigns and courts, their officials, assemblies, and courts of law, or to promulgate or publish in print pertinent reports that he manages to obtain. For a private person is not at all capable of making such a judgment, because he lacks complete knowledge of circumstances and motives."[25] By praising the king for his enlightenment, Kant thus prescribes—publicly—the king's duties and obligations: "argue as much as you please, about whatever you please; only obey!" (ww, 11:61; HR, 59).[26] For the fact is, this obedience is valid only up to the time when whatever is making circumstances intolerable gets remedied. This is expressed by Kant's concluding sentence, where he designates the freedom to think as ultimately representing a preliminary stage of the freedom to act (ww, 11:61; HR, 59).

The idea of a public realm as a space in which opinions are freely exchanged, takes on a dynamic character, for it serves to propagate, as it were, the literary manifestation of the *volonté générale*. Kant is very aware of the paradoxical dialectic by which oppression can engender spirit, whereas freedom can stupefy it. For programmatic reasons, however, he touches on this point only very gently. Yet for understanding the Kantian distinction between the public and private use of reason, this point may actually provide an indispensible key:

> So zeigt sich hier ein befremdlicher nicht erwarteter Gang menschlicher Dinge; so wie auch sonst, wenn man ihn im grossen betrachtet, darin fast alles paradox ist. Ein grösserer Grad bürgerlicher Freiheit scheint der Freiheit des *Geistes* des Volks vorteilhaft, und setzt ihr doch Schranken; ein Grad weniger von jener verschafft hingegen diesem Raum, sich nach allem seinen Vermögen auszubreiten.

> Thus a puzzling and unexpected course of human affairs shows itself here; as is also the case otherwise, when one views this process in larger terms, almost everything in it is paradoxical. A greater degree of civil freedom seems advantageous to the freedom of the *spirit* of the people, and yet sets limits for it, too; a lesser degree of such freedom, in contrast, generates the space for this spirit to extend itself to its full capacity. (ww, 11:61; HR, 59)

The restrictive definition of public use of reason would then have the function of creating precisely the intellectual climate in which spirit, and more specifically democratic spirit ("the spirit of the people"), would meet its necessary conditions. Self-critique would then be a pragmatic precondition, as well, in order to render governmental censorship obsolete. This is one of the programmatic points of the "Answer." In this respect, it follows the *Critique* exactly. This conclusion would imply, however, that Kant's distinctions between public and private thought and expression would take on a more comprehensive critical potential than is generally allowed for.

The role of the scholar as a writer therefore consists in freely raising discussion about adverse circumstances, and in transmitting such topics of discussion into the space defined as the public realm. This realm is conceived as a coercion-free medium, as a place where conflicts of interest are settled. Kant, in conceiving it thus, considers the act of introducing something into the public realm to mean simultaneously placing it under the jurisdiction of the tribunal of the (critique of) reason, the tribunal of the consent of all citizens of the realm of reason. It is at this juncture that the differentiation of private from public use of the faculty of reason has to be grasped in its own, specific dialectic. In and of itself, it designates the *public* use—and hence the public-realm-producing use—of a *private* person's faculty of reason. The fact that this distinction has been largely misunderstood is a sign of Kant the writer's specifically "private" conception of himself *as* a writer *qua* scholar. This is the core idea that Kant's contemporaries never grasped. In it, Kant's understanding of himself in relation to his philosophical preconceptions, in a simultaneously critical and political sense, is articulated most exactly: the writer's public voice emerges from his private activity, which now takes on a public dimension. And the point of division in this public-private border dispute is occupied by the writer himself.

In further exposition of the formulations developed in the "Idea for a Universal History," Kant's "Enlightenment" essay comes to define enlightenment as a philosophical-historical category. This means, however, that in respect to the *one* history our era is to be distinguished, not qualitatively as *the* "Enlightenment," but at most "quantitatively," as an era of increasing enlightenment; instead of denoting a *perfectum* (of being already "enlightened," as the *Prolegomena* maintains [ww, 5:263; lwb, 130]), the word enlightenment [*Aufklärung*] thus shows itself to be a term of process, a progressive *substantivum*.

Kant situates the concept of enlightenment in the discursive field stretching not only to the political realm, but also, fundamentally, to that of critical philosophy and the philosophy of history as well. This establishes the essay on Enlightenment as the decisive point of transition, whereby the philosopher, consistent with his theory, defines himself as an author. Foucault describes this interconnection of the three *Critiques* with the enlightenment essay exactly, when he writes,

> that this little text is located in a sense at the crossroads of critical reflection and reflection on history. It is a reflection by Kant on the contemporary status of his own enterprise. No doubt it is not the first time that a philosopher has given his reasons for undertaking his work at a particular moment. But it seems to me that it is the first time that a philosopher has connected in this way, closely and from the inside, the significance of his work with respect to knowledge, a reflection of history and a particular analysis of the specific moment at which he is writing and because of which he is writing. It is in the reflection on "today" as difference in history and as a motive for a particular philosophical task that the novelty of this text appears to me to lie.[27]

And it is precisely in this that Foucault sees what he designates the attitude of modernity.[28]

Although Kant's distinction between the private and public use of reason is often cited as inadequate, its systematic importance is made clear by his contribution a half-year later to the *Berlinische Monatsschrift*, in May 1785, "On the Illegality of Reprinting Books" ["Von der Unrechtmässigkeit des Büchernachdrucks"].[29] This text is a key to understanding Kant's self-conception as a writer, and it is indeed remarkable that this essay has attracted so little attention in connection with Kant's concept of enlightenment. Instead, it is generally assumed that with "An Answer to the Question: What is Enlightenment?" Kant has answered the question completely and placed it *ad acta*, considering the matter resolved. But the case is rather that, from the time of the *Critique* at the latest, Kant explicitly opens up a discourse on enlightenment. This discourse is anchored in the "Idea for a Universal History," in philosophical-historical terms that lend it theoretical dignity. In the "Answer," it is given its exoteric certification of relevance. This does not simply bring the discourse to an end, however. On the contrary, the discussion about enlightenment continues, uninterrupted. It takes on the role of a constant in Kant's thinking.

When Kant takes a position on authorial rights, the passionate harshness of his diction is striking. Executed as a legal deduction, it ostensibly takes on the cool form of a judiciary procedure of evidence. Yet this formality seems to be only an outward necessity, the rigor of expression allowing the author to seize the opportunity to have his say amidst such an uproar. The issue is treated as a question of justice and, furthermore, in the conceptual framework of a judicial-theoretical definition of personal property. Taken together, the various strains of the argument cast a revealing light on Kant's conception of himself as a writer.

Kant brackets out the whole economic aspect of the problem. This only further emphasizes that for him, significantly enough, it is not a matter of securing and dividing profits but, exclusively, a question of justice. His concern is the preservation of authorial rights, as such. In this respect, Kant's self-contained reformulation of the relation among author, publisher, and public audience is not to be misunderstood as a theory of ownership, but must rather be seen as an act of reflective, practical enlightenment. It is a deduction of how things ought to be, when justice is justly understood. Although the word "enlightenment" does not appear even once (because its use is restricted to the practice of philosophic-historical reflection), the deduction of authorial rights nonetheless formulates Kant's self-conception exactly in terms of the pragmatic function of enlightenment: the process of philosophical discourse is intimately bound up with publication. This is nicely illustrated by *Reflexion* §5028, which ends with the following remark: "In such conflicts, whoever has the last word is always right. But the last word goes every time to whoever asserts the orthodox proposition. For either the publisher [crossed out: book dealer] is already being investigated fiscally, etc" (AA, 18:66). The distinction between private and public use of reason introduced in the "Answer" is now made fully transparent and productive in its systematic significance. Accordingly, Kant reduces the publisher's legal function to that of mediator between the author and general public, so that the publisher only represents the author: "In a book as a text, the author *speaks* to his reader; and he who has printed it *speaks* through his copies, not for himself, but rather entirely in the name of the author" (AA, 8:80). The publisher is allowed no independent rights whatsoever aside from the right to represent the author's interests. This means that the author's rights are understood as inviolably justified.

By subjugating the merely economic rights of publishers, Kant attempts to constitute the public realm as the locus of free speech for authors. This follows from the definition of a book or a text as public speech. This definition is now familiar from the "Answer," but it is nonetheless hardly ready for public consumption without further refinement, for it is not inherently compelling on its own. The systematic consideration that it receives from Kant in "On the Illegality of Reprinting Books" must be taken into account. Considered together, a meaning emerges from the distinction of public from private use of reason that brings authorial rights and enlightenment into close relationship. This has such a central significance for Kant that the question "What is a book?" reappears in a central position in the *Metaphysics of Morals*.[30] Indeed, authorial rights are considered in direct connection to the question, "What is money?" whereby even formally, in the iterative formulation of the two questions, an analogy is suggested—so that what they have in common is brought to the fore. Both are defined by the sphere of circulation that is their shared ground, namely the public realm. Understood as the universal medium for the traffic of commodities (in the case of money), and of enlightenment (in the case of books), circulation is the essence of the public sphere in both cases (ww, 8:404ff.; MG, 106ff.). Thus the author is part of the *Wealth of Nations*. What is true for money—Kant quotes Adam Smith here—is therefore by analogy true for the book, as well. In the case of author's rights, what is peculiar is the confluence of property rights and personal rights. The book has a double aspect, being both a possession and an instrument of the author's (personal) speech, and this engenders the legal confusion whereby whoever owns the book can claim to own the speech, as well.[31] Opposing this, Kant repeats in utter, and even typographical, clarity, "The Unauthorized Publishing of Books Is Forbidden as a Matter of Right" (ww, 8:404, 405; MG, 106).[32]

Out of this fusion of authorial rights and enlightenment, the pragmatic purpose of Kant's concept of enlightenment finally emerges along with his conception of himself as an author, so that each conditions the other reciprocally. The categories "private" and "public" thus take on a constitutive meaning for the self-definition of the writer. The autonomy of the writer is derived from this categorical disjunction, which admittedly is as a result encumbered with a theoretical debt. It is not by accident that this procedure is analogous to the Kantian thought process of recognizing possibilities at all times only by linking them simultaneously to a set of conditions. The extent to which Kant is willing to understand the book as the author's free speech to a public audience is shown by his consistency in disallowing alteration, revision, or even translation into another language to count as the original any longer, "for it is not the same speech of the author, even though the thoughts may be exactly the same" (aa, 8:87). A footnote makes it clear what he means: "The author and the owner of a copy can each say, with an equal amount of right: it is my book! but in a different sense. The former takes the book to be text, or speech; the latter takes it merely as the mute instrument transporting the speech to him or to the public, i.e., as a copy" (aa, 8:86).

A half-year later, in the essay "Determination of the Concept of a Human Race" ["Bestimmung des Begriffs einer Menschenrasse"], Kant elaborates what the specific function of a critical essay, or *Versuch*, will consist of henceforth. Considering the problem of the genetic definition of a human being, Kant formulates the *non liquet* of the "magical power of imagination": "For if I allow even one instance of this sort [the intervention of imagination into genetic material, through humans or events] then it would be as if I were to concede one ghost story or magic spell" (ww, 11:72). Thus Kant conjures the situation in the *Dreams*, with its challenge to epistemological theory, and now speaks the same ban against it: "But as pertains to this type of thing [a story or spell]—that, although it is capable of an experiment, it cannot endure even a single one, or it avoids it continually with every possible excuse—it is nothing but delusion and fiction [*Wahn und Erdichtung*]" (ww, 11:72). If one holds to the limits of reason, then a definition of concepts that is aware of its own *a priori* character will contribute directly to enlightenment: "Quite a lot rests upon having previously, by oneself, defined adequately the concept one wishes to enlighten oneself about through observation, before one turns to examine experience, for you find in experience what you need only when you know beforehand what you seek" (ww, 11:65).

What is true for the physical nature of human beings should be true for the spiritual, as well. This is the theme of "A Conjecture on the Beginning of Human History" ["Mutmasslicher Anfang der Menschengeschichte"],[33] which appeared in January 1786 in the *Berlinische Monatsschrift*. This text specifically draws the line between enlightenment and the novel and poetic fiction in general. But Kant's efforts in this direction draw attention, once again, more to alert one to the precarious proximity of philosophy and fiction than to defuse any suspicion of their intermingling. To far too great a degree, conjectures are "a movement of the imagination, accompanied by reason, that is allowed for the sake of the mind's recuperation and health, but not for serious business" (ww, 11:85; hr, 221). Indeed, conjectures should not "place too high a demand on definition" (ww, 11:85; hr, 221). Hence, Kant builds his distinction between fiction and conjecture upon the dubious basis of a plausible but also unproven conjecture of a continuity and equality of world experience in history. This presumption seems to be so little grounded in experience that Kant calls his essay "a mere pleasure trip" [*eine blosse Lustreise*] (ww, 11:85; hr, 221). With this reference to travel literature, however, Kant is clearly directing us to his preferred interspace between fiction and truth.

Read with the "Answer" in mind, this "mere pleasure trip" presents us with a secularization theory in a theological costume. The story of Creation becomes a text of enlightenment theory, which authorizes, as it were, Kant's concept of emancipation from tutelage and his entire theory of culture. Kant's text is not based on the impulse to give a piece of secularized

Bible exegesis. On the contrary, and in a playful way—and only thus can his approach be explained in light of his resolute theory of religion—Kant is running an experiment to see how a theological jacket fits the thought of enlightenment. This literary dalliance explains Kant's easy tone regarding the interpretation of such inevitably ponderous themes as those touched upon by the story of Creation. This unseriousness—which is anything other than cheap ridicule or disingenuousness, however—proves itself to be an instance of enlightenment. Contrary to the assumptions of orthodoxy and neology, one must always assume, on the basis of Kant's theory of religion, that what is involved here is projection, and hence fiction. The idea that enlightenment would want to seek authorization for itself even in the story of Creation is Kant's way of concretely testing enlightenment's inherent limits. In proceeding with a Bible commentary that is both playful, from a literary perspective, and has pretensions toward enlightenment, Kant renders the whole problem of a secularized theory of religion explicit. Once again, Kant rigorously carries out the theme of the separation of belief and knowledge, only this time accompanied by an ironic undertone as well.

Kant conceives his concept of enlightenment more sharply in an essay marking his intervention in the Spinoza dispute, "What Does It Mean, to Orient Oneself in Thinking?" ["Was heisst: sich im Denken orientieren?"].[34] Appearing in the October 1786 issue of the *Berlinische Monatsschrift*, the essay is a monument to one of the preeminent enlighteners, Moses Mendelssohn, who had died somewhat prematurely in January of the same year. It was generally known that the dispute against Jacobi's allegations that Lessing had become a Spinozist at the end of his life, which must have wounded Mendelssohn deeply, was one of the factors that accelerated Mendelssohn's demise.[35] Hence personal reasons were what finally motivated Kant, after waiting patiently for so long, to begin putting an end to Jacobi's feud, which was developing into an Enlightenment crusade. Whereas the attempts by Mendelssohn, Biester, and Schütz to impel Kant to take a position in the Spinoza dispute had been fruitless,[36] Mendelssohn's death brought about a new situation. Kant now saw himself impelled to take on the common cause of enlightenment publicly, in the place of his now-silenced friend. Mendelssohn, after all, had not only been an uncompromising proponent of the Enlightenment but was also considered its undisputed representative. Now he was suddenly subject to hostility from all sides. Then, on February 27, 1786, Marcus Herz wrote to Kant: "What do you say to the uproar that, since Moses's death, and centered around it, has begun among preachers and geniuses, exorcists and farcical poets, fanatics and musicians, all of which was instigated by the Privy-

Councilor from Pimplendorf? If only a man like you would call out a stern *Be quiet!* to this tawdry swarm; I bet it would disperse like chaff in the wind" (Kant, *Briefwechsel*, 285). Kant (a chronically slow correspondent) responded to this on April 7: "Jacobi's fad is not serious, but rather just the *fanaticism of genius* [*Genieschwärmerei*], in order to make his name known, and therefore it hardly merits serious refutation. Perhaps I will have something inserted in the Berl. M. [*Berlinische Monatsschrift*], in order to expose this charlatanry" (292).[37]

Called upon by all sides to state his position, Kant decided only with difficulty to publish his tensely awaited judgment on this issue.[38] Although Kant remains civil in his encounter with Jacobi and his followers, this does not mean that he is less than singularly committed to the defense of enlightenment, and thus of Moses Mendelssohn. Rather, it reflects a posture marked by indifference and contempt toward people like Jacobi, to whom he does not want to give further incentive with a polemical response, as his letter to Marcus Herz shows. In the end, Kant finds himself beyond the debates that erupted in the conflict surrounding the Spinoza dispute, because his position is grounded in critical philosophy. The language is clear enough: both sides are wrong when considered from the perspective of epistemological theory, because they exhibit a dogmatism that the *Critique* has rendered obsolete. Nonetheless, Kant gives clear enough indication of where his sympathies lie regarding the attitude of each side with respect to practical reason.[39] The significance of the text consists in the way Kant, in very few moves, steers a polemic poisoned by personal attacks back to its "rational" contents. By thus bringing to light what was hidden by partisan tactics, he reformulates the Spinoza dispute, now on the reflective level of the *Critique*, as a dispute about the meaning of enlightenment.

The genuine *homage* to Mendelssohn, however, consists in Kant's incorporating Mendelssohn's concept of enlightenment into his own. Until this point, Kant's concept had been, in its essential aspects, a category of the philosophy of history; now it is enriched with an individual, concretely pragmatic side. This is most clearly distinguishable in the long concluding note of "What Does It Mean to Orient Oneself in Thinking." Here, enlightenment is defined as thinking for oneself. Mendelssohn's definition of enlightenment as a process carried out individually, as well as his insight into the danger of a "dialectic of enlightenment," are brought together with Kant's own undertaking in the *Critique* and fused into one concept. Even Mendelssohn's historical pessimism, which Kant otherwise opposes,[40] is included in the note as a memory: "But to enlighten an *era* is something quite protracted, for so many external hinderances arise" (ww, 5:283; HR, 249, note). Kant reformulates the metaphysically diffuse Spinoza dispute as a question of freedom of thought, which he conceives of as equivalent to the freedom to express one's opinions: "Perhaps one can therefore say that the sort of external force which robs men of their freedom to *communicate* their thoughts publicly also robs them of their freedom to *think*" (ww, 5:280; HR, 247). This clarity and directedness of purpose in such a volatile and confusing issue shows once again what kind of role enlightenment plays in Kant's self-conception as a writer.

Further explication of the concept of enlightenment comes in the 1793 essay, "On the Common Saying: 'This May Be True in Theory, But It Does Not Apply in Practice' " ["Über den Gemeinspruch: Das mag in der Theorie richtig sein, taugt aber nicht für die Praxis"],[41] which once again appears in the *Berlinische Monatsschrift*. Kant takes vehement aim here against the relegation of theory, as the private pursuit of scholars, to the academic margins (ww, 11:130; HR, 63):

> Diese, in unsern spruchreichen und tatleeren Zeiten, sehr gemein gewordene Maxime richtet nun, wenn sie etwas Moralisches (Tugend- oder Rechtspflicht) betrifft, den grössten Schaden an. Denn hier ist es um den Kanon der Vernunft (im Praktischen) zu tun, wo der Wert der Praxis gänzlich auf ihrer Angemessenheit zu der ihr untergelegten Theorie beruht, und alles verloren ist, wenn die empirischen und daher zufälligen Bedingungen der Ausführung des Gesetzes zu Bedingungen des Gesetzes selbst gemacht, und so eine Praxis, welche auf einen nach *bisheriger* Erfahrung wahrscheinlichen Ausgang berechnet ist, die für sich selbst bestehende Theorie zu meistern berechtigt ist.

> In our times, so rich in slogans and so poor in deeds, this maxim has become quite commonplace, and now causes the greatest damage when directed towards ethical matters (duties of virtue and lawfulness). For here it affects the canon of reason (in practical matters), where the value of practice rests entirely on its conformity with the theory that underlies it, and where everything is lost when empirical and hence incidental conditions of the enactment of the law are made into conditions of the law itself, so that a practice calculated according to a probable outcome based upon *previous* experience is justified in overruling the self-sufficient theory. (ww, 11:129; HR, 63)

For Kant, theory's independence from empirical data is what gives it emancipatory potential. To see theory as a nonempirical undertaking—and be conscious of its autonomy, unlike those who hold that theory is predicated on experience (the French encyclopedists, for example)—is precisely the concern of the "enlighteners," as well. However, the proponents of enlightenment who are so committed to draping themselves in experience stand in danger of expending themselves in the legitimation of existing conditions. Just as Kant invokes the figures of the officer and the cleric in the "Answer," here he invokes the "private man (who is) nonetheless a businessman," the "statesman," and the "worldly man (or world-citizen in general)" (ww, 11:130; hr, 63). With these, the three realms of human interaction are delineated: the individual (ethics), national (constitutional law), and international (international law). Opposed to these is the academic [*Schulmann*], just as it was the scholar [*Gelehrte*] in the "Answer." One never outgrows the "school of wisdom" (ww, 11:143; hr, 72). And the realization, "that everything in morals that is correct in theory must also hold true for practice" (ww, 11:143; hr, 72), holds just as true for constitutional and international law. The concluding sentence is thus formulated categorically: "What is valid for theory on rational grounds, is valid also in practice" (ww, 11:172; hr, 92). With this proposition, Kant demonstrates a practical relevance for philosophy whose radicality is unsurpassed.[42]

The distinction between the private and the public use of reason that was unsatisfying in the "Answer" because it remained insufficiently motivated only now gets clarified in regard to its political sense. The balance that upholds the state and makes the legal concept of a *volonté générale* possible is an equilibrium growing out of a dialectic, one which was already necessarily a problem for Rousseau, and for which Kant now provides a sort of regulation. The tension between obedience (the totalizing tendencies in Rousseau) and freedom (the anarchic tendencies in Rousseau) is irresolvable. This is the reason it resurfaces in the concept of enlightenment: "In every communal organization, there must be *obedience*, under the mechanism of a civic constitution containing compelling laws (which apply to all), but simultaneously there must be a *spirit of freedom*" (ww, 11:163; hr, 85). Because Kant does allow the common people [*dem Volke*] rights, but no "compelling rights" [*Zwangsrechte*], meaning no right to active resistance, the right to freedom becomes particularly important. "Thus the *freedom of the pen* is . . . the only palladium of the people's rights" (ww, 11:161; hr, 85). Thus the writer, the philosopher as scholar—for this is whom Kant has in mind (and therefore himself, as well)—is assigned a fundamental role. It becomes clear that the compelling force tying the citizen to the law is what first liberates him, giving him an "inalienable right against the state," even if this is only the freedom of the pen. It is this that comprises the function of the public sphere, the way it constitutes legality (ww, 11:161; hr, 85).

Kant opens up a decidedly deeper dimension of this idea in the text published two years later, in 1795, *Perpetual Peace* [*Zum ewigen Frieden*].[43]

Previously, perhaps, we have been accustomed to Kant often expressing his most profoundly crucial concerns only in indirect form, in an ironic medium, cast as a *Versuch*. In this case, then, *Perpetual Peace* perfects this method, presenting a thoroughly formalized composition.[44]

The preface operates as a *clausula salvatoria*, introducing the text's basic movement. What presents itself as a humble precautionary measure is actually the attack itself. Already, in the third word of the preface, we encounter "satirical." Kant is stipulating that satire serves only as the starting point for what is to follow. The text's pervasive irony[45] becomes the formal literary principle for representing the transcendental-philosophical standpoint. This irony is neither Socratic, nor is it permanent, like its Romantic counterpart. Rather, it continues and builds upon the mode of philosophizing developed since the *Dreams*, to become a genuine Kantian irony.

Therefore the decisive moment is expressed parenthetically, by way of clauses, for such stipulations act as a basis and a defense, a fool's freedom, within which the *Versuch* is able to formulate itself.[46] Kant carries on his play with the conventions of diplomatic peace treaties precisely because it suddenly turns bitterly serious at the end. What enters the discourse in the colorful costume of preliminary considerations and stipulations [*Präliminar- und Definitivartikel*] ultimately turns out to be incisive criticism. The imitation of conventions is, literally, what allows Kant's peace plan even to be circulated, as a text.

The second edition of *Perpetual Peace* carries, as a second appendix, the parody of a "secret article." This irrevocably leads *ad absurdum*, something that previously may not have been clearly enough the case for Kant's argument. Now it arrives at its final implication, namely, the *secret* acknowledgment of the right to *public* discussion of political issues, as well as the right to an audience. The secret article is the publicity clause for philosophers, whose indispensability is here legally anchored, as it were—as writers.

The refinement of Kant's irony is expressed in its innocence, which is free of guilt only so long as it is forced by the guilt of oppression to put on an innocent face:

> Also wird der Staat die [Philosophen] *stillschweigend* (also, indem er ein Geheimnis daraus macht) *dazu auffordern*, welches soviel heisst, als: er wird sie frei und öffentlich über die allgemeinen Maximen der Kriegsführung und Friedensstiftung *reden lassen* (denn das werden sie schon von selbst tun, wenn man es ihnen nur nicht verbietet) . . .

> Thus the state will *tacitly* (by making a secret of it) *require* them
> [philosophers] to do this, which basically means: it will *let them
> speak* freely and publicly about the general maxims of conducting
> war and of establishing peace (for they will do that already on
> their own, if only they are not forbidden to do so) . . . (ww,
> 11:227; HR, 115)

This second appendix elaborates Kant's theory of practice. In so doing,
moreover, it clearly shows what the practice of his theory is, by articulating
its ultimate intentions within the context of authorship: public rights are
constituted on the grounds of their publicizability. The "transcendental
formula of public right" reads: "All actions relating to the rights of other
men and whose maxims are not compatible with their being made public
are unlawful" (ww, 11:245; HR, 126).[47] This "transcendental principle of
publicity," as Kant formulates it, in language almost reminiscent of Kleist,
is "like an axiom, unprovably certain" (ww, 11:245; HR, 126). Nevertheless,
it is "merely negative," exclusively a criterion of unlawfulness. The application of this criterion, however, is not unproblematic. Kant argues that
every rebellion is unlawful because its preparations must be carried out in
secret, and he would like to prove this to be a logical consequence of the
transcendental principle. But already, to the first reviewers of this essay,
among them Friedrich Schlegel, this appears to be an incorrect use of the
principle. Schlegel, in fact, sees this principle as potentially expressing the
duty to rebel.[48]

Alongside the negative principle, Kant sets an "affirmative principle of
public right": "All maxims that *require* publicity (in order not to fail in their
purpose) accord with right and politics combined" (ww, 11:250; HR, 130).
Only taken together do the two principles guarantee the unanimity of
politics and ethics, theory and practice. The transcendental principle of
publicity illuminates one of the primary motifs of Kantian philosophy,
publicity in general. In the second transcendental principle, the philosopher
as a writer finds his justification from the viewpoint of legal philosophy. In
this second principle, Kant's conception of himself as a writer is precisely
described. The fact that Kant defers "the further exposition and discussion
of this principle" to some other time (ww, 11:251; HR, 130) suggests the
limitations of the *a priori* of this principle, which represents the standpoint
from which Kant has always already been writing.

The Conflict of the Faculties [*Der Streit der Fakultäten*] (1798) is an exposition of the rightful claim of philosophers to an autonomous role
within academic faculties, a claim that Kant sees as comprising a genuine
scientific demand. Whereas theology and jurisprudence occupy themselves

with given textual *corpora*, and medicine has its knowledge of scientific facts in respect to their usefulness, philosophy, by contrast, represents the discipline embodying pure reason, which implies a claim to "autonomy, i.e., to judge freely (according to principles of thought in general)" (ww, 11:290). This faculty is "an opposition party (the left side)" (ww, 11:299), and hence also the sole guarantor of enlightenment for the people [*Volksaufklärung*]. The philosophers—always understood as writers who appeal to the public audience and thus seek to formulate a consensus beyond the university—are therefore the free teachers of the law and the enlighteners (ww, 11:362f.).[49] The theses formulated in *Perpetual Peace* are given further explication here and are grounded from within the sciences through the delineation of borders between philosophy and the three dominant faculties. Theology, jurisprudence, and medicine are energetically set within their limits, and their scientific gains are illuminated first of all in their philosophical application.

The third section, entitled "On the Power of the Mind to Master Its Morbid Feelings by Sheer Resolution" ["Von der Macht des Gemüts, durch den blossen Vorsatz seiner krankhaften Gefühle Meister zu sein"], was also published as a self-contained *Versuch* in the *Journal der practischen Arzneykunde und Wundarzneykunst*. In it, Kant addresses the malady *par excellence* of philosophers and writers: hypochondria. The "fictionalizing melancholia" [*dichtende Grillenkrankheit*] consists in poetic imagination beginning to function independently. Once more, Kant traces the familiar demarcations of reason forcefully here and even adds to them by pointing out the necessity for a "diet in thinking" (ww, 11:385). In light of the advanced age of the author, the conclusion of the essay is both significant and touching. In his postscript Kant expresses his desire to protect the eyes of readers, assailed by poor print, and gives concrete suggestions for improvement (larger type, easily readable printing ink). Far more than simply an obsession with typography, this final note is once more a writer's appeal (now reduced to the merest formalization) for the conditions of the possibility—in printing technology—of reception by the reader.[50]

In his disputational texts, Kant proceeds polemically. But these texts also derive their philosophical motivation from the process of distinguishing the private from the public use of reason.[51] Kant takes topics that might otherwise be considered private uses of reason, to be carried on under the cover of darkness, away from the public, insofar as they are cast as private scholastic quarrels, and transforms them into a discourse worthy and capable of public discussion. By doing so, he forces the parties involved to decide the proper forum in which to seek their solution. In the case of scholarly conflicts, this could come in a disputation. But in many other cases (as

Kant's own selection of topics illustrates), they may actually require publicity, that is, they may be issues that belong in the forum of practical reason. In their very activity, Kant's polemical writings represent the praxis of enlightenment. They present enlightenment in its pragmatic aspect. In the fulfillment of its public use, reason subjects itself to proof.

It is important for Kant's conception of writing as public speech to a public audience that he consider rhetorical quality to be by no means irrelevant. And this applies not only to the logical requirement for clarity and distinctness but also, and here he agrees with antiquity, to tonal quality. In their diction, Roman rhetoricians had to attain the correct pitch in the cadences structuring their sentences, so that the overall aural image would achieve the right tone. Kant's differentiated grasp of tonal qualities is closely related to those based in Latin. From this, his predilection for Latin poetry may be explained, as well. Moreover, his habit of giving Latin equivalents in parentheses, which are not always strict terminological equivalents, often serves less for clarification than as a sort of "setting the tone," as a stylistic means of tuning the tone through "bracketing."[52]

The consonance of the tone takes on a decisive meaning because it exhibits the authenticity of one's philosophical claims. Like a litmus test, the quality of the discourse diminishes as the tone escalates; the higher, the more noble and extravagant the tone becomes, the more insubstantial the claims behind it. Already in the *Critique,* Kant explains that it can "in no way be harmful to the good cause . . . to tone down the dogmatic language of the scornful sophist to one of moderation and humility" (A, 624f./B, 653f.; S, 520f.). And in the appendix to the *Prolegomena,* Kant asks of the reviewer of the *Critique* in the *Göttingische Gelehrte Anzeigen,* "what could justify taking on such a tone" as the reviewer does, and denounces the reviewer's "lofty tone" (WW, 5:256; LWB, 126).[53] In "On the Common Saying" Kant describes the view that theory does not apply to practice as being expressed "in a superior and dismissive tone, full of pretension" (WW, 11:129; HR, 63). In *Perpetual Peace,* he remarks of the Machiavellians "that it is not justice, but rather force that they advocate, and in this they assume the tone, just as though they themselves thereby were issuing some command" (WW, 11:238f.; HR, 121).

Kant addresses the conflict with Eberhard, who wanted to see in Kant's transcendental philosophy merely a reformulation of Leibniz, in "On a Discovery according to Which Any New Critique of Pure Reason Has Been Made Superfluous by an Earlier One" ["Über eine Entdeckung, nach der alle neue Kritik der reinen Vernunft durch eine ältere entbehrlich gemacht werden soll"] (1790).[54] Kant uses a remark by Eberhard as an occasion to distinguish polemically between a gentle and a raw tone: "He is even inclined . . . to use most often the latter. I choose to remain with the former, which suits him who has the preponderance of reasons on his side" (ww, 5:337; Allison (ed.), *The Kant-Eberhard Controversy*, 135). Tone and comportment (ww, 5:368; Allison, 135) are not adiaphora; instead, in Kant's understanding, they are closely connected to the act of philosophizing itself. But they are able to function as a criterion for the validity of claims only because they are thought of as actually constitutive of these claims.

For the fine arts, the *Critique of Judgment* explicitly ascribes such a constitutive role to tone. There one reads that "only the connection of these three types of expression [word, comportment, and tone as articulation, gesticulation, and modulation]" comprises "the complete communication of the speaker" (ww, 10:258, §51; CJ, 164). Not only poetry, but eloquence as well belongs to the "rhetorical arts." As a written work is defined in terms of authorial rights (the right of free speech to a public audience), so tone gets formulated as an ethical-aesthetic condition of discourse. Aesthetics, as it is formulated by the *Critique of Judgment*, defines the fundamental meaning of taste "as a type of *sensus communis*" (heading from §40, ww, 10:224; CJ, 135).

The tension between taste and genius is indicative not only of Kant's conception of the problem of the artist but also equally of the problem of the self-definition of the writer (*qua rhetor*), as it has been presented in the course of this investigation. Thus in his argument with Goethe's brother-in-law Schlosser, in the article "On a Newly Arisen Superior Tone in Philosophy" ["Von einem neuerdings erhobenen vornehmen Ton in der Philosophie"] (1796),[55] published in the *Berlinische Monatsschrift*, Kant merely expands upon what has been implicit since the *Critique*. This could be described as the *Critique*'s critical potential, taken in a comprehensive sense, as it is contained in its manner of proceeding. Now, in its unfolding, the genuine democratic thrust becomes fully explicit. In Kant's concept of tone, a class consciousness is given expression that is able to take a critical stance toward concepts like labor, scholasticism, and scholarship (today we would call it *professionalism*), the "Herculean labor of self-knowledge from the bottom up," the illegitimate claims of aristocracy ("leisure class"), and genius.[56] A tendentiously portrayed Plato is unmasked as a "club member," who parades his alleged philosophy with a haughty air (ww, 6:388; Fenves (ed.), *Raising the Tone*, 63). A superior tone obviously betrays a deficiency and arrogance in philosophy, but also the lack of these qualities: "But that would-be philosophers act *superior* is in no way to be condoned, because they elevate themselves over their fellow *guild members* [Zunftgenossen], and injure their inalienable right to freedom and equality in matters of reason alone" (ww, 6:383; Fenves, 57f.). As for Lessing, [57] so too for Kant:

truth is not a possession but rather labor. Thus Kant speaks ironically for the purported "owner" of truth: "I can therefore speak in the tone of a lord who is elevated above the complaint of having to prove his title of ownership (*beati possidentes*)" (ww, 6:384; Fenves, 58). But an entirely different tone is struck by the "voice of reason (*dictamen rationis*), which speaks clearly to everyone and is capable of being known scientifically" (ww, 6:392; Fenves, 67). In reason we find the idea of duty whose voice is "adamant"; hearing it makes a person shiver, for it is severe and pitiless. This is the moral "law in me" in all its greatness and sublimity, as it is invoked in the conclusion of the *Critique of Practical Reason*:

> Hier ist nun das, was Archimedes bedurfte, aber nicht fand: ein fester Punkt, woran die Vernunft ihren Hebel ansetzen kann, und zwar, ohne ihn weder an die gegenwärtige, noch eine künftige Welt, sondern bloss an ihre innere Idee der Freiheit, die durch das unerschütterliche moralische Gesetz, als sichere Grundlage darliegt, anzulegen, um den menschlichen Willen, selbst beim Widerstande der ganzen Natur, durch ihre Gegensätze zu bewegen. Das ist nun das Geheimnis, welches nur nach langsamer Entwickelung der Begriffe des Verstandes und sorgfältig geprüften Grundsätzen, also nur durch Arbeit, *fühlbar* werden kann.
>
> Here, now, is what Archimedes needed, but did not find: a fixed point upon which reason could set its lever, and this is found to rest neither upon the present, nor upon a future world, but rather simply upon reason's innate idea of freedom, which lies available to us because it has unshakable moral law as its secure basis, in order to move the human will through its antitheses, even given the resistance of all of nature. This therefore is the secret, which can be *felt*, but only after the gradual development of the concepts of understanding and of carefully tested principles, thus only through labor. (ww, 6:393; Fenves, 69)

Having been brought this far, tone now takes on its full character, the systematic meaning of which has been prepared in a passage, only the first part of which has been quoted. Here, it continues, giving tone its duly rich orchestration:

> Der Ton des sich dünkenden Besitzers dieses wahren Geheimnisses kann nicht vornehm sein; denn nur das dogmatische oder historische Wissen bläht auf. Das durch Kritik seiner eigenen Vernunft herabgestimmte des ersteren nötigt unvermeidlich zur Mässigung in Ansprüchen (Bescheidenheit); die Anmassung des

letzteren aber, die Belesenheit im Plato und den Klassikern, die nur zur Kultur des Geschmacks gehört, kann nicht berechtigen, mit ihr den Philosophen machen zu wollen.

The tone of the self-purported owner of this true secret cannot be superior; for only dogmatic or historical knowledge inflates. Dogmatic knowledge, having lowered its tone through the critique of its own reason, inevitably is compelled to moderate its claims (modesty); as for the pretensions of historical knowledge, however, being well-read in Plato and the classics, which belongs merely to the culture of taste, cannot justify wanting to use it in order to act the philosopher. (ww, 6:393f.; Fenves, 69)

Because there is "no classical author of philosophy" (ww, 5:334; Allison, 133, note), there can also be no "classical" tone. Thus there can be no pompous display of might and splendor in philosophical discourse, as Kant never tires of repeating, but only the lowered tone of modesty. This "toning down," however, is a metaphor for the gesture of critical philosophy, the transcendental-reflective philosophical form, as the *epoché* was for the Skeptics. As Kant's long concluding note maintains, contrary to any poetic imputations, this "toning-down" is prosaic: "In principle, probably all philosophy is prosaic; and a recommendation that we now begin once again to philosophize poetically ought to be understood perhaps like a recommendation to a merchant: that in the future he should keep his books in verse, rather than prose" (ww, 6:397; Fenves, 72).

Even in his last published contribution, a short "Postscript of a Friend" for Christian Gottlieb Mielke's *Littauisch-deutsches und deutsch-littauisches Wörterbuch* of 1800, tone plays a decisive role. Now its practical, political side is addressed directly when Kant speaks of the "tone of equality and confidential open-heartedness" (AA, 8:445), namely here in the native language of the "Prussian Lithuanian." The particular character of a people is mirrored in its language. Enlightenment, as self-enlightenment, leads through the enlightenment of language. And this transpires through the act of upholding exemplary, outstanding language. It is not to be pursued as a historicizing Romanticism, but rather as the genuine sort of enlightenment that consists of reflection upon one's own origins:

Überhaupt, wenn auch nicht an jeder Sprache eine eben so grosse Ausbeute zu erwarten wäre, so ist es doch zur Bildung eines jeden Völkleins in einem Lande, z.B. im preussischen Polen, von Wichtigkeit, es im Schul- und Kanzelunterricht nach dem Muster der reinsten (polnischen) Sprache, sollte diese auch nur ausserhalb des Landes geredet werden, zu unterweisen und diese nach und

nach gangbar zu machen: weil dadurch die Sprache der Eigen-
thümlichkeit des Volks angemessener und hiemit der Begriff desselben aufgeklärter wird.

In general, even if we cannot expect such a great yield from every
language, it is nonetheless important, for the education of every
little group in a country, for example in Prussian Poland, to instruct them in the school and in the church according to the
example of the purest (Polish) language, even if this is spoken
only outside of the country, and eventually to make this language
prevalent; for in this way the language becomes more suited to
the particular character of the people, and with this its concept of
itself becomes more enlightened. (AA, 8:445)

As a writer, Kant had a highly developed feeling for tone. This, along with
the consistently maintained stylistic realization of his writings, all lead to a
consistent style that we might wish to call the transcendental-reflective
style. As such, however, it has assumed the power to create, shape, and
inform succeeding styles. Perhaps it is this that inspired Goethe's fine
observation in a conversation with Schopenhauer, that when he reads a
page of Kant, he feels as if he were entering a bright room.[58]

BIBLIOGRAPHIC ESSAY

T HE SUBJECT ''KANT, THE WRITER'' is not unfamiliar, and is addressed often, even with a certain regularity; but just as regularly, once it is brought up, it is abandoned again in the course of inquiry. In the best cases, where it is confirmed, and in various *aperçus*, it exists as a problematic issue. But never is it raised as the subject of investigation itself. This is particularly astonishing in light of the general consensus that Kant's style and language merit consideration, and that they should not simply be separated from their propositional claims. Karl Jaspers, and in some respects Ernst Cassirer as well, who will both be discussed in their turn below, are among the rare exceptions to this practice. Among literary authors, it is Dürrenmatt who once noted, in the persona of his Inspector Bärlach: "I say leave Kant in peace. His writing is difficult, but not bad."[1] And E. Y. Meyer's novel, *In Trubschachen*, deals with someone who sets out to write a paper on Kant and to come to an understanding of Kant's language.[2]

The complaints about Kant's style are as old as Kantian philosophy. And it is a part of the underlying irony in Kant that he already prefigured these himself.[3] Even Wieland, with his mild demeanor, felt that "Kant has a poor style."[4] The same chord is struck later by Madame de Staël, who summarizes the contemporary criticism on Kant, as she encountered it, when she writes (in 1813), "In his metaphysical treatises, he takes the words for tokens and ascribes them the value he desires, without burdening themselves with the value they have otherwise."[5] In the meantime, when discussing art, or particularly ethics, his writing can be utterly clear, simple, and "energetic."[6] Alongside this generally assumed stance, there is another view, admittedly, but it is one that never entirely prevailed. Thus already in 1794, Wilhelm Mackensen maintained in his *Beiträge zur Kritik der deutschen Sprache*:

In the history of German letters, Kant's writings will be just as epochal as they were in philosophy, even if they can never be as successful in the former. The German language has perhaps never displayed more strongly what it is capable of than when it gives itself over to its taciturn seriousness and proceeds with only the strictest definition. It is impossible to find one sentence in the entire *Critique of Pure Reason* that does not entirely say what it is supposed to say. In every aspect, one sees the idea as it is thought with the utmost clarity, and expressed with the meticulousness that one commonly admires in the craftsmanship of a work of art.[7]

It is Goethe who perhaps first recognized the significance of Kant's specific irony. As Goethe reflects, it "seemed to me that the precious man proceeds with mischievous irony, in that at one moment he seems committed to restricting the capacity of knowledge as narrowly as possible, and in the next, with a wink, he is pointing beyond the borders he had drawn himself."[8] And even more clearly in his *Maximen und Reflexionen:* "Kant restricts himself by design to a certain sphere, and always points beyond it ironically."[9] A philosophical potential is hidden in this observation that would be worthwhile to bring to fruition. And it shows as well that Goethe was entirely able to follow Kant, when he wished.[10] In this regard, Goethe's style in his later years is in certain ways congenial with Kant's.[11] In a passage that has strangely gone unnoticed, Goethe points out Kant's decisive influence on the overall development of German literature. In his memorial address, "Zu brüderlichem Andenken Wielands" (1813), Goethe names the precise historical demarcation line drawn by Kant's philosophy as the turning point for German literature as well:

Whereas earlier, in his shorter writings, Kant was merely preluding his more significant insights, and seemed to express himself in merry yet complex form about even the most important subjects, still then, he stood close enough to our friend [Wieland]; but when the colossal theoretical structure had been erected, then all those who had until then passed their lives freely, in poetry as well as in philosophy, had to perceive in this edifice a threat, a stronghold from whence their merry excursions over the field of experience were to be restricted. Not only for the philosopher, however, but for the poet, too, much—indeed all—was to be feared in the face of this new intellectual direction, the moment a great mass allowed itself to be drawn by it . . . and in poetry, a new epoch began to emerge.[12]

In this way, Goethe not only indicates, with a gentle touch, the reason for Wieland's being tied to a certain historical period, but also precisely describes Kant's significance for intellectual history in general. Translated into normative terms, in *Winkelmann und sein Jahrhundert* (1805), this means, "that no scholar has repudiated, resisted, or despised that great philosophical movement begun by Kant, without regretting it."[13] For Goethe, it was self-evident that Kant's writings were distinguished by a particular style. Writing to Schiller about the *Verkündigung des nahen Abschlusses eines Traktats zum ewigen Frieden in der Philosophie,* Goethe generously forgives the attack it contains on his brother-in-law Johann Georg Schlosser and maintains rather that "a quite valuable product of his well-known way of thinking, which like everything coming from him contains the most masterful passages, but which is also, in *composition* and *style,* more Kantian than Kant himself [*Kantischer als Kantisch*]."[14] Twenty years later, in a conversation with Victor Cousin, Goethe remarks: "A few months ago, I reread Kant; nothing is so clear, once one draws all the consequences from all his principles. . . . Kant's method is a principle of humanity and tolerance."[15]

Hegel rains down his ridicule on the lack of descriptive exposition and Kant's "barbaric terminology."[16] He compares the inherent difficulty of Kant's approach "with wanting to swim before going into the water,"[17] and with catching a bird with a lime-twig.[18] Hegel's opponent Schopenhauer counters this, however, with the rejoinder that, in the *Critique*, one finds "the most important work of German literature."[19] Indeed Schopenhauer, the master of the German style, maintains "Kant's style altogether bears the mark of a superior mind, of genuine, firm characteristics, and of an utterly uncommon intellectual vigour. Its character can perhaps be accurately described as a *brilliant dryness,* on account of which he is able to single out concepts with great confidence and to grasp them firmly, and afterwards he is capable of tossing them to and fro with great freedom, to the reader's astonishment. I find this same brilliant dryness again in the style of Aristotle, although he is much easier."[20] This generously given praise, however, is taken back immediately when Kant's exposition is named "often unclear, indefinite, unsatisfying, and occasionally obscure" (*Die Welt,* 578f.). Schopenhauer then claims on the contrary that whoever clearly understands a matter is also able to express it clearly, distinctly, and simply: "Such a person will generally not repeat himself incessantly, and even then, in doing so, in every new exposition of an idea already covered a hundred times, nonetheless leave the very same passages obscure" (*Die Welt,* 579). However, the thought that the whole transcendental-philosophical point is hidden precisely in these passages is something that is first addressed by Jaspers. Heine, who promised to spill the school secret of German philosophy and thereby had his eye on Hegel, coined the harsh phrase about Kant's "wrapping-paper style" [*Packpapierstyl*].[21]

Thomas de Quincey makes repeated references to Kant's language and style. As a style-conscious writer himself, profoundly impressed by Kant's philosophy, and having translated some of Kant's shorter texts into English, he pours out his complaints to the reader. In his autobiography (1836), he dedicates one whole chapter to Kant. There, in a graphic image, he describes Kant's syntactical strategy:

> His idea of a sentence was as follows:—We have all seen, or read of, an old family coach, and the process of packing it for a journey to London some seventy or eighty years ago. Night and day, for a week at least, sate the housekeeper, the lady's maid, the butler, the gentleman's gentlemen, &c., packing the huge ark in all its recesses, its "imperials," its "wells," its "Salisbury boots," its "sword-cases," its front pockets, side pockets, rear pockets, its "hammer-cloth cellars" (which a lady explains to me as a corruption from *hampercloth*, as originally a cloth for hiding a hamper, stored with *viaticum*), until all the uses and needs of man, and of human life, savage or civilized, were met with separate provision by the infinite chaos. Pretty nearly upon the model of such an old family coach packing did Kant institute and pursue the packing and stuffing of one of his regular sentences. Everything that could ever be needed in the way of explanation, illustration, restraint, inference, by-clause, or indirect comment, was to be crammed, according to this German philosopher's taste, into the front pockets, side pockets, or rear pockets, of the one original sentence.[22]

Although de Quincey expresses himself in an extremely reserved way about the obscurity of Kant's style and remarks that Kant's popularity in Germany is apparently due to this obscurity (*Collected Writings*, 2:87), in his conclusion he nonetheless sees in Kant's towering intellectual power "not an enchanter's, but the power of a disenchanter—and a disenchanter the most profound" (2:108). Six years earlier, in his article "Kant in His Miscellaneous Essays" (1830), he had already noted, "In reality Kant was a bad writer, and in some respects a pedant, and also, in a qualified sense (and without meaning the least disrespect to him), something of a brute."[23] In his essay "Rhetoric" (1828), he had mercilessly named him "a monster of vicious diction."[24] In his article on style (1840), he complains about Kant's style as a "formidable barrier to the study of his writings" (*Collected Writings*, 10:160), and mocks, "Kant might naturally enough have written a book from beginning to end in one vast hyperbolical sentence" (10:161). Then, in "Language" (1858), he states in conclusion: "Kant was a great man, but he was obtuse and deaf as an antediluvian boulder with regard to language and its capacities."[25]

Hermann Hettner, in his literary history that set the standard in the nineteenth century, granted Kant a prominent place, but treated him exclusively as a philosopher, and says nothing about the specific form of Kantian philosophy.[26] The qualities of the young Kant are extolled, however, and the *Dreams of a Spirit-Seer* is designated a classic (*Geschichte der deutschen Literatur*, 167). Otherwise, Hettner restricts himself to pages-long quotations. It is worth noting that he grants Kant a central place in his literary history as having established the ideal of humanity in the classical age of German literature.[27] In his portrayal of Kant, which was widely circulated in the nineteenth century, Kuno Fischer also comes to speak of Kant's style of working:

> He demonstrated just this sort of precision and order in his works. First, he would conceive the plan in silence, and he thought through the object he intended to treat mostly during his solitary strolls. Then he sketched the plans in writing on single sheets of paper, following this with the comprehensive working out of the issue in its particulars. When this was completed, he repeated it with the written draft intended for print, which had to be ready in every last point before the manuscript could make its way to press. Hence the maturity and the thought-out character of Kantian texts, through which they claim such an outstanding place in philosophical literature overall, and the unconditional first place in German philosophy.[28]

However, Kant's character is also mirrored, as Fischer continues, directly in his language:

> Kant . . . did not want to surprise, either, but instead, always, to convince. And his way of writing accorded perfectly with this meticulously upright way of thinking: never deceptive, always thorough and thus . . . often unwieldy. In order to be perfectly upright, everything belonging to the matter had to be expressed as well. In this way, the load carried by one sentence often became great, some things had to be packed into parentheses, in order to come away at all within the same sentence; such Kantian periods stride along in an unwieldy way, like freight wagons; they have to be read and reread, and sentences that are wrapped together have to be taken apart, in short, the whole period actually has to be unpacked if one wishes to understand it thoroughly. This stylistic unwieldiness is not really clumsiness, for Kant was also capable of writing in an easy and flowing way, when his object allowed it. It is the thoroughness and love of truth of a conscientious thinker who wishes to withhold nothing in his judgments that may contribute to their completeness. (*I. Kant und seine Lehre* 1:120f.)

It should hardly be astonishing that one of the best stylists of the German language, who after all himself knew, "Why I Write Such Good Books," believed himself compelled to vent his anger at Kant. Nietzsche

conceded to Schopenhauer having even been able to "draw in . . . the Kantian philosophy itself . . . as an extraordinary rhetorical instrument."[29] In
the *Gay Science* (1882), he remarks with witty accuracy: "*Kant's joke.—*
Kant wanted to prove to the 'whole world,' in a slap-in-the-face way, that
the 'whole world' was right:—that was the secret joke of this mind. He
wrote against scholars for the benefit of popular preconceptions, but for
scholars, and not for the people."[30] In his notes from the years 1876 to 1877,
the following remark appears: "Thus, through the scholarly manner of
making books, Kant . . . let himself be induced to communicate in that
prolix sort of way, which is doubly regrettable in his case, because there was
(because of his academic duties) never enough time: frequently he had to
think his way back into his train of thought while already writing."[31] In
Beyond Good and Evil (1886), Nietzsche mocks Kant's long-windedness,
which he comes to speak of repeatedly: "How are synthetic judgments a
priori *possible?* Kant asks himself—and what was his answer, really?
Thanks to the *faculty of a faculty:* but not in so many words, unfortunately,
but rather so long-windedly, imposingly, and with such an expenditure of
German profundity and verbal flourish that one hardly hears the comical
niaiserie allemande hidden in such an answer."[32] Repeatedly, Nietzsche
amuses himself with the "bulky pedantry and the small-town mentality of
old Kant, the grotesque tastelessness of this Chinaman from Königsberg."[33] This complaint constitutes the repetitive element in Nietzsche's
critique of Kant, which condenses into an *aperçu:* "Kant, a concept machine,
the entire eighteenth century, with an underside of theologian-cunning
and a ——".[34]

In his speech, "Von Kants Einfluss auf die deutsche Kultur" (1883),
Hermann Cohen deepens the image of Kant in one essential aspect, when
he maintains:

> In the whole wide field of the so-called humanities [*Geisteswis-
> senschaften*], it would first of all have to be *style,* through which
> Kant exercised an effect on us, more powerfully than *Klopstock* or
> *Lessing,* and in any case engaging us with wider scope than
> *Winckelmann.* Audaciously, I claim that neither *Schiller,* nor *Plato*
> himself, *wrote more beautifully than Kant, measuring the expres-
> sion by the thought.* All form must be the form of its sub-
> stance. . . . Nobody in recent times, besides Kant, has conducted a
> matter in the omnipresence of all standpoints and parties in such
> a way that one "although" [*Zwar*] in the preceding clause takes
> hold of the spiritualist, and one "but" [*Aber*] in the subsequent
> clause manages to include the empiricist, while the variously
> named intermediate groupings, which labor to bridge the gap
> between these views of the world, are distributed into the inter-
> vening clauses and adverbial ornaments. . . . Kant's closest and

most immediate effect consists in this. With him, the nation has received a *great author*.[35]

And in 1914, Cohen once again points to Kant's significance not only for the content, but also for the specific form of German literature: "To describe the *German style* at all in its uniqueness—who today would feel himself to be adequate to this task. But whoever undertakes it will succeed only if he is able to establish the origin of the German type of historical inquiry and thought with reference to the spirit of *Kantian* philosophy."[36]

Wilhelm Windelband, in his portrayal of Kant in his *Geschichte der neueren Philosophie* (1880), directs attention to the agility of Kant's language in his early essays. These, he says, written in the English genre, betray the influence of English literature and of Rousseau: "Even the specifically philosophical texts stemming from this period in time show the same particularities and the same striving to free himself no less from scholastic language than from scholastic opinion."[37] According to Windelband, this striving can be described as the "Kantian spirit's liberation of itself from the shackles of the traditional ways of thinking and writing" (*Geschichte,* 2:11). With the breakthrough to critical philosophy, however, Windelband notes that his style changes as well, and in place of the flowing, light, and mobile way of writing comes a thought-heavy gait, "with its intricate periods, its compartmentalized sentences, its cautious stipulations, its tortuous repetitions."[38] The chains of conceptual connection always continue onward indefinitely, and the closure of the totality is broken up (*I. Kant und seine Weltanschauung,* 15). Forming its own style, there is a double movement running through Kant's work from that point on: a negative and a positive movement, "and these two trains of thought cross each other continually with ever-new twists and turns" (Ibid., 11).

Friedrich Paulsen (1898) compares the style of the *Critique of Pure Reason* with a palimpsest: "[F]rom an original, half-obscured text, a new text has been written, whose clarity is diminished by the underlying text."[39] Paulsen subsequently dedicates a section to "Kant as a Thinker and a Writer." He describes the precritical writings, particularly those from the 1760s, as Kant's "best accomplishments as a writer," whereas the later writings are thought and written "in the strict style of scholastic philosophy" (*I. Kant. Seine Leben und seine Lehre,* 73). Paulsen's thesis is that "ever since [Kant] found the standpoint of his own system, he (turned) back to the strict systematic-scholastic form" (73). Because of this, thoughts would often get "squashed and garbled" (74). Thus the verdict also reads, "Kant does not belong to the masters of the German style. He could have become one. . . . But if everyone has the vices of his virtues, then this counts too for Kant as a writer" (77f.).

It is Rudolf Eucken's accomplishment to have been the first to dedicate a study to Kant's imagery and allegories (at first in the *Fichtezeitschrift,*

[1883]). But although Eucken brings together a number of metaphors used by Kant, he does not grant them any inherent value. If they are an expression of Kant's thought, nonetheless they have "more significance for Kant's individuality than for his philosophy."[40] According to Eucken, Kant used images and allegories to illustrate ideas, preferably near the beginning and at the end of investigations, in order to lend them a new sense. The playful aspect of such displacements of meaning indicate the sense of nuance that cannot be accounted for conceptually.

K. A. Rosikat delves into Kant's relation to poetry in his inquiry, *Kants Kritik der reinen Vernunft und seine Stellung zur Poesie*. He speaks of a "new poetic moment that appears relatively often in the *Critique of Pure Reason*,"[41] and also of the "sensual coloring of his language" (23). "*Dichten*," to compose or fabricate, turns up often in Kant, mostly in a negative sense. Because the faculty of imagination is granted a decisive place in Kant, he sees himself compelled to distinguish poetry and fiction from philosophy, to a degree that often amounts to a compensatory overreaction.

Wichert[42] was the first to treat Kant as a poet. But only the first pages of his essay deal with Kant's verse. No analysis is given. (This would require, for instance, tracing the influence of Haller in Kant's own poems.) Jünemann subsequently says more on this theme in "Kant als Dichter."[43] Yet his article consists primarily in reprinting several of Kant's poems. In Jünemann, as in Wichert, they have the air of being curiosities—and this is not entirely unjustified. What results from such an approach is the old refrain that had already been struck up by Kant's contemporaries, that Kant could write "beautifully," even poetically, if he wanted to. But the assertion acts as a fixative: the claim about Kant's otherwise poor style thereby enjoys a legitimized preeminence.

Wilhelm Uhl's study on Kant's vocabulary and use of language, "Wortschatz und Sprachgebrauch bei Kant" (1904) is quite important. Uhl directs attention to the fact that a monograph on Kant's way of writing has yet to be produced. Although Kant's writerly activities have been scrutinized from the most varied standpoints, "the so-profitable theme, 'Kant as a stylist' has been touched upon only occasionally, here and there."[44] This would be explained in no small part by the fact of "the almost utter lack of any sort of preliminary studies" (166). The Grimm dictionary is, as Uhl points out, ultimately unsatisfying in respect to Kant, even if Jacob Grimm did recognize Kant's significance in regard to language. Hence in the first volume of the *Deutsches Wörterbuch* (1854), Grimm speaks of Kant's "lively manner of expression," which "a dictionary cannot neglect to include, to the extent that it falls within the area of the German language" (xxxii). Grimm thus acknowledged quite clearly Kant's creative accomplishments in language. Uhl directs notice to the immense investigative effort that a critical study of metaphors and images in Kant would require, and which has yet to be accomplished, as for example a comprehensive collection and evaluation of the complete Kantian vocabulary.[45] Anyway, only the categorical imperative has managed thus far to make its way into the thesaurus of German proverbs, *Büchmann*, but Uhl notes, "A work on the categorical imperative in world literature would be quite appreciated" ("Wortschatz und Sprachgebrauch bei Kant," 173). Along the analogy of the critical and precritical periods, Uhl distinguishes two stylistic epochs. Without succumbing to the old prejudice regarding the supposed worsening of Kant's style, he makes every effort to remain "free of values" as a historian of German literature. In agreement with Schopenhauer, therefore, he speaks of a "correct, transparent style": "Precisely this correctness in his style elevates our philosopher high above his century" (175). The so-called scholastic mannerism (167) of the critical period should not be condemned as a lack of ability, if one concedes that Kant consciously chose this style. Rather, this needs to be investigated first of all. "That Kant everywhere followed the received philosophical terminology quite narrowly" (173), thus becomes the stylistic distinguishing mark of a specialized, professional language. As such, this language develops according to its own rules and should not be judged according to criteria imported from outside.

H. Ernst Fischer's monograph, *Kants Stil in der Kritik der reinen Vernunft*, moves between two extremes. The first is one of numerical exactness, in counting out the various dependent clauses of first, second, and third order, the pleonasms, paraphrases ("c'est-que-clauses"), the uniformities of expression, and anacolutha. On the other hand, he applies a diffuse, "linguistic-psychological method." This work distinguishes itself by not allowing itself the slightest conclusion in regard to Kant's philosophy, but otherwise it seems itself to blunder stylistically. Fischer beautifully describes the effect of Kantian syntax, however, when he writes: "We enter the structure as we enter a maze, each enclosed space leads us quickly to the next, we lose sight of the entryway and hurry onward, until suddenly we can go no further and stand before a wall, so we go back, trying our luck in another series of enclosures anew—and the same game is repeated, but then after a sometimes long, futile search, some happy coincidence leads us to the main path, which leads from main clause to main clause, finally allowing us to reach the exit from the maze."[46] Indeed, Fischer occasionally speaks of the "malevolent essence of the Kantian sentence-monster" (42). He touches upon philosophical relevance only once, when he observes: "The subsyntactical connection, however, emerges from an overall idea in the writer's consciousness, and this intimately posited relationship in apperception establishes itself in the various structural changes in the syntax. Through these, then, receptive attention becomes the apperceptive positing of relationships, which is caused to form an overall idea, something that can happen only under the influence of an active apperception that compares and connects" (69). The difficulty in Fischer perhaps consists ultimately in the fact that he is intent upon a unified law of style, which can only be derived speculatively, and which certainly seems to keep him from being interested in a close reading. But little is served by such abstract lines of thought, particularly since the issue remains—as Uhl pointed out—primarily one of a first sifting-through of Kant's style.

Arnold Kowalewski, in his essay "Die verschiedenen Arbeitsformen der Philosophie und ihre Bewertung bei Kant," also touches upon the "poetic way of working."[47] In opposition to Eucken, he maintains that "a firmly circumscribed participatory role in mental operations" must be ascribed to images and allegories (111): "In addition, it can be observed that Kant does not always adopt figurative expressions in their conventional sense, but instead often attempts through critical analysis to give them precision, sometimes even a new meaning. In such cases, obviously, the methodical valence of the poetic element in Kant can no longer be doubted." A study that made this into the object of its inquiry would promise "interesting revelations about the more refined history of this philosopher's development" (111), hence something Kowalewski would designate as desirable.

It would require an intellectual-historical approach to philosophy, such as Dilthey developed, to comprehend Kant's precritical writings in their literary-historical significance. Certainly, Dilthey does interpret the breakthrough to the critical epoch—following prevalent opinion—as such a radically new beginning that it has to be grasped as a break in continuity, much the way Kant himself wished to understand his own development. By doing so, Dilthey closes himself off from gaining a perspective on Kant's *literary* development *within* his philosophical development: "But then when Lessing died and, soon after him, Friedrich passed away, and then when Kant, after a long period of silence, emerged once more into public as an esoteric philosopher, with a hardly understandable, artificial language and architectonic, the great era of the literature of Enlightenment in Germany had reached its end."[48] Nonetheless, Dilthey's important insight remains, that Kant—even if for Dilthey only the early Kant—deserves a definitive place in literary history: "In his development, there is only a too-short time in which he appeared alongside Lessing as a major author: the time of the great shift in his inner life brought on by Rousseau's writings. This upheaval raised his descriptive powers to the highest pitch of energy" (172). Yet this passage, in Dilthey's *Friedrich der Grosse und die deutsche Aufklärung*, has hardly been given serious consideration, not to mention that it has never given cause for further investigation.

In a letter from October 22, 1917, to his friend Gershom Scholem, Walter Benjamin, who was at that time still searching for interpretive inroads to the core of Kantian philosophy, writes:

> It is my conviction: whoever does not feel Kant's struggle with
> *the thinking of theory itself,* and whoever thus fails to grasp him

with the utmost reverence down to the letter as a *tradendum,* as something to be handed down (however far one may have to reformulate him later), knows absolutely nothing about philosophy. Therefore any finding fault with his philosophical style is utter philistinism and profane babble. It is entirely true that in the great scientific creations, art must be taken into account (and *vice versa*), and thus it is also my conviction that Kant's prose itself represents a *limes* of high artistic prose.[49]

In his portrayal of Kant in *Kants Leben und Lehre* (1918), Ernst Cassirer observes a change in style from the precritical to the critical works: "[A] deeper and more far-reaching stylistic shift than that which transpires in Kant in the decade between 1770 and 1780 has probably never been seen in the history of literature and philosophy."[50] In particular, Cassirer notes, the drafts from 1775 show the uniqueness and style of Kantian thinking as it originates: the content itself generating the form (146f.). The conscious avoidance of visual representation brings with it a change in style that indicates a new type of thinking (151). "Concepts develop and become other ones according to the position where they stand in the progressing construction of the whole" (152). Thus whoever expects to find a clearly minted coin in Kant will inevitably only become confused by Kant's mode of presentation. On the contrary, it is precisely this consistently maintained congruence of content and form that distinguishes Kant's style, particularly following the Copernican turn, and it must be considered an intrinsic part of the philosophical proposition.[51]

In the second volume of his work, *Immanuel Kant. Der Mann und das Werk* (1924), Karl Vorländer comes to speak of "Kant as a writer, a stylist, and a correspondent." Although he offers nothing fundamentally new, the balanced way he handles the theme is worthy of note. Genuine humor and ironic wit, along with inner clarity, are addressed there as characteristics of Kant's style.[52]

Karl Jaspers raises precisely this problem in his chapter on Kant in *Die grossen Philosophen* (1957), making it for the first time the object of philosophical contemplation. "With the writerly cultivation of his language," Kant belonged to the Enlightenment. "Beautiful brightness and irony," along with "agility of thought"[53] mark the style of the precritical epoch. Thus Kant was considered, "the most elegant and impressive philosophical author" (409). In progressing toward the critical epoch, he surrendered this position, "in favor of a penetrating, dense, soberly specialized language" (404). This does not mean, however, that this language was "understandable," that is, resolvable into its elements. Just the opposite is the case. And the sense that this was Kant's actual desire becomes the centerpoint of Jaspers's observations. He formulates this in a Kafkaesque manner: "The reader can become confused and dizzy, until out of precisely this dizziness there emerges that clarity which cannot be grasped in any of the objective definitions" (444). The fact that "all sorts of expressions (require) a translation, not into some other way of saying them, but rather into the consciousness of something all-encompassing, within which all those definite formulations first receive their meaning" (443), points to the philosophical reasons for the Kafkaesque element inherent in Kant.[54] The thesis Jaspers develops leads to an overturning of the generally shared view that the style of the younger Kant compares favorably with that of the "critical" Kant. On the precritical writings, Jaspers notes, "They lack that enlivening aura of the later works, generated by the conceptuality itself, and lack having unforseeable depths illuminated by clear concepts. Only thus, through the weight and inexhaustability of its contents, does the outstanding style of the great critical works arise" (516). Circles, tautologies, and contradictions are hence not "accidents" that may have somehow been avoided; rather, they designate the only adequate medium of philosophical thinking. Philosophy as labor, as Kant wished it to be understood, thus reaches no conclusion, and the results are, as he never tires of emphasizing, "only" negative. "In his usage of words, and in the immediate representational sense of his sentences," contradictions necessarily arise (587). It is a "grand conceptual dialectic that bursts forth" (586); not a self-circling dialectic, but one that opens up and out (579). As an aporetical movement of thought seeking to set out the conditions of all objectivity, the transcendental method can pursue its aim only in objective thought itself, and this means in objects that are not themselves objects. This happens, however, only by once again upholding the strictly drawn limits of objective thought itself, within which we always already move, and which we cannot transcend (except, perhaps, in a practical aim, wherein is hidden the real thrust of Kantian thought) (439). The result of this is that Kant cannot restrict himself to a single way of expressing himself. Thus he brings to bear "psychological," "logical," "methodological," and "metaphysical" elements in his language. The result of this is an "intermingling of directions of thought, which can indeed be sorted out, but which retain the force of their language as a whole" (435). "Such concepts cannot be treated simply as definable clumps, ready, in their invariable significance, for use by a formal operation of the understanding. It is much more a question of their realization" (587). This explains why Kant's work shows "the greatest clarity in each particular train of thought, within an inevitable lack of conceptual clarity from an overall perspective" (435). And this does not preclude, rather quite the opposite requires, "a masterpiece of conceptual exposition" (435). Through repeated emphasis on the "negativity" of his thinking, Kant places himself in a philosophical tradition that is also confronted with the same problem, in all its complexity, when it appears in the form of negative theology, as Jaspers shows in his book on Cusanus.[55]

In his Leipzig lectures on the history of philosophy from 1950 to 1956, which now have been published under the title *Neuzeitliche Philosophie 2: Deutscher Idealismus. Die Philosophie des 19. Jahrhunderts,* Ernst Bloch raises the issue of Kant's language and states categorically: "It is humbug to say that Kant wrote bad German."[56] Bloch directs particular notice to the Latinity of Kant's German, and to his almost Ciceronian use of periods. He assigns the early writings a place among the "most beautiful German literary rococo" (17). Of particular interest is what he says about Kleist's relation to Kant: "The language has been learned from Kant, with all of its retractions, commas, restrictions, with all this insolent precision, whereby something is screwed down tight right on the spot, with all this *chut des mots,* the cadence of words, the rhythm. Whoever has read Kant will recognize the tone immediately, and if you have an ear for Kleist, you will be able to read Kant more easily." (17)

Within the framework of an investigation into the history of German book criticism, Anni Carlssohn assigns Kant a key position. She writes, "Alongside the establishment of the sublime style of writing by Klopstock, Kant's strict and clear thinker's language, primarily in the three great philosophical critiques, stands as the most significant founding accomplishment in language in the eighteenth century; even until today, it has remained a sturdy foundation of the human sciences."[57] Hence the critical interpretation and self-interpretation of German Classicism has already had its theoretical underpinning from Kant's transcendental-reflective philosophy (85).

Dieter Henrich has pointed repeatedly to the literary shape of Kant's work, particularly for a more precise understanding of his development: "It would be a useful undertaking to write a stylistic history of Kant's literary production."[58] This would not only render his concept of philosophy explicit, but also enable it first possible to be adequately understood: "Whoever reads Kant's main work with regard only to the subject matter that it deals with will therefore never escape the feeling of strangeness and uncertainty in their understanding of it. What is true for every philosophical work is true for the *Critique* to an especially high degree: it is defined by the subject matter, but also, just as much, by a definite style in its exposition."[59] How work style, style of thinking, and writing style leave their mark on each other is a question that is still speculated about, in a way that frequently exceeds any proof. This is necessarily so, particularly when, as Henrich especially points out, the state of research is so extraordinarily poor. The discussion of Kant is primarily constituted by the preconceptions we bring to him. It is unlikely this will change much in the forseeable future.

David Tarbet's "The Fabric of Metaphor in Kant's *Critique of Pure Reason*" compiles a series of the central metaphors of the *Critique,* and strives to develop a typology of these metaphors. While Tarbet does not concede any philosophically relevant inherent value to Kant's use of metaphor, he does tease out a continuous strand of metaphors that he designates as at least biographically relevant. "The metaphor around which the entire work is constructed draws its associations from the field of jurisprudence, and might for convenience be called the legal metaphor."[60] Fundamental concepts such as deduction (266), and constitutive and regulative (269), are taken from the realm of jurisprudence. But the structure and the mode of argumentation are also oriented toward this field. Lewis W. Beck has directed attention to the fact that this is also true to a certain degree for the military metaphors,[61] which are mentioned by Tarbet. Beck speaks of Kant's two-front war against empiricism and rationalism.[62]

That the Cartesian criteria of clearness and distinctness for philosophical truth can no longer be applied in an unrestricted way but instead are themselves under suspicion of being latently ideological, is the insight of the *Dialectic of Enlightenment* by Horkheimer and Adorno. Adorno's *Negative Dialectics*, with its critique of thinking grounded in identity logic, has made possible a sensibility regarding the difficulty of texts that precisely in relation to Kant has lead to a newly motivated interest in his works. A textual practice schooled in Adorno's interpretive tenacity has proved itself to be especially helpful in this regard. Two studies, Martin Puder's *Kant—Stringenz und Ausdruck*,[63] and Manfred Sommer's *Die Selbsterhaltung der Vernunft*[64] show both the possibilities and the limits of the Frankfurt School's reading of Kant. In both cases, these studies distinguish themselves through their system-resistant analysis, probing linguistic peculiarities for philosophical relevance. Thus Puder maintains: "If the style is the philosopher, then Kant was more materialistic than most professed materialists. Instead of commanding the idea, his language presses it" (64). This can be demonstrated in the "earthly gravity" of Kant's syntax, as well as in his metaphors (64). In this respect, Benjamin's comment that "any finding fault with his philosophical style is utter philistinism and profane babble,"[65] is to be taken as a touchstone of Kant interpretation.

Kant's "ironic stance towards definition, as well as to the ideal of clearness in general," much like "the irony of what one tends to call the overall result of the first *Critique*," (Puder, *Kant,* 109) must be recognized as such if they are to be understood. Constituting a style, they betray neither carelessness nor excessive caution, but instead an aesthetic element designed to render any fixedness of thought impossible. Manfred Sommer traces the "systematic relationship between the use of metaphors and the self-preservation of a faculty of reason that must reconcile itself to the deficiency of its primary means for accomplishing its purpose."[66] Thus he analyses concepts, figures, and metaphors for what they contribute to Kant's philosophical systematics.[67]

The only monograph that exclusively thematizes Kant as a writer is Jean-Luc Nancy's *Le discours de la syncope* (1976), whose first volume is entitled *Logodaedalus* (more has not appeared).[68] Nancy does indeed lead the reader around in the labyrinth made for us by the "Logodaedalus" Kant, but, by its very nature, this does not produce any sort of "results." The accomplishment of this book is rather to have brought some somewhat fresh air back into Kant research. Nancy, however, is too much of an artistic writer himself to be aiming at conceptual precision. Hence his investigation offers little to our understanding of the details but enriches critical understanding with a new perspective. That Kant both criticizes and legitimates himself as a writer can, according to Nancy, be followed like a *leitmotiv* through Kant's work (28). Kant was the first to regret his stylistic failure, all the more so since it proved to be an inability conditioned by the subject matter of philosophy itself: "Kant, the writer, marks, of all the possibilities, the beginning of a singular literary fortune, and misfortune. Or rather, it is as if Kant's literature, by producing and completing the philosophical separation of philosophy and literature, had at the same time inscribed literature with the indelible mark of its origin." (29) Thus the philosopher is also the poet of the sublime (109). "The *Critique of Pure Reason* is the first treatise of philosophy that conceives and determines itself as a 'work,' which necessarily means that the *Critique* conceives itself as a 'work of art'—be it negatively or problematically" (52).

"If you (want) to imagine his tone and the way he speaks, just so—right down to the smallest turns of phrase, just as it is without contrived warmth," writes the Austrian Count and Jacobin, Gottfried Wenzel von Purgstall, in a letter, "then read his *Metaphysics of Morals* or the preface to the *Critique of Practical Reason*—again" (by the former meaning, in 1795, the *Foundation to the Metaphysics of Morals*).[69] This is precisely what Jean-Louis Galay does in *Philosophie et invention textuelle. Essai sur la poétique d'un texte kantien.* His investigation is a highly acute reading borne by the insight that philosophy, in order to be critical, must submit to poetological analysis.[70] It is precisely because Galay understands his poetological critique as an approach grounded in philosophical concerns, hence a continuation of critical philosophy by other means, that his insights are so productive. He seeks to demonstrate through Kant his thesis that philosophy is conditioned on language. The inherent poetics of the philosophical text reveal its givenness in what is given as the other of its self (324): "With regard to discursivity and a particular project, philosophy has a foundation of a different nature than that of the truth which it proposes: the foundation of its discursivity is grounded in the projects and the discursivity of everyday life" (315). What results from immersing oneself in the details of the text is insight into the moment wherein writing, expression, and formulation are constituted for philosophy in general. The fictional as such, composition, redundancies, the mimetic, rhetorical, and artistic elements of the Kantian discourse operate as the conditions framing and constituting the text in which philosophy formulates itself. Doublings [*dittologie*] and negations[71] are stylistic characteristics that, beyond the repetitions hastily diagnosed as the failure of style, first allow knowledge to be generated. "The philosophical text does not proceed . . . like a narrative (passing from one fact to another), but returns always to the same facts, in order to penetrate what appears, by that very movement, as their "essence." Repetition has, as Lausberg writes, the intellectual value of perspicacity [*Vereindringlichung*].[72] In regard to this function, it seems better to speak of recurrence than of repetition, for the fact of remaining within the same is, for this type of discourse, the condition for progress and recognition" (298). Kant's language and style are thus—and in this consists their poetic thrust—themselves already epistemologically significant. Not to be understood simply as supplementary illustration, they are, rather, what they themselves already designate: critique of knowledge.

> This discourse cannot function in a concept ("theme") unless it speaks of the other, that is, of one of its dialectical oppositions (which play the role of the "theme"). In other words, the identity of the concept—the text shows it—is assured in a play of cross-references which are its own inverted image; for example, the determination of purity [*Reinigkeit*] is produced by way of a constant, absolute reference of the text to the empirical under the aspect of the "mixed" [*vermengt*]. There is no productive difference there but the setting to work of a discursivity whose total is produced in a play of difference. (311)

A "dialogical-dialectical procedure," one that makes the history of Kant's thought into an exemplary case of the dialogical self-enlightenment of reason, is what Gerhardt and Kaulbach recognize in Kant's writing.[73] They even speak of Kant's "dia-logic" (69), something that Henrich has shown, for example, using the model "Hutcheson and Kant." Whereas the older interpretations of Kant atomized language and thought philologically, and precisely in doing so, "missed the overarching consistency of Kantian speech and thought,"[74] the method of conceptual analysis, on the other hand, does not reach far enough (Henrich, "Hutcheson and Kant," 23ff., 33). Kaulbach repeatedly points to the "dialogical-dialectical" aspect of reason.[75] But this does not lead to further reflection on the philosophical implications of the "dialogic," which has meanwhile gained a footing in philosophy.[76]

The ferocious attack against Kant launched by Walter Kaufmann in his work, *Discovering the Mind*,[77] may seem somewhat astonishing. But it is essentially just a variation, spilled out over thirty pages, of Nietzsche's dictum that Kant is "the greatest misfortune in recent philosophy."[78] Translated into American terms, Kant is a "disaster."[79] In terms that prove repetitive, Kant's style is labeled "a contagious disease" (166), "scandalous" (167), "a stylistic atrocity" (171), and, obviously, "obscure" (195). Kaufmann's argument is sustained by incomprehension that spills over, almost somersaults, into interpretive short-circuits. Indeed, it becomes tiresome, the way Kaufmann constantly twists various *dicta Kantiana*. Kaufmann's discussion essentially disqualifies itself from serious consideration. In place of substantiation, nonbinding generalized claims are served up with a certain brilliance borrowed from Nietzsche. What Nietzsche was still able to carry off to some degree, however, degenerates here into idle rhetoric, which finds itself vulnerable when it runs aground on Kantian reefs.[80]

In his large-scale *Biographie*, Wolfgang Ritzel comes to speak of Kant's self-conception as a writer.[81] Comparisons and images—often from seafaring and construction—are carefully selected by Kant, and do not serve as ornamental accessories, but rather contribute to understanding.[82] Ritzel's emphasis on the systematic significance of the faculty of imagination for Kant, which after all is the power of sensual poetic imagination, indicates not only why Kant has poetic qualities but also why he made such an effort at screening them out (cf. what Kant wrote about Rousseau in this regard).

In his essay, "Kant and the Novel. A Study of the Examination Scene in Hippel's *Lebensläufe nach aufsteigender Linie*," Hamilton Beck seeks to provide evidence that Hippel, "with remarkable consistency works out the implications of Kant's positions for the theory of the novel."[83] Although he does not entirely deliver on this promise, his inquiry does succeed in illuminating an association already suggested by Nancy, namely Kant's link to Hippel. Of particular interest is Beck's exposition of the theme "Kant and the Narrative First Person" (282ff.). In *The Elusive "I" in the Novel: Hippel, Sterne, Diderot, Kant*, Beck repeats the claim just quoted.[84] Hippel's attempt to, as it were, popularize Kant and his nearly incomprehensible philosophy by recasting it into easily consumed, literarily diluted appetizers is undoubtedly as laudable as it proves to be problematic in the end. The program formulated by Hippel, to communicate the contents of Kantian philosophy while bypassing his "poor" style, becomes questionable in light of the fact that the naive separation of form and content is precisely what the *Critique of Pure Reason* fundamentally calls into question. Hence Hippel's distinction between the "art philosopher" [*Kunstphilosoph*] and the "nature philosopher" [*Naturphilosoph*]—and with this distinction, one sees already where he is headed—is rendered obsolete in advance by Kant's critical philosophy. Hippel's popularization, as a desystematization of Kant's philosophy, thus rests upon the misunderstanding that in Kant's philosophy one is still dealing with a system in the conventional sense. For this reason, by splitting the very point of inception of Kant's thinking, as Hippel's fictional staging does, Hippel misses the innermost intent of such thinking; he circumvents the critical way of proceeding that fundamentally constitutes Kant's thinking: the transcendental-reflective method of philosophizing. For Kant's philosophy is not comprised of a number of individual, more or less truthful fragments of knowledge, or even some random arrangement of such fragments; it is the form that makes it what it is.

It can hardly come as a surprise, then, that Kant sought to distance himself from Hippel's nonetheless well-meaning efforts. This alone makes Kant's quite decided but protracted distancing of himself from Hippel comprehensible, in his "Explanation on Account of the Authorship of von Hippel" ["Erklärung wegen der v. Hippelschen Autorschaft"], where he renounced the rumors that he himself was the coauthor of Hippel's novels. This is also, to some degree, an expression of Kant's irritation over Hippel, whose misunderstanding of the intentions of the *Critique of Pure Reason* were broadcast by his somewhat clumsy attempt at popularizing them. The play of various motives in Kant's written style, and the way this style reflects such a complexity, are leveled into fiction by Hippel, thereby committing precisely the conflation that Kant's entire undertaking of a critique of reason set out to oppose. Ultimately, the point was to derive a critical way of ascertaining the truth that would be both methodologically secure and self-reflective. Hippel uses Kant merely as a literary springboard for his own, independent flights into the world of fiction, which actually neither have, nor need, any theoretical underpinning from Kant.

In his article, "The Philosopher as Essayist: Leibniz and Kant,"[85] John McCarthy directs attention to the quasi-journalistic essays of both philosophers. Whether Leibniz's writings on the German language can legitimately be counted as essays is another question. McCarthy provides an excellent study of Kant's classic essay on enlightenment. Yet the decisive essay writing of the young Kant, essays that are in a real sense *attempts,* goes unmentioned. Stephen Barker, in his essay, "The Style of Kant's Critique of Reason,"[86] maintains that the reason for the artistic weaknesses and inadequacies of Kant's mode of presentation lies in the extreme difficulty he had in formulating his thoughts, or in the thoughts themselves. In taking such an approach, Barker moves within the traditional argumentative framework, one still defined by the Cartesian epistemological ideal that whatever is clearly thought can be clearly stated, otherwise no cognitive value can be ascribed to it. As accurate as some of Barker's observations are, they likewise betray a general shortcoming in the Anglo-Saxon analytic tradition that ignores foreign language—and especially here German—literature. Barker's "close reading" is unable to penetrate the flexible, often obstinate texture of Kantian prose. His reading of the *Critique of Pure Reason* as a soap opera may very well be original, but it is imported into Kant from Hegel, and contributes little to understanding of the text.

Claudia Brodsky, in the chapter "Kant and Narrative Theory" in her comparative study *The Imposition of Form: Studies in Narrative Representation and Knowledge,*[87] develops—for the first time, as far as I know—the genuine relevance of Kant's transcendental-philosophical method for a theory of narrative. In doing so, she does not seek to distill retrospectively a narratology from Kant, but rather examines his project of the critique of reason as one that, on its own, and in a fundamental way, thematizes narrative, as such: "Kant's system of knowledge can therefore be seen to describe a system of narrative—and to describe experience as *'the'* narrative—par excellence" (10). For, as Kleist's "Kant crisis" shows—if it was really a Kant crisis at all, rather than a Kleist crisis—Kant's criticism strikes precisely the root of the problem of representation; his strict division between *noumenon* and *phenomenon* insists, in a philosophically radical way, upon the aporia of representation, namely the impossibility of grasping discursive reality immediately. Brodsky's point is that what is critical about Kant is precisely what narratology makes into its object of knowledge, the division between the telling and what is told, between representation and what is represented.

Kant's decidedly non-Aristotelian concept of representation as a pure product of thought throws an anti-aesthetic light on his philosophy, while at the same time it revolutionizes the concept of aesthetics by casting it in transcendental-philosophical terms. The analysis of the concepts of nominal and real definition in Kant's *Logic,* which are so central to narrative theory, argues already in a truly trailblazing fashion: "As no word can be considered final in the course of representing experience, no discursive knowledge of experience can be considered sufficient and no definition of experiential concepts thus truly definitive" (Brodsky, *Imposition of Form,* 38). Experience is therefore always already narrative: conditioned *a priori* through the pure intuition of space and time and through the connections accomplished by the category of causality (50). This is one of the implications of Kant's concept of experience, which is so productively complex. And thus Brodsky can also formulate, rightly, "[T]he formal suppositions underlying all current epistemic systems of 'narratology' can be recognized to owe no more fundamentally, if also no less consciously, to any other single philosophical work than Kant's *Critique*" (24).

Particular significance is attributed subsequently to the concept of the sublime, the decisive point of Kantian aesthetics; from this concept is generated, as Brodsky delicately reveals, fiction and poetry [*Dichten*]. The paradigmatic role of Albrecht von Haller for Kant's concept of poetry, it is worth noting, receives thereby its precise significance. In Kant, the power of poetic invention seems to follow from the critique of reason as a matter of logical consistency: as a pure capacity of reason. The concept of freedom in the *Critique of Practical Reason,* with its epistemologically precarious function as the "cornerstone" of the entire edifice of Kant's system of reason, hence is given its own narratological thrust. Freedom is that instance wherein the will to impose form assembles the mass of data into the form of experience, and thus into the form of discourse and poetic fiction [*Dichtung*]: " 'Freedom,' the only critical basis for our linking logic to any form of knowledge, is said to be made known to us solely by the 'imposition' of the 'moral law' 'upon us' " (80). What imposes the concept of freedom upon us is nonetheless not freedom itself, but rather its form—

ethical or moral law (81). But again this cannot be grounded or justified with recourse to the real, as such—this is strictly disallowed by the critical approach—and so narration emerges from this instead, by necessity. At the architectonic place that has been reserved for the cornerstone, there appears, instead of an argumentative grounding, an inserted "story" (84) upon which the edifice establishes itself.

Marco Baschera's *Das dramatische Denken. Studien zur Beziehung von Theorie und Theater anhand von I. Kants "Kritik der reinen Vernunft" und D. Diderots "Paradoxe sur le comédien"*[88] contains a few interesting observations on stylistic features in the *Critique*. Baschera's freestyle approach engages in a reading that is as productive as it is provocative. His reading opens one's eyes to some idiosyncratic moments in Kant. Unburdened by any discussion of Kant literature, the study suffers from an ultimately ahistorical approach. Tobia Bezzola, meanwhile, reads Kant's work, in his *Die Rhetorik bei Kant, Fichte und Hegel. Ein Beitrag zur Philosophiegeschichte der Rhetorik,*[89] from an exclusively rhetorical point of view. Not surprisingly, such an approach must end in disappointment over Kant's allegedly poor rhetorical qualities. Kant's sophisticated negotiating with the rhetorical nature of all writing must necessarily escape an investigation that views Kant only in regard to the surface phenomena of directly observable rhetorical features. Baschera and Bezzola both read Kant exclusively as a stylist and rhetorician. The philosophical-critical dimension of Kant's praxis of writing remains screened out. Consequently, the intricately complicated philosophical argumentation complex that permeates Kant's writing, including his ethical and practical deliberations, is lost sight of. Yet it is precisely Kant's highly differentiated project of publicizing enlightenment, backed by epistemological-critical theory, that defines the framework in which Kant's writing style has to be understood. Rather, it is this philosophical-critical context that shapes Kant's theory and praxis of writing.

As a survey of the literature shows, there are plenty of provocative ideas. But almost all the investigations occupy themselves exclusively with the *Critiques,* and primarily the *Critique of Pure Reason* or with the "critical" Kant, as such (whatever or whoever that may be). Therefore an investigation based on the complexity of Kant's historical development seems to be a *desideratum.* In this regard, there is much in the present literature that would be useful, but much would have to be newly organized on the basis of what such a theme demands. This means that the main task remains to undertake a close reading of Kant's texts, and from them, particularly from their key passages, to develop the theses that will guide the reading and understanding of Kant and Kantian thought.

NOTES

A Note on Translations

All translations in the text and notes are original, unless otherwise noted. English translations used are listed under Kant editions in the Bibliography. Editorial emendations are enclosed in brackets.

One   Project Career Trajectory

1   Letter of August 18, 1791, in Kant, *Briefwechsel*, ed. O. Schöndörffer (Hamburg, 1986), 515.

2   See Kant's letters to Leonhard Euler and to an unknown reviewer, where he gives reasons for the delay in publication (*Briefwechsel*, 925f., cf. also 1); also cf. Harald-Paul Fischer, "Eine Antwort auf Kants Brief von 23. August 1749," *Kant-Studien* 76 (1985): 79–89; there one also finds a reprint and discussion of the first review of *Thoughts* from the *Franckfurtische Gelehrte Anzeigen*, November 14, 1749. In the *Göttingische Zeitungen von gelehrten Sachen*, which was run at the time by Albrecht von Haller, a review did not appear until April 1750, and it made reference to the 1749 review. See also H.-P. Fischer, "Kant an Euler," *Kant-Studien* 76 (1985): 214–9.

3   See Ernst Cassirer, *Kants Leben und Lehre*, 2d ed. (1921; reprint, Darmstadt, 1977), 28. On the other hand, W. H. Werkmeister, *Kant: The Architectonic and Development of His Philosophy* (La Salle, 1980), 1–6; and H. Böhme and G. Böhme, *Das Andere der Vernunft* (Frankfurt, 1983), 87 and n. o [sic], 499, both point out that not until 1758 was d'Alembert able to provide the correct mathematical solution to the problem of moving force and that the honor of discovery thus goes to Boscovich. In any case, as Erdmann has pointed out, it is very likely that as of 1746 or 1747, d'Alembert's *Traité de Dynamique* (Paris, 1743) had not yet reached Königsberg; see Benno Erdmann, *Martin Knutzen und seine Zeit: Ein Beitrag zur Geschichte der wolffischen Schule und insbesondere zur Entwicklungsgeschichte Kants* (Leipzig, 1876), 8. Königsberg's remoteness from the literary scene must have motivated Kant to make close contacts with bookdealers, the sole traders and transporters to and from the "book metropolis," Leipzig. On the insular character of Königsberg, see Kurt Stavenhagen, *Kant und Königsberg* (Göttingen, 1949), 9. Lessing's mocking

verse is well known: "K unternimmt ein schwer Geschäfte,/ der Welt zum Unterricht./ Er schätzet die lebendgen Kräfte;/ Nur seine schätzt er nicht." [K's assumed a heavy task,/ to teach the world a lesson./ He measures every living force,/ but leaves his own unquestioned.] From "Das Neueste aus dem Reich des Witzes," July 1751, in G. E. Lessing, *Sämtliche Werke,* ed. Karl Lachmann-Franz Muncker (Stuttgart, 1886), 1:41.

4   Opinions diverge here, even within current research, which rather brings to mind the aporia of a judgment passed, *post festum,* that itself seems both historically and philosophically conditioned.

5   Erich Adickes, *Kant als Naturforscher* (Berlin, 1924), 1:69.

6   The idea that an author could be greater than his or her work had already become a topos in Kant's time and was often accompanied by the claim that this was itself a prerequisite for a (philosophical) work. This is the perspective from which the biographies by Borowski, Jachmann, and Wasianski were written. See also L. E. Borowski, *Immanuel Kant: Sein Leben in Darstellungen seiner Zeitgenossen,* ed. F. Gross (Berlin, 1912), as well as the recounted impressions of Johann Friedrich Abegg, *Reisetagebuch von 1798,* ed. W. Abegg and J. Abegg with Zwi Batscha (Frankfurt, 1976), esp. 142 and 247, and Stavenhagen, *Kant und Königsberg,* 58, 65, 77; see also Cassirer, *Kants Leben und Lehre,* 39ff., where reference is made to Poerschke's claim that this is indeed the defining mark of Kant's originality. While a book may be more scholarly than its author among conventional scholars, the depth and uniqueness of one who truly thinks for himself, on the other hand, is shown precisely by the fact that his texts never stand above him, but instead lag behind him.

7   Emil Arnoldt, "Kants Jugend und die ersten fünf Jahre seiner Privatdozentur," in *Gesammelte Schriften,* (Berlin, 1908), 3:159.

8   It seems that Adickes, and others with him, begrudge Kant the fact that he ventured into the natural sciences so assuredly and with so little preparation. But it would be a gross misrecognition of Kant's genuine point of departure, were one to take those moments when Kant first blazed a new trail, philosophically, and chalk them up as mere errors.

9   The titles of Wolff's German works promise "reasonable thoughts": *Vernünftige Gedanken von den Kräften des menschlichen Verstandes* [Reasonable thoughts on the powers of human understanding] (1713); *Vernünftige Gedanken von Gott, der Welt und der Seele des Menschen, auch allen Dingen überhaupt* [Reasonable thoughts on God, the world, and the soul of man, and on all things in general] (1720); *Vernünftige Gedanken von den Würckungen der Natur* [Reasonable thoughts on the effects of nature] (1723). Two books that appeared in Königsberg just before Kant's are C. G. Fischer, *Vernünftige Gedanken von der Natur* [Reasonable thoughts on nature] (1743), and Martin Knutzen, *Vernünftige Gedanken von den Kometen* [Reasonable thoughts on comets] (1744). For both, see Erdmann, *Martin Knutzen,* 41, 53.

10   Friedrich Nietzsche, *Sämtliche Werke,* Kritische Studienausgabe, ed. G. Colli, and M. Montinari (Berlin and Munich, 1980), 1:248. Nietzsche is mentioned *en passant* in Karl Vorländer, *Immanuel Kant. Der Mann und das Werk* (Hamburg, 1977), 1:57.

11   Adickes, *Kant,* 1:66. On the question of Kant's estimation of himself during this period, H.-P. Fischer ("Kant an Euler," 216) fittingly notes: "The question is always asked, in connection with this first work, what sort of self-consciousness and what expectations guided Kant. The interpretations range from confidence and humbleness, through youthfully cheeky audacity, to an act of grandiose self-display. These two letters [from 1749] also do not provide an equivocal answer, but instead point much more to Kant's *fluctuating* self-esteem" (emphasis added).

12 On the dedication and its subject, Bohlius (who seems to have been a benefactor of the family and who to that extent merits some of the credit for this first work), see Arnoldt, "Kants Jugend," 164. Page numbers given in this chapter refer, when not otherwise noted, to Kant, *Werkausgabe*, vol. 1, ed. W. Weischedel (hereafter cited as ww); the number of the paragraph cited will also sometimes be given.

13 *Bahn* in German can mean both "track," as well as, more abstractly, "course" or "trajectory." *Lauf* also ranges in meaning, from "career" to "orbit." Thus it is necessary to render *Laufbahn*, at times, as both "career track" and "career trajectory," to capture both aspects of the word. [*Translator's note*]

14 G. Gerland, "Immanuel Kant, seine geographischen und anthropologischen Arbeiten," *Kant-Studien* 10 (1905): 1–43; 417–547; quotation is from ibid., 35.

15 I call this a joke in Freud's sense. See Sigmund Freud, "Der Witz und seine Beziehung zum Unbewussten," in S. Freud, *Studienausgabe*, ed. A. Mitscherlich, A. Richards, and J. Strachey (Frankfurt, 1969).

16 See the letter of Dec. 17, 1796, in Kant, *Briefwechsel*, 721, where Kant excuses his delay in answering with the explanation that "in one's seventy-third, it is not easy to get back into the groove of things, when one has allowed oneself to stray, more than once, from the prescribed track."

17 Contrast Mendelssohn's restrained comportment: "It has never occurred to me to become my own era in the world's wisdom, or to become famous through a system of my own. Where I see a well-worn track [*Bahn*] ahead of me, I do not seek to forge a new one" (Moses Mendelssohn, appendix to *Phädon oder die Unsterblichkeit der Seele*, 3d ed. [1769; reprint, Hamburg, 1979], 143).

18 Arnoldt continues, "This always ran counter to people's commonplace views, and disappointed the expectations of those around him who observed him. For whatever one expected from him in the form of an undertaking, was either not undertaken, or else he undertook it only after any expectations had already been given up, and then he would carry it out so grandiosely and completely that his accomplishment brought forth utter astonishment, and thus again defied all expectations, and this time rightfully so" ("Kants Jugend," 205).

19 Cf. Kant, *Theoretical Philosophy, 1755–1770*, ed. and trans. David Wolford (New York, 1992), 354 (hereafter cited as DW).

20 If the truth really has sought him out as her exclusive lover, as Kant so proudly announces, then he could at least offer some reason why this is so. He is, after all, the youngest of her suitors, among whom such prominent names as Leibniz and Wolff figured as well. This "erotic undertone" is also pointed out by Böhme and Böhme, *Das Andere*, 87.

21 Cassirer, *Kants Leben und Lehre*, 28.

22 According to Werkmeister, Kant's trailblazing work on the distinction between mathematical and philosophical modes of knowledge has already begun here (*Kant*, 5).

Two Cosmological Family Romance

1 Heinz Heimsoeth has rightfully called this Kant's "first major work," in his essay "Astronomisches und Theologisches in Kants Weltverständnis," in H. Heimsoeth, *Studien zur Philosophie Immanuel Kants II*, Kantstudien Ergänzungsheft 100 (Bonn, 1970), 86.

2 Hans Blumenberg, *Das Lachen der Thrakerin. Eine Urgeschichte der Theorie* (Frankfurt, 1987), 112.

3   F. A. Paneth, "Die Erkenntnis des Weltbaus durch Thomas Wright und Immanuel Kant," *Kant-Studien* 47 (1955/56): 337. On p. 346, n. 9, Paneth mentions that the Königsberg University Observatory was not established until six years after Kant's death. But "even in 1718 (there was) a small . . . wooden tower built on the roof of the school building [the Collegium Fredericianum that Kant attended] as an 'observatory,' the first of its kind in Königsberg" (Vorländer, *Immanuel Kant,* 1:30). Whether Kant ever used it is hard to say, and perhaps Heimsoeth is correct in remarking, "Kant's conception and the individual problems he considers came about, it can be assumed, without his ever having had a telescope at his disposal"—or his ever having used it, for that matter (Heimsoeth, "Astronomisches und Theologisches in Kants Weltverständnis," 91, n. 11).

4   It appeared in 1751 in parts I, II, and III; cf. Kant, *Gesammelte Schriften,* ed. the Berliner Akademie der Wissenschaften (hereafter cited as AA), 1:547; published in an English translation as an appendix to Milton K. Munitz's English edition of Kant, *Universal Natural History and Theory of the Heavens,* trans. W. Hastie (Glasgow, 1900; Ann Arbor, 1969), 169–80.

5   Hans-Joachim Waschkies, *Physik und Physikotheologie des jungen Kant. Die Vorgeschichte seiner Allgemeinen Naturgeschichte und Theorie des Himmels* (Amsterdam: Grüne, 1987), 28, mentions only the years from 1748 to 1751 when Kant stayed in Judtschen.

6   Kant, *Geographische und andere naturwissenschaftliche Schriften,* ed. Jürgen Zehbe (Hamburg, 1985), 9.

7   Kuno Fischer expresses the same opinion in his portrayal, *Immanuel Kant und seine Lehre* (Heidelberg, 1898). One indication that Kant prepared the journal articles only *after* conceiving the entire *Universal Natural History* comes from Kant himself, when, in the *Universal Natural History* (WW, 1:103), he "sets aside" the discussion of a question to answer it later in 1754 (Kant, *Geographische Schriften,* 3).

8   Erich Adickes, *Kant also Naturforscher,* (Berlin, 1925), 2:207. Harvard University's Houghton Library contains a copy of the *Allgemeine Naturgeschichte* of 1755, as well as an edition of his rare first work of 1746 (actually printed in 1749).

9   Kant, *Der einzig mögliche Beweisgrund zu einer Demonstration des Daseins Gottes* [*The Only Possible Argument in Support of a Demonstration of the Existence of God*] (1763). Letters to Biester, June 8, 1781; to Bode, September 2, 1790; to Gensichen, April 19, 1791, in Kant, *Briefwechsel.* H. Böhme and G. Böhme see the reason for Kant's refusal in the idea that, after the development of his philosophical critique, he could only accept those parts of the *Universal Natural History* that still accorded with a now fully articulated, strictly discursive line of argumentation. Thus it was important for Kant to assert the priority of the scientific-cosmological hypothesis he had formulated, but he was simultaneously concerned with suppressing the predominantly imaginative portion of the text. From this perspective, the otherwise puzzling acerbity of his Herder review (WW 12:781ff.) can perhaps best be understood as a self-criticism by the "critical" Kant of his "precritical" self (Böhme and Böhme, *Das Andere,* 174, 207 and n. 40, 504f.).

10   This according to Kuno Fischer, *I. Kant,* 174; opposing this view is Gerland, "I. Kant," 420f. S. Sambursky calls Kant the "father of modern cosmology" (quoted in J. Zehbe, Introduction to Kant, *Geographische und andere naturwissenschaftliche Schriften,* vii). See also Jürgen Hamel, *Zur Entstehungs- und Wirkungsgeschichte der Kantischen Kosmogonie,* Mitteilungen der Archenhold-Sternwarte Berlin-Treptow, no. 130 (Berlin-Treptow, 1979), 2f., 66.

11   The German word *Versuch* can, in various contexts, mean "attempt," "experiment," or "essay." It is not completely interchangeable with *essay,* here, nor is the English term

attempt a recognizable designation for a literary form. Thus, in most instances, I have left *Versuch* untranslated, in the hope that the reader will bear in mind the term's multivalence. [*Translator's note*]

12 Theodor W. Adorno, "Der Essay als Form," in *Noten zur Literatur* (Frankfurt, 1974), 25, 27. On the essay in general, see Ludwig Rohner, ed., *Der deutsche Essay. Materialien zur Geschichte und Ästhetik einer literarischen Gattung* (Neuwied and Berlin, 1966); Max Bense, "Über den Essay und seine Prosa," in *Der deutsche Essay,* ed. Rohner; Georg Lukacs, "Über Wesen und Form des Essays," in *Der deutsche Essay,* ed. Rohner.

13 As opposed to these communication-oriented forms, which are subject to heteronomous formal rules, the essay is autonomous in its form of thought.

14 On the significance for Kant of Leibniz's *Nouveaux Essais* in the history of the form, see Ernst Cassirer's introduction to Leibniz's *Neue Abhandlungen über den menschlichen Verstand,* vol. 6 (Leipzig, 1915). On the literary quality of this text, Nicholas Jolley, *Leibniz and Locke: A Study of the "New Essays on Human Understanding"* (Oxford, 1984), 9, expresses reservations.

15 Swift does just this, in "A Tale of a Tub," in *The Prose Works of Jonathan Swift,* ed. T. Scott (London, 1907–1925), vol. 1.

16 It is an essential aspect of the essay that it cannot be defined with respect to its length. Such a definition would only prove to be arbitrary and unhistorical. In the eighteenth century one finds essays that are, by our standards, quite extensive, for instance Freiherr Adolph von Knigge, *Über den Umgang mit Menschen,* ed. G. Ueding (Frankfurt, 1987). See Willi Goetschel, "Zur Neuausgabe des 'Knigge,'" *Zeitschrift für Religions- und Geistesgeschichte* 40 (1988): 359ff.

17 On this idea in general, see Cassirer's description of "forms of thought" in the Enlightenment, in *Die Philosophie der Aufklärung* (Tübingen, 1973), 1–48, especially 16.

18 Kant habitually cited authoritative earlier writers. Christoph Friedrich Heilsberg, a friend of Kant's in his youth, reports: "When met with the reproach that he himself laughed little or not at all, he admitted this as a failing of his, and added, that no metaphysician would ever bring about as much good in the world as Erasmus of Rotterdam and the famous Montaigne in France had brought about; and recommended the latter's essays to us as the choice for extensive reading; and he could recite by heart many passages from them himself" (in *Immanuel Kant in Rede und Gespräch,* ed. R. Malter (Hamburg, 1990), 19. In his remarks on Samuel Gottlieb Wald's "Memorial Speech for Kant on April 23, 1804," Kraus notes: "Even in [Kant's] professorial years, he still read Seneca, Lucretius, etc. He was practically overflowing with beautiful sentences from his favorite author, Montaigne." Christian Jacob Kraus, note on S. Wald, "Gedächtnisrede auf Kant am 23. April 1804," in *Immanuel Kant zu Ehren,* ed. J. Kopper and R. Malter, (Frankfurt, 1974), 71, n. 7. On Kant and Montaigne, see Cassirer, *Kants Leben und Lehre,* 89f.

19 Malter, ed., *I. Kant in Rede und Gespräch,* 218.

20 Böhme and Böhme, *Das Andere,* 196f.

21 Friedrich Wilhelm Schelling, *Philosophie der Kunst,* quoted in Böhme and Böhme, *Das Andere,* 171.

22 Lucretius had, "as we know, a very early and very deep effect on Kant" (Heimsoeth, "Astronomisches und Theologisches," 92, n. 17). Wald names Lucretius first in the list of classical poets admired by Kant, in "Gedächtnisrede" in *I. Kant zu Ehren,* ed. Kopper and Malter, 62.

23 Böhme and Böhme, *Das Andere,* abbreviate the title to "Theory of the Heavens." But this once again places the emphasis back on theory, and forces into the background the fact

that "natural history" is what is eminently the issue here. This is given graphic expression in the original printing, where "Natural History" is printed in letters twice as large as those of "Theory of the Heavens."

24 Gerland, Adickes, and others have performed just such an exercise. Such a *spiel* only confirms that to miss its literary character is to miss its essence.

25 Gerland, "I. Kant," 34.

26 Munitz, introduction to Kant, *Universal Natural History*.

27 Paragraphs I, III, V, VII (paragraph I begins "Because I.").

28 Sentences 1, 4, 5, 6, 8, 9 ("My zeal"), 10, ww, 1:227. Page numbers in this chapter refer, when not otherwise specified, to ww, vol. 1.

29 Paragraphs, I, II, V, XIII, XVI, XVII, XX, XXII.

30 Paragraphs IV ("if I"), XI ("henceforth I will"), XVIII ("These are causes, to which I"), XIX ("After I"), XXI ("In the second section . . . I will seek"), XXIII ("If one will allow me"), XXIV ("if I").

31 Paragraphs IV, V, X ("Let us now see").

32 Within individual paragraphs, the "I" appears occasionally in overtly concentrated formations. See in particular paragraphs I, II, XI, XVII, XX–XXIV.

33 Hans Blumenberg, *Die Genesis der kopernikanischen Welt* (Frankfurt, 1975), 678: "A cheeky tone runs throughout Kant's book, one that he may not have been entirely comfortable with later on. In some of his more daring "I"-sentences, the author appears as the Prometheus of his own *Weltkunstwerk*."

34 J. W. Goethe, *Sämtliche Werke*, ed. E. Beutler (Zürich, 1950), 16:395. On this note, one could refer as well to Freud, who draws the connection between Copernicus's discovery (and, following the second offence—by Darwin—comes the third, the psychoanalytic one) and the ego's loss of dominance in its own household (Freud, *Studienausgabe,* 1:283).

35 Herman Schmalenbach, *Kants Religion* (Berlin, 1929), 27.

36 Ibid., 37. See also 81: "Not only did this early pantheistic-metaphysical interest have lasting repercussions in Kant, but even the concept of God in the *Critique of Pure Reason,* in astonishing concordance with the one from the *Only Possible Argument* from 1763, is still essentially pantheistic."

37 Vorländer, *I. Kant,* 1:96.

38 There are two translations of Kant's *Allgemeine Naturgeschichte* generally available: W. Hastie's, ed. K. Munitz (Glasgow, 1900; reprint, Ann Arbor, 1969); and Stanley L. Jaki's (Edinburgh, 1981). Hastie's translation, while the more readable, is simply incomplete, leaving off the seventh chapter of the second section and the entire third section. Jaki's translation is complete, but its language is a somewhat stilted and mechanical attempt to mimic Kant's German syntax. Moreover, Jaki is a professedly anti-Kantian scientific positivist, which gives his reading a rather reductive perspective. But his comments regarding Kant's exact place in the history of science are themselves clear, detailed, and very readable. His footnotes are often highly amusing as they follow Kant's every argument and point out his difficulties with data, calculation, and even logic, and Jaki is especially merciless with Kant's attempts at scientific posturing. See also note 41. [*Translator's note*]

39 Compare too the talmudic designation "*apikorez*" for heretics. On Mendelssohn, see Willi Goetschel, *Zur Spinozarezeption bei Moses Mendelssohn* (Master's thesis, University of Zürich, 1982).

40 Friedrich Albert Lange, in *Geschichte des Materialismus* (Frankfurt, 1974), does deal extensively with Kant in his classic study, even arranging his work around Kant's place in

the history of philosophy (ibid., 453), but he only deals with the "critical" Kant. Tendencies in Kant's early work that could very well be termed materialistic seem to have escaped him.

41 The products of Kant's fantasy seem to have created such difficulties for Kant's English translators that they simply suppressed them. Only in 1977 did a translation finally appear, Stanley L. Jaki's "An English Translation of the Third Part of Kant's 'Universal Natural History and Theory of the Heavens,'" in *Cosmology, History, and Theology*, ed. Wolfgang Yourgrau and Allen D. Breck (New York and London, 1977). In the introduction to his translation, where Jaki gives an overview of previous translations, he writes: "To a careful reader of Kant's cosmology it should be clear that apart from his explanation of the visual appearance of the Milky Way—the first correct one to appear in print—each and every step in Kant's explanation of the evaluation of the planetary system is patently a priori and invariably wrong" (ibid., 389). See also what C. V. L. Charlier (quoted by Jaki) writes: "I mean that the *Naturgeschichte des Himmels* is, scientifically, of very small value; that the comparison of it with the planetary cosmogony of Laplace is highly unjust and misleading; also that it cannot be used as a working hypothesis, which, however, may be the case with the atom theory of Democritus. As a popular treatise on cosmogony I consider the *Naturgeschichte* of Kant unsuitable and even dangerous as inviting feeble minds to vain and fruitless speculations" (ibid.). Jaki himself concludes his introductory remarks with words no less harsh: "If the Third Part of Kant's cosmology is read in that broader perspective, it will not only titillate by its bizarre details and reasoning, but will also instruct as few pieces from the writings of major philosophers ever will" (ibid., 390), namely, "how not to write," as can be inferred from the context. A more conciliatory tone is struck by Edward R. Harrison, *Cosmology: The Science of the Universe* (Cambridge, 1981): "Kant . . . described the most stupendous picture of the universe that had ever been imagined" (83f.). Ibid., 86, fig. 4.19, even gives an illustration of how Kant and Lambert imagined the cosmos to look.

42 Böhme and Böhme point this out as well in *Das Andere*, 198, 208, and passim.

43 Even "addictively," according to Böhme and Böhme, *Das Andere*, 85. Thomas de Quincey notes, cleverly enough, that Kant read nothing *except* travelogues. Despite being paradoxical and somewhat extravagant, de Quincey's polemic does have some truth to it: that Kant's own writings take travelogues as their schema. See T. de Quincey, *The Collected Writings*, ed. D. Masson (Edinburgh, 1889), 8:93.

44 Schmalenbach, *Kants Religion*, 41: "This passion for travelogues would be a problem even if we didn't know what Kant thought about travel, and what he did with all his readings of travel-reports. The yearning to travel that he carried inside himself, and that could not be realized directly because of other, even more hidden internal resistances, was transformed and given an outlet in reading great quantities of travelogues. But this act of transference could be made possible only if descriptions of travel could accomplish what Kant would have been able to expect from travelling himself. This would include features not only of what he read—which must have suited him only to varying degrees, given that scores of widely different texts are involved here—but also characteristics of the reader: an extraordinary fantasy, an uncommonly intricate sensual imagination. Thus, as bold as it may seem to say this about the 'abstract' Kant, it must be pointed out that the travel-descriptions Kant read were actually mostly lacking in descriptions of actual, lived experience."

45 It is known that Kant used Brockes's translation from 1740. Brockes, in his "preface," introduces Pope as one who has succeeded in combining poetry and metaphysics. He

describes Pope as a philosopher who utilizes simply the light of his reason in his writings, and by this means seeks to prepare himself for a more elevated light. Brockes also maintains that there is no Spinozism in Pope's work. See Barthold Heinrich Brockes, *Aus dem Englischen übersetzter Versuch vom Menschen des Herrn Alexander Pope* (Hamburg, 1740).

Kant's use of Brockes's translation of Pope poses a minor difficulty for the translator, because these translations are not terribly accurate. Jaki points this out in his translation of the *Universal Natural History* and quotes Pope's original verses in his footnotes: "Is the great chain, that draws all to agree/ And drawn supports, upheld by God, or thee?" (253) [*Translator's note*]

46 See Arthur O. Lovejoy, *The Great Chain of Being* (Cambridge, Mass., 1961). Lovejoy's claim that Kant "was simply giving a temporalized version of the principle of plenitude" (ibid., 265) is heavily reductive. This too, when he notes, "It would be hardly excessive to say that much of Kant's cosmology is a prose amplification and extension of the 'philosophy' of the First Epistle of the Essay of Man" (ibid., 357, n. 24). The word "hardly" could rightfully be crossed out—and indeed has been in the library copy from the Widener Library.

47 Cf. ww, 1:363, 380.

48 Pope's original verse, quoted by Jaki:

> See plastic Nature working to this end,
> The single atoms each to other tend,
> Attract, attracted to, the next in place
> Formed and impelled its neighbor to embrace.
> See Matter next, with various life endued,
> Press to one centre still, the gener'l Good. (Jaki, 256)

49 A psychoanalytic interpretation of these projections is given by Böhme and Böhme, *Das Andere*.

50 On Kant's later sun parable as a reformulation of Plato's parable of the cave, and the consequences that result for a theory of knowledge, see Blumenberg, *Genesis,* 69f. Kant's parable of the sun is found in *On a Superior Tone Recently Adopted in Philosophy* (1796).

51 "Die Sterne sind vielleicht ein Sitz verklärter Geister,/ Wie hier das Laster herrscht, ist dort die Tugend Meister."

52 The same effect is accomplished, under the guise of trivial literature—and certainly with other intentions philosophically—by Douglas Adams's *Hitchhiker's Guide to the Galaxy* and its sequels.

53 Compare Alexander Altmann, *Trostvolle Aufklärung. Studien zur Metaphysik und politischen Theorie Moses Mendelssohns* (Stuttgart-Bad Cannstatt, 1982), 278f. See also Willi Goetschel, "Ergebnisse des Lessing-Mendelssohn-Jahrs," *Studia Philosophica* 42 (1983): 299. *Clear up* [*aufheitern*] turns up in the eighteenth century as a synonym for *enlighten* [*aufklären*]. For a discussion of the emblematic and metaphorical imagery of meteorology, see Werner Schneiders, *Hoffnung auf Vernunft. Aufklärungsphilosophie in Deutschland* (Hamburg, 1990), chap. 2.

54 Rudolf Unger, " 'Der bestirnte Himmel über mir . . . ,' Zur geistesgeschichtlichen Deutung eines Kant-Wortes," in *Immanuel Kant. Festschrift zur zweiten Jahrhundertfeier seines Geburtstages,* ed. Albertus University in Königsberg (Leipzig, 1924), 244, notes the connection between the period of Sentimentality and the unmistakable echoes of Klopstock. Unger's research traces the history of this resonant remark in Kant's work, and shows

that this metaphor is a common thread throughout Kant's writings, reappearing constantly and each time revealing significant shifts in its meaning. For models from antiquity (Seneca, Marcus Aurelius, Cicero), see Edmund von Lippmann, "Zu 'Zwei Dinge erfüllen das Gemüt," *Kant-Studien* 34 (1929). Reference to the pantheistic background of this classic formula is made by Schmalenbach, *Kants Religion*, 81. Of course, the formula has its own reception history. Ferdinand Busson, for instance, a minister of education in nineteenth-century France, suggested that schoolteachers take their class to an open field on a summer evening, to meditate on this most sublime observation of Kant's. See Robert Minder, *Die Entdeckung deutscher Mentalität. Essays* (Leipzig, 1992), 193.

Three   Short Essays

1 Kant, *Geographische Schriften*, chaps. 1–8. Page numbers in this chapter refer, when not otherwise specified, to this edition.

2 Vorländer, *Kant*, 1:110.

3 Cf. the remarks, in aphoristic form: "The very same driving-force [*Trieb*] that makes trees grow, brings about their death when their growth is completed" (*Geographische Schriften*, 14); "The very mechanism [*Mechanismus*] by which a creature or a human lives and grows, brings it its death as well, when the growth is complete" (ibid., 15).

4 See Kant, "On the Causes of Earthly Tremors" ["Von den Ursachen der Erderschütterungen"], "History and Description of the Nature of the Earthquake That in 1755 Caused Tremors in Part of the Earth" ["Geschichte und Naturbeschreibung des Erdbebens, welches 1755 einen Teil der Erde erschüttert hat"], "Continued Observation of Earthly Tremors" ["Fortgesetzte Betrachtung der Erderschütterungen"], in Kant, *Geographische Schriften*, 33–89.

5 For the argument that thankfulness is a form of acquiescence to contingency, see Odo Marquard, "Skeptiker. Dankrede," in *Apologie des Zufälligen* (Stuttgart, 1986), 6.

6 On the actual threat of war in the year 1756, see Arsenij Gulyga, *Immanuel Kant* (Frankfurt, 1981), 46ff.

7 Vorländer, *Kant*, 1:114.

8 His "Nova dilucidatio" contains a short dialogue on freedom of the will. But this is also kept well within the bounds of academic norms (ww, 1:454ff.).

9 Vorländer, *Kant*, 1:76.

10 ww, 2:585–95. For background, see Fischer, *I. Kant*, 1:195ff.; Ludwig Borowski, *Immanuel Kant*, ed F. Gross (Berlin, 1912), 37. For an English translation, see Kant, *Theoretical Philosophy, 1755–1770*, ed. and trans. David Walford (New York, 1992), 67–83 (cited as DW).

11 For background on this prize competition, see Adolf Harnack, *Geschichte der königlich preussischen Akademie der Wissenschaften zu Berlin* (Berlin, 1900), 1:403–9; for the formulation of the prize question, ibid., 404. A German translation was carried by the *Freye Urtheile und Nachrichten* (Hamburg, July 27, 1753), quoted in AA, 17:229: "[E]ine Untersuchung des Systematis des Herrn Pope, welches sich in dem Satze befindet: Alles ist gut." ["An examination of the system of Mr. Pope, contained in the proposition: Everything is good."]

12 Mendelssohn and Lessing, "Pope, ein Metaphysiker!" in Lessing, *Sämtlich Werke*, 23–57. See also Alexander Altmann, *Moses Mendelssohns Frühschriften zur Metaphysik* (Tübingen, 1959), 184–208.

13 Lessing, *Sämtliche Werke*, 3:53.

14 Ibid., 57.

15 "Der Philosoph, welcher auf den Parnass hinaufsteiget, und der Dichter, welcher sich in die Täler der ernsthaften und ruhigen Weisheit hinabbegeben will, treffen einander gleich auf dem halben Wege, wo sie, so zu reden, ihre Kleidung verwechseln, und wieder zurückgehen. Jeder bringt des anderen Gestalt in seine Wohnung mit sich; weiter aber nichts, als die Gestalt. Der Dichter ist ein philosophischer Dichter, und der Weltweise ein poetischer Weltweise geworden. Allein ein philosophischer Dichter ist darum noch kein Philosoph, und ein poetischer Weltweise ist darum noch kein Poet."

16 Cf. ibid., 45f.

17 AA, 17:229–39; *Reflexionen* §§3703–5.

18 Kant's argument is that the best of all possible worlds implies no infinite regress, because, as opposed to the mathematical infinity, it represents a real thing.

19 Vorländer, *Kant*, 1:88; similarly Arnoldt, *Kants Jugend*, 200.

20 See especially Wolfgang Ritzel, *Immanuel Kant. Eine Biographie* (Berlin, 1985), 78f.

21 Especially AA, 2:40f.

22 Kügelgen designates it "as a sort of sermon," in C. W. von Kügelgen, "Kant als Prediger und seine Stellung zur Homiletik," *Kant-Studien* 1 (1897): 202.

23 For the significance of Kant's mother for his development, cf. Reinhold Jachmann, *Immanuel Kant. sein Leben in Darstellungen von Zeitgenossen,* ed. Felix Gross (Berlin, 1912), 170f.; Böhme and Böhme, *Das Andere,* 486f.

Four System Crisis

1 Dieter Henrich, "Kants Denken 1762/3. Über den Ursprung der Unterscheidung analytischer und synthetischer Urteile," in *Studien zu Kants philosophischer Entwicklung,* ed. H. Heimsoeth, D. Henrich, and G. Tonelli (Hildesheim, 1967), 11.

2 Kuno Fischer has already pointed this out in his book *I. Kant,* 1:200f.

3 English translations of all of these essays are contained in Kant, *Theoretical Philosophy, 1755–1770,* ed. and trans. David Walford. References to this edition will hereafter appear as DW, following the citation to the German edition (WW). However, for the sake of stylistic and terminological consistency, all translations of Kant in this chapter are original. [*Translator's note*]

4 The title vignette shows an open rococo shell, while the first paragraph, "General Concept of the Nature of Rational Deductions" ["Allgemeiner Begriff von der Natur der Vernunftschlüsse"] has, as its frontispiece, its own symbolic representation: a somewhat bigger ammonite shell, coiling on itself (see the first edition; one is housed in the Houghton Library).

5 "Krise des Systembegriffs von 1762"; Henrich, "Kants Denken," 11.

6 See Rousseau's first discourse, "Discours sur les Sciences et les Arts"; cf. the English translation, *The First and Second Discourses Together with the Replies to Critics and Essay on the Origin of Languages,* ed. Victor Gourevitch (New York, 1986).

7 WW, 2:610; DW 100f.

8 See also Kant, *Critique of Pure Reason,* in general for its intention and its "negative" results, particularly *Kritik der reinen Vernunft* (Riga, 1st ed. [A] 1781, 2d ed. [B] 1787), B, 859/A, 831; *Critique of Pure Reason,* trans. Norman Kemp Smith (New York, 1965), S, 651–2. On editions of the *Critique* and abbreviations used, see chap. 8, n.2.

9 On this, see Rudolf Eucken, "Über Bilder und Gleichnisse bei Kant," in *Beiträge zur Einführung in die Philosophie* (Leipzig, 1906); Ritzel, *I. Kant,* 94f.

10   *Noonautica,* the ship of Reason, sails upon the tide of prejudice between the cliffs of Error and Ignorance safely into the harbor of *Alethopolis,* the city of Truth—in any case on the frontispiece to Samuel Grosser, *Pharus intellectus sive logica electiva* (1697). Reproduced in Werner Schneiders, *Aufklärung und Vorurteilskritik. Studien zur Vorurteilskritik* (Stuttgart–Bad Cannstatt, 1983), 8.

11   The text had an immediate effect. Within that same year, a dissertation appeared in Tübingen, *Observationes ad commentationem M. J. Kantii de uno possibili fundamento demonstrationis existentiae Dei* (1763). But it probably had the greatest effect on Friedrich Heinrich Jacobi, who began to study Spinoza because of it (see Kuno Fischer, *I. Kant,* 1:234).

12   Conversely, the *Only Possible Argument* may have had an effect on the *Inquiry* as well, simply because Kant must have been reading proof sheets of the former while finishing writing the latter. In fact, the construction and formation of the prize text show a high degree of transparency, especially when compared with Mendelssohn's first-prize text, which contains numerous heavy-handed passages.

13   The last two lines (emphasis added) comprise the epigraph. Lucretius, *De rerum natura,* bk. 1, ll. 50–4; the English translation is from the Loeb Classical Library, 2d rev. ed., trans. W. H. D. Rouse, ed. Martin Ferguson Smith (Cambridge, Mass., 1982).

14   Ibid., bk. 1, ll. 54f.

15   Adolf Harnack, *Geschichte der königlich preussischen Akademie der Wissenschaften zu Berlin* (Berlin, 1900), 2:410; AA, 2:492ff.

16   For background on the distribution of prizes, see Harnack, *Geschichte,* 2:410; Moses Mendelssohn, "Über die Evidenz in metaphysischen Wissenschaften" (last paragraph of the introduction), in Mendelssohn, *Gesammelte Schriften. Jubiläums-Ausgabe* (Stuttgart–Bad Cannstatt, 1971 ff.), 2:272.

17   In fact, Kant had already successfully applied for permission from Formey, the secretary of the academy, to revise his treatise, but he never put it to use. See Kant, *Briefwechsel,* 32f.

18   Lucretius, *De rerum natura,* 403f.; Rouse's translation.

19   Unless, of course, one takes the next verse as an allusion: "namque *canes* ut montivagae persaepe ferai/naribus inveniunt intectas fronde quietes" (emphasis added); "For as hounds [*canes*] very often find by their scent the leaf-hidden resting place of the mountain-ranging quarry" (Ibid., 1, ll. 404f.).

20   A summary comparison of both texts and an important evaluation of the lifelong relationship of Kant and Mendelssohn is given by Walter Kinkel, "Moses Mendelssohn und Immanuel Kant," *Kant-Studien* 34 (1929). Also see Sylvain Zac, "Le prix et la mention. Les Preisschriften de Mendelssohn et de Kant," *Revue de Métaphysique et de Morale* 79 (1974). On Mendelssohn's prize text, see the detailed exposition by Alexander Altmann, *Moses Mendelssohns Frühschriften zur Metaphysik* (Tübingen, 1969), chap. 5, 252–391; and Alexander Altmann, *Moses Mendelssohn. A Biographical Study* (London, 1973), 112–30. Hans Jürgen Engfer, *Philosophie als Analysis. Studien zur Entwicklung philosophischer Analysiskonzeptionen unter dem Einfluss mathematischer Methodenmodelle im 17. und frühen 18. Jahrhundert* (Stuttgart–Bad Cannstatt, 1982), 26ff., compares the 1763 competition texts of Kant, Mendelssohn, and Lambert only in those passages where analysis definitions are explicitly discussed. A more thorough treatment would have involved the discussion implied in the texts, which would have required consideration of them in their entirety and in context. The full significance of the Kant-Mendelssohn relationship still requires reworking. It would have to begin with a new evaluation of Mendelssohn, which

will become possible once the complete edition of Mendelssohn's works is finished, along with a reappraisal of Kant's works.

21   In Mendelssohn, compare the third section of "Von der Evidenz in den Anfangsgründen der Mathematik" ["On Evidence in the First Principles of Mathematics"], in *Gesammelte Schriften*, 2:297ff., and Kant, ww, 2:84ff.

22   In Mendelssohn, compare especially the first section of "On Evidence" and Kant, ww, 2:50ff.

23   Kinkel, "Moses Mendelssohn," points this out as well.

24   Moses Mendelssohn, *Gesammelte Schriften*, 2:316ff.; Kant, dw, 771.

25   Mendelssohn defines moral philosophy here as "the science of the constitution of a being with free will, in so far as it has a free will," *Gesammelte Schriften*, 2:322.

26   Harnack, *Geschichte*, 411.

27   For particulars, see Henrich's discussion in his "Kants Denken."

28   It is conceived thus by Hobbes, Spinoza, and, of course, Wolff.

29   This recognition, having been won, is maintained even in the *Critique of Pure Reason* (*Kritik*, b, 756ff./a, 728ff.; *Critique*, s, 586ff.).

30   The word turns up in the letter to Lambert, of December 31, 1765, in Kant, *Briefwechsel*, 41.

31   Kant introduces the designation "ontological" for the proof of God that he attributed to Descartes, but which is actually Anselm's.

32   "den erhabensten unter allen"—This passage seems to have been overlooked by Schmalenbach, who otherwise regards the connection of sublimity and religion as a central point.

33   Cf. ww, 2:643, 710, 714, 720, 727.

34   The reformulation of the cosmogonic hypothesis occurs in Kant's two "postulates of energy preservation" [*Energieerhaltungssätzen*], that (1) if A exists, then a $-A$ must exist, with the result $= 0$ (ww, 2:808f.), and (2) the sum of all existing reality $= 0$ (ww, 2:811). This corresponds exactly to the condition of flux, the balancing of positive and negative, in the *Universal Natural History*.

35   "Paradoxical intention" is a term introduced by Paul Watzlawick. It means that whatever is said intends just its opposite.

36   For the background in the history of philosophy, see Louis I. Bredvold, "The Invention of the Ethical Calculus," in *The Seventeenth Century: Studies in the History of English Thought and Literature from Bacon to Pope*, by Richard Foster Jones and others writing in his honor (Stanford, 1951), 165–80. He comes to the conclusion, admittedly sounding somewhat poor, especially after Kant, that "this brief survey of their [ethical and political] history and application may suggest some tentative reservations as to their theoretical and practical soundness" (ibid., 180). For an argument against the attempt to introduce the calculus of proportional relations into moral philosophy, see David Hume, *An Enquiry Concerning the Principles of Morals*, ed. J. B. Schneewind (Indianapolis, Hackett, 1983), 84f.

37   In general, Kant's examples illustrating the significance of introducing negative magnitudes into philosophy merit some attention. Applied to happiness, for example, "the calculation [Maupertius]," produces, is "a negative sum, and I cannot concur with it in this" (ww, 2:794). Concur, however, is what he subsequently does, in the *Critique of Judgment*, paraphrasing Maupertius's calculation word for word in the footnote to §83 ("the value of life . . . sinks below zero"), although this is merely to argue for the separation of noumena and phenomena. That Kant tries to get a grip on the major

questions with a "calculation" (*Kalkül*) of negative magnitudes probably relates to what he is looking for here, something that Hegel later developed further into the dialectic: "In such a way, things that are regarded as the one being the negative of the other are both positive when regarded for themselves" (Kant, ww, 2:789). The question whether the sum of happiness balances the one of unhappiness, or to which account the deficit would go, was a popular Enlightenment topic. It is connected with the economy of secularization. Kant could also find a discussion of it in Rousseau's *Discours sur l'inégalité* (in n. i of the first part). As Kurt Weigand points out, in a footnote in Rousseau, *Schriften zur Kulturkritik*, ed. K. Weigand (Hamburg, 1978), 339, n. 9, it was a topic widely discussed at the Berlin Academy.

38 Kant understands this term more keenly than preceding philosophers. Already here (ww, 2:805), it is given an epistemological significance.

39 See note 34.

40 M. Mendelssohn, *Gesammelte Schriften*, 5.1:602–16, 657–69.

Five   Observation as Indirect Literary Strategy

1 "We call that kind of knowledge experience which we receive by giving heed to our sensations. . . . The object of our sensation is produced either by nature, without our assistance . . . or we have to prepare it ourselves. In the first case, the experience is called a perception (*observatio*) . . . , whether it simply offers itself on its own, crossing the eye of anyone having as much attentiveness as is commonly necessary for all human functions; or whether it requires a high degree of attentiveness, such as can be acquired through practice, or awakened by knowledge already gained, or enhanced by the use of future instruments. We name the former a common perception or apprehension [*Wahrnehmung*], the latter an artificial perception or observation (*observatio vulgaris, artificialis*). In the second case, the experience is called an experiment [*Versuch*] (*experimentum*)." These words originate from the pen of the Wolff disciple and coeditor Andreas Böhm, "Erfahrung," in *Deutsche Encyclopädie oder Allgemeines Real-Wörterbuch*, ed. Gesellschaft Gelehrten (Frankfurt, 1782), vol. 8; on this, see Willi Goetschel, Catriona McLeod, and Emery Snyder, "The *Deutsche Encyclopädie* and Encyclopedism in Eighteenth-Century Germany," in *The Encyclopédie and the Age of Revolution*, ed. Clorinda Donato and Robert Maniquis (Boston, 1992); and Goetschel, McLeod, and Snyder, "The *Deutsche Encyclopädie*," in *Notable Encyclopedias of the Late Eighteenth Century: Twelve Successors of the Encyclopédie*, ed. Frank Kafker (Oxford, 1994).

2 Evidence of this is Johann Georg Hamann's letter of February 1, 1764 (AA, 2:482), where he writes, "At this very moment I am working on Kant's *Observations on the Feeling*, which I would like to see somewhat extensively and preferentially reviewed." The review appeared on April 30; on the date of publication, see also Vorländer, *Kant*, 1:158.

3 Citations in this chapter are to ww; G refers to Kant, *Observations on the Feeling of the Beautiful and the Sublime*, trans. and intro. John T. Goldthwait (Berkeley, 1960). Goldthwait's translations have been modified here for the sake of stylistic and terminological consistency. [*Translator's note*]

4 "Es wäre eine recht artige Schrift, wenn die Worte schön und erhaben auf dem Titel gar nicht stünden und im Büchlein selbst seltner vorkämen. Es ist voll allerliebster Bemerkungen über die Menschen, und man sieht seine Grundsätze schon keimen." Goethe to Schiller, February 18, 1795, in *Briefwechsel zwischen Schiller und Goethe*, ed. Franz Muncker (Stuttgart, n.d.), 1:70.

5   "Was Sie von der kleinen Schrift Kants schreiben, erinnere ich mich bei Lesung derselben auch empfunden zu haben. Die Ausführung ist bloss anthropologisch, und über die letzten Gründe des Schönen lernt man darin nichts. Aber als Physik und Naturgeschichte des Erhabenen und Schönen enthält es manchen fruchtbaren Stoff. Für die ernsthafte Materie schien mir der Stil etwas zu spielend und blumenreich; ein sonderbarer Fehler an einem Kant, der aber wieder sehr begreiflich ist." Schiller to Goethe, February 19, 1795, in ibid., 71.

6   On this, see James T. Boulton's introduction to Edmund Burke's *A Philosophical Enquiry into the Origin of our Ideas of the Sublime and Beautiful* (Notre Dame, 1968), cxxff. Just as with the *Universal Natural History and Theory of the Heavens,* where a review became the basis for writing a book (in the same way Jean-Paul's Schulmeisterlein Wutz would write the books corresponding to the titles he found in the bookfair catalogues but could not afford to buy), this time it may have been Moses Mendelssohn's 1758 review of Burke's theory that provided the impetus. Although Kant differs in many cases from Burke in terms of content, Boulton determines in reference to Kant, "The method is Burkean" (ibid., cxxv).

7   AA, 20:44.

8   "Der Verfasser . . . ist ein grosser Beobachter der Natur. Er häuft Beobachtungen auf Beobachtungen, die alle eben so gründlich als scharfsinnig sind; allein so oft es darauf ankommt, diese Beobachtungen aus der Natur unserer Seele zu erklären, so zeigt sich seine Schwäche." Mendelssohn, *Gesammelte Schriften,* 1:400. See the discussion itself in Mendelssohn's review, ibid., 3:216–236, where the first paragraph already introduces the word "observation" redundantly. Mendelssohn's discussion also contains the encouragement to pursue further the themes just raised by Burke, "which could give a systematic thinker abundant opportunity for contemplation" (ibid., 3:228). Still in the *Rhapsodie,* he repeats, "With this essay, I wish much more to have encouraged a philosophical thinker to pursue this worthy investigation" (ibid., 1:401). Mendelssohn may have had Lessing in mind, but pursuing such an investigation is precisely what Kant does, and he differs in this from Burke and Mendelssohn (who still proceed rhapsodically) by introducing a philosophically motivated organization to the material. Concerning Mendelssohn and Lessing, cf. Eva Engel's discussion of Mendelssohn's review of Burke, in Mendelssohn, *Gesammelte Schriften,* 3:lxxiii–lxxxiii.

9   On this, see especially Georg Gurwitsch, "Kant und Fichte als Rousseau-Interpreten," *Kant-Studien* 27 (1922); Ernst Cassirer, "Kant and Rousseau," in *Rousseau, Kant, Goethe* (Princeton, 1970).

10   On Francis Hutcheson, see Wolfgang Leidhold's detailed introduction to his translation of Hutcheson's *Über den Ursprung unserer Ideen von Schönheit und Tugend* (Hamburg, 1986). A good discussion of Hutcheson is provided by Jürgen Sprute, "Der Begriff des Moral Sense bei Shaftesbury und Hutcheson," *Kant-Studien* 71 (1980), 221–37. The first to point out Hutcheson's significance for Kant's philosophy was Dieter Henrich, "Hutcheson und Kant," *Kant Studien* 49 (1957/58); see also D. Henrich, "Der Begriff der sittlichen Einsicht und Kants Faktum der Vernunft," in *Kant. Zur Deutung seiner Theorie von Erkennen und Handeln,* ed. G. Prauss (Cologne, 1973). Also cf. Joseph Schmucker, *Die Ursprünge der Ethik Kants in seinen vorkritischen Schriften und Reflektionen,* vol. 23 of *Monographien zur philosophischen Forschung* (Meisenheim am Glan, 1961), 87ff., 125ff.

11   Cassirer, "Kant and Rousseau," 32.

12   On the fixing of dates, see G. Lehmann (AA, 20:472f.), who assumes the years to be 1764 to 1765, contrary to Adickes (and Schubert).

13 Cf. Schmucker, *Ursprünge*, who claims that Rousseau's influence on Kant first reached a decisive stage *after* the *Observations* were written. His claim is directed against Foerster, Paul Menzer, "Der Entwicklungsgang der Kantischen Ethik in den Jahren 1760 bis 1785," *Kant Studien* 2 (1898) and 3 (1899), and against Paul Arthur Schilpp, *Kant's Pre-Critical Ethics* (Evanston, 1960). But his argument fails to convince. Schmucker is no doubt to be sided with in maintaining, contrary to Menzer, Schilpp, and others, that the discursive encounter with Rousseau was not concluded with the *Observations*. But his emphasis is nonetheless misleading when he sees the Rousseau reception beginning first with the *Bemerkungen*, and separates these completely from the *Observations*. This is already contradicted by the fact that Kant wrote his remarks in his personal copy of the *Observations*, and gave up this practice soon afterward, so that it seems more sensible here to view the *Observations* and the *Bemerkungen* as a unit. All investigations prior to Schmucker are obviously outdated, simply because Kant's remarks were not published in their entirety until 1942, which first made possible a scientific interpretation (Kant, AA, vol. 20). So to summarize, in light of Kant's legendary reading of *Emile*, which made him skip his regular afternoon walk, it can be said that Kant was in all likelihood familiar with Rousseau by 1762 (consider what was said in chap. 4 about *False Subtlety*). Given the general sensation Rousseau's first discourse caused on its publication in 1750 and the prolonged debates by Mendelssohn and others about the first and second discourses, Kant's involvement with Rousseau must have started early on. His reading of *Emile* presents an already advanced stage in Kant's Rousseau reception. Kant's involvement was not the sort that could be concluded just one or two years later, if the currents of Rousseau run as deep in Kant's thought as he himself repeatedly acknowledged. Remarkably, Schmucker seems to have overlooked Cassirer's, "Kant and Rousseau," a short essay that nonetheless clarifies many of these points. See also Henrich, "Hutcheson und Kant," 65: "Considered in the framework of the Latin remarks, one sees that the work as it was published is indeed a popular piece, following Rousseau, behind which the systematic thinker conceals himself, not completely in the clear about his new principle." A view critical of Schmucker comes from H.-J. Schings, *Melancholie und Aufklärung. Melancholiker und ihre Kritiker in Erfahrungsseelenkunde und Literatur des 18. Jahrhunderts* (Stuttgart, 1977), 319, n. 60: "Schmucker would like to situate Rousseau's great effect as coming only after the *Observations*, and maintains rather Francis Hutcheson's influence for these. Kant's thought-provoking revalorization of the melancholy disposition is not given further consideration in any of this, even though it links up quite nicely later on with his evaluation of Rousseau." (On melancholy, see the next chapter.) On Kant's reading of Rousseau, see the meticulous work by Jean Ferrari, *Les sources françaises de la philosophie de Kant* (Paris, 1979).

14 A detailed overview of Kant's Rousseau reception is given by Ferrari, *Les sources*, who anyway sets an earlier beginning to it than Schmucker, whom he seems, moreover, not to know.

15 Cf. the discussion below of the fragment from the *Bemerkungen* concerning the zetetic method.

16 Johann Gottfried Herder, "Viertes Wäldchen," in *Sämtliche Werke*, ed. B. Suphan (Berlin, 1877–1913), 4:176.

17 Jean-Jacques Rousseau, *Emile ou de l'éducation* (Paris, 1964), 1: "La première de toutes les utilités, qui est l'art de former les hommes, est encore oubliée." See Schmucker, *Ursprünge*, 138.

18 Johann Georg Hamann, *Sämtliche Werke*, ed. J. Nadler (Vienna, 1949–57), 4:292.

19   Two months previously, Hamann had been the impetus for Kant's *Essay on the Sicknesses of the Head,* which was preceded by a short "*Raisonnement.*" On these points, see the next chapter.

20   See especially ww, 2:857f.

21   He later provides a contrasting image: "for example, books that stand neatly arrayed in long rows in bookcases, and an empty head that looks at them and takes delight" (ww, 2:846; G, 71).

22   Schmucker, *Ursprünge,* 123.

23   The comparison that follows shortly, pairing *galimatias* (nonsense) with splendor as a relation analogous to the relation of whim or capriciousness to the serious-sublime, does nothing to alter this disdain, for splendor and the serious-sublime are not equivalent here. Instead, they are supposed to illustrate how much of a stretch this opposition is to begin with. In order to show this unmistakably, Kant speaks here of the serious-sublime. This would seem to make splendor into a sublime that lacks seriousness and thus its *differentia specifica* as well, rendering it practically absurd. In the fourth section, Kant positions splendor between nobility and false glitter, and names the Romans as an example (ww, 2:883; G, 114).

24   On style, see Vorländer, *Kant,* 1:158ff, whose opinion of the text as a whole is that it is "old-fashioned" [*zopfig*]: "This text, along with Kant's literary-aesthetic taste in general, quite simply still belongs to the older tendencies of its time" (ibid., 161).

25   Hamann, *Sämtliche Werke,* 4:289; Johann Gottfried Herder, "Über die neuere Deutsche Litteratur. Fragmente," in Herder, *Sämtliche Werke,* 2:103.

26   Herder, "Kritische Wälder. Oder Betrachtungen, die Wissenschaft und Kunst des Schönen betreffend, nach Massgabe neurer Schriften" (1769), in Herder, *Sämtliche Werke,* 3:281.

27   These are also brought into relation with the erotic. The passage reads: "[Of someone who] is bored with beautiful music [it can be presumed with some certainty] that the beauties of written style and the delicate enchantments [*feine Bezauberungen*] of love will have little power over him" (ww, 2:846; G, 71).

28   Thus the irony seems to have utterly eluded Schmucker in *Ursprünge* and Menzer in "Der Entwicklungsgang." The reason this is remarkable is that, in view of the weight placed upon principles earlier in the second section (ww, 2:836, 837, 839; G, 60–3), and particularly in view of the concluding sentence, the entire concluding passage cannot be understood other than ironically.

29   Schilpp, *Kant's Pre-Critical Ethics,* 60f., claims that Kant has no use for the concept *moral sense.*

30   We find this same ironic turn of phrase concerning principles in Burke: "It is, I own, not uncommon to be wrong in theory and right in practice; and we are happy that it is so. Men often act right from their feelings, who afterwards reason but ill on them from principle; but as it is impossible to prevent an attempt at such reasoning, and equally impossible to prevent its having some influence on our practice, surely it is worth some pains to have it just, and founded on the basis of sure experience." in Burke, *Philosophical Enquiry,* 53.

31   This metaphor is taken up again later, ww, 2:857f; G, 84f.

32   Especially, "that all the other merits of a woman [*Frauenzimmer*] *should* unite solely to enhance the character of the beautiful" (ww, 2:850; G, 77, emphasis added), and "the fair sex has just as much understanding as the male, but it is a beautiful understanding, whereas ours *should* be a deep understanding, an expression that signifies identity with the sublime" (ww, 2:851; G, 78, emphasis on *should* added).

33 As if any human being generally—not to speak of one with an even more developed sense of individuality—could be reduced to such monocausality, such as the concept of reason, for example. This displays astonishing anthropological naïveté and ultimately a shockingly barbaric sort of bluntness. In light of the theme, one is forced to wonder: how is such carelessness, in light of the complexity of Kant's methodological deliberations, still possible at all?

34 Kant, *Briefwechsel*, 108f, 412, 557. This work appeared between 1778 and 1781, anonymously and in three volumes, and in excerpts in 1782. The author was C. F. Germershausen (see the note to letter 104, *Briefwechsel*, 834).

35 For Mendelssohn, rhetoric and eroticism are geneologically related: "Divine eloquence . . . transforms all guiding impulses [*Triebfedern*] into penetrating arrows, and dips them into the enchanting nectar that the goddess Suada received, if I may express myself poetically, from her mother, Venus." In Mendelssohn, *Gesammelte Schriften*, 1:422. Mendelssohn invented this himself, of course: only one daughter of Venus has been "authenticated," and she is Harmonia.

36 "Indeed so little does poetry depend for its effect on the power of raising sensible images, that I am convinced it would lose a very considerable part of its energy, if this were the necessary result of all description. Because that union of affecting words which is the most powerful of all poetical instruments, would frequently lose its force along with its propriety and consistency, if the sensible images were always excited" (Burke, *Philosophical Enquiry*, 170).

37 "Ermahnung an die Teutsche, ihren Verstand und sprache besser zu üben," in Gottfried Wilhelm Leibniz, *Politische Schriften*, ed. H. H. Holz (Frankfurt, 1966–67), 2:73; "Unvorgreifliche Gedanken, betreffend die Ausübung und Verbesserung der teutschen Sprache," in Leibniz, *Hauptschriften zur Grundlegung der Philosophie*, ed. E. Cassirer (Hamburg, 1966), 2:519.

38 See Gotthold Ephraim Lessing, *Laokoon oder die Grenzen der Malerei und Poesie* (1766), in *Werke*, ed. Otto Mann (Munich, 1972), vol. 2. Lessing mainly just draws the consequences of the observations made by Burke. See also Boulton's introduction to Burke, *Philosophical Enquiry*, 120ff. For Lessing, cf. William Guild Howard, "Burke among the forerunners of Lessing," *PMLA* 22 (1907): 608–32, who emphasizes Mendelssohn's role in the reception and discussion of Burke for Lessing.

39 Lehmann's assumption that all of the *Bemerkungen* stem from 1764 and 1765 (AA, 20:472) appears to be supported by the conjecture that Kant used his personal copy primarily as a notebook, and that therefore the period of its usefulness would be subject to time constraints.

40 Kant, *Bemerkungen in den "Beobachtungen über das Gefühl des Schönen und Erhabenen,"* vol. 3 of *Kant-Forschungen*, ed. Marie Rischmüller (Hamburg, 1991).

41 Rischmüller correctly points out that Kant was no aphorist (ibid., xxi). Cf. also Hermann Cohen's remarks on the aphorism's immodest style, in his "Ethik des reinen Willens," in *Werke*, ed. Helmut Holzhey (Hildesheim: 1981), 7:535.

42 Mendelssohn, *Gesammelte Schriften*, 2:81–109.

43 Ibid., 2:83.

44 Ibid., 2:93.

45 Ibid., 5.1:366–89.

46 Ibid., 5.1:366.

47 Ibid., 5.1:369.

48 See also what Cassirer writes on Rousseau and Newton in "Kant and Rousseau," 18ff.

49 Cassirer, ibid., 18, writes that Rousseau must have appeared to Kant as "a philosophical liberator."

50 Ibid., 6.

51 See also Kant, AA, 20:181, and what was said above about §6 of the preface of Kant's first text. The nightgown marks the point of intersection between the philosopher's other-worldly dignity and his worldly inclinations toward eroticism.

52 Even in his letters, he avoids any personal expressions. See Joachim Kopper's remarks in the introduction to Kant, *Briefwechsel,* 49ff., and my review of this edition in *Lessing Yearbook* 20 (1988): 322–4.

53 Kant emphasizes the difference between error and ignorance pragmatically: "Everything considered, error is never more useful than the truth, but this is often so with ignorance" ["Der Irrthum ist niemals alles ineinander gerechnet nützlicher als die Wahrheit aber die Unwissenheit ist es oft"] (AA, 20:114).

54 Certainly, at the latest by the time of his next book, the *Dreams of a Spirit-Seer,* Kant makes the transition to satire. It may also be that Kant's critical stance toward satire is due in part to his feeling drawn to it, even though for other reasons he believes himself compelled to resist it. As Samuel Gottlieb Wald said in his "Memorial Speech," "He loved satire in general and enjoyed reading satirical writings. He was intimately familiar with Hudibras, Don Quixote and Lichtenberg's explanation of Hogarth's copper-engravings." Kraus, to whom Wald, among others, gave his speech for editing, noted this about the term *satire* in the margin: "Wit and even caustic wit. One of Kant's predominant person-ality traits was good-naturedness, and for this reason he was not fond of satire as such. But he loved wit, *well-aimed* and *true,* and that is not the same as what people mean by satire, and he was also very fond of Swift." Speech and marginalia reprinted in Kopper and Malter, eds., *I. Kant zu Ehren,* 60, 73.

55 Among the numerous laments about the explosion of book production in the latter half of the eighteenth century, at least one is worth noting here: the remark in the *Deutsche Encyclopädie* (under the keyword "Bücherkenntnis") that even knowing simply the books' titles is hardly possible anymore.

56 See Kant, AA, 20:175: "The ultimate purpose is to find the destiny of man." ["Der letzte Zweck ist die Bestimmung des Menschen zu finden."] See also ibid., 41, 45.

57 Cf. ibid., 190, lines 16ff., 181, where themes from the next book are already introduced.

58 "Mich dünkt, dass man bisher in Frankreich die philosophische und in Deutschland die historische Sittenlehre zu gering geachtet. Daher fehlet es dem tiefsinnigen System eines Wolfs an pragmatischer Anwendung auf die Geschichte, und den feinen Beobachtungen eines Montesquieu an allgemeinen systematischen Grundsätzen. Ein Werk, das den gründlichen Tiefsinn eines Wolfs mit dem scharfsinnigen Beobachtungsgeist eines Mon-tesquieu verbände, wäre meines Erachtens das vollkommenste Meisterstück der men-schlichen Vernunft; vielleicht ein Ideal, das die menschliche Kräfte übersteigt, dem sich aber die grössten Genies unsrer Zeit, so viel als möglich nähern suchen sollten." Men-delssohn, *Gesammelte Schriften,* 5.1:506.

Six   Wit as a Formal Principle

1 Hamann, *Sämtliche Werke,* 4:269.

2 The opening sentence of an excerpt provided by Borowski, in *I. Kant,* 104, differs from this one: "In the opinion of one local scholar, in regard to the above report on our inspired Faunus, it may well be in the eyes of those who . . . " ["Nach dem Urtheil eines hiesigen

Gelehrten, möchte in obiger Nachricht von unserm begeisterten Faunus, für Augen, welche . . . "]. It may well be that the format of the *Königsbergische Gelehrte und Politische Zeitung* affected the wording of Kant's introduction.

3 All translations of Kant in this chapter are original. [*Translator's note*]

4 See Rohner, *Der deutsche Essay.*

5 On *Experimentalphilosophie,* see the articles by G. Frey, "Experiment," and by R. Kuhlen and U. Schneider, "Experimentalphilosophie," in *Historisches Wörterbuch der Philosophie,* ed. J. Ritter, 2:867ff., 870ff. On the concept of *experimentelle Philosophie,* see Gernot Böhme, Wolfgang van den Daele, and Wolgang Krohn, *Experimentelle Philosophie* (Frankfurt, 1977).

6 Page references in this chapter, unless otherwise specified, are to ww, vol. 2.

7 "Tout est bien sortant des mains de l'Auteur des choses, tout dégénère entre les mains de l'homme . . . il bouleverse tout, il défigure tout, il aime la difformité, les monstres" [Everything is good as it leaves the hands of the Creator of the world, everything degenerates in the hands of man . . . he reverses everything, he disfigures everything, he loves deformity, monsters].

8 A half-year later, Voltaire's *Dictionnaire philosophique* appeared, whose entry *"folie"* comes to the same conclusion: "Ils [*docteurs*] se croiront sages, et ils seront aussi fous que lui [*le fou*] ["They think they are wise men, but are as crazy as the fool"] (Paris, 1964), 198.

9 Kant is viewed as a "hair-splitter" (*logodaedalos*) by Jean-Luc Nancy, in *Le discours de la syncope,* vol. 1, *Logodaedalos* (Paris, 1976). To mistake Kant's systematics for a system belongs to the *topoi* of uncritical, but still popular, Kant interpretations.

10 This classification approaches the later system of the three critiques: (1) the *Critique of Pure Reason* as the *catharcticon* of concepts of experience, (2) the *Critique of Practical Reason* as the *catharcticon* of madness, and (3) the *Critique of Judgment* as that of insanity.

11 To pursue such interconnections would be the task of a biography such as Ritzel demands, albeit without ultimately satisfying this demand himself (see my review of Ritzel's *Immanuel Kant: A Biography,* in *Lessing Yearbook* 19 (1987). Their relevance to the formulation of philosophy should not be underestimated.

12 On Montaigne, see M. A. Screech, *Montaigne and Melancholy: The Wisdom of the Essays* (London, 1983).

13 On Kant's more reflective view of melancholy, see also Wolf Lepenies, *Melancholie und Gesellschaft* (Frankfurt, 1981), 101–14.

14 G. W. F. Hegel, *Grundlinien der Philosophie des Rechts* (Hamburg, 1955), 17.

15 Schings, *Melancholie und Aufklärung,* 53ff. Kant's reorientation of the traditional concept of melancholy is overlooked by H.-U. Lessing, "Melancholie," in *Historisches Wörterbuch,* 5:1041, who takes only the *Observations* into account.

16 Raymond Klibansky, Erwin Panofsky, and Fritz Saxl, *Saturn and Melancholy: Studies in the History of Natural Philosophy, Religion, and Art* (London, 1964), 122.

17 See Kant's *The Conflict of the Faculties [Streit der Fakultäten],* whose third part is an article that appeared simultaneously in a medical journal (*Journal der practischen Arzneykunde und Wundarzneykunst*). See Kant, "Anthropologie," ww, 12:628ff. Also Kant, *The Conflict of the Faculties,* intro. Mary J. Gregor, trans. Mary J. Gregor and Robert E. Anchor (New York, 1979). See also Hans Vaihinger, "Kant als Melancholiker," *Kant-Studien* 2 (1898); Vorländer, *Kant,* 1:159; Schilpp, *Kant's Pre-Critical Ethics;* and Odo Marquard's article, "Anthropologie," in *Historisches Wörterbuch,* 1:365.

18 See Hamann, *Sämtliche Werke:* "This man's transfiguration is said to be the fault of a

sickness that befell him 7 years ago and that consisted of an indigestion or stomach-spasm with haemmorhages." With this, the circle of the *Versuch* is completed, which took this human spectacle as its starting point, and now returns to it at the end, albeit only hintingly, in order to conclude with a "medical" outlook.

19   The passage by Swift is in "A Letter of Advice to a Young Poet; together with a Proposal for the Encouragement of Poetry in this Kingdom," in *The Prose Works of Jonathan Swift,* ed. T. Scott 11:107f.

Seven   Double Satire and Double Irony

1   Kant, *Briefwechsel,* 50.

2   Liliane Weissberg, "*Catarcticon* und der schöne Wahn. Kants *Träume eines Geistersehers, erläutert durch die Träume der Metaphysik,*" *Poetica* 18 (1986): 110: "Kant is fascinated by literature, but the elegant garb conceals dubious contents. Literature turns out to be a moral question for philosophy. Philosophy and literature, Kant and Swedenborg, have to exclude one another mutually." On clothing metaphors in general, see also Nancy, *Le discours de la syncope.*

3   Reprinted in Kant, *Träume eines Geistersehers, erläutert durch die Träume der Metaphysik,* ed. Rudolf Malter (Stuttgart, 1976), 120.

4   "Das Ganze der Schrift dörfte nicht gnug Einheit, und ein Theil nicht gnug Beziehung auf den andern haben. Der Verfasser trägt die Wahrheiten von beiden Seiten vor, und sagt wie jener Römer: einer sag nein! der andere: ja! ihr Römer, wem glaubt ihr? Indessen schärft es die Aufmerksamkeit desto mehr, und man sieht allenthalben, dass der Verf. den Genius der Philosophie zu seinem Freunde habe, als Sokrates sich mit seinem Dämon auch in heiligen Träumen besprach" ibid., 123f.

5   Ibid., 118.

6   Friedrich Ueberweg, *Grundriss der Geschichte der Philosophie* (Berlin, 1924), 3:510.

7   Kuno Fischer, *I. Kant,* 276.

8   Cassirer, *Kants Leben und Lehre,* 81.

9   Schilpp correctly designates the text as an essay, albeit without delving any further into the term, in *Kant's Pre-Critical Ethics,* 79, 86.

10   Keith Ward, *The Development of Kant's View of Ethics* (Oxford, 1972), 34.

11   Julius Ebbinghaus, "Kant und Swedenborg," in *Gesammelte Aufsätze, Vorträge, Reden* (Hildesheim, 1968), 60.

12   Herman-J. de Vleeschauwer, *The Development of Kantian Thought* (London, 1962), 41f. The question of whether Hume or Rousseau stands behind the "scepticism" in the *Dreams* (as Fischer, Vleeschauwer, and others have agreed) cannot be decided conclusively. Traces of a Hume reception in Kant can be found beginning early on. On the other hand, the celebrated awakening of Kant from his dogmatic slumber probably did not occur before 1768 or 1769, the year that gave him "great light" [*Reflexion* §5037; AA, 18:69]; see the chapter on "Manifeste und apokryphe Hume-Rezeption bei Kant," in Günter Gawlick and Lothar Kreimendahl, *Hume in der deutschen Aufklärung* (Stuttgart–Bad Cannstatt, 1987), 174–98. Rousseau's profound significance for the *Dreams* is confirmed in some of its particulars by Schmucker in *Ursprünge,* 154ff.

13   "Like the dreams of a sick man, empty semblances are fashioned" (DW, 449).

14   At first glance, the *Dreams* presents itself (in the version published by Johann Jacob Kanter, Königsberg 1766; see Kant, AA, 2:500) as a literary work even on the title page. The title vignette shows "Genius, sitting naked, with a garland in the left hand, and a lyre

in the right." From the viewer's perspective, he is turned to the right, and proffers the garland with an extended arm, in order to offer it possibly to the author, or to the winner of a poetical contest. The opening of the book, it can be speculated, would let that winner appear.

15 All further page references in this chapter, unless otherwise noted, are first to ww, vol. 2; then to DW. Passages of the English translation have been modified or retranslated for the sake of terminological and stylistic consistency. [*Translator's note*]

16 Individual motifs are discussed by H. Ernst Fischer, *Kants Stil in der Kritik der reinen Vernunft*, Kant-Studien Ergänzungsheft 5 (Berlin, 1907), 286ff.; Ernst Benz, *Swedenborg in Deutschland* (Frankfurt, 1947), 266ff.; C. D. Broad, "Immanuel Kant and Physical Research," in *Religion, Philosophy, and Physical Research* (London, 1953), 125ff.; and Böhme and Böhme, *Das Andere*, 260. Schmucker's talk of the "hardly balanced or rounded character of the treatise," and its being merely an "occasional text" [*Gelegen-heitsschrift*] (Schmucker, *Ursprünge*, 155f.), does not hold up under close analysis. It is remarkable that the hermeneutic circle drawn around the *Dreams* by Kant's preface has until now been overlooked. That Kant returns to one or another of the reasons he gives during the preface in the course of the *Dreams* does not constitute an argument for the text being merely the whim of a moment. This is because the preface sets a satirical tone for everything that follows. So, from the outset, every claim to interpretive justification on the part of the reader is preempted.

17 As someone deeply impressed by Kant, Adolf Freiherr von Knigge remarks in his essay, *Über den Umgang mit Menschen*, in the section entitled, "On Mystical Deceivers, Spirit-Seers, Gold-Makers": "The more enlightened the times become, and the more assidu-ously we strive to get to the ultimate basis of the truth, the clearer it becomes to us that we will not find this ultimate basis here on earth, and so we find our way that much more easily onto the path we used to despise, as long as there were new discoveries to be made along the healthy path of theories. I believe that this is an unforced explanation of the phenomenon that seems so marvelous to so many, and that even in times of the greatest enlightenment can elicit blind faith in what would otherwise be considered fairy-tales" (Knigge, *Über den Umgang*, 386f.).

18 Letter to Boxel of September 1674, in Baruch de Spinoza, *Briefwechsel*, ed. Carl Gebhardt (Hambrug, 1977), 212f.

19 Letter to Boxel of October 1674 (ibid., 221).

20 Ibid., 222.

21 Fischer, *Kant*, 276.

22 The reader is directly addressed, or referred to on ww, 2:924, 925ff; DW, 307ff. The opponents/interlocutors are addressed for extended periods with "you" ["*ihr*"], and over twenty-four times (ww, 2:941–83; DW, 305–59) overall.

23 Voltaire had just recently made light of this idea in his *Dictionnaire philosophique*: "[O]n ne sait pas précisément où les anges se tiennent, si c'est dans l'air, dans le vide, dans les planètes: Dieu n'a pas voulu que nous en fussions instruits" ["It is not known where precisely the angels dwell, whether in the air, in the void, or in the planets: God did not want us to be informed about this"] (Voltaire, "Ange," *Dictionnaire philosophique*, 41).

24 "Ein Fragment der geheimen Philosophie"—Indeed, part of the very point of this heading is that it is not entirely clear to which of the fragments—the framework, or what is framed—this heading applies. It applies to both—but to the *Versuch* itself only *cum grano salis*.

25 Cf. Schilpp, *Kant's Pre-Critical Ethics*, 84: "He is directly on the road to the Dissertation of

1770 and to its analysis of the 'form and principles of the intelligible world' in which he places the processes of moral concepts and judgments. It is in these tendencies towards the formal as method and process that the real significance of the passages is to be found"; and Schmucker, *Ursprünge*, 168: "The decisive thing here is that, with the law of a general will, the principle of formalism is made statutory for the first time. With this, a completely new starting point is gained for solving the question of the supreme principle of obligation, in the sense of a genuine formal principle of what *ought* to be done."

26 By defining dreams as a sleeper's thoughts that are remembered upon awakening, Kant anticipates what Freud designated as "manifest dreams."

27 "Guter Herr, auf den Himmel mögt ihr euch wohl verstehen, hier aber auf der Erde seid ihr ein Narr."—Kant stresses the whole sentence. On this point, compare Hans Blumenberg's laconic comment: "Not an admonition, but rather a compromise as to the separation of realms of competence" (Blumenberg, *Das Lachen der Thrakerin*, 109).

28 Cf. Montaigne's ironic remark, that Aristotle is "le Dieu de la science scholastique"— Montaigne, "Apologie de Raimond Sebond," in *Essais*, book 2, chap. 12, *Oeuvres complètes*, ed. A. Thibaudet and M. Rat (Paris, 1962), 521.

29 Plutarch, *De superstitione*, trans. F. C. Babbitt (Cambridge, Mass., 1928), 463.

30 This passage is a quotation from Samuel Butler's *Hudibras*, as Kant himself notes.

31 This has to be opposed, in particular, to the series of treatises that see the argument with Swedenborg as the main topic of discussion, instead of understanding it as a pretext for Kant to deepen his understanding of himself and his approach to philosophizing. The Swedenborg fixation has received an inordinate amount of emphasis. The fact that Kant— in contrast to the position he had previously taken in the letter to Fräulein Knobloch— now calls the author "Schwedenberg" throughout the text, cannot be construed (only) as disparaging. Instead it must be viewed, just like in the biographical sketches he gives, as an effort to elevate individual qualities into universal ones. The polemic runs much less along a personal level than along an argumentative one, where Swedenborg merely represents to Kant an attitude, albeit one to be fought mercilessly. Kant writes "Schwedenberg" in a letter to Moses Mendelssohn on April 8, 1766 (*Briefwechsel*, 51 and 54). This may have become Kant's customary spelling by this time.

32 On the divergences between the *Dreams* and the letter to Fräulein von Knobloch, see Kant, *Briefwechsel*, 926ff., and also Benz, *Swedenborg*, 235ff., Broad, "I. Kant and Psychical Research," 116ff., and Robert E. Butts, *Kant and the Double Government Methodology* (Dordrecht, 1984), 64ff.

33 Vergil, *Aeneid*, bk. 6, l. 266.

34 Vergil, *Bucolica*, bk. 3, l. 63: "and [she] flees towards the willow trees, hoping to be seen before she disappears" (DW, 455).

35 On the connection of honesty and foolishness, see ww, 2:969; DW, 343.

36 See Helmut Holzhey, "Kritik," in *Historisches Wörterbuch der Philosophie*, ed. J. Ritter, 4:1267–82, especially 1267.

37 Carlos Fuentes analysed this function of literature in his seminar, "The Novel of the Time and the Time of the Novel" (Harvard, 1984). Also see the important study by Norbert Elias, *Über die Zeit* (Frankfurt, 1984), which first analysed time as being generated by experience.

38 "Courage, meine Herren, ich sehe Land."—Kant continues to proclaim this in his old age, as an expression of impatience at the end of dinner, when finally coffee was served. With regard to Böhme and Böhme, *Das Andere*, 469, it should be noted that this proclamation— a sort of fixed locution and self-citation of Kant's—is used by him continually, and that it

signals homecoming, or also "all's well that ends well." But it is also worth noting in the margin that this motto-like saying is used by Kant in the context of reading a boring book to its end.

39 Thus Hamann and Mendelssohn, for example, to name only two prominent writers who identified themselves with Socrates. Johann Georg Hamann, "Sokratische Denkwür-digkeiten," in *Sämtliche Werke;* Moses Mendelssohn, *Phädon* 15f., especially the appendix to the 3d ed., 150f. Mendelssohn, who was also Kant's role model as a writer, was celebrated by his contemporaries as a "German Socrates." On this, see Beate Berwin, *Moses Mendelssohn im Urteil seiner Zeitgenossen,* Kant-Studien Ergänzungsheft 49 (1919; reprint, Vaduz, 1978).

40 David Langdon, "On the Meanings of the Conclusion of *Candide,*" *Studies on Voltaire and the Eighteenth Century* 238 (1985): 408.

41 For positive opinions on this, see K. Fischer, *I. Kant,* 290ff., where he brings Kant's *Dreams* into proximity with Hume's skepticism; see also Butts, *Double Government,* 88. For doubtful opinions, see Vleeschauwer, *Development of Kantian Thought,* 38; Giorgio Tonelli, "Kant und die antiken Skeptiker," in *Studien zu Kants philosophischer Entwick-lung,* ed. H. Heimsoeth, D. Henrich, and G. Tonelli (Hildesheim, 1987), 110.

42 Tonelli, "Kant und die antiken Skeptiker," 110.

43 Sextus Empiricus, *Grundriss der Pyrrhonischen Skepsis,* ed. M. Hossenfelder (Frankfurt, 1986): "Skepticism is the art of setting things as they appear against each other in every possible way, from which, because of the equivalence of the contrasting issues and argu-ments, we attain first a sense of detachment, and then afterward a peacefulness of the soul" (94).

44 Butts, *Double Government,* intro. and 88.

45 Weissberg, "*Catarcticon,*" 108, has correctly pointed out that "Kant's problem with meta-physics appears as the lack of an appropriate 'form,' as the search for the right body for his text. His attempt to define the truth, and his own straying attempts to distance and separate himself, are all connected with the problem of representation: setting outside of oneself, making visible, defining. With the question of the representability as a text, Kant nonetheless enters into that realm of experience that he reiterates with Swedenborg's stories: that of literature."

46 Ibid., 103.

47 Letter from Kant to Johann Heinrich Lambert, December 31, 1765, in Kant, *Briefwechsel,* 42f. Also see, especially, Kant, *Briefwechsel,* 41, where Kant claims, after "various over-turnings" ["*so mancherlei Umkippungen*"], to have now found, definitively, the method by which knowledge can be attained.

Eight   Toward the Form of Critique

1 Mikhail Bakhtin, "Discourse in the Novel," in *The Dialogic Imagination,* ed. M. Holquist (Austin, 1981), 301ff. Bakhtin names Kant's friend Hippel as the first German author to use the device of *heteroglossia* in his novels.

2 This complaint is as old as the *Critique,* and it turns out to be anticipated by Kant himself in the preface (A, xviiif; s, 12). The *Critique of Pure Reason* is cited from the first edition of 1781 (A) and the second edition of 1787 (B). Textual passages quoted that appear in both editions will be cited throughout as A/B, respectively. The B/A method of citation that has made its way to the fore seems, even as a technical convention, to opt for a reading that leads to doxographical implications, of which it is worth taking critical notice here.

[Following the A/B citations here will be the corresponding citations from the standard translation (s), by Norman Kemp Smith: Kant, *Critique of Pure Reason* (1929; paperback, New York, 1965). These citations are for the reader's reference, although in most cases, Kant passages quoted in this chapter have been modified or retranslated for the sake of stylistic and terminological consistency and flavor. Although Smith's translation is eminently useful and readable, and has proved itself indispensable to this translator, it is obviously grounded in the need for philosophical accuracy, rather than literary quality. *Translator's note*] Shortly after the publication of *Critique*, Kant writes in a letter to Johann Erich Biester: "This work has indeed been thought over by me for various years, but it was brought to paper in its present form in just a short time, which is also why a few negligent points or hasty formulations, and in part a few obscurities will have been left over" (June 8, 1781, in Kant, *Briefwechsel*, 199). See also the letter to Christian Garve of August 7, 1783, in Kant, *Briefwechsel*, 227.

3 "Die Beweisstruktur der transzendentalen Deduktion der reinen Verstandesbegriffe—eine Diskussion mit Dieter Henrich," in *Probleme der "Kritik der reinen Vernunft*," ed. B. Tuschling (Berlin, 1984), 59. See also Dieter Henrich, *Identität und Objektivität* (Heidelberg, 1976), 9, 14.

4 Hereafter LWB refers to citations from Kant, *Prolegomena to Any Future Metaphysics*, trans. and intro. Lewis White Beck (Indianapolis, 1950).

5 The report begins, "I therefore attempted, first of all . . . " ["Ich versuchte also zuerst . . . "] (WW, 5:119; LWB, 8).

6 On this point, see the preceding passage (WW, 5:120) and *Reflexion*, §5040: "Even if I had all the powers of embellishment, like Hume, I would still have reservations about making use of them. It is true that some readers are frightened off by dryness. But is it not necessary to frighten away a few, so that this material does not end up in the wrong hands?" (AA, 18:70). Further, *Reflexion* §5031, likewise stems from the time of preliminary work on the *Critique:* "I have chosen the scholastic method, in preference to ["the free flight"—crossed-out] the free movement of spirit and wit, even though I did find that, since I wished that every thoughtful mind should take part in this inquiry, the dryness of this method would frighten off precisely the sort of readers who seek some connection to the practical. Even if I were in possession of the greatest amounts of wit and a writer's charms, I would have kept them out of it, for it means very much to me to allow no suspicion to remain that I should want to engage and to persuade the reader, but rather, I expect (from him) either no assent whatever, or only what comes by the strength of the insights." Just how closely connected the *Versuch* is to the act of writing itself is illustrated by the following paragraph of this *Reflexion*, which simply states, "The method, too, came to me through attempts [*Versuche*]" (AA, 18:67). See also *Reflexionen* §§4989, 5015, 5020, 5025, 5028, 5035, 5036, 5084.

7 Vergil, *Georgics*, bk. 4, 168: "They defend the hives against the drones, those indolent creatures" (translation from LWB, 12).

8 A similar passage: A, 831/B, 859; S, 651f.

9 By drawing the connection between the matron Metaphysics and Hecuba, Kant is playfully spinning out Mendelssohn's words: "That poor matron! says Shaftesbury, She has been expelled from the larger world and restricted to the schools and colleges. And lately she has had to move out of that dusty corner, as well" (Mendelssohn, *Literaturbriefe* [1759], quoted by Hans Vaihinger, *Kommentar zu Kants Kritik der reinen Vernunft* [reprint; Aalen, 1970], 1:92f.). Hecuba herself is a sort of composite; to describe her in terms of a concept (matron), Kant uses his literary intuition here: "modo maxima rerum,/ tot

generis natisque potens—nunc trahor exul, inops" (A, ix). The lines come from Ovid's *Metamorphoses:* "But late on the pinnacle of fame, strong in my many sons, my daughters, and my husband, now, exiled, penniless, torn from the tombs of my loved ones" (Ovid, *Metamorphoses,* Loeb Classical Library, 2d ed., trans. F. I. Miller [Cambridge, Mass., 1984], bk. 13, ll. 508–10). Whether Kant had Hamlet's oft-quoted words about Hecuba in mind—or even knew them—can hardly be answered definitively. In view of the widespread but rather late reception of Shakespeare in Germany, it seems doubtful.

10   The sequence of *leitmotifs* determines the construction of the *Critique:* the battlefield is the locus of skepticism and the metaphors of armor serve to expose the faulty epistemic model of knightliness, so at the end of the *Critique* only the critical path remains open.

11   [D]*as Zeitalter der Kritik*—Smith translates *Kritik* here as *criticism,* and adds a note explaining that his translation alternates between the two words. Here, *critique* will be preferred whenever possible, to maintain focus on questions of method and genre, not only intellectual comportment. [*Translator's note*]

12   Hume had already made use of this metaphor, but it is questionable whether Kant got it from him, as claimed by Kathleen Wright, "Kant und der Kanon der Kritik," in *Kanon und Zensur. Archäologie der literarischen Kommunikation,* ed. A. Assmann and J. Assmann (Munich, 1987), 2:332. He probably knew the conclusion of the first book of the *Treatise* in Hamann's translation, and, from discussions with Hamann and Kraus, perhaps the contents as well. But in Hume, this metaphor surfaces in the preface. Admittedly, the metaphor of the tribunal has a tradition. On that, see Hans Blumenberg, "Paradigmen zu einer Metaphorologie," *Archiv für Begriffsgeschichte* 6 (1960): 24: "The medieval-scholastic disputation lives, down to its very details, from the background conception of a truth that prevails through the medium of a procedural order." For reasons of methodological affinity—considering the *Critique*'s epigraph—one might sooner think of Francis Bacon, for whom man is the judge and instigator of the harsh interrogation that nature must undergo, and who calls understanding's jurisdiction "the judicial palace or palace of the mind" (Blumenberg, "Paradigmen," 27). This passage is found in Bacon, *Of the Advancement of Learning* (1605; London and New York, n.d.), 2:85. The "political-metaphorical background" is already important for Bacon (Blumenberg, "Paradigmen," 28). In Kant, what is decisive is the specific reflective context of the transcendental meaning expressed by the tribunal as a model of knowledge.

13   Kant condenses here a number of considerations that he had been struggling to clarify for years. On this, see his remarks on Georg Friedrich Meier's *Logic* (AA, vol. 16; *Reflexionen* §§1688–1715, especially 1694, 1696). Also *Reflexion* §1590: "On the illusion of clearness, by either saying nothing except what is already known in other words, or indeed what can be thought according to the same methods we are accustomed to." Also cf. Kant's differentiated concept of clarity in the *Critique,* B, 414f; S, 372f.

14   The earliest reception can be found in Hamann's letters. Hamann, as one of the first, received the *Critique* when it was still in the form of editor's proofs; see Johann Georg Hamann, *Briefwechsel,* ed. A. Henkel (Wiesbaden, 1959), 4:278ff. He probably did not withhold his commentary *vis-à-vis* Kant in a more diplomatic form. For the first reactions and reviews, see Kant's correspondence from the 1780s. Already shortly before the publication of the *Critique of Pure Reason,* Theodor Gottlieb von Hippel took aim at Kant's style in his novel *Lebensläufe.* The gentle but decided way Kant distances himself from this, expressed in his "Erklärung wegen der v. Hippelschen Autorschaft," although he otherwise proclaims his loyalty to his friend, is based at least partially on the fact that Kant considered himself misunderstood as an author by Hippel (AA, 12:386f.; the "Erklä-

rung" appeared in two newspapers on January 5 and 21, 1797). On this, see Hamilton Beck, *The Elusive "I" in the Novel* (New York, 1987), 18 and 123, n. 14.

15   The virulence of this thought is evident in the redundancy of the word *Versuch,* which runs like a guiding thread through the *Critique,* appearing over forty times. Frequently used in connection with "vain attempts," *Versuch* nonetheless does not have simply negative connotations. Its significance shows itself in the ambivalence of the concept. Thus people who are naive are called the "untried" [*Unversuchten*], and an occasional procedure within the *Critique* itself is called a *Versuch.* Gerd Buchdahl rightly notes "that the Kantian philosophy is less systematic than it may appear at first glance; that it much rather has more of a trying-out and looking-around quality to it than usually is assumed" (Gerd Buchdahl, "Der Begriff der Gesetzmässigkeit in Kants Philosophie der Naturwissenschaft," in *Zur Kantforschung der Gegenwart,* ed. P. Heintel and L. Nagel [Darmstadt, 1981], 93). For an analysis of Montaigne's essay as a model for the concept of essay and experiment in the dialectic of the *Critique of Pure Reason,* cf. Rüdiger Bittner, "Über die Bedeutung der Dialektik Immanuel Kants" (Ph.D. diss., University of Heidelberg, 1970), 78ff.

16   There may even be a legal connotation hidden in the title. On "critique" as a legalistic concept, see the entry from 1782, "Critic (juristische)," in *Deutsche Encyclopädie,* 1:514f.

17   It is remarkable that besides *deduction,* concepts of methodically central significance, such as "constitutive" and "regulative," are also legal terms. In Roman law, *constitutio* means an imperial edict, order, or decree—as opposed to *lex, senatus consultum,* etc.—which is a legal form that rests only upon the will of the emperor. *Regula* can be traced to the *regula generis,* which designate an ensemble of rules that the courts devise from time to time to regulate jurisdiction. The legal context of these terms is pointed out by David Tarbet, "The Fabric of Metaphor in Kant's *Critique of Pure Reason,*" *Journal of the History of Philosophy* 6 (1968): 266, 269. With regard to the legal expression *non liquet,* Voltaire had the following to say: "Mettons à la fin de presque tous les chapitres de métaphysique les deux lettres des juges romains quand ils n'entendaient pas une cause: *N.L., non liquet,* cela n'est pas clair" [Let's add at the end of almost all chapters of metaphysics the two letters the Roman judges would use when they did not understand a case: *N.L., non liquet,* this is not clear] (Voltaire, "Bien (tout est)," in his *Dictionnaire philosophique,* 72).

18   We may better understand how crucial it is for Kant to tie down the *Critique*'s net of justification with legal metaphors if we consider that for Kant, justice is not a state of being, but rather an ideal toward which we must strive. Like Hobbes, Kant speaks of how reason ought to be conducted from the state of nature, as it were, into that of legality (A, 752/B, 780; S, 601f.). On this point in general, see Tarbet, "Fabric of Metaphor" who speaks in this regard of a "legal metaphor."

19   "The apagogic method of proof . . . is like the champion who wants to prove the honor and the indisputable right of his adopted party by threatening to brawl whoever wants to doubt it, even though such braggadocio resolves nothing of the matter, and only shows the respective strength of the opponents" (A, 793/B, 821; S, 628).

20   Kant uses the knightly combat metaphor of the tournament for a literary preview whenever he is about to speak of the skeptical method (A, viiif.; S, 7f., A, 422f./B, 450f.; S, 394f., A, 747ff./B, 775ff.; S, 598f., A, 793f./B, 821f.; S, 627f.).

21   Jurij Striedter, *Die Fragmente des Novalis als "Präfigurationen" seiner Dichtung* (Munich, 1985), 28, calls the antinomy a dialogue, and maintains: "In this, the 'tournament' Kant stages (as a means of the skeptical method) is an immediate predecessor of the literary-philosophical dialogues of Romanticism (as an expression of Romantic irony)."

22 Tarbet, "Fabric of Metaphor," 260; Lewis W. Beck, "Kant's Strategy," *Journal of the History of Ideas* 28 (1967), even speaks of Kant's two-front war, namely, against empiricism and against rationalism. Such a view is nonetheless misleading, if we consider Kant's intentions. It becomes clear, for instance, if we draw Pierre Bayle's concept of reason into comparison. For Bayle, reason is, "a fair where the most diametrically opposed sects procure their arms; subsequently, they fight each other without reserve under the auspices of reason, each one rejecting some evident axioms" (quoted by Eucken, "Bayle und Kant," in *Beiträge*, 91, note).

23 On the particulars of this point, see Hans Saner, *Kant's Political Thought: Its Origins and Development*, trans. E. B. Ashton (Chicago and London, 1973).

24 *Representation* is arguably the translation for both *Darstellung* and *Vorstellung*. In Smith, and in traditional philosophical translations of Kant in general, *representation* is treated as the terminological equivalent for *Vorstellung*, and designates the product of thought, the mental act. This may be in part derived from Kant's use of *repraesentatio* as a Latin equivalent, in parentheses, for *Vorstellung* (cf. A, 320/B, 377; S, 314). An English translation should not necessarily be strictly bound by Kant's understanding of a Latin term (cf. p. 162), however, and the exclusive use of "representation" in this context turns a conventional term in German into unconventional English. For the sake of clarity, *Vorstellung* will be translated here as *mental image/representation*. *Darstellung* will be rendered as *mode of/literary representation* or merely *presentation*. [*Translator's note*]

25 See Kant, *Prolegomena*, in WW, 5:135f.; LWB, 37f. (cf. A, 65): "that sensibility consists, not in this logical distinction of clearness and obscurity, but in the genetic one of the origin of knowledge itself."

26 For a discussion of its progression of ideas, see Henrich, *Identität und Objektivität*; Wilfried Hinsch, *Erfahrung und Selbstbewusstsein* (Hamburg, 1986).

27 This is also the result reached by the meticulous investigation of Hermann Mörchen, *Die Einbildungskraft bei Kant* (Tübingen, 1970), especially 75f.

28 The function of imagination and its schematism in constituting knowledge has been analysed by Mörchen as the problem Kant never solved: "The question concerning the essence of imagination is thus not an absurdly specialized question, but instead the fundamental question of the deduction, ultimately left open by Kant" (ibid., 948). And this, as Mörchen makes clear, is actually the question of the definition of subjectivity. In this regard, imagination proves itself to be a "necessary ingredient" of the concept, and even of perception (ibid., 128).

29 Cf. especially A, 222/B, 269, A, 223/B, 270, A, 255/B, 310, A, 292/B, 348, A, 770ff./B, 798ff., A, 799/B, 827, A, 827/B, 855.

30 Nancy, *Le discours de la syncope*, has analyzed this implicit message of the *Critique*.

31 A, 278/B, 334; A, 346f./B, 404; A, 366; A, 378. The self is "ascertained only as a logical requirement—that it has no other existence attributed to it, than the being of a condition," as Ernst Cassirer, *Das Erkenntnisproblem in der Philosophie und Wissenschaft der neueren Zeit* (Darmstadt, 1974), 2:732, notes.

32 Manfred Riedel, "Kritik der reinen Vernunft und Sprache. Zum Kategorienproblem bei Kant," *Allgemeine Zeitschrift für Philosophie* 7 (1982): 1–15.

33 In parentheses, B, 278 brings together dreams and insanity as mere effects of the imagination. Further passages: A, 376, A, 491/B, 519, A, 492/B, 520, A, 624/B, 652, A, 780/B, 808.

34 Kant continuously associates Plato and ideas with metaphors of flight. The flight of a dove (A, 5/B, 8; S, 47) and the "wings of ideas" (A, 630/B, 658; S, 524) suggest Pegasus.

Readers will stop at nothing; an amusing misunderstanding of the metaphor of the dove is brought to light by a letter to Kant (letter from Doctor and Privy Councillor Christoph Friedrich Hellwag, of December 13, 1790, in Kant, *Briefwechsel,* 501.

35   "Of the power of worth and wisdom, he has set before us an instructive pattern" (Horace, *Epistles,* Loeb Classical Library, trans. H. R. Fairclough [Cambridge, Mass., 1926], 1, bk. 2, 17f.).

36   It is particularly revealing that even Wieland, by his own admission, requires the fiction, within his novel, that the novel is not actually a novel. Thus the fictitious "publisher" of the story of Agathon claims, "that he had never given a thought to writing a novel, as many people perhaps had set their minds upon believing, regardless of the title and the preface—and since this book, to the extent the publisher had a part in it, is not a novel, nor ought to be" (Christoph Martin Wieland, *Werke,* ed. F. Martini and H. W. Seiffert [Munich, 1964], 1:831).

37   The distinction between example and idea represents a crucial moment in Kant's critique of reason. Cf. his *Grounding for the Metaphysics of Morals* (ww, 7:36f.), where Kant explains why the example of role models does not by itself provide an argument to act morally: "There is no imitation in the sphere of morals; examples may have exhortative power but they can never legitimate actions themselves. Only reason is capable of doing this."

38   Wright, "Kant und der Kanon der Kritik," 330.

39   By now, the metaphor of a journey at sea constitutes its own *topos* in the history of philosophy. Compare chap. 4, n. 10. In the preface to the first edition of his *Gründe der Weisheit,* Johann Christoph Gottsched states: "My experience here has been like that of someone who comes from a wild sea of disagreeable opinions into a secure harbor, and after much undulation and drifting finally sets his feet upon firm ground" (quoted in Erdmann, *Martin Knutzen,* 18).

40   Wright, "Kant und der Kanon der Kritik," 331.

41   Ibid., 330f.

42   Kant read every work by Hume that was available in translation. Moreover, he knew Hume's work from conversations with Hamann and Kraus. See especially Gawlick and Kreimendahl, *Hume in der deutschen Aufklärung.*

43   Ibid.

44   David Hume, *A Treatise of Human Nature,* ed. L. A. Selby-Bigge (Oxford, 1978), 263.

45   Ibid.; Johann Georg Hamann, *Sämtliche Werke,* 4:364.

46   Compare the "Herculean labor of self-knowledge," in "Von einem neuerdings erhobenen vornehmen Ton in der Philosophie" ["On a Newly Arisen Superior Tone in Philosophy"] (ww, 6:379).

47   Wright, "Kant und der Kanon der Kritik," 330.

48   This is pointed out by Martin Puder, *Kant—Stringenz und Ausdruck* (Freiburg, 1974), 71ff. On 767 printed pages of the *Critique* (in the Meiner edition), I counted 81 of these or related constructions, for instance "never more than," "nowhere other than," "no other than," etc. Kant obviously valued this figure extraordinarily, and even added it to the second edition in three places. It appears with increasing frequency in the course of the *Critique,* a change that probably can be explained by the fact that, as the work progresses, this figure, as a genuine critical gesture, develops into a stylistic trademark.

49   Jean-Louis Galay, *Philosophie et invention. Essai sur la poétique d'un texte kantien* (Paris, 1977), 252, and see also 311.

50   The significance that this seafaring metaphor possesses for Kant is shown by his letter to

Friedrich Heinrich Jacobi, of August 30, 1789: "He who shows you the reefs is nonetheless not the one who put them there, and even if, at the same moment, he declares the impossibility of passing through them with full sails (of Dogmatism), nonetheless he has not denied all possibility of a successful passage. I do not think that you will judge the compass of reason to be unnecessary here, or even misleading" (Kant, *Briefwechsel,* 413). See also the *Prolegomena,* ww, 5:121; lwb, 10 (a, 17).

51 The progression from system to systematics lay in the tendency of the time. Johann Heinrich Lambert's preparatory work in systematization were as decisive for Kant as was the general drift of the times toward giving up the paradigm of a system, in the Cartesian and Leibniz-Wolffian sense, in favor of an orientation toward experimental philosophy. Newton's paradigm was the decisive example for this trend. On the virulence of system critique as a mode of thought, see Cassirer, *Die Philosophie der Aufklärung,* 6ff., and the *Deutsche Encyclopädie*'s harsh criticism of its French prototype: Goetschel et al., "The Deutsche Encyclopädie." See also J. H. Lambert, *Texte zur Systematologie und zur Theorie der wissenschaftlichen Erkenntnis,* ed. Geo Siegwart (Hamburg, 1988), especially Siegwart's detailed introduction.

52 On this point, see also the important passage, a, 831/b, 859; s, 651f.

53 See n. 23.

54 Onora O'Neill, "The Public Use of Reason," in *Constructions of Reason: Explorations of Kant's Practical Philosophy* (Cambridge, 1989), 29.

55 In a similar vein this strategy has been shown to be at work in Spinoza: Fatma Haddad-Chamakh, *Philosophie systématique et système de philosophie politique chez Spinoza* (Tunis, 1980); Toni Negri, *The Savage Anomaly: The Power of Spinoza's Metaphysics and Politics,* trans. Michael Hardt (Minneapolis, 1991).

56 On the skeptical method (which precedes the critical), see a, 756–69/b, 784–97; s, 604–12.

57 On this, also see the remarks by Karl Jaspers, quoted below, chap. 10.

58 It is a self-quotation of Kant's, from *The Only Possible Argument in Support of a Demonstration of the Existence of God* (Kant, ww, 2:724; dw 191).

59 It is worth noting that the maxim form that became famous through Goethe holds strictly to the Kantian definition.

60 Friedrich Schlegel, *Kritische Ausgabe,* ed. E. Behler (Paderborn and Zürich, 1958ff.), Sec. 2, 16:160; quoted in Puder, *Kant,* 54.

61 On "nothing other than," see note 47; on "merely," the passage a, 771f/b, 799f; s, 613f. could be cited, as one among many. "As if" naturally becomes significant only near the end of the *Critique.* "In general" is found mostly following the substantive noun. On this, see Hans Amrhein, "Die Bedeutung der Verallgemeinerungspartikel 'überhaupt' in Kants Philosophie," in *Kants Lehre vom "Bewusstsein überhaupt" und ihre Weiterbildung bis auf die Gegenwart,* Kant-Studien Ergänzungsheft 10 (Berlin, 1909), 10:53–68: "In places in Kant's language, the 'in general' [*überhaupt*] is used like a sharp blade, a practice whereby, not infrequently, pleonasms slice the air" (54). Also see Kant, *Reflexion* §5107, aa, 18:90.

62 On this, see the compilation and tables in H. Ernst Fischer, *Kants Stil.*

63 Consider Kant's verdict against neologisms, a, 312/b, 369; s, 309.

64 For Kant's position on real definition: a, 241ff; s 260f., a, 727ff/b, 755ff; s, 586ff.

65 To illustrate that the length of Kant's sentences represented a hindrance for Kant's contemporaries as well, the following anecdote, told to Goethe by Zelter (Letter of December 4–6, 1825), should suffice: "Our now-deceased Privy-Councillor of Finance

Wlömer, who was highly esteemed by old Fritz, was once sent to Königsberg to audit the local bank. Once there, he reencounters his one-time roommate, old Kant, after forty years, and they celebrate present and bygone years. 'But,' says Kant, 'do you, the businessman, have any interest in reading my work at some point?' 'Oh, yes, and I would do it more often, but I haven't got the fingers for it.' 'What's that supposed to mean?' 'Well, my dear friend, your writing style is so full of parentheses and qualifications that I have to keep an eye on; so then I place a finger on the first word, then one on the second, the third, the fourth, and before I turn the page, I'm all out of fingers' " (quoted in Kant, *Briefwechsel*, 827, n. 2 to letter 63).

66   Ten years after the publication of the *Critique*, Kant writes to a student "that mere mathematics does not fulfill the soul of a thinking man, that there must be something else, even if, as for Kästner, it is only (!) poetry, so that, by occupying the remaining faculties, it partially just refreshes, but also partially gives our whole constitution alternative nourishment" (letter to Jacob Sigismund Beck of September 27, 1791, in Kant, *Briefwechsel*, 528).

Nine   Publicizing Enlightenment

1   Kant, *Political Writings*, ed. Hans Reiss, trans. H. B. Nisbet (Cambridge, 1991), 41–53; cited hereafter as HR. English translations are cited in this chapter for the reader's reference; however, most Kant passages have been retranslated here for the sake of stylistic and terminological consistency. [*Translator's note*]

2   Five times in all: ww, 11:35 (twice), 38, 46, 49; HR, 43, 44, 51, 52.

3   On "enlightenment" as an operative concept, see Peter Weber, "Die Berlinische Monatsschrift als Organ der Aufklärung," in *Berlinische Monatsschrift (1783–1796)*, ed. P. Weber (Leipzig, 1986), 372. Horst Stuke, in his important study of the history of the concept of enlightenment, determines "that Kant's use of language is nonuniform, and 'enlightenment' is not a fixed term in his works" (H. Stuke, "Aufklärung," in *Geschichtliche Grundbegriffe* (Stuttgart, 1972), 1:267). To this claim should be added in passing that Kant subsequently developed a quite concise concept of enlightenment. The real difficulty in getting a handle on this concept, however, is that it can serve as a category for grasping Kant's work as a whole and thus is closely connected with an interpretation of Kant.

4   Kant maintains right at the beginning that the article was elicited from him through a notice in a journal (ww, 11:33; HR, 41, note).

5   This has been shown by Hans Saner, through to its offshoots in Kant's work as a whole (Saner, *Kant's Political Thought*).

6   On this, see also Manfred Riedel, "Geschichte als Aufklärung. Kants Geschichtsphilosophie und die Grundlagenkrise der Historiographie," *Neue Rundschau* 84 (1973).

7   On overturnings, cf. Kant's letter to Lambert of December 31, 1765 (Kant, *Briefwechsel*, 41).

8   On this, see the discussion of the metaphors concerning heavenly orbits in passages from Kant's early writings, in chaps. 1 and 2 above.

9   The chapter on ideas in the *Critique* is for this reason of central significance for Kant's conception of himself as a writer.

10   Cf. the very same delineating mechanism by the philosopher against the poet, in this instance in relation to the idea of teleology in nature: "Von den verschiedenen Rassen der

Menschen" ["On the Different Races of Humankind"] (1775), ww, 11:26, and "Über den Gebrauch teleologischer Prinzipien in der Philosophie" ["Concerning the Use of Teleological Principles in Philosophy"] (1788), ww, 11:142f.

11 Jürgen Habermas speaks of the "remarkable self-implication of the philosophy of history": "it took into account the effect of a theory of history on the course of this history itself. . . . Thus, by virtue of the fact that its insights entered into the public's processes of critical reflection, the philosophy of history itself was to become a part of the enlightenment diagnosed as history's course" (J. Habermas, *The Structural Transformation of the Public Sphere. An Inquiry into a Category of Bourgeois Society*, trans. T. Burger [Cambridge, Mass., 1989], 116). Philosophy's self-implication in the philosophy of history thereby manages to expand the concept of enlightenment to include reflection on history, as such. From this reflection—and not only from history itself—enlightenment derives its self-reflectedness. The Kantian concept of enlightenment bypasses the others in this regard, because such reflectivity comes into play only on the basis of what the *Critique* had accomplished.

12 Moses Mendelssohn, "Über die Frage: was heisst aufklären?" in *Gesammelte Schriften*, 6.1:113–9. For Mendelssohn, culture is the practical side, and enlightenment the theoretical side of education [*Bildung*].

13 "What Is Enlightenment," HR, 54–60.

14 Johann Friedrich Zöllner, "Ist es rathsam, das Ehebündniss nicht ferner durch die Religion zu sancieren?" reprinted in *Was ist Aufklärung? Beiträge aus der Berlinischen Monatsschrift*, ed. N. Hinske and M. Albrecht (Darmstadt, 1981), 115.

15 This has been made clear by Günter Schulz, "Kant und die Berliner Aufklärung," in *Akten des 4. Internationalen Kant-Kongresses*, ed. G. Funke (Berlin, 1974), pt 2; also now James Schmidt, "The Question of Enlightenment: Kant, Mendelssohn, and the Mittwochgesellschaft," *Journal of the History of Ideas* (1989) 50; further, Norbert Hinske, preface and epilogue to *Was ist Aufklärung?* ed. Hinske and Albrecht; Werner Schneiders, *Die wahre Aufklärung. Zum Selbstverständnis der deutschen Aufklärung* (Freiburg, 1974); Weber, *Berlinische Monatsschrift*.

16 Thus Gisbert Beyershaus, "Kants 'Programm' der Aufklärung aus dem Jahre 1784," *Kant-Studien* 26 (1921): 1–16. Beyershaus is severely, and rightfully, called to task by Hinske, *Was ist Aufklärung?* 541ff.

17 This tendency is encouraged, for English readers, by the conventional elision of the first half of the essay's title, so that it is called simply, "What Is Enlightenment?" [*Translator's note*]

18 Cf. Schneiders, *Die wahre Aufklärung;* Hinske, *Was ist Aufklärung?*

19 On the concept of legal majority, which stems from Germanic legal thought, and on this concept's horizon of meaning, which is differently stratified from the concept of emancipation stemming from Roman jurisprudence, cf. M. Sommer, "Mündigkeit," in *Historisches Wörterbuch der Philosophie*; see Norbert Hinske, *Kant als Herausforderung an die Gegenwart* (Freiburg, 1980), 70ff., on the distinction between majority/minority as a legal and philosophical concept.

20 Cf. Moses Mendelssohn's "Votum in der Mittwochgesellschaft, Öffentlicher und Privatgebrauch der Vernunft," in *Gesammelte Schriften*, 8:225–229: "What Kant names the public and private use of reason, simply has something odd about it, in the way it is expressed" (227). Also see the discussions in Habermas, *Structural Transformation;* Schneiders, *Die wahre Aufklärung;* Hinske, *Kant als Herausforderung*. Lucian Hölscher points out the polemical significance of using this pair of concepts ("Öffentlichkeit," in

Historisches Wörterbuch der Philosophie, 6:1137). On the motivation behind Kant's distinction, cf. Schulz, *Kant und die Berliner Aufklärung*, 66.

21   Lucian Hölscher, *Öffentlichkeit und Geheimnis. Eine begriffsgeschichtliche Untersuchung zur Entstehung der Öffentlichkeit in der frühen Neuzeit* (Stuttgart, 1979), 101.

22   Ibid., 102.

23   Onora O'Neill, "Enlightenment as Autonomy: Kant's Vindication of Reason," in *The Enlightenment and Its Shadows*, ed. P. Hulme and L. Jordanora (London, 1990), points out that "private" uses of reason are *privatus*, that is, deprived or partial, viz., controlled by some interior or exterior authority other than reason itself. See also O'Neill's brilliant discussion, "The Public Use of Reason," in her *Constructions of Reason: Explorations of Kant's Practical Philosophy* (Cambridge, 1989).

24   This is done by Schneiders in *Die wahre Aufklärung*. On this, see also the harsh criticism in Hinske, *Kant als Herausforderung*. Habermas, in *Structural Transformation*, indicates the dilemma with more subtlety: "A series of fictions in which the self-understanding of the bourgeois consciousness as 'public opinion' was articulated extended right into the Kantian system, and therefore it was possible to derive from it in turn the idea of the bourgeois public sphere precisely in its connection with the presupposition of a natural basis of the juridical condition. It was no accident that the concept of public sphere, as soon as this connection became questionable, turned against the foundations of the system itself" (117). In this regard, it is to be noted that the compactness of Kant's initial intentions drives even the critic into a circle, which can indeed serve to express the discontent with Kant's concept of the public, without however being able to hit upon its essence.

25   Quoted in Habermas, *Structural Transformation*, 25.

26   Cf. the passage preceding this one, which with a thrice-repeated "rather" [*sondern*] sensitizes the ear for the "but" [*aber*] that follows, but that therefore sounds strange, syntactically (ww, 11:55; HR, 54f.).

27   Michel Foucault, "What is Enlightenment?" in *The Foucault Reader*, ed. P. Rabinow (New York, 1984), 38.

28   Ibid.

29   On the background of the contemporaneous discussion of authorial rights in relation to property law, cf. John A. McCarthy, "Literatur als Eigentum: Urheberrechtliche Aspekte der Buchhandelsrevolution," *Modern Language Notes* 104 (1989); Martha Woodmansee, "The Genius and the Copyright: Economic and Legal Conditions of the Emergence of the 'Author,'" *Eighteenth-Century Studies* 17 (1984), leaves Kant unaccounted for, even though the title of the article circumscribes Kant's situation exactly.

30   Kant, *The Metaphysics of Morals*, trans. Mary J. Gregor (New York, 1991). Hereinafter cited as MG.

31   Kant cites as an example of a similar confusion, in another area of law, a case of lease law. By doing so, he demonstrates the right of an author in its legally systematic connection, as a formal right.

32   On the publication aspects of book production, cf. also Kant's polemic against Nicolai from 1798: Kant, "Über die Buchmacherei. Zwei Briefe an Herrn Friedrich Nicolai" (AA, 8:433–8).

33   Translated in HR, 221–34.

34   Translated as "What Is Orientation in Thinking," in HR, 237–49.

35   Mendelssohn's walking to his publisher's on a cold December night, to deliver him a text against Jacobi, whereby he caught a fatal cold, has been named as the immediate cause of

his death. Already among his contemporaries, this was seen as containing a symbolism that transcends medical facts. Cf. Altmann, *Moses Mendelssohn: A Biographical Study,* 729ff.

36 Mendelssohn's indirect demand (Kant, *Briefwechsel,* 272); Johann Erich Biester's request (ibid., 273); Christian Gottfried Schütz's entreaty (ibid., 283).

37 On this, also see the further letters from Biester (ibid., 299ff., 309). When Kant therefore speaks against the excesses of the cult of genius in the *Berlinische Monatsschrift,* this can also be seen as an encoded renunciation of Jacobi.

38 On the details of this, see the journal style reports from Hamann in his letters, and also Hippel and others, collected in Malter, ed., *Kant in Rede und Gespräch,* 270ff.

39 Frederick C. Beiser, *The Fate of Reason: German Philosophy from Kant to Fichte* (Cambridge, Mass., 1987), proposes the interesting thesis that the breakthrough of Kantian philosophy is to be understood in the framework of the pantheism conflict that dominated the last two decades of the eighteenth century, against which Kant's critical philosophy posed the only tenable alternative. Cf. on Beiser, my review essay, "Neue Literatur zur Aufklärung," *German Quarterly* 62 (1989).

40 Kant, "Über den Gemeinspruch: Das mag in der Theorie richtig sein, taugt aber nicht für die Praxis," ww, 11:165f., 168. For an English translation, see "On the Common Saying: 'This May Be True in Theory, But It Does Not Apply In Practice'," in HR, 87f, 92.

41 On this in general, see Dieter Henrich, "Über den Sinn des vernünftigen Handelns im Staat," intro. to *Über Theorie und Praxis,* ed. D. Henrich (Frankfurt, 1967), which contains, along with Kant's essay, the contributions to the discussion of Kant's "Über den Gemeinspruch" by his contemporaries, Gentz and Rehberg.

42 In a note to §40 of the *Critique of Judgment,* Kant remarks "One soon sees that enlightenment is indeed an easy thing in *thesi,* but in *hypothesi* it is a difficult matter, and slow to accomplish" (ww, 10:226). Cf. Kant, *Critique of Judgment,* 137, hereafter cited as CJ. The "maxim" is often expressed in the same terms: "this or that sentence is valid in *thesi,* but not in *hypothesi*" (ww, 11:128; HR, 62); also see *Perpetual Peace* (ww, 11:212f; HR, 105f.); on the conflict of theory and practice, in this work as well, ww, 11:229, 242; HR, 116f., 125f.

43 In HR, 93–130.

44 The first reviewers of this text already point out its literary qualities. Kant, *Zum ewigen Frieden. Mit Texten zur Rezeption 1796–1800,* ed. Manfred Buhr and Steffen Dietzsche (Leipzig, 1984). See there, in particular, Fichte (93); the reviewer in *Deutschland* (102f.); Friedrich Schlegel (104).

45 Karl Jaspers, "Kants *Zum ewigen Frieden,*" in *Philosophie und Welt. Reden und Aufsätze* (Munich, 1958), 131ff.

46 The French translation, which appeared in 1796, carries the designation "Essai philosophique." Cf. Kant, *Zum ewigen Frieden,* 76.

47 Hölscher points out the novelty of this legal proposition. This consists in the fact that the morality of the content of the laws is for the first time linked to the publication of the laws (Hölscher, *Öffentlichkeit,* 147). For an excellent discussion of the terms of publicizability, see Onora O'Neill, "The Public Use of Reason," in her *Constructions of Reason.*

48 On this, see the reviews in Kant, *Zum ewigen Frieden,* including the one by Schlegel (104ff; on insurrection, 119); by Fichte (93ff.), as well as the reviewer from the *Gothaische gelehrte Zeitungen* (77ff.; on insurrection, 86). Further, see the discussion by Zwi Batscha in the introduction of A. Bergk, J. L. Ewald, J. G. Fichte et al., *Aufklärung und*

Gedankenfreiheit. Fünfzehn Anregungen aus der Geschichte zu lernen, ed. Zwi Batscha (Frankfurt, 1977).

49   Jacques Derrida analyzes the implications of Kant's argument in "Mochlos, ou le conflit des facultés" in *Du droit à la philosophie* (Paris, 1990) [*Logomachia: The Conflict of the Faculties,* trans. and ed. Richard Rand (Lincoln, 1992)]. Derrida shows to what degree Kant's separation of competences in the faculties has become questionable. Kant argued that separation guaranteed intellectual autonomy in academia, but the practice can lead to involuntary complicity among the faculties in upholding the ideology of free research, which is in fact run by political and institutional mechanisms. In a rigorous reading, Derrida shows how the Kantian framework must be turned around in order to set its critical intention into motion. Cf. also Derrida's argument for a new enlightenment, "Les pupilles de l'Université. Le principe de raison et l'idée de l'Université" (ibid., 461–98).

50   On the role of this theme for Kant as he grew older, cf. Malter, ed., *Kant in Rede und Gespräch,* 290.

51   Cf. Saner on Kant's concept of polemic and its fundamental significance for his thought (Saner, *Kant's Political Thought*).

52   On bracketing and parentheses, also see *Reflexion* §5108, AA, 18:90.

53   Cf. also *Prolegomena* §31 (ww, 5:182; LWB, 61) and ww, 5:263; LWB, 130.

54   Cf. the English translation by Henry E. Allison, *The Kant-Eberhard Controversy* (Baltimore, 1973).

55   Trans. and ed. Peter Fenves, *Raising the Tone in Philosophy: Late Essays by Immanuel Kant, Transformative Critique by Jacques Derrida* (Baltimore, 1993). In this volume, cf. also the somewhat free associations of Jacques Derrida, "Of an Apocalyptic Tone Recently Adopted in Philosophy" (originally publ. in *Semeia* 23 [1982]: 63–97).

56   Cf. *Reflexion* §5089 (quoted above, chap. 8), on Kant's not uncritical attitude regarding scholastic philosophy.

57   Cf. Lessing's rejoinder to Johann Melchior Goeze ("Eine Duplik," in Lessing, *Werke,* ed. Otto Mann, 3:148f.), but also *Nathan the Wise,* whose whole tenor is that the truth consists of an interminable process of realization.

58   W. von Biedermann, ed., *Goethes Gespräche* (Leipzig, 1891), 9:113.

Bibliographic Essay

1   Friedrich Dürrenmatt, *Der Verdacht* (Zürich, 1980), 176. This same formulation had appeared, almost word for word, as the paraphrase of a review of a Japanese commentary on Kant by Kiyono, reviewed by Nohara, who finds that, "Kant was only a difficult writer, not a bad one" ["Kant sei nur ein schwerer, nicht aber ein schlechter Schriftsteller"]. "Kant in Japan," *Kant-Studien* 2 (1898): 493.

2   E. Y. Meyer, *In Trubschachen* (Frankfurt, 1973).

3   On this, see the prefaces to the first and second editions of the *Critique of Pure Reason,* and their discussion in chap. 8, "Toward the Form of Critique."

4   In a conversation with Johann Friedrich Abegg (J. F. Abegg, *Reisetagebuch von 1798,* 305).

5   Madame de Staël, *De l'Allemagne,* ed. J. de Pagne (Paris, 1959), 4:149 [author's translation].

6   Cf. also the numerous, frequently ironic remarks by Friedrich Schlegel on Kant's style, in *Schriften zur Literatur,* ed. W. Rasch (Munich, 1970), 47, 60, 64, and passim.

7   Wilhelm Mackensen, *Beiträge zur Kritik der deutschen Sprache,* quoted in A. Carlsson, *Die deutsche Buchkritik,* (Stuttgart, 1963), 79f.

8   "[Es] wollte mir manchmal dünken, der köstliche Mann verfahre schalkhaft ironisch, indem er bald das Erkenntnisvermögen aufs engste einzuschränken bemüht schien, bald über die Grenzen, die er selbst gezogen hatte, mit einem Seitenwink hinausdeutete" Goethe, *Sämtliche Werke*, 16:877f.; cf. also 16:874ff.

9   Goethe, *Sämtliche Werke*, 9:650, §1198; cf. also §1201.

10 Goethe's private lessons in Kant's philosophy, given by Reinhold, were not in vain. Cf. W. von Biedermann, ed., *Gespräche Goethes* (Leipzig, 1889), 3:250.

11 In this context, the comment Goethe made to Eckermann is also worth recalling: "Kant is the most preeminent (of the new philosophers), without any doubt. He is also the one whose theory has proved itself to have a continuing effect, and which has penetrated our German culture the most deeply. He has also had an effect upon you, without your having read him. Now you do not need him any more, for you already possess what he could give you. If you ever want to read something from him later on, then I would recommend to you the *Critique of Judgment,* in which he treats rhetoric superbly, poetry passably, but the visual arts unacceptably" (conversation of April 11, 1827, in Johann Peter Eckermann, *Gespräche mit Goethe in den letzten Jahren,* ed. E. Beutler [Zürich, 1948], 248).

12 "Wenn früher Kant in kleinen Schriften nur von seinen grössern Ansichten präludierte, und in heitern Formen selbst über die wichtigsten Gegenstände sich problematisch zu äussern schien, da stand er unserm Freunde noch nah genug; als aber das ungeheure Lehrgebäude errichtet war, so mussten alle die, welche sich bisher in freiem Leben, dichtend so wie philosophierend ergangen hatten, sie mussten eine Drohung, eine Zwingfeste daran erblicken, von woher ihre heitern Streifzüge über das Feld der Erfahrung beschränkt werden sollten. Aber nicht allein für den Philosophen, auch für den Dichter war, bei der neuen Geistesrichtung, sobald eine grosse Masse sich von ihr hinziehen liess, viel, ja alles zu befürchten . . . und in der Poesie tat sich eine neue Epoche hervor" (Goethe, *Sämtliche Werke*, 12:711f).

13 Ibid., 13:440.

14 Ibid., 12:163 (September 12, 1797; emphasis added). Even Goethe's definition of style, by the way, shows clear traces of Kant's: "Thus style rests upon the deepest foundations of knowledge, upon the essence of things, insofar as we are allowed to know this in visible and graspable forms [*Gestalten*]" (Goethe, "Einfache Nachahmung der Natur, Manier, Stil," in *Sämtliche Werke*, 13:68).

15 "Il y a quelques mois, je me suis mis à relire Kant; rien n'est si claire [*sic*] depuis que l'on a tiré toutes les conséquences de tous ses principes. . . . La méthode de Kant est un principe d'humanité et de tolérance" (conversation of October 20, 1817, quoted in *Gespräche Goethes,* ed. Biedermann, 3:290).

16 G. W. F. Hegel, *Vorlesungen über die Geschichte der Philosophie,* reprinted in J. Kopper and R. Malter, *Materialien zu Kants "Kritik der reinen Vernunft"* (Frankfurt, 1975), 100ff.

17 Ibid., 99

18 G. W. F. Hegel, *Phänomenologie des Geistes* (1807), ed. J. Hoffmeister (Hamburg, 1952), 64.

19 Arthur Schopenhauer, *Die Welt als Wille und Vorstellung* (1819), ed. W. von Löhneysen (Darmstadt, 1974), 1:587.

20 Ibid., 20. Kant himself once points to Aristotle as a literary forerunner, in "Von einem neuerdings erhobenen vornehmen Ton in der Philosophie" (ww, 6:382). This is closely connected to his concept of philosophy; cf. Dieter Henrich, "Zu Kants Begriff der Philoso-

phie," in *Kritik und Metaphysik, Festschrift für H. Heimsoeth,* ed. F. Kaulbach and J. Ritter (Berlin, 1966).

21   Heinrich Heinze, *Zur Geschichte der Religion und Philosophie in Deutschland,* in *Historisch-kritische Gesamtausgabe der Werke,* ed. M. Windfuhr (Hamburg, 1979), 8.1:83.

22   Thomas de Quincey, *The Collected Writings,* ed. D. Masson (Edinburgh, 1889), 2:83f.

23   Ibid., 8:90.

24   Ibid., 10:122.

25   Ibid., 10:259. Cf. the note on "Transcendental," 10:262f.

26   Hermann Hettner, *Geschichte der deutschen Literatur im achtzehnten Jahrhundert,* ed. G. Witkowski (Leipzig, 1928).

27   Ibid., sec., 4, 3ff.

28   Kuno Fischer, *Immanuel Kant und seine Lehre,* 1:119.

29   Nietzsche, *Sämtliche Werke,* 1:410.

30   Ibid., 3:504.

31   Ibid., 8:446.

32   Ibid., 5:24. The translation adapts Nietzsche's words slightly in order to make the sentence consistent. Where the English reads "*faculty of a faculty:* but not in so many words," Nietzsche has "*Vermöge eines Vermögens:* leider aber nicht mit drei Worten."

33   Ibid., 11:175; cf. also 11:100, 262; 10:646; 12:340.

34   Ibid., 13:442.

35   Hermann Cohen, "Von Kants Einfluss auf deutsche Kultur," in *Schriften zur Philosophie und Zeitgeschichte,* ed. H. Cohen, A. Görland, and E. Cassirer (Berlin, 1928), 1:376f., especially 369, 378ff.: "There is no time today to speak of the impact on that literature, which has reached classical quality in wrestling with the problems of Kantian philosophy, in order to reach moral legitimation as well as clarification of its peculiar principles" (Ibid., 1:380).

36   H. Cohen, "Über das Eigentümliche des deutschen Geistes," ibid., 1:567.

37   Wilhelm Windelband, *Geschichte der neueren Philosophie* (Leipzig, 1880), 2:11.

38   Wilhelm Windelband, *Immanuel Kant und seine Weltanschauung* (Heidelberg, 1904), 10.

39   Friedrich Paulsen, *Immanuel Kant. Seine Leben und seine Lehre* (1898; 4th ed., Stuttgart, 1904), xxi.

40   Rudolf Eucken, "Über Bilder und Gleichnisse bei Kant," in *Beiträge zur Einführung in die Geschichte der Philosophie* (Leipzig, 1906), 80.

41   K. A. Rosikat, *Kants Kritik der reinen Vernunft und seine Stellung zur Poesie* (Königsberg, 1901), 21.

42   Ernst Wichert, "Verse Kants und an Kant," *Altpreussische Monatsschrift* 15 (1878): 383ff.

43   Franz Jünemann, *Kantiana. Vier Aufsätze zur Kantforschung und Kantkritik* (Leipzig, 1909).

44   Wilhelm Uhl, "Wortschatz und Sprachgebrauch bei Kant," in *Zur Erinnerung an Immanuel Kant,* ed. University of Königsberg (Halle, 1904), 166.

45   Ibid., 172.

46   H. Ernst Fischer, *Kants Stil in der Kritik der reinen Vernunft,* Kant-Studien Ergänzungsheft 5 (Berlin, 1907), 32.

47   Arnold Kowalewski, "Die verschiedenen Arbeitsformen der Philosophie und ihre Bewertung bei Kant," in *I. Kant. Festschrift zur zweiten Jahrhundertfeier seines Geburtstages,* ed. Albertus University in Königsberg (Leipzig, 1924), 111.

48   Wilhelm Dilthey, *Friedrich der Grosse und die deutsche Aufklärung,* in *Gesammelte Schriften,* ed. P. Ritter (Stuttgart-Göttingen, 1959), 3:173f.

49 Walter Benjamin, *Briefe*, ed. Gershom Scholem and Theodor W. Adorno (Frankfurt, 1966), 150. Cf. also the letter of December 7, 1917, ibid., especially 158f.

50 Cassirer, *Kants Leben und Lehre*, 149.

51 In connection to his argument concerning Heidegger's book on Kant, Cassirer speaks of Kant's "principle of style" [*Stilprinzip*]: "From the very beginning, on the contrary, Heidegger's philosophy stands under a different *principle of style*, as it were." Cassirer, "Kant und das Problem der Metaphysik. Bemerkungen zu Martin Heideggers Kant-Interpretation," *Kant-Studien* 36 (1931): 24 (emphasis added by Cassirer).

52 Vorländer, *Immanuel Kant. Der Mann und das Werk*, 2:110f.

53 Karl Jaspers, *Die Grossen Philosophen*, ed. Hans Saner (1957; 3d ed., Munich, 1981), 404.

54 It is remarkable that only with Theodor Adorno's *Aesthetic Theory*, which seeks to use its negative dialectics as a basis for pinning down Kafka's poetics, does the demand arise for what Kant, as a writer, maintained with overt obstinacy—namely "to say what it cannot say, even though it can only say it by not saying it," to paraphrase Adorno. Although Derrida quotes Kant at length in his Kafka essay, "Devant la Loi" (in *Philosophy and Literature*, ed. A. Phillips Griffiths [Cambridge, 1984], 173–88), in doing so he brings Kafka into connection with Kant only in a secondary way, in relation to the concepts of duty and law. The decisive connection here too, however, would be the poetological aspect of writing, as suggested by the paraphrase of Adorno, wherein Kafka is "conceptualized"—to the extent that is possible. For Kafka, cf. Willi Goetschel, "Kafka's Negative Dialectics," *Journal of the Kafka Society* 9 (1985): 83–106.

55 Karl Jaspers, *Nikolaus Cusanus* (Munich, 1964).

56 Ernst Bloch, *Neuzeitliche Philosophie 2: Deutscher Idealismus.* in *Die Philosophie des 19. Jahrhunderts (Leipziger Vorlesungen)* (Frankfurt, 1985): 4:14.

57 A. Carlssohn, *Die deutsche Buchkritik*, 80. Cf. there as well the chapter dedicated to the *Allgemeine Literaturzeitung*, the Kantians' mouthpiece, pp. 86–118, which investigates the discussion of Kant in the context of the contemporary literature.

58 Henrich, "Zu Kants Begriff der Philosophie," 51.

59 Henrich, "Kants Denken 1762/3. Über den Ursprung der Unterscheidung analytischer und synthetischer Urteile," 9.

60 David Tarbet, "The Fabric of Metaphor in Kant's *Critique of Pure Reason*," *Journal of the History of Philosophy* 6 (1968): 265.

61 Lewis W. Beck, "Kant's Strategy," *Journal of the History of Ideas* 28 (1967).

62 Ibid., 224.

63 Puder, *Kant—Stringenz und Ausdruck.* "Stringency and expression" is a quotation from Adorno, *Negative Dialektik*, in *Gesammelte Schriften* (Frankfurt, 1973), 6:29.

64 Manfred Sommer, *Die Selbsterhaltung der Vernunft* (Stuttgart, 1977).

65 Quoted in Puder, *Kant*, 90, n. 23, full passage cited above.

66 Sommer, *Selbsterhaltung*, 16.

67 Cf. the register of concepts, figures, and metaphors, ibid., 265–70.

68 Nancy, *Le discours de la syncope.*

69 Malter, *I. Kant in Rede und Gespräch*, 420.

70 Jean-Louis Galay, *Philosophie et invention textuelle* (Paris, 1977), 324.

71 Cf. chap. 8 above, "Toward the Form of Critique," notes 48 and 49.

72 Galay is referring here to Heinrich Lausberg, *Handbuch der literarischen Rhetorik. Eine Grundlegung der Literaturwissenschaft* (Munich, 1973).

73 Volker Gerhardt and Friedrich Kaulbach, *Kant. Erträge der Forschung* (Darmstadt, 1979), 105:69, 63.

74　Dieter Henrich, "Hutcheson und Kant," 8.

75　Friedrich Kaulbach, *Immanuel Kant* (Berlin, 1969), and Kaulbach, *Das Prinzip der Handlung in der Philosophie Kants* (Berlin, 1978).

76　There are important contributions by Rosenzweig and Buber on "dialogical thinking," which formulate the theoretical framework employed by Habermas, who, in turn, seems subsequently simply to have instrumentalized it for sociology. Dialogic, as a philosophically systematic concept, was introduced by Hermann Levin Goldschmidt. Cf. Goldschmidt, *Philosophie als Dialogik. Frühe Schriften,* vol. 1 of *Werke,* ed. W. Goetschel (Vienna, 1993); *Freiheit für den Widerspruch,* vol. 6 of *Werke,* ed. W. Goetschel (Vienna, 1993).

77　Walter Kaufmann, *Discovering the Mind,* vol. 1, *Goethe, Kant, and Hegel* (New York, 1980).

78　Nietzsche, *Studienausgabe,* 13:536.

79　Kaufmann, *Discovering the Mind,* 191, 194; also 171, 201.

80　This is especially ironic because Nietzsche's strategy of tackling Kant must be seen in the light of his own indebtedness to Kantian epistemological critique. Cf. Hans Vaihinger, *Die Philosophie des Als Ob* (Leipzig, 1927), 778, n. 1: "Nietzsche took much more from Kant than is generally assumed." (I owe this reference to Peter Claessens.)

81　Ritzel, *Immanuel Kant,* 76ff.

82　Ibid., 94f.

83　Hamilton Beck, "Kant and the Novel: A Study of the Examination Scene in Hippel's *Lebensläufe nach aufsteigender Linie,*" *Kant-Studien* 74 (1983): 282.

84　H. Beck, *The Elusive "I" in the Novel: Hippel, Sterne, Diderot, Kant,* American University Studies, ser. 1 (New York, 1987), 46:110.

85　In *The Philosopher as Writer: The Eighteenth Century,* ed. Robert Ginsberg (Selingrove, 1987).

86　Ibid.

87　Claudia Brodsky, *The Imposition of Form: Studies in Narrative Representation and Knowledge* (Princeton, N.J., 1987).

88　(Heidelberg, 1989).

89　(Tübingen, 1993).

BIBLIOGRAPHY

Abbreviations

A   *Kritike der reinen Vernunft*, 1st ed.
AA: *Gesammelte Schriften*
B: *Kritik der reinen Vernunft*, 2d ed.
CJ: *Critique of Judgment*, trans. J. H. Bernard
DW: *Theoretical Philosophy, 1755–1770*, trans. David Walford
G: *Observations on the Feeling of the Beautiful and the Sublime*, trans. John T. Goldthwait
HR: *Political Writings*, ed. Hans Reiss, trans. H. B. Nisbet
LWB: *Prolegomena to Any Future Metaphysics*, trans. Lewis White Beck
MG: *The Metaphysics of Morals*, trans. Mary J. Gregor
S: *Critique of Pure Reason*, trans. Norman Kemp Smith
WW: *Werkausgabe*

Editions of Works by Immanuel Kant

Bemerkungen in den "Beobachtungen über das Gefühl des Schönen und Erhabenen." Kant-Forschungen 3. Edited by Marie Rischmüller. Hamburg: Felix Meiner, 1991.

Briefwechsel. 3d ed. Edited by Otto Schöndörffer, revised by Rudolf Malter, introduced by Rudolf Malter and Joachim Kopper. Hamburg: Felix Meiner, 1986.

The Conflict of the Faculties (1798). Introduced by Mary J. Gregor, translated by Mary J. Gregor and Robert E. Anchor. New York: Abaris, 1979.

Critique of Judgment (1790). Translated by J. H. Bernard. New York: Hafner, 1972.

Critique of Pure Reason (1781). Translated by Norman Kemp Smith. 1929. New York: St. Martin's Press, 1965.

Geographische und andere naturwissenschaftliche Schriften. Edited by Jürgen Zehbe. Hamburg: Felix Meiner, 1985.

Gesammelte Schriften. Edited by the Berliner Akademie der Wissenschaften. Berlin: de Gruyter, 1900ff.

Immanuel Kant in Rede und Gespräch. Edited by Rudolf Malter. Hamburg: Felix Meiner, 1990.

Kritik der reinen Vernunft (1781). Riga: Johann Friedrich Hartknoch, 1st ed., 1781 (A); 2d ed., 1787 (B).

The Metaphysics of Morals (1795). Translated by Mary J. Gregor. New York: Cambridge University Press, 1991.

Observations on the Feeling of the Beautiful and the Sublime (1764). Translated and introduced by John T. Goldthwait. Berkeley: University of California Press, 1960.

On a Discovery According to Which Any New Critique of Pure Reason Has Been Made Superfluous by an Earlier One (1790). Translated by Henry E. Allison. In *The Kant-Eberhard Controversy,* edited by Henry E. Allison. Baltimore, Md.: Johns Hopkins University Press, 1973.

On a Recently Arisen Superior Tone in Philosophy (1796). Translated by Peter Fenves. In *Raising the Tone in Philosophy: Late Essays by Immanuel Kant, Transformative Critique by Jacques Derrida,* edited by Peter Fenves. Baltimore, Md.: Johns Hopkins University Press, 1993.

Political Writings. Edited by Hans Reiss, translated by H. B. Nisbet. Cambridge: Cambridge University Press, 1991. The following essays are cited:
> "Idea for a Universal History with a Cosmopolitan Purpose" (1784)
> "An Answer to the Question: 'What Is Enlightenment?' " (1784)
> "On the Common Saying: "This May Be True in Theory, but It Does Not Apply in Practice' " (1793)
> *Perpetual Peace: A Philosophical Sketch* (1795)
> "Conjectures on the Beginning of Human History" (1786)
> "What Is Orientation in Thinking?" (1786)

Prolegomena to Any Future Metaphysics (1783). Translated and introduced by Lewis White Beck. Indianapolis: Bobbs-Merrill, 1950.

Theoretical Philosophy, 1755–1770. Translated and edited by David Walford. New York: Cambridge University Press, 1992. The following essays are cited:
> *The False Subtlety of the Four Syllogistic Figures* (1762)
> *The Only Possible Argument in Support of a Demonstration of the Existence of God* (1762)
> *Attempt to Introduce Negative Magnitudes into Philosophy* (1763)
> *Inquiry Concerning the Distinctiveness of the Principles of Natural Theology and Morality* (1764)
> *Dreams of a Spirit-Seer, Elucidated by Dreams of Metaphysics* (1766)

Universal Natural History and Theory of the Heavens (1755). Translated by Stanley L. Jaki. Edinburgh: Scottish Academy Press, 1981. (This translation, unlike Kunitz's, contains the complete essay, including the third part.)

Universal Natural History and Theory of the Heavens (1755). Edited by Milton K. Munitz, translated by W. Hastie. Ann Arbor: University of Michigan Press, 1969.

Werkausgabe. Edited by Wilhelm Weischedel. Wiesbaden: Insel, 1958.

Zum Ewigen Frieden. Mit Texten zur Rezeption 1796–1800. Edited by Manfred Buhr and Steffan Dietzsch. Leipzig: Reclam, 1984.

Abegg, Johann Friedrich. *Reisetagebuch von 1798.* Edited by Walter Abegg and Jolanda Abegg, with Zwi Batscha. Frankfurt: Insel, 1976.

Adams, Douglas. *The Hitchhiker's Guide to the Galaxy.* New York: Pocket Books, 1979.

Adickes, Erich. *Kant als Naturforscher.* Berlin: de Gruyter, 1924/25.

Adorno, Theodor W. *Negative Dialektik,* vol. 6 of *Gesammelte Schriften.* Frankfurt: Suhrkamp, 1973.

——. "Der Essay als Form." In *Noten zur Literatur.* Frankfurt: Suhrkamp, 1974.

——. *Ästhetische Theorie.* Frankfurt: Suhrkamp, 1974.

Adorno, Theodor W., and Max Horkheimer. *Dialektik der Auflärung. Philosophische Fragmente.* Frankfurt: Fischer, 1971.

Allison, Henry E., ed. *The Kant-Eberhard Controversy.* Baltimore, Md.: Johns Hopkins University Press, 1973.

Altmann, Alexander. *Moses Mendelssohns Frühschriften zur Metaphysik.* Tübingen: J. C. B. Mohr (Paul Siebeck), 1969.

——. *Moses Mendelssohn: A Biographical Study.* London: Routledge & Kegan Paul; Tuscaloosa: University of Alabama Press, 1973.

——. *Trostvolle Aufklärung. Studien zur Metaphysik und politischen Theorie Moses Mendelssohns.* Stuttgart-Bad Cannstatt: Frommann-Holzboog, 1982.

Amrhein, Hans. *Kants Lehre von "Bewusstsein überhaupt" und ihre Weiterbildung bis auf die Gegenwart.* Kant-Studien Ergänzungsheft 10. Berlin: Reuther & Reichard, 1909.

Arnoldt, Emil. "Kants Jugend und die fünf ersten Jahre seiner Privatdozentur." In *Gesammelte Schriften,* vol. 3. Berlin: Bruno Cassirer, 1908.

Bacon, Francis. *Of the Advancement of Learning.* 1605. Edited by G. W. Kitchin, Everyman's Library. London: Dent; New York: Dutton, n.d.

Bakhtin, Mickail. "Discourse in the Novel." In *The Dialogic Imagination,* edited by Michael Holquist. Austin: University of Texas Press, 1981.

Barker, Stephen. "The Style of Kant's Critique of Reason." In *The Philosopher as Writer: The Eighteenth Century,* edited by Robert Ginsberg. Selingrove, Pa.: Susquehanna University Press, 1987.

Baschera, Marco. *Das dramatische Denken. Studien zur Beziehung von Theorie und Theater anhand von I. Kants 'Kritik der reinen Vernunft' und D. Diderots 'Paradoxe sur le comedien.'* Heidelberg: Carl Winter, 1989.

Beck, Hamilton. "Kant and the Novel: A Study of the Examination Scene in Hippel's *Lebensläufe nach aufsteigender Linie.*" *Kant-Studien* 74 (1983).

——. *The Elusive "I" in the Novel: Hippel, Sterne, Diderot, Kant.* American University Studies, ser. 1, vol. 46. New York: Peter Lang, 1987.

Beck, Lewis White. "Kant's Strategy." *Journal of the History of Ideas* 28 (1967).

Beiser, Frederick C. *The Fate of Reason: German Philosophy from Kant to Fichte.* Cambridge, Mass.: Harvard University Press, 1987.

Bense, Max. "Über den Essay und seine Prosa." In *Deutsche Essays,* edited by Ludwig Rohner. Neuwied and Berlin: Luchterhand, 1968.

Benz, Ernst. *Swedenborg in Deutschland.* Frankfurt: Vittorio Klostermann, 1947.

Bergk, Adam, J. L. Ewald, J. G. Fichte, et al. *Aufklärung und Gedankenfreiheit. Fünfzehn Anregungen aus der Geschichte zu lernen.* Edited by Zwi Batscha. Frankfurt: Suhrkamp, 1977.

Berwin, Beate. *Moses Mendelssohn im Urteil seiner Zeitgenossen.* Kant-Studien Ergänzungsheft 49. 1919. Reprint, Vaduz: Topos, 1978.

Beyershaus, Gisbert. "Kants 'Programm' der Aufklärung aus dem Jahre 1784." *Kant-Studien* 26 (1921).

Bezzola, Tobia. *Die Rhetorik bei Kant, Fichte und Hegel. Ein Beitrag zur Philosophiegeschichte der Rhetorik.* Tübingen: Max Niemeyer, 1993.

Bittner, Rüdiger. *Über die Bedeutung der Dialektik Immanuel Kants.* Ph.D. diss., University of Heidelberg, 1970.

Bloch, Ernst. *Neuzeitliche Philosophie 2: Deutscher Idealismus. Die Philosophie des 19. Jahrhun-*

derts. *Leipziger Vorlesungen zur Geschichte der Philosophie,* vol. 4. Frankfurt: Suhrkamp, 1985

Blumenberg, Hans. "Paradigmen zu einer Metaphorologie." *Archiv für Begriffsgeschichte* 6 (1960).

——. *Die Genesis der kopernikanischen Welt.* Frankfurt: Suhrkamp, 1975.

——. *Das Lachen der Thrakerin. Eine Urgeschichte der Theorie.* Frankfurt: Suhrkamp, 1987.

Böhme, Hartmut, and Gernot Böhme. *Das Andere der Vernunft. Zur Entwicklung von Rationalitätsstrukturen am Beispiel Kants.* Frankfurt: Suhrkamp, 1983.

Böhme, Hartmut, Wolfgang van den Daele, and Wolfgang Krohn. *Experimentelle Philosophie.* Frankfurt: Suhrkamp, 1977.

Borowski, Ludwig Ernst. "Darstellung des Lebens und Charakters Immanuel Kants." *Immanuel Kant. Sein Leben in Darstellungen seiner Zeitgenossen,* edited by Felix Gross. Berlin: Deutsche Bibliothek, 1912.

Broad, C. D. "Immanuel Kant and Psychical Research." In *Religion, Philosophy and Psychical Research.* London: Routledge & Kegan Paul, 1953.

Brockes, Barthold Hinrich. *Aus dem Englischen übersetzter Versuch vom Menschen des Herrn Alexander Pope.* Hamburg: Christian Herold, 1740.

Brodsky, Claudia. *The Imposition of Form: Studies in Narrative Representation and Knowledge.* Princeton, N.J.: Princeton University Press, 1987.

Bredvold, Louis I. "The Invention of the Ethical Calculus." *The Seventeenth Century: Studies in the History of English Thought and Literature from Bacon to Pope: Richard Foster Jones and Others Writing in His Honor.* Stanford, Calif.: Stanford University Press, 1951.

Buchdahl, Gerd. "Der Begriff der Gesetzmässigkeit in Kants Philosophie der Naturwissenschaft." In *Zur Kantforschung der Gegenwart,* edited by Peter Heintel and Ludwig Nagl. Darmstadt: Wissenschaftliche Buchgesellschaft, 1981.

Burke, Edmund. *A Philosophical Enquiry into the Origin of Our Ideas of the Sublime and Beautiful.* Edited by James T. Boulton. Notre Dame, Ind.: University of Notre Dame Press, 1968.

Butts, Robert E. *Kant and the Double Government Methodology.* Dordrecht: D. Reidel, 1984.

Carlsson, Anni. *Die deutsche Buchkritik.* Stuttgart: Kohlhammer, 1963.

Cassirer, Ernst. *Einleitung zu Leibniz' Neuen Abhandlungen über den menschlichen Verstand.* 3d ed. Leipzig: Felix Meiner, 1915.

——. *Das Erkenntnisproblem in der Philosophie und Wissenschaft der neueren Zeit.* Vol. 2. Darmstadt: Wissenschaftliche Buchgesellschaft, 1974.

——. *Kants Leben und Lehre.* 1918. 2d ed. 1921. Reprint, Darmstadt: Wissenschaftliche Buchgesellschaft, 1977.

——. "Kant und das Problem der Metaphysik. Bemerkungen zu Martin Heideggers Kant-Interpretation." *Kant-Studien* 36 (1931).

——. "Kant and Rosseau." In *Rousseau, Kant, Goethe.* 1945. Princeton, N.J.: Princeton University Press, 1970.

——. *Die Philosophie der Aufklärung.* Tübingen: Mohr, 1973.

Cohen, Hermann. *Schriften zur Philosophie und Zeitgeschichte.* Edited by A. Görland und E. Cassirer. Berlin: Akademie-Verlag, 1928.

Derrida, Jacques. "Of an Apocalyptic Tone Recently Adopted in Philosophy." *Semeia* 23 (1982).

——. "Devant la Loi." *Philosophy and Literature.* Edited by A. Phillips Griffiths. Cambridge: Cambridge University Press, 1984.

——. *Du droit à la philosophie.* Paris: Galilée, 1990.

Deutsche Encyclopädie oder Allgemeines Real-Wörterbuch. Edited by a "Gesellschaft Gelehrten." Frankfurt: Varrentrapp & Wenner, 1782.

Dilthey, Wilhelm. *Gesammelte Schriften*. Vol. 3. 3d ed. Edited by D. Ritter. Stuttgart: Vandenhoeck & Ruprecht and Göttingen: Teubner, 1959.

Dürrenmatt, Friedrich. *Der Verdacht*. Zürich: Arche, 1980.

Eckermann, Johann Peter. *Gespräche mit Goethe in den letzten Jahren seines Lebens*. 3d ed. Edited by Ernst Beutler. Zürich: Artemis, 1976.

Elias, Norbert. *Über die Zeit*. Frankfurt: Suhrkamp, 1984.

Engfer, Hans Jürgen. *Philosophie als Analysis. Studien zur Entwicklung philosophischer Analysiskonzeptionen unter dem Einfluss mathematischer Methodenmodelle im 17. und frühen 18. Jahrhundert*. Stuttgart–Bad Cannstatt: Frommann-Holzboog, 1982.

Erdmann, Benno. *Martin Knutzen und seine Zeit. Ein Beitrag zur Geschichte der wolfischen Schule und insbesondere zur Entwicklungsgeschichte Kants*. Leipzig: Leopold Voss, 1876.

Eucken, Rudolf. *Beiträge zur Einführung in die Geschichte der Philosophie*. Leipzig: Dürr, 1906.

Ferrari, Jean. *Les sources françaises de la philosophie de Kant*. Paris: Klincksieck, 1979.

Fischer, H. Ernst. *Kants Stil in der Kritik der reinen Vernunft*. Kant-Studien Ergänzungsheft 5. Berlin: Reuther and Reichard, 1907.

Fischer, Harald-Paul. "Eine Antwort auf Kants Brief vom 23. August 1749." *Kant-Studien* 76 (1985).

——. "Kant an Euler." *Kant-Studien* 76 (1985).

Fischer, Kuno. *Immanuel Kant und seine Lehre*. 4th ed. Heidelberg: C. Winter, 1898.

Foucault, Michel. *The Foucault Reader*. Edited by Paul Rabinow. New York: Pantheon, 1984.

Freud, Sigmund. *Studienausgabe*. Edited by A. Mitscherlich, A. Richards, J. Strachey. Frankfurt: S. Fischer, 1969.

Frey, G. "Experiment." In *Historisches Wörterbuch der Philosophie*. Vol. 2. Basel: Schwabe, 1972.

Fuentes, Carlos. "The Novel of Time and the Time of the Novel." Seminar delivered at Harvard University, 1984.

Galay, Jean-Louis. *Philosophie et invention textuelle. Essai sur la poétique d'um texte kantien*. Paris: Klincksieck, 1977.

Gawlick, Günter, and Lothar Kreimendahl. *Hume in der deutschen Aufklärung*. Stuttgart–Bad Cannstatt: Frommann-Holzboog, 1987.

Gerhardt, Volker, and Friedrich Kaulbach. *Kant*. Erträge der Forschung, vol. 105. Darmstadt: Wissenschaftliche Buchgesellschaft, 1979.

Gerland, G. "Immanuel Kant, seine geographischen und anthropologischen Arbeiten." *Kant-Studien* 10 (1905).

Goethe, Johann Wolfgang. *Sämtliche Werke*. Edited by Ernst Beutler. Zürich: Artemis, 1949.

——. *Briefwechsel zwischen Schiller und Goethe*. Edited by Franz Muncker. Stuttgart: Cotta, n.d.

——. *Gespräche Goethes*. Edited by W. von Biedermann. Leipzig: F. W. von Biedermann, 1889–1896.

Goetschel, Willi. "Zur Pragmatik von Aufklärung. Die Spinozarezeption bei Moses Mendelssohn." Master's thesis, University of Zürich, 1982.

——. "Ergebnisse des Lessing-Mendelssohn-Jahrs." *Studia Philosophica* 42 (1983).

——. "Kafka's Negative Dialectics." *Journal of the Kafka Society* 9 (1985).

——. "Zur Neuausgabe des 'Knigge'." *Zeitschrift für Religions- und Geistesgeschichte* 40 (1988).

——. "Neue Literatur zur Aufklärung." *German Quarterly* 62 (1989).

Goetschel, Willi, Catriona MacLeod, and Emery Snyder. "The *Deutsche Encyclopädie* and

Encyclopedism in Eighteenth-Century Germany." In *The Encyclopédie and the Age of Revolution*, edited by Clorinda Donato and Robert Maniquis. Boston: G. K. Hall, 1992.

———. "The *Deutsche Encyclopädie*." In *Notable Encylopedias of the Late Eighteenth Century: Twelve Successors of the Encylopédie*, edited by Frank Kafker. Oxford: Oxford University Press, 1994.

Goldschmidt, Hermann Levin. *Philosophie als Dialogik. Frühe Schriften. Werke.* Vol. 1. Edited by Willi Goetschel. Vienna: Passagen, 1993.

———. *Dialogik—Philosophie auf dem Boden der Neuzeit.* Frankfurt: Europäische Verlagsanstalt, 1964.

———. *Freiheit für den Widerspruch. Werke.* Vol. 6. Edited by Willi Goetschel. Vienna: Passagen, 1993.

Grimm, Jacob. "Einleitung." In *Deutsches Wörterbuch*. Leipzig: 1854.

Gulyga, Arsenij. *Immanuel Kant.* Frankfurt: Insel, 1981.

Gurwitsch, Georg. "Kant und Fichte als Rousseau-Interpreten." *Kant-Studien* 27 (1922).

Haagen, Bernhard. "Auf den Spuren Kants in Judtschen." *Altpreussische Monatsschrift* 48 (1911).

Habermas, Jürgen. *The Structural Transformation of the Public Sphere: An Enquiry into a Category of Bourgeois Society.* Translated by Thomas Burger with Frederick Lawrence. Cambridge, Mass.: MIT Press, 1989.

Haddad-Chamakh, Fatma. *Philosophie systématique et système de philosophie politique chez Spinoza.* Tunis: Publications de l'Univérsité Tunis, 1980.

Hamann, Johann Georg. *Sämtliche Werke.* Vol. 4. Edited by Josef Nadler. Vienna: Herder, 1952.

———. *Briefwechsel.* Vol. 4. Edited by Arthur Henkel. Wiesbaden: Insel, 1959.

Hamel, Jürgen. *Zur Entstehungs- und Wirkungsgeschichte der Kantischen Kosmogonie.* Mitteilungen der Archenhold-Sternwarte Berlin-Treptow, no. 130. Berlin-Treptow, 1979.

Harnack, Adolf. *Geschichte der königlich preussischen Akademie der Wissenschaften zu Berlin.* Berlin: Reichsdruckerei, 1900.

Harrison, Edward R. *Cosmology: The Science of the Universe.* Cambridge: Cambridge University Press, 1981.

Hegel, Georg Wilhelm Friedrich. *Phänomenologie des Geistes.* 6th ed. Edited by J. Hoffmeister. Hamburg: Felix Meiner, 1952.

———. *Grundlinien der Philosophie des Rechts.* Edited by J. Hoffmeister. Hamburg: Felix Meiner, 1955.

Heimsoeth, Heinz. "Astronomisches und Theologisches in Kants Weltverständnis." In *Studien zur Philosophie Immanuel Kants* II. Kant-Studien Ergänzungsheft 100. Bonn: Bouvier, 1970.

Heine, Heinrich. *Historisch-kritische Gesamtausgabe der Werke.* Vol. 8, pt. 1. Edited by Manfred Windfuhr. Hamburg: Hoffmann and Campe, 1979.

Henrich, Dieter. "Hutcheson und Kant." *Kant-Studien* 49 (1957/58).

———. "Zu Kants Begriff der Philosophie." In *Kritik und Metaphysik. Festschrift für H. Heimsoeth.* Edited by F. Kaulbach und J. Ritter. Berlin: de Gruyter, 1966.

———. "Kants Denken 1762/3. Über den Ursprung der Unterscheidung analytischer und synthethischer Urteile." In *Studien zu Kants philosophischer Entwicklung*, edited by H. Heimsoeth, D. Henrich, and G. Tonelli. Hildesheim: Olms, 1967.

———. "Über den Sinn vernünftigen Handelns im Staat." In *Über Theorie und Praxis*, edited by Dieter Henrich. Frankfurt: Suhrkamp, 1967.

———. "Der Begriff der sittlichen Einsicht und Kants Faktum der Vernunft." In *Kant. Zur*

Deutung seiner Theorie von Erkennen und Handeln, edited by G. Prauss. Köln: Kiepenheuer & Witsch, 1973.

——. *Identität und Objektivität.* Heidelberg: Carl Winter, 1976.

——. "Die Beweisstruktur der transzendentalen Deduktion der reinen Verstandesbegriffe—eine Diskussion mit Dieter Henrich." In *Probleme der 'Kritik der reinen Vernunft',* edited by Burkhard Tuschling. Berlin: de Gruyter, 1984.

Herder, Johann Gottfried. *Sämtliche Werke.* Edited by Bernhard Suphan. Berlin: Weidmann, 1877ff.

Hettner, Hermann. *Geschichte der deutschen Literatur im achtzehnten Jahrhundert.* Edited by G. Witkowski. Leipzig: List, 1928.

Hinsch, Wilfried. *Erfahrung und Selbstbewusstsein.* Hamburg: Felix Meiner, 1986.

Hinske, Norbert, und Michael Albrecht. *Was ist Aufklärung? Beiträge aus der Berlinischen Monatsschrift.* 2d ed. Darmstadt: Wissenschaftliche Buchgesellschaft, 1977.

——. *Kant als Herausforderung an die Gegenwart.* Freiburg: Alber, 1980.

Hölscher, Lucian. *Öffentlichkeit und Geheimnis. Eine begriffsgeschichtliche Untersuchung zur Entstehung der Öffentlichkeit in der frühen Neuzeit.* Stuttgart: Klett-Cotta, 1979.

——. "Öffentlichkeit." In *Historisches Wörterbuch der Philosophie,* vol. 6.

Holzhey, Helmut. "Kritik." In *Historisches Wörterbuch der Philosophie,* vol. 3.

Howard, William Guild. "Burke among the Forerunners of Lessing." *PMLA* 22 (1907).

Hume, David. *A Treatise of Human Nature.* Edited by L. A. Selby-Bigge. Oxford: Clarendon Press, 1978.

Hutcheson, Francis. *Über den Ursprung unserer Ideen von Schönheit und Tugend.* Edited by W. Leidhold. Hamburg: Meiner, 1986.

Jachmann, Reinhold Bernhard. "Immanuel Kant geschildert in Briefen an einen Freund." *Immanuel Kant. Sein Leben in Darstellungen von Zeitgenossen.* Edited by Felix Gross. Berlin: Deutsche Bibliothek, 1912.

Jaki, Stanley L. "An English Translation of the Third Part of Kant's *Universal Natural History, and Theory of the Heavens.*" In *Cosmology, History, and Theology,* edited by Wolfgang Yourgrau and Allen D. Breck. New York and London: Plenum Press, 1977.

Jaspers, Karl. *Die Grossen Philosophen.* 3d ed. Edited by Hans Saner. Munich: Piper, 1981.

Jolley, Nicholas. *Leibniz and Locke: A Study of the "New Essays on Human Understanding."* Oxford: Clarendon Press, 1984.

Jünemann, Franz. *Kantiana. Vier Aufsätze zur Kantforschung und Kantkritik.* Leipzig: Demme, 1909.

Kaufmann, Walter. *Discovering the Mind.* Vol. 1, *Goethe, Kant, and Hegel.* New York: McGraw-Hill, 1980.

Kaulbach, Friedrich. *Immanuel Kant.* Berlin: de Gruyter, 1969.

——. *Das Prinzip Handlung in der Philosophie Kants.* Berlin: de Gruyter, 1978.

Kinkel, Walter. "Moses Mendelssohn und Immanuel Kant." *Kant-Studien* 34 (1929).

Klibansky, Raymond, Erwin Panofsky, and Fritz Saxl. *Saturn and Melancholy: Studies in the History of Natural Philosophy, Religion and Art.* London: Nelson, 1964.

Knigge, Adolph von. *Über den Umgang mit Menschen.* Edited by G. Ueding. Frankfurt: Insel, 1987.

Kopper, J., and R. Malter, eds. *Materialien zu Kants 'Kritik der reinen Vernunft.'* 2d ed. Frankfurt: Suhrkamp, 1975.

——, eds. *Immanuel Kant zu ehren.* Frankfurt: Suhrkamp, 1974.

——. "Einleitung." Introduction to *Briefewechsel,* by Immanuel Kant.

Kowalewski, Arnold. "Die verschiedenen Arbeitsformen der Philosophie und ihre Bewertung bei Kant." In *I. Kant. Festschrift zur zweiten Jahrhundertfeier seines Geburtstages.* Edited by Albertus University of Königsberg. Leipzig: Dieterich, 1924.

Kügelgen, C. W. von. "Kant als Prediger und seine Stellung zur Homiletik." *Kant-Studien* 1 (1897).

Kuhlen, R., and U. Schneider. "Experimentalphilosophie." In *Historisches Wörterbuch der Philosophie*, vol. 2.

Langdon, David. "On the Meanings of the Conclusion of *Candide*." *Studies on Voltaire and the Eighteenth Century* 238 (1985).

Lange, Friedrich Albert. *Geschichte des Materialismus.* Frankfurt: Suhrkamp, 1974.

Leibniz, Gottfried Wilhelm. *Hauptschriften zur Grundlegung der Philosophie.* 3d ed. Edited by Ernst Cassirer. Hamburg: Felix Meiner, 1966.

——. *Politische Schriften.* Edited by Hans Heinz Holz. Frankfurt: Europäische Verlagsanstalt, 1966/67.

Lepenies, Wolf. *Melancholie und Gesellschaft.* 2d ed. Frankfurt: Suhrkamp, 1981.

Lessing, Gotthold Ephraim. *Lessings Sämtliche Werke.* Vol. 1. Edited by Karl Lachmann and Franz Muncker. Stuttgart: Göschen, 1886.

——. *Werke.* Edited by Otto Mann. Munich: Winkler, 1972.

Lessing, H.-U. "Melancholie." In *Historisches Wörterbuch der Philosophie*, vol. 5.

Lichtenberg, Georg Christoph. *Schriften und Briefe.* Vol. 1. 3d ed. Edited by W. Promies. Munich: Hanser, 1980.

Lippmann, Edmund von. "Zu 'Zwei Dinge erfüllen das Gemüt . . . ' " *Kant-Studien* 34 (1929).

Lovejoy, Arthur O. *The Great Chain of Being.* Cambridge, Mass.: Harvard University Press, 1961.

Lukács, Georg. "Über Wesen und Form des Essays." In *Deutsche Essays*, edited by Ludwig Rohner. Neuwied and Berlin: Luchterhand, 1968.

McCarthy, John. "The Philosopher as Essayist: Leibniz and Kant." In *The Philosopher as Writer: The Eighteenth Century*, edited by Robert Ginsberg. Selingrove, Pa.: Susquehanna University Press, 1987.

——. "Literatur als Eigentum: Urheberrechtliche Aspekte der Buchhandelsrevolution." *Modern Language Notes* 104 (1989).

Marquard, Odo. "Anthropologie." In *Historisches Wörterbuch der Philosophie*, vol. 1.

——. "Skeptiker. Dankrede." In *Apologie des Zufälligen.* Stuttgart: Reclam, 1986.

Mendelssohn, Moses. *Gesammelte Schriften. Jubiläums-Ausgabe.* Edited by Alexander Altmann et. al. Stuttgart–Bad Cannstatt: Frommann-Holzboog, 1929ff. and 1971ff.

——. *Phädon oder über die Unsterblichkeit der Seele.* 3d ed. Edited by D. Bourel. Hamburg: Felix Meiner, 1979.

Menzer, Paul. "Der Entwicklungsgang der Kantischen Ethik in den Jahren 1760 bis 1785." *Kant-Studien* 2 (1898); 3 (1899).

Meyer, E. Y. *In Trubschachen.* Frankfurt: Suhrkamp, 1973.

Minder, Robert. *Die Entdeckung deutscher Mentalität.* Leipzig: Reclam, 1992.

Mörchen, Hermann. *Die Einbildungskraft bei Kant.* 2d ed. Tübingen: Niemeyer, 1970.

Montaigne, Michel de. *Oeuvres complètes.* Edited by Albert and Maurice Rat. Paris: Gallimard, 1962.

Munitz, Milton K., ed. Introduction to *Universal Natural History and Theory of the Heavens*, by Immanuel Kant. Ann Arbor: University of Michigan Press, 1969.

Nancy, Jean-Luc. *Le discours de la syncope.* Vol. 1, *Logodaedalus.* Paris: Aubier-Flammarion, 1976.

Negri, Antonio. *The Savage Anomaly: The Power of Spinoza's Metaphysics and Politics.* Translated by Michael Hardt. Minneapolis: University of Minnesota Press, 1991.

Nietzsche, Friedrich. *Sämtliche Werke. Kritische Studienausgabe.* Edited by G. Colli and M. Montinari. Berlin: de Gruyter; Munich: DTV, 1980.

Nisbet, H. B. " 'Was ist Aufklärung?': The Concept of Enlightenment in Eighteenth-Century Germany." *Journal of European Studies* 12 (1982).

O'Neill, Onora. *Constructions of Reason: Explorations of Kant's Practical Philosophy.* Cambridge: Cambridge University Press, 1989.

——. "Enlightenment as Autonomy: Kant's Vindication of Reason." In *The Enlightenment and Its Shadows*, ed. Peter Hulme and Ludmilla Jordanora. London: Routledge, 1990.

Paneth, F. A. "Die Erkenntnis des Weltbaus durch Thomas Wright und Immanuel Kant." *Kant-Studien* 47 (1955/56).

Paulsen, Friedrich. *Immanuel Kant. Sein Leben und seine Lehre.* 1898. 4th ed. Stuttgart: Frommann, 1904.

Puder, Martin. *Kant—Stringenz und Ausdruck.* Freiburg: Rombach, 1974.

Quincey, Thomas de. *The Collected Writings.* Edited by D. Masson. Edinburgh: Adam and Charles Black, 1889.

Riedel, Manfred. "Kritik der reinen Vernunft und Sprache. Zum Kategorienproblem bei Kant." *Allgemeine Zeitschrift für Philosophie* 7 (1982).

——. "Geschichte als Aufklärung. Kants Geschichtsphilosophie und die Grundlagenkrise der Historiographie." *Neue Rundschau* 84 (1973).

Ritzel, Wolfgang. *Immanuel Kant. Eine Biographie.* Berlin: de Gruyter, 1985.

Rohner, Ludwig. *Der deutsche Essay. Materialien zur Geschichte und Ästhetik einer literarischen Gattung.* Neuwied and Berlin: Luchterhand, 1966.

Rosikat, K. A. *Kants Kritik der reinen Vernunft und seine Stellung zur Poesie.* Königsberg: Hartung, 1901.

Rousseau, Jean-Jacques. *Emile ou de l'éducation.* 1762. Paris: Garnier, 1964.

——. *The First and Second Discourses together with the Replies to Critics and Essay on the Origin of Languages.* Edited by Victor Gourevitch. New York: Perennial Library, 1986.

——. *Schriften zur Kulturkritik.* 3d ed. Edited by Kurt Weigand. Hamburg: Felix Meiner, 1978.

Saner, Hans. *Kant's Political Thought: Its Origins and Development.* Translated by E. B. Ashton. Chicago: Chicago University Press, 1973.

Schilpp, Paul Arthur. *Kant's Pre-critical Ethics.* 2d ed. Evanston, Ill.: Northwestern University Press, 1960.

Schings, H.-J. *Aufklärung und Melancholie. Melancholiker und ihre Kritiker in Erfahrungsseelenkunde und Literatur des 18. Jahrhunderts.* Stuttgart: Metzler, 1977.

Schlegel, Friedrich. *Kritische Ausgabe.* Edited by Ernst Behler. Sec. 2, vol. 16 (1981). Edited by Hans Eichner. Paderborn: F. Schöningh; Zurich: Thomas, 1958ff.

——. *Schriften zur Literatur.* Edited by W. Rasch. Munich: Carl Hanser, 1970.

Schmalenbach, Herman. *Kants Religion.* Berlin: Junder & Dünnhaupt, 1929.

Schmid, Friedrich Albert. "Kant im Spiegel seiner Briefe." *Kant-Studien* 9 (1904).

Schmidt, James. "The Question of Enlightenment: Kant, Mendelssohn, and the *Mittwochsgesellschaft.*" *Journal of the History of Ideas* 50 (1989).

Schmucker, Josef. *Die Ursprünge der Ethik Kants in seinen vorkritischen Schriften und Reflexionen.* Monographien zur philosophischen Forschung, vol. 23. Meisenheim am Glan: A. Hain, 1961.

Schneiders, Werner. *Die wahre Aufklärung. Zum Selbstverständnis der deutschen Aufklärung.* Freiburg: Karl Alber, 1974.

——. *Aufklärung und Vorurteilskritik. Studien zur Vorurteilskritik.* Stuttgart–Bad Cannstatt: Frommann-Holzboog, 1983.

——. *Hoffnung auf Vernunft. Aufklärungsphilosophie in Deutschland.* Hamburg: Felix Meiner, 1990.

Schopenhauer, Arthur. *Die Welt als Wille und Vorstellung.* Edited by W. von Löhneysen. Darmstadt: Wissenschaftliche Buchgesellschaft, 1974.

Schulz, Eberhard Günter. "Kant und die Berliner Aufklärung." Pt. 2 of *Akten des 4. Internationalen Kant-Kongresses.* Edited by G. Funke. Berlin: Walter de Gruyter, 1974.

Screech, M. A. *Montaigne and Melancholy: The Wisdom of the Essays.* London: Duckworth, 1983.

Sextus Empiricus. *Grundriss der pyrrhonischen Skepsis.* Edited by Malte Hossenfelder. Frankfurt: Suhrkamp, 1968.

Sommer, Manfred. *Die Selbsterhaltung der Vernunft.* Stuttgart: Frommann-Holzboog, 1977.

Spinoza, Baruch de. *Briefwechsel.* 2d ed. Edited by Carl Gebhardt. Hamburg: Felix Meiner, 1977.

Sprute, Jürgen. "Der Begriff des Moral Sense bei Shaftesbury und Hutcheson." *Kant-Studien* 71 (1980).

Staël, Madame de. *De l'Allemagne.* Edited by Jean de Pange. Paris: Hachette, 1958–60.

Stavenhagen, Kurt. *Kant und Königsberg.* Göttingen: Deuerlich, 1949.

Striedter, Jurij. *Die Fragmente des Novalis als "Präfigurationen" seiner Dichtung.* Munich: Wilhelm Fink, 1985.

Stuke, Horst. "Aufklärung." In *Geschichtliche Grundbegriffe,* vol. 1. Stuttgart: Ernst Klett, 1972.

Swift, Jonathan. *The Prose Works.* Edited by Temple Scott. London: George Bell & Sons, 1907–25.

Tarbet, David. "The Fabric of Metaphor in Kant's *Critique of Pure Reason.*" *Journal of the History of Philosophy* 6 (1968).

Tonelli, Giorgio. "Kant und die antiken Skeptiker." *Studien zu Kants philosophischer Entwicklung.* Edited by Heinz Heimsoeth, Dieter Henrich, and Giorgio Tonelli. Hildesheim: Olms, 1967.

Ueberweg, Friedrich. *Grundriss der Geschichte der Philosophie.* Vol. 3. 12th ed. Berlin: Mittler, 1924.

Uhl, Wilhelm. "Wortschatz und Sprachgebrauch bei Kant." In *Zur Erinnerung an Immanuel Kant.* Edited by the University of Königsberg. Halle an der Saale: Verlag der Buchhandlung des Waisenhauses, 1904.

Unger, Rudolf. " 'Der bestirnte Himmel über mir . . . ' Zur geistesgeschichtlichen Deutung eines Kant-Wortes." *Immanuel Kant. Festschrift zur zweiten Jahrhundertfeier seines Geburtstages.* Edited by Albertus University of Königsberg. Leipzig: Dieterich, 1924.

Vaihinger, Hans. "Kant als Melancholiker." *Kant-Studien* 2 (1898).

——. *Kommentar zu Kants Kritik der reinen Vernunft.* 1922. Reprint, Aalen: Scientia, 1970.

——. *Die Philosophie des Als Ob.* 10th ed. Leipzig: Felix Meiner, 1927.

Vleeschauwer, Herman Jean de. *The Development of Kantian Thought.* Translated by A. R. C. Duncan. London: T. Nelson, 1962.

Voltaire. *Dictionnaire philosophique.* Paris: Garnier-Flammarion, 1964.

Vorländer, Karl. *Immanuel Kant. Der Mann und das Werk.* 2d ed. Hamburg: Felix Meiner, 1977.

Ward, Keith. *The Development of Kant's View of Ethics.* Oxford: Basil Blackwell, 1972.

Wasianski, E. A. C. "Immanuel Kant in seinen letzten Tagen." In *Immanuel Kant. Sein Leben in Darstellungen von Zeitgenossen*, edited by Felix Gross. Berlin: Deutsche Bibliothek, 1912.

Weber, Peter. "Die *Berlinische Monatsschrift* als Organ der Aufklärung." In *Berlinische Monatsschrift (1783–1796)*, edited by P. Weber. Leipzig: Reclam, 1986.

Weissberg, Liliane. "*Catarcticon* und der schöne Wahn. Kants *Träume eines Geistersehers, erläutert durch die Träume der Metaphysik.*" *Poetica* 18 (1986).

Werkmeister, William Henry. *Kant: The Architectonic and Development of his Philosophy.* La Salle, Ill.: Open Court, 1980.

Wichert, Ernst. "Verse Kants und an Kant." *Altpreussische Monatsschrift* 15 (1878).

Wieland, Christoph Martin. *Werke.* Edited by Fritz Martini and Hans Werner Seiffert. Munich: Carl Hanser, 1964.

Windelband, Wilhelm. *Geschichte der neueren Philosophie.* Vol. 1. Leipzig: Breitkopf and Härtel, 1880.

——. *Immanuel Kant und seine Weltanschauung.* Heidelberg: C. Winter, 1904.

Woodmansee, Martha. "The Genius and the Copyright: Economic and Legal Conditions of the Emergence of the 'Author.'" *Eighteenth-Century Studies* 17 (1984).

Wright, Kathleen. "Kant und der Kanon der Kritik." In *Kanon und Zensur. Archäologie der literarischen Kommunikation*, vol. 2, edited by Aleida Assmann and Jan Assmann. Munich: Wilhelm Fink, 1987.

Zac, Sylvain. "Le prix et la mention. Les Preisschriften de Mendelssohn et de Kant." *Revue de Métaphysique et de Morale* 79 (1974).

INDEX

About the Author. Willi Goetschel is Assistant Professor
of German at Columbia University.
About the Translator. Eric Schwab is a graduate student
in the Department of Germanic Languages and Literature,
Yale University.

Library of Congress Cataloging-in-Publication Data
Goetschel, Willi, 1958–
[Kant als Schriftsteller. English]
Constituting critique : Kant's writing as critical praxis / Willi
Goetschel ; translated by Eric Schwab.
p.   cm. — (Post-contemporary interventions)
Translation of: Kant als Schriftsteller.
Includes bibliographical references and index.
ISBN 0–8223–1534–3 (cloth : alk. paper). —
ISBN 0–8223–1543–2 (paper : alk. paper)
1. Kant, Immanuel, 1724–1804. 2. Criticism (Philosophy)
I. Title. II. Series.
B2798.G59413   1994
193—dc20   94-22054 CIP